FORENSIC TOXICOLOGY

ENCYCLOPAEDIA OF FORENSIC SCIENCE - IV

FORENSIC TOXICOLOGY

By

Ashok Kumar

Dept. of Zoology
Bundelkhand University
Campus Department
Jhansi

First Published – 2010

Reprinted – 2025

ISBN: 978-81-8356-422-9 (Set)
978-81-8356-567-7

Forensic Toxicology

Published by:

DISCOVERY PUBLISHING HOUSE
4383/4B, Ansari Road, Darya Ganj
New Delhi-110 002 (India)
Phone: +91-11-23279245; 23253475; 43596065
Mobile: +91 9811179893 / +91 9871656464
E-mail: discoverybooksindia@gmail.com
orderdphbooks@gmail.com
namitwasan9@gmail.com
web: www.discoverypublishinggroup.com

Printed at:
Infinity Imaging Systems
Delhi

Preface

The present title *"Encyclopaedia of Forensic Science"* has been written for undergraduate, post-graduate students and those engaged in pharmaceutical, pathological, and clinical research. Actually the explosion of new technologies with their vast potential has brought with it the need for forensic scientists to equip themselves and their laboratories with a whole array of new expertise. With the high discriminating power of the DNA systems has come high potential in evidentiary terms, high profile status for many investigations, and not least, a high degree of professional scruting of evidence produced by such technology. The present book provides protocols for the major methods of DNA analysis that have been introduced for identity testing in forensic laboratories. It also deals with the developments intersecting with the neighbouring fields of law inforcement and the justice system. This book will prove a useful guide for public awareness, health authorities, professional and industrial organizations. The aim of writing this book has .been to show how it is possible to enjoy the benefits of technology in detecting the criminals. The language used in it is simple and lucid, and illustrations are clear and labelled.

To make the work more comprehensive and informative, the author has consulted many authoritative books, research journals, abstracts, monographs etc., so there can be no claim to originality except in the .manner of treatment.

The author expresses his thanks to his friends and colleagues whose continue inspirations have initiated him to bring out this book.

The author expresses his gratitude to Mr. Wasan and staff of M/s Discovery Publishing House Pvt. Ltd. for their whole hearted co-operation in the publication of this book.

In the mean time, the author will remain sincerely responsible for any shortcomings of the book and be grateful to the readers for their suggestions and constructive criticism for the continuous betterment of the book. He takes this opportunity to appeal to the readers to send their suggestions straightaway to his Publisher.

Author

CONTENTS

1

Introduction

A *poison*, or *toxicant*, is a substance that is harmful to living organisms because of its detrimental effects on tissues, organs, or biological processes. *Toxicology* is the science of poisons. A *toxicologist* deals with toxic substances, their effects, and the probabilities of these effects. These definitions are subject to a number of qualifications. Whether a substance is poisonous depends on the type of organism exposed, the amount of the substance, and the route of exposure. In the case of human exposure, the degree of harm done by a poison can depend strongly on whether the exposure is to the skin, by inhalation, or through ingestion. For example, a few parts per million of copper in drinking water can be tolerated by humans. However, at that level it is deadly to algae in their aquatic environment, whereas at a concentration of a few parts per billion copper is a required nutrient for the growth of algae. Subtle differences like this occur with a number of different kinds of substances.

History of Toxicology

The origins of modern toxicology can be traced to M.J.B. Orfila (1787–1853), a Spaniard born on the island of Minorca. In 1815 Orfila published a classic book, the first ever devoted to the harmful effects of chemicals on organisms. This work discussed many aspects of toxicology recognized as valid today. Included are the relationships between the demonstrated presence of a chemical in the body and observed symptoms of poisoning, mechanisms by which chemicals are eliminated from the body, and treatment of poisoning with antidotes.

Since Orfila's time, the science of toxicology has developed at an increasing pace, with advances in the basic biological, chemical, and biochemical sciences. Prominent among these advances are modern instruments and techniques for chemical analysis that provide the means for measuring chemical poisons and their metabolites at very low levels and with remarkable sensitivity, thereby greatly extending the capabilities of modern toxicology.

This chapter deals with toxicology in general, including the routes of exposure and clinically observable effects of toxic substances. The information is presented primarily from the viewpoint of human exposure and readily observed detrimental effects of toxic substances on humans. To a somewhat lesser extent, this material applies to other mammals, especially those used as test organisms. It should be kept in mind that many of the same general principles discussed apply also to other living organisms. Although LD is often the first parameter to come to mind in discussing degrees of toxicity, mortality is usually not a good parameter for toxicity measurement. Much more widespread than fatal poisoning, and certainly more subtle, are various manifestations of morbidity (unhealthiness). As discussed in this chapter, there are many ways in which morbidity is manifested. Some of these, such as effects on vital signs, are obvious. Others, such as some kinds of immune system impairment, can be observed only with sophisticated tests. Various factors must be considered, such as minimum dose or the latency period (often measured in years for humans) for an observable response to be observed. Furthermore, it is important to distinguish *acute toxicity*, which has an effect soon after exposure, and *chronic toxicity*, which has a long latency period.

Future of Toxicology

As with all other areas of the life sciences, toxicology is strongly affected by the remarkable ongoing advances in the area of mapping and understanding the deoxyribonucleic acid (DNA) that directs the reproduction and metabolism of all living things. This includes the human genome, as well as those of other organisms. It is known that certain genetic characteristics result in a predisposition for .certain kinds of diseases and cancers. The action of toxic substances and the susceptibility of organisms to their effects have to be strongly influenced by the genetic makeup of organisms. The term *chemical idiosyncrasy* has been applied to the abnormal reaction of individuals to chemical exposure. An example of chemical idiosyncrasy occurs with some individuals who are affected very strongly by exposure to nitrite ion, which oxidizes the iron(II) in hemoglobin to iron(III), producing methemoglobin, which does not carry oxygen to tissues. These individuals have a low activity of the NADH–methemoglobin reductase enzyme that converts methemoglobin back to hemoglobin. An understanding of the reactions of organisms to toxic substances based on their genetic makeup promises tremendous advances in toxicological science.

Specialized Areas of Toxicology

Given the huge variety of toxic substances and their toxic effects, it is obvious that toxicology is a large and diverse area. Three specialized areas of toxicology should be pointed out. *Clinical toxicology* is practiced primarily by physicians who look at the connection between toxic substances and the illnesses associated with them. For example, a clinical toxicologist would be involved in diagnosing and treating cases of poisoning. *Forensic toxicology* deals largely with the interface between the medical and legal aspects of toxicology and seeks to establish the cause and responsibility for poisoning, especially where criminal activity is likely to be involved. *Environmental toxicology* is concerned with toxic effects of environmental pollutants to humans and other organisms. Of particular importance are the sources, transport, effects, and interactions of toxic substances within ecosystems as they influence population dynamics within these systems. This area constitutes the branch of environmental toxicology called *ecotoxicology*.

Toxicological Chemistry

Toxicological chemistry relates chemistry to toxicology. It deals with the chemical nature of toxic substances, how they are changed biochemically, and how xenobiotic substances and their metabolites react biochemically in an organism to exert a toxic effect.

Kinds of Toxic Substances

Toxic substances come in a variety of forms from a number of different sources. Those that come from natural sources are commonly called *toxins*, whereas those produced by human activities are called *toxicants*. They may be classified according to several criteria, including the following:

1. Chemically, such as heavy metals or polycyclic aromatic hydrocarbons, some of which may cause cancer
2. Physical form, such as dusts, vapors, or lipid-soluble liquids
3. Source, such as plant toxins, combustion by-products, or hazardous wastes produced by the petrochemical industry
4. Use, such as pesticides, pharmaceuticals, or solvents
5. Target organs or tissue, such as neurotoxins that harm nerve tissue

6. Biochemical effects, such as binding to and inhibiting enzymes or converting oxygen-carrying hemoglobin in blood to useless methemoglobin
7. Effects on organisms, such as carcinogenicity or inhibition of the immune system.

Usually several categories of classification are appropriate. For example, parathion is an insecticide that is produced industrially, to which exposure may occur as a mist from spray, and that binds to the acetylcholinesterase enzyme, affecting function of the nervous system.

Since toxicological chemistry emphasizes the chemical nature of toxic substances, classification is predominantly on the basis of chemical class. Therefore, there are separate chapters on elemental toxic substances, hydrocarbons, organonitrogen compounds, and other chemical classifications of substances.

Toxicity Influencing Factors

Classification of Factors

It is useful to categorize the factors that influence toxicity within the following three classifications: (i) the toxic substance and its matrix, (ii) circumstances of exposure, and (iii) the subject and its environment. These are considered in the following sections.

Form of the Toxic Substance and Its Matrix

Toxicants to which subjects are exposed in the environment or occupationally, particularly through inhalation, may be in several different physical forms. Gases are substances such as carbon monoxide in air that are normally in the gaseous state under ambient conditions of temperature and pressure. Vapors are gas-phase materials that can evaporate or sublime from liquids or solids. Benzene or naphthalene can exist in the vapor form. Dusts are respirable solid particles produced by grinding bulk solids, whereas fumes are solid particles from the condensation of vapors, often metals or metal oxides. Mists are liquid droplets. Generally a toxic substance is in solution or mixed with other substances. A substance with which the toxicant is associated (the solvent in which it is dissolved or the solid medium in which it is dispersed) is called the *matrix*. The matrix may have a strong effect on the toxicity of the toxicant.

Numerous factors may be involved with the toxic substance itself. If the substance is a toxic heavy metal cation, the nature of the anion with which it is associated can be crucial. For example, barium ion, Ba^{2+}, in the form of insoluble barium sulfate, $BaSO_4$, is routinely used as an x-ray opaque agent in the gastrointestinal tract for diagnostic purposes (barium enema x-ray). This is a safe procedure; however, *soluble* barium salts such as $BaCl_2$ are deadly poisons when introduced into the gastrointestinal tract.

The pH of the toxic substance can greatly influence its absorption and therefore its toxicity. An example of this phenomenon is provided by aspirin, one of the most common causes of poisoning in humans. The chemical name of aspirin is sodium acetylsalicylate, the acidic form of which is acetylsalicylic acid (HAsc), a weak acid that ionizes as follows:

$$HAsc \rightleftarrows H^+ + Asc^- \quad K_a = \frac{[H^+][Asc^-]}{[HAsc]} = 6 \times 10^{-4} \qquad ...(1)$$

The K_a expression is expressed in molar concentrations (denoted by brackets) of the neutral and ionized species involved in the ionization of the acetylsalicylic acid. The pK_a (negative log of K_a) of HAsc is 3.2, and at a pH substantially below 3.2, most of this acid is in the neutral HAsc form. This neutral form is easily absorbed by the body, especially in the stomach, where the contents have a low pH of about 1. Many other toxic substances exhibit acid–base behavior and pH is a factor in their uptake.

Solubility is an obvious factor in determining the toxicity of systemic poisons. These must be soluble in body fluids or converted to a soluble form in the organ or system through which they are introduced into the body. Some insoluble substances that are ingested pass through the gastrointestinal tract without doing harm, whereas they would be quite toxic if they could dissolve in body fluids.

As noted at the beginning of this section, the degree of toxicity of a substance may depend on its matrix. The solvent or suspending medium is called the *vehicle*. For laboratory studies of toxicity, several vehicles are commonly used. Among the most common of these are water and aqueous saline solution. Lipid-soluble substances may be dissolved in vegetable oils. Various organic liquids are used as vehicles. Dimethylsulfoxide is a solvent that has some remarkable abilities to carry a solute dissolved in it into the body. The two major classes of vehicles for insoluble substances are the natural gums and synthetic colloidal materials. Examples of the former are tragacanth and acacia, whereas methyl cellulose and carboxymethylcellulose are examples of the latter.

Some drug formulations contain *excipients* that have been added to give a desired consistency or form. In some combinations excipients have a marked influence upon toxicity. *Adjuvants* are excipients that may increase the effect of a toxic substance or enhance the pharmacologic action of a drug. For example, dithiocarbamate fungicides may have their activities increased by the addition of 2-mercaptothiazole.

A variety of materials other than those discussed above may be present in formulations of toxic substances. *Dilutents* increase bulk and mass. Common examples of these are salts, such as calcium carbonate and dicalcium phosphate; carbohydrates, including sucrose and starch; the clay, kaolin; and milk solids. Among the *preservatives* used are sodium benzoate, phenylmercuric nitrate, and butylated hydroxyanisole (an antioxidant). "Slick" substances such as cornstarch, calcium stearate, and talc act as *lubricants*. Various gums and waxes, starch, gelatin, and sucrose are used as *binders*. Gelatin, carnauba wax, and shellac are applied as *coating agents*. Cellulose derivatives and starch may be present as *disintegrators* in formulations containing toxicants.

Decomposition may affect the action of a toxic substance. Therefore, the stability and storage characteristics of formulations containing toxicants should be considered. A toxic substance may be contaminated with other materials that affect toxicity. Some contaminants may result from decomposition.

Circumstances of Exposure

There are numerous variables related to the ways in which organisms are exposed to toxic substances. Another important factor is the *toxicant concentration*, which may range from the pure substance (100%) down to a very dilute solution of a highly potent poison. Both the duration of exposure per exposure incident and the *frequency* of exposure are important. The *rate* of exposure, inversely related to the duration per exposure, and the total time period over which the organism is exposed are both important situational variables. The exposure *site* and *route* strongly affect toxicity. Toxic effects are largely the result of metabolic processes on substances that occur after exposure, and much of the remainder of this book deals with these kinds of processes.

It is possible to classify exposures on the basis of acute vs. chronic and local vs. systemic exposure, giving four general categories. *Acute local* exposure occurs at a specific location over a time period of a few seconds to a few hours and may affect the exposure site, particularly the skin, eyes, or mucous membranes. The same parts of the body can be affected by *chronic local* exposure, but the time span may be as long as several years. *Acute systemic* exposure is a brief exposure or exposure to a single dose and occurs with toxicants that can enter the body, such as by inhalation or ingestion, and affect organs such as the liver that are remote from the entry site. *Chronic systemic* exposure differs in that the exposure occurs over a prolonged time period.

Subject

The first of two major classes of factors in toxicity pertaining to the subject and its environment consists of factors inherent to the subject. The most obvious of these is the *taxonomic classification* of the subject, that is, the species and strain. With test animals it is important to consider the *genetic status* of the subjects, including whether they are littermates, half-siblings (different fathers), or the products of inbreeding. Body mass, sex, age, and degree of maturity are all factors in toxicity. *Immunological status* is important. Another area involves the general well-being of the subject. It includes disease and injury, diet, state of hydration, and the subject's psychological state as affected by the presence of other species and/or members of the opposite sex, crowding, handling, rest, and activity.

The other major class consists of *environmental factors*. Among these are ambient atmosphere conditions of temperature, pressure, and humidity, as well as composition of the atmosphere, including the presence of atmospheric pollutants, such as ozone or carbon monoxide. Light and noise and the patterns in which they occur are important. Social and housing (caging) conditions may also influence response of subjects to a toxicant.

Exposure to Toxic Substances

Perhaps the first consideration in toxicology is *exposure* of an organism to a toxic substance. In discussing exposure sites for toxicants, it is useful to consider the major routes and sites of exposure, distribution, and elimination of toxicants in the body. The major routes of accidental or intentional exposure to toxicants by humans and other animals are the skin (percutaneous route), the lungs (inhalation, respiration, pulmonary route), and the mouth (oral route); minor means of exposure are the rectal, vaginal, and parenteral routes (intravenous or intramuscular, a common means for the administration of drugs or toxic substances in test subjects). The way that a toxic substance is introduced into the complex system of an organism is strongly dependent upon the physical and chemical properties of the substance. The pulmonary system is most likely to take in toxic gases or very fine, respirable solid or liquid particles. In other than a respirable form, a solid usually enters the body orally. Absorption through the skin is

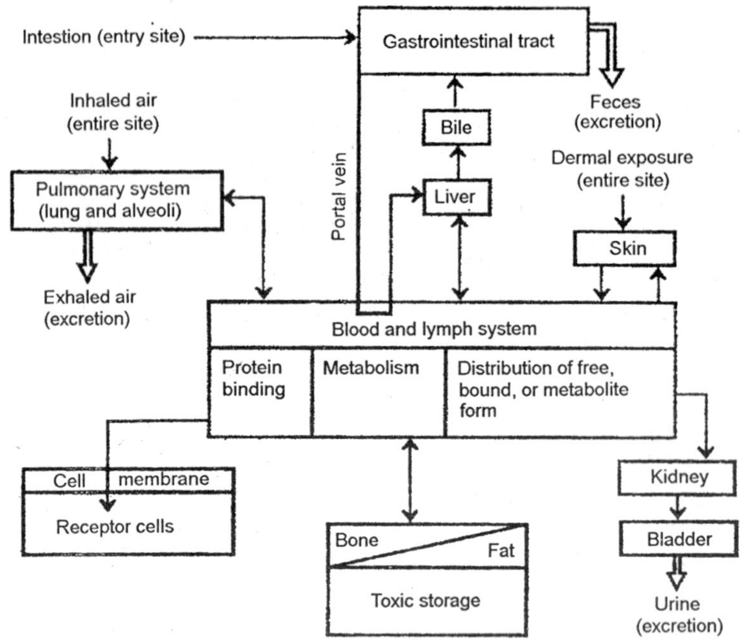

Fig. 1.1. Major sites of exposure, metabolism and storage, and routes of distribution and elimination of toxic substances in the body.

most likely for liquids, solutes in solution, and semisolids, such as sludges.

The defensive barriers that a toxicant may encounter vary with the route of exposure. For example, elemental mercury is more readily absorbed, often with devastating effects, through the alveoli in the lungs than through the skin or gastrointestinal tract. Most test exposures to animals are through ingestion or gavage (introduction into the stomach through a tube). Pulmonary exposure is often favored with subjects that may exhibit refractory behavior when noxious chemicals are administered by means requiring a degree of cooperation from the subject. Intravenous injection may be chosen for deliberate exposure when it is necessary to know the concentration and effect of a xenobiotic substance in the blood. However, pathways used experimentally that are almost certain not to be significant in accidental exposures can give misleading results when they avoid the body's natural defense mechanisms.

Percutaneous Exposure

Toxicants can enter the skin through epidermal cells, sebaceous gland cells, or hair follicles. By far the greatest area of the skin is composed of the epidermal cell layer, and most toxicants absorbed through the skin do so through epidermal cells. Despite their much smaller total areas, however, the cells in the follicular walls and in sebaceous glands are much more permeable than epidermal cells.

Skin permeability

The absorption of a toxic substance through the skin and its entry into the circulatory system, where it may be distributed through the body. Often the skin suffers little or no harm at the site of entry of systemic poisons, which may act with devastating effects on receptors far from the location of absorption.

The permeability of the skin to a toxic substance is a function of both the substance and the skin. The permeability of the skin varies with both the location and the species that penetrates it. In order to penetrate the skin significantly, a substance must be a liquid or gas or significantly soluble in water or organic solvents. In general, nonpolar, lipid-soluble substances traverse skin more readily than do ionic species. Substances that penetrate skin easily include lipid-soluble endogenous substances (hormones, vitamins D and K) and a number of xenobiotic compounds. Common examples of these are phenol, nicotine, and strychnine. Some military poisons, such as the nerve gas sarin, permeate the skin very readily, which greatly adds to their hazards. In addition to the rate of transport through the skin, an additional factor that influences toxicity via the percutaneous route is the blood flow at the site of exposure.

Barriers to Skin Absorption

The major barrier to dermal absorption of toxicants is the *stratum corneum*, or horny layer. The permeability of skin is inversely proportional to the thickness of this layer, which varies by location on the body in the following order: soles and palms > abdomen, back, legs, arms > genital (perineal) area. Evidence of the susceptibility of the genital area to absorption of toxic substances is to be found in accounts of the high incidence of cancer of the scrotum among chimney sweeps in London described by Sir Percival Pott, Surgeon General of Britain during the reign of King George III. The cancer-causing agent was coal tar condensed in chimneys. This material was more readily absorbed through the skin in the genital areas than elsewhere, leading to a high incidence of scrotal cancer. (The chimney sweeps' conditions were aggravated by their lack of appreciation of basic hygienic practices, such as bathing and regular changes of underclothing.) Breaks in epidermis due to laceration, abrasion, or irritation increase the permeability, as do inflammation and higher degrees of skin hydration.

Measurement of dermal toxicant uptake

There are two principal methods for determining the susceptibility of skin to penetration by toxicants. The first of these is measurement of the dose of the substance received by the organism using chemical analysis, radiochemical analysis of radioisotope-labeled substances, or observation of clinical symptoms. Secondly, the amount of substance remaining at the site of administration may be measured. This latter approach requires control of nonabsorptive losses of the substance, such as those that occur by evaporation.

Pulmonary exposure

The pulmonary system is the site of entry for numerous toxicants. Examples of toxic substances inhaled by human lungs include fly ash and ozone from polluted atmospheres, vapors of volatile chemicals used in the workplace, tobacco smoke, radioactive radon gas, and vapors from paints, varnishes, and synthetic materials used for building construction.

The major function of the lungs is to exchange gases between the bloodstream and the air in the lungs. This especially includes the absorption of oxygen by the blood and the loss of carbon dioxide. Gas exchange occurs in a vast number of alveoli in the lungs, where a tissue the thickness of only one cell separates blood from air. The thin, fragile nature of this tissue makes the lungs especially susceptible to absorption of toxicants and to direct damage from toxic substances. Furthermore, the respiratory route enables toxicants entering the body to bypass organs that have a screening effect (the liver is the major "*screening organ*" in the body and it acts to detoxify numerous toxic substances). These toxicants can enter the bloodstream directly and be transported quickly to receptor sites with minimum intervention by the body's defense mechanisms.

There are several parts of the pulmonary system that can be affected by toxic substances. The upper respiratory tract, consisting of the nose, throat, trachea, and bronchi, retains larger particles that are inhaled. The retained particles may cause upper respiratory tract irritation. Cilia, which are small hair-like appendages in the upper respiratory tract, move with a sweeping motion to remove captured particles. These substances are transported to the throat from which they may enter the gastrointestinal tract and be absorbed by the body.

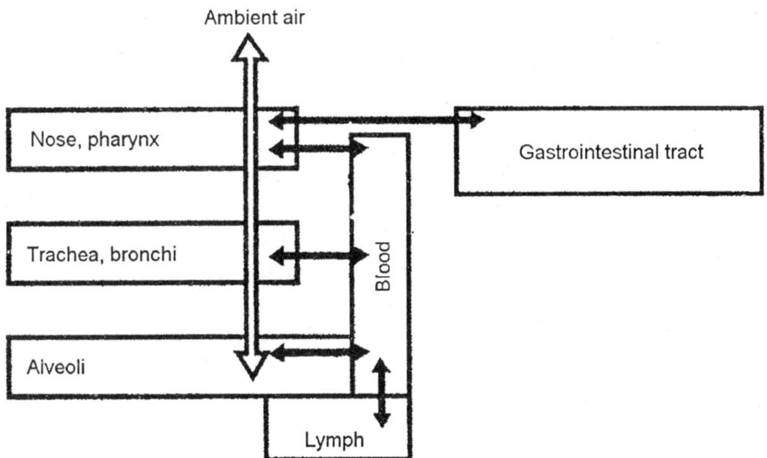

Fig. 1.2. Pathways of toxicants in the respiratory system.

Gases such as ammonia (NH_3) and hydrogen chloride (HCl) that are very soluble in water are also removed from air predominantly in the upper respiratory tract and may be very irritating to tissue in that region.

Gastrointestinal Tract

The gastrointestinal tract may be regarded as a tube through the body from the mouth to the anus, the contents of which are external to the rest of the organism system. Therefore, any systemic effect of a toxicant requires its absorption through the mucosal cells that line the inside of the gastrointestinal tract. Caustic chemicals can destroy or damage the internal surface of the tract and are viewed as nonkinetic poisons that act mainly at the site of exposure.

Mouth, Esophagus, and Stomach

Most substances are not readily absorbed in the mouth or esophagus; one of several exceptions is nitroglycerin, which is administered for certain heart disfunctions and absorbed if left in contact with oral tissue. The stomach is the first part of the gastrointestinal tract where substantial absorption and translocation to other parts of the body may take place. The stomach is unique because of its high content of HCl and consequent low pH (about 1.0). Therefore, some substances that are ionic at pH values near 7 and above are neutral in the stomach and readily traverse the stomach walls. In some cases, absorption is affected by stomach contents other than HCl. These include food particles, gastric mucin, gastric lipase, and pepsin.

Intestines

The small intestine is effective in the absorption and translocation of toxicants. The pH of the contents of the small intestine is close to neutral, so that weak bases that are charged (HB^+) in the acidic environment of the stomach are uncharged (B) and absorbable in the intestine. The small intestine has a large surface area favoring absorption. Intestinal contents are moved through the intestinal tract by peristalsis. This has a mixing action on the contents and enables absorption to occur the length of the intestine. Some toxicants slow down or stop peristalsis (paralytic ileus), thereby slowing the absorption of the toxicant itself.

Intestinal Tract and the Liver

The intestine–blood–liver–bile loop constitutes the *enterohepatic circulation* system. A substance absorbed through the intestines goes either directly to the lymphatic system or to the *portal circulatory system*. The latter carries blood to the portal vein that goes directly to the liver. The liver serves as a screening organ for xenobiotics, subjecting them to metabolic processes that usually reduce their toxicities, and secretes these substances or a metabolic product of them back to the intestines. For some substances, there are mechanisms of active excretion into the bile in which the substances are concentrated by one to three orders of magnitude over levels in the blood. Other substances enter the bile from blood simply by diffusion.

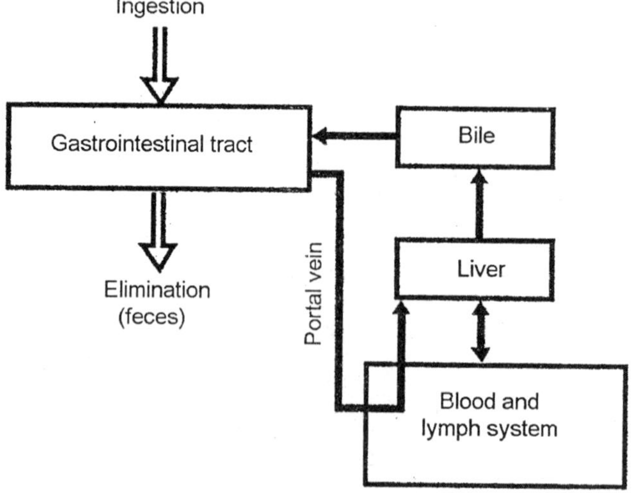

Fig. 1.3. Representation of enterohepatic circulation.

Dose-Response Relationships

Toxicants have widely varying effects on organisms. Quantitatively, these variations include minimum levels at which the onset of an effect is observed, the sensitivity of the organism to small increments of toxicant, and levels at which the ultimate effect (particularly death) occurs in most exposed organisms. Some essential substances, such as nutrient minerals, have optimum ranges above and below which detrimental effects are observed.

Factors such as those just outlined are taken into account by the *dose–response* relationship, which is one of the key concepts of toxicology. *Dose* is the amount, usually per unit body mass, of a toxicant to which an organism is exposed. *Response* is the effect on an organism resulting from exposure to a toxicant. In order to define a dose–response relationship, it is necessary to specify a particular response, such as death of the organism, as well as the conditions under which the response is obtained, such as the length of time from administration of the dose. Consider a specific response for a population of the same kinds of organisms. At relatively low doses, none of the organisms exhibit the response (for example, all live), whereas at higher doses, all of the organisms exhibit the response (for example, all die). In between, there is a range of doses over which some of the organisms respond in the specified manner and others do not, thereby defining a dose–response curve. Dose–response relationships differ among

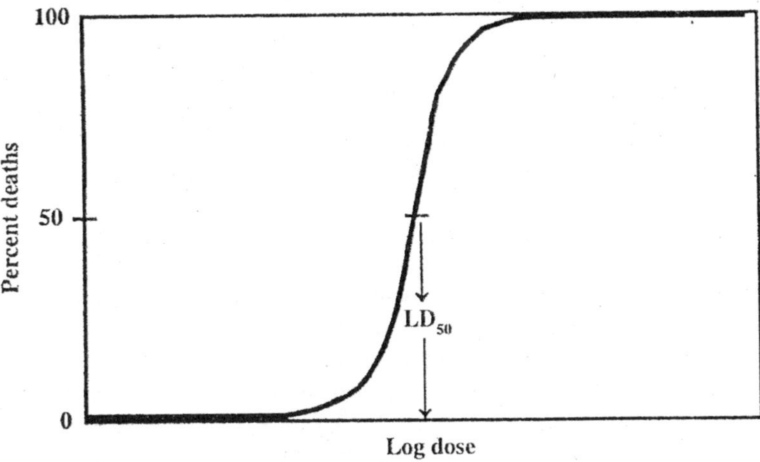

Fig. 1.4. Illustration of a dose-response curve in which the response is the death of the organism. The cumulative percentage of deaths of organisms is plotted on the y axis.

different kinds and strains of organisms, types of tissues, and populations of cells.

Figure 1.4 shows a generalized dose–response curve. Such a plot may be obtained, for example, by administering different doses of a poison in a uniform manner to a homogeneous population of test animals and plotting the cumulative percentage of deaths as a function of the log of the dose. The result is normally an S-shaped curve. The dose corresponding to the midpoint (inflection point) of such a curve is the statistical estimate of the dose that would cause death in 50% of the subjects and is designated as LD_{50}. The estimated doses at which 5% (LD_5) and 95% (LD_{95}) of the test subjects die are obtained from the graph by reading the dose levels for 5 and 95% fatalities, respectively. A relatively small difference between LD_5 and LD_{95} is reflected by a steeper S-shaped curve and vice versa. Statistically, 68% of all values on a dose–response curve fall within ± 1 standard deviation of the mean at LD_{50} and encompass the range from LD_{16} to LD_{84}.

The midrange of a dose–response curve is virtually a straight line. The slope of the curve in this range may vary. A very steep slope reflects a substance and organisms that have an abrupt onset of toxic effects, and only a small increase in dose causes a marked increase in response. A more gradual slope reflects a relatively large range, from a small percentage to a large percentage of responses. The LD_{50} might be the same in both cases, but with a sharp dose–response curve there is a small difference in dose between LD_5 and LD_{95}, whereas with a gradual curve the difference between these values is larger.

When exposure to toxic substances is in the air that animals breathe or in the water in which aquatic animals swim, exposure is commonly expressed as concentration. In such cases, LC_{50} values are obtained, where C stands for concentration, rather than dose.

Thresholds

An important concept pertinent to the dose–response relationship is that of *threshold* dose, below which there is no response. Threshold doses apply especially to acute effects and are very hard to determine, despite their crucial importance in determining safe levels of exposures to chemicals. In an individual, the response observed as the threshold level is exceeded may be very slight and subtle, making the threshold level very hard to determine. In a population, the number of subjects exhibiting the particular response at the threshold limit is very small and may be hard to detect above background effects (such as normal mortality rates of test organisms). For chronic effects, the determination of a threshold value is very difficult. This is especially true of cancer-causing substances that act by altering cellular DNA. For some of these substances, it is argued that there is no threshold and that the slightest exposure entails a risk.

Relative Toxicities

In terms of fatal doses to an adult human of average size, a "*taste*" of a supertoxic substances (just a few drops or less) is fatal. A teaspoonful of a very toxic substance could have the same effect. However, as much as a quart of a slightly toxic substance might be required to kill an adult human.

When there is a substantial difference between LD_{50} values of two different substances, the one with the lower value is said to be the more *potent*. Such a comparison must assume that the dose–response curves for the two substances being compared have similar slopes. If this is not the case, the substance for which the dose–response curve has the lesser slope may be toxic at a low dose, where the other substance is not toxic at all. Put another way, the relative LD_5 values of the substances may be reversed from the relative LD_{50} values.

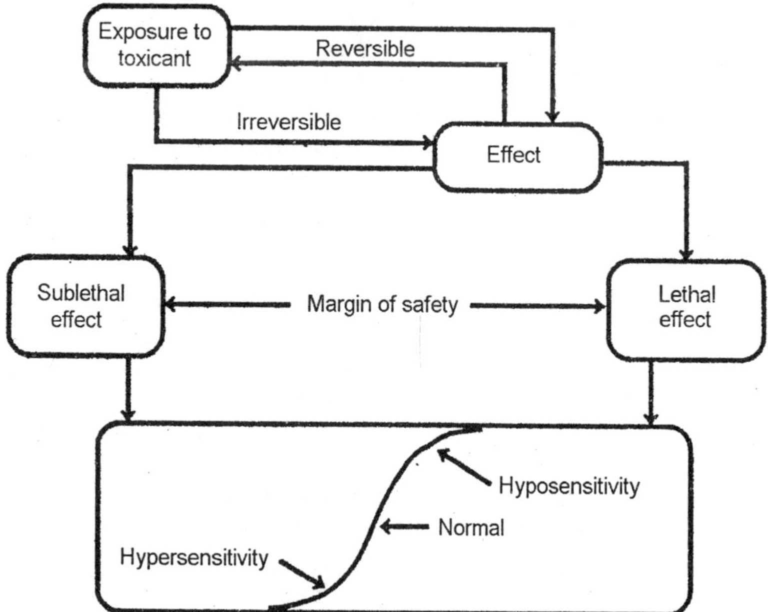

Fig. 1.5. Effects of and response to toxic substances.

Nonlethal Effects

It must be kept in mind that the acute toxicities of substances as expressed by LD_{50} values have limited value in expressing hazards to humans. This is because death from exposure to a toxic substance is a relatively rare effect that is irreversible. Of much more concern are *sublethal effects* that are often *reversible*, such as allergies, and birth defects. Of particular concern is the development of cancer from exposure to toxic substances (carcinogenicity) that, although often fatal, is not an acute effect and does not register on tables of LD_{50} values.

Sublethal reversible effects are obviously important with drugs, where death from exposure to a registered therapeutic agent is rare, but other effects, both detrimental and beneficial, are usually observed. By their very nature, drugs alter biologic processes; therefore, the potential for harm is almost always present. The major consideration in establishing drug dose is to find a dose that has an adequate therapeutic effect without undesirable side effects. The difference between the effective dose and harmful dose reflects the *margin of safety*.

When substances are used as pharmaceuticals to destroy disease-causing microorganisms or cancer tissue, or as pesticides to kill insects, weeds, or other pests, there is obviously an organism or tissue that is to be destroyed, commonly called the *uneconomic form*, and an organism or tissue that should remain unharmed, commonly called the *economic form*. Much of the ongoing research in pharmaceuticals and pesticides is designed to maximize the ratio of toxicities to uneconomic forms to those of economic forms. Several approaches are used. Some agents are about as toxic to both forms, but are accumulated more readily by the uneconomic form. Other agents take advantage of the higher susceptibility of receptors in tissues of the uneconomic form, which is therefore harmed more by the toxic agent. The selective toxicity of antibiotic penicillin to bacteria is due to the fact that it inhibits formation of cell walls, which bacteria have and need, whereas animals do not have cell walls. Another example is provided by genetically engineered soybeans that are not harmed by the hugely popular Roundup herbicide, whereas competing plants are destroyed by it.

In some cases there are striking differences between species in susceptibilities to toxic substances. One notable example is the 1000-fold greater susceptibility of guinea pigs over hamsters — both rodent species — to the effects of 2,3,7,8-tetrachlorodibenzo-*p*-dioxin (TCDD), commonly called "*dioxin*." Such differences may arise from the absence in the less susceptible species of receptors affected by the toxic substance. More commonly, they are due to the presence in the less susceptible organism of more effective mechanisms, usually detoxifying enzyme systems, for counteracting the effects of the toxic substance.

Individuals of the same species may differ significantly in their susceptibilities to various toxic agents. These differences are often genetic in nature. For example, some individuals lack tumor suppressor genes that other individuals possess and are thus more likely to develop some kinds of cancers, some of which are initiated by carcinogens. With increased knowledge of the human genome, these kinds of susceptibilities may become more apparent and appropriate preventive measures may be applied in some cases.

Reversibility and Sensitivity

Sublethal doses of most toxic substances are eventually eliminated from an organism's system. If there is no lasting effect from the exposure, it is said to be *reversible*. However, if the effect is permanent, it is termed *irreversible*. Irreversible effects of exposure remain after the toxic substance is eliminated from the organism. For various chemicals and different subjects, toxic effects may range from the totally reversible to the totally irreversible.

Hypersensitivity and Hyposensitivity

Examination of the dose–response curve, reveals that some subjects are very sensitive to a particular poison (for example, those killed at a dose corresponding to LD_5), whereas others are very resistant to the same substance (for example, those surviving a dose corresponding to LD_{95}). These two kinds of responses illustrate *hypersensitivity* and *hyposensitivity*, respectively; subjects in the midrange of the dose–response curve are termed *normals*. These variations in response tend to complicate toxicology in that there is not a specific dose guaranteed to yield a particular response, even in a homogeneous population.

In some cases hypersensitivity is induced. After one or more doses of a chemical, a subject may develop an extreme reaction to it. This occurs with penicillin, for example, in cases where people develop such a severe allergic response to the antibiotic that exposure results in death if counter-measures are not taken.

A kind of hyposensitivity is that induced by repeated exposures to a toxic substance leading to *tolerance* and reduced toxicities from later exposures. Tolerance can be due to a less toxic substance reaching a receptor or to tissue building up a resistance to the effects of the toxic substance. An example of the former occurs with repeated doses of toxic heavy metal cadmium. Animals respond by generating larger quantities of polypeptide *metallothionein*, which is rich in –SH groups that bind with Cd^{2+} ion, making it less available to receptors.

Xenobiotic and Endogenous Substances

Xenobiotic substances are those that are foreign to a living system. It should be kept in mind that xenobiotic substances may come from natural sources, such as deadly botulinus toxin produced by bacteria. Substances that occur naturally in a biologic system are termed *endogenous*. Endogenous substances are usually required within a particular concentration range in order for metabolic processes to occur normally. Levels below a normal range may result in a toxic response or even death, and the same effects may occur above the normal range.

Examples of Endogenous Substances

Examples of endogenous substances in organisms include various hormones, glucose (blood sugar), some vitamins, and some essential metal ions, including Ca^{2+}, K^{+}, and Na^{+}. Calcium in human blood serum exhibits the kind of behavior, with an optimum level that occurs over a rather narrow range of 9 to 9.5 mg/dL. Below these values, a toxic response known as hypocalcemia occurs, manifested by muscle cramping. At serum levels above about 10.5 mg/dL, hypercalcemia occurs, the major effect of which is kidney malfunction. Vitamin A is required for proper nutrition, but excessive levels damage the liver and may cause birth defects. Selenium, essential at low levels, can be toxic to the brain at higher levels.

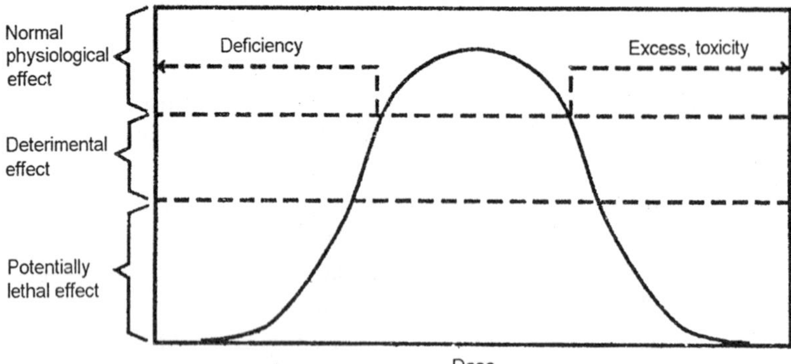

Fig. 1.6. Biologic effect of an endogenous substance in an organism showing optimum level, deficiency, and excess.

Kinetic and Nonkinetic Toxicology

Nonkinetic toxicology deals with generalized harmful effects of chemicals that occur at an exposure site; a typical example is the destruction of skin tissue by contact with concentrated nitric acid, HNO_3. Nonkinetic toxicology applies to those poisons that are not metabolized or transported in the body or subject to elimination processes that remove them from the body. The severity of a nonkinetic insult depends on both the characteristic of the chemical and the exposure site. Injury increases with increasing area and duration of the exposure, with the concentration of the toxicant in its matrix (for example, the concentration of HNO_3 in solution), and with the susceptibility of the exposure site to damage. The toxic action of the substance ceases when its chemical reaction with tissue is complete or when it is removed from the exposure site. Nonkinetic toxicology is also called *nonmetabolic* or *nonpharmacologic* toxicology.

Kinetic Toxicology

Kinetic toxicology, also known as *metabolic* or *pharmacologic* toxicology, involves toxicants that are transported and metabolized in the body. Such substances are called *systemic poisons* and they are studied under the discipline of *systemic toxicology*. Systemic poisons may cross cell membranes and act on *receptors* such as cell membranes, bodies in the cells, and specific enzyme systems. The effect is dose responsive, and it is terminated by processes that may include metabolic conversion of the toxicant to a metabolic product, chemical binding, storage, and excretion from the organism.

In an animal, a xenobiotic substance may be bound reversibly to a plasma protein in an inactivated form. A polar xenobiotic substance, or a polar metabolic product, may be excreted from the body in solution in urine. Nonpolar substances delivered to the intestinal tract in bile are eliminated with feces. Volatile nonpolar substances such as carbon monoxide tend to leave the body via the pulmonary system. The ingestion, biotransformation, action on receptor sites, and excretion of a toxic substance may involve complex interactions of biochemical and physiological parameters. The study of these parameters within a framework of metabolism and kinetics is called *toxicometrics*.

Receptors and Toxic Substances

A toxic substance that enters the body through any of the possible entry sites (ingestion, inhalation, skin) undergoes biochemical transformations that can increase or decrease its toxicity, affect its ability to traverse cell membranes, or enable its elimination from the body. A substance involved in a kinetic toxicological process generally enters the blood and lymph system before it has any effect. Plasma proteins may inactivate the toxic substance by binding reversibly to it. The substance often undergoes biotransformation, most commonly in the liver, but in other types of tissue as well. These reactions are catalyzed by enzymes, most frequently mixed-function oxidases. Toxicants can either stimulate or inhibit enzyme action. It is obvious that biochemical actions and transformations of toxicants are varied and complex.

Receptors

As noted in the preceding section, there are various *receptors* upon which xenobiotic substances or their metabolites act. In order to bind to a receptor, the substance has to have the proper structure or, more precisely, the right *stereochemical molecular configuration*. Receptors are almost always proteinaceous materials, normally enzymes. Nonenzyme receptors include opiate (nerve) receptors, gonads, or the uterus.

One of the most commonly cited examples of an enzyme receptor that is adversely affected by toxicants is that of *acetylcholinesterase*. It acts on *acetylcholine* as shown by the reaction. Acetylcholine is a neurotransmitter, a key substance involved with transmission of nerve impulses in the brain, skeletal muscles, and other areas where nerve impulses occur. An essential step in the proper function of any nerve impulse is its cessation, which requires hydrolysis of acetylcholine. Some xenobiotics, such as organophosphate compounds and carbamates inhibit acetylcholinesterase, with the result that acetylcholine accumulates and nerves are over-stimulated. Adverse effects may occur in the central nervous system, in the autonomic nervous system, and at neuromuscular junctions. Convulsions, paralysis, and finally death may result.

Phases of Toxicity

Having examined the routes by which toxicants enter the body, it is now appropriate to consider what happens to them in the body and what their effects are. The action of a toxic substance can be divided into two major phases. The *kinetic phase* involves absorption, metabolism, temporary storage, distribution, and, to a certain extent, excretion of the toxicant or its precursor compound, called the *protoxicant*. In the most favorable scenario for an organism, a toxicant is absorbed, detoxified by metabolic processes, and excreted with no harm resulting. In the least favorable case, a protoxicant that is not itself toxic is absorbed and converted to a toxic metabolic product that is transported to a location where it has a detrimental effect. The *dynamic phase* is divided as follows: (i) the toxicant reacts with a receptor or target organ in the *primary reaction* step, (ii) there is a biochemical response, and (iii) physiological or behavioral manifestations of the effect of the toxicant occur.

Toxification and Detoxification

As shown for the kinetic phase, a xenobiotic substance may be detoxified by metabolic processes and eliminated from the body, made

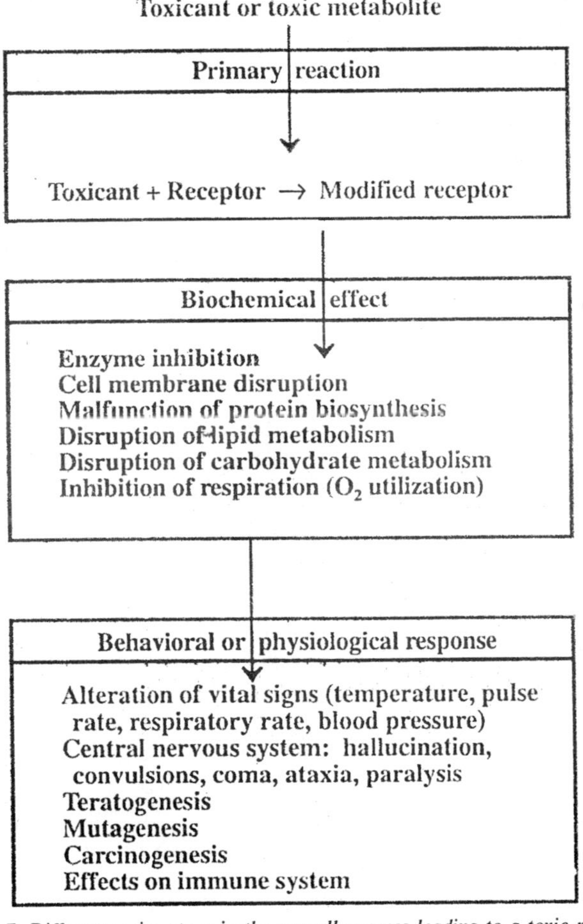

Fig. 1.7. Different major steps in the overall process leading to a toxic response.

more toxic (toxified) by metabolic processes and distributed to receptors, or passed on to receptors as a metabolically unmodified toxicant. A metabolically unmodified toxicant is called an *active parent compound*, and a substance modified by metabolic processes is an *active metabolite*. Both types of species may be involved in the dynamic phase.

During the kinetic phase an active parent compound can be present in blood, liver, or nonliver (extrahepatic) tissue; in the latter two, it may be converted to inactive metabolites. An inactive parent metabolite may produce a toxic metabolite or metabolites in the liver or in extrahepatic tissue; in both these locations a toxic metabolite may be changed to an inactive form. Therefore, the kinetic phase involves a number of pathways by which a xenobiotic substance is converted to a toxicant that can act on a receptor or to a substance that is eliminated from the organism.

Synergism, Potentiation, and Antagonism

The biological effects of two or more toxic substances can be different in kind and degree from those of one of the substances alone. One of the ways in which this can occur is when one substance affects the way in which another undergoes any of the steps in either the kinetic phase or the dynamic phase. Chemical interaction between substances may affect their toxicities. Both substances may act on the same physiologic function, or two substances may compete for binding to the same receptor. When both substances have the same physiologic function, their effects may be simply *additive* or they may be *synergistic* (the total effect is greater than the sum of the effects of each separately). *Potentiation* occurs when an inactive substance enhances the action of an active one, and *antagonism* when an active substance decreases the effect of another active one. Antagonism falls into several different categories. *Functional antagonism* occurs when two different substances have opposite functions and tend to balance each other. When a toxic substance reacts chemically with another toxic substance and is neutralized, the phenomenon is called *chemical antagonism*. The degree to which a toxic substance reaches a target organ can be reduced by the presence of another substance, a phenomenon called *dispositional antagonism*. The effects of a toxic substance can be reduced by the action of another substance (called a *blocker*) that competes with it for binding to a receptor, a phenomenon called *receptor antagonism*.

Behavioral and Physiological Responses

The final part of the overall toxicological process consists of *behavioral* and *physiological responses*, which are observable symptoms of poisoning. These are discussed here, primarily in terms of responses seen in humans and other animals. Nonanimal species exhibit other kinds of symptoms from poisoning; for example, plants suffer from leaf mottling, pine needle loss, and stunted growth as a result of exposure to some toxicants.

Vital Signs

Human subjects suffering from acute poisoning usually show alterations in the *vital signs*, which consist of *temperature*, *pulse rate*, *respiratory rate*, and *blood pressure*. These are discussed here in connection with their uses as indicators of toxicant exposure.

Among those that increase body temperature are benzadrine, cocaine, sodium fluoroacetate, tricyclic antidepressants, hexachlorobenzene, and salicylates (aspirin). In addition to phenobarbital and ethanol, toxicants that decrease body temperature include phenothiazine, clonidine, glutethimide, and haloperidol.

Toxicants may have three effects on pulse rate: *bradycardia* (decreased rate), *tachycardia* (increased rate), and *arrhythmia* (irregular pulse). Alcohols may cause either bradycardia or tachycardia. Amphetamines, belladonna alkaloids, cocaine, and tricyclic antidepressants may cause either tachycardia or arrhythmia. Toxic doses of digitalis may result in bradycardia or arrhythmia. The pulse rate is decreased by toxic exposure to carbamates, organophosphates, local anesthetics, barbiturates, clonidine, muscaric mushroom toxins, and opiates. In addition to the substances mentioned above, those that cause arrhythmia are arsenic, caffeine, belladonna alkaloids, phenothizine, theophylline, and some kinds of solvents.

Among the toxicants that increase respiratory rate are cocaine, amphetamines, and fluoroacetate, nitrites (compounds containing the NO_2^- ion), methanol (CH_3OH), salicylates, and hexachlorobenzene.

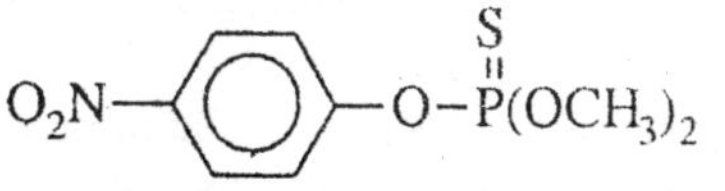

Methyl parathion

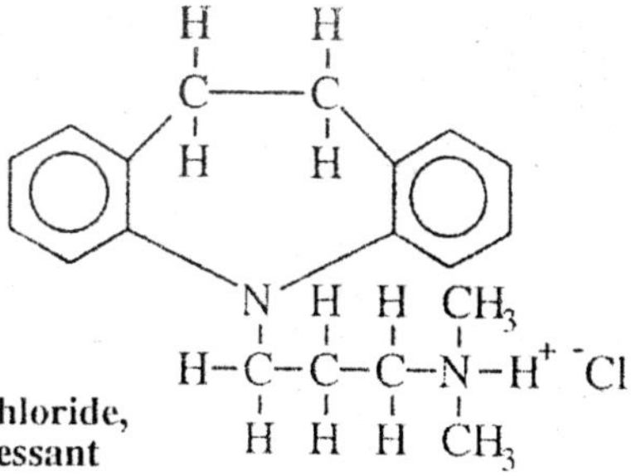

Imiprimine hydrochloride, a tricyclic antidepressant

Fig. 1.8. Structures of toxicants that can affect pulse rate.

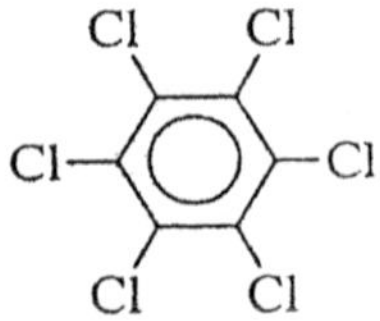

Hexachlorobenzene

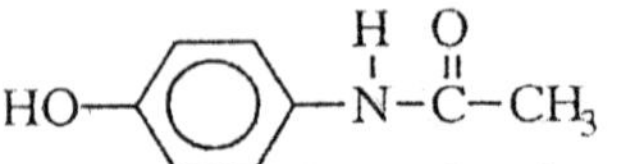

Acetaminophen

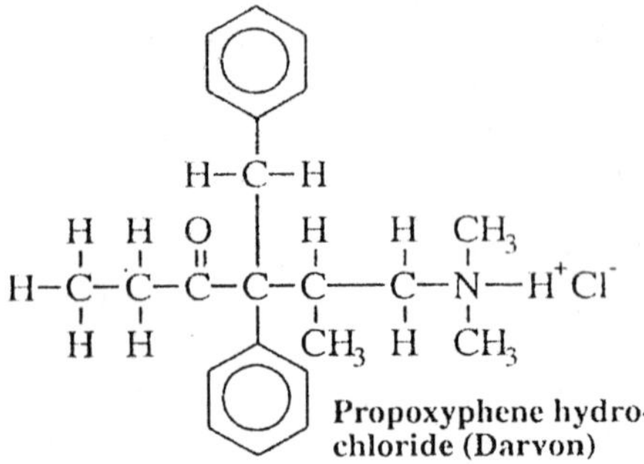

Propoxyphene hydrochloride (Darvon)

Fig. 1.9. Some compounds that affect respiratory rate.

Cyanide and carbon monoxide may either increase or decrease respiratory rate. Alcohols other than methanol, analgesics, narcotics, sedatives, phenothiazines, and opiates in toxic doses decrease respiratory rate.

Amphetamines and cocaine, tricyclic antidepressants, phenylcyclidines, and belladonna alkaloids at toxic levels increase blood pressure. Overdoses of antihypertensive agents decrease blood pressure, as do toxic doses of opiates, barbiturates, iron, nitrite, cyanide, and mushroom toxins.

Skin Symptoms

In many cases the skin exhibits evidence of exposure to toxic substances. The two main skin characteristics observed as evidence of poisoning are skin color and degree of skin moisture. Excessively dry skin tends to accompany poisoning by tricyclic antidepressants, antihistamines, and belladonna alkaloids. Among the toxic substances for which moist skin is a symptom of poisoning are mercury, arsenic, thallium, carbamates, and organophosphates. The skin appears flushed when the subject has been exposed to toxic doses of carbon monoxide, nitrites, amphetamines, monsodium glutamate, and tricyclic antidepressants. Higher doses of cyanide, carbon monoxide, and nitrites give the skin a *cyanotic* appearance (blue color due to oxygen deficiency in the blood). Skin may appear *jaundiced* (yellow because of the presence of bile pigments in the blood) when the subject is poisoned by a number of toxicants, including arsenic, arsine gas (AsH_3), iron, aniline dyes, and carbon tetrachloride.

Odors

Toxic levels of some materials cause the body to have unnatural *odors* because of parent compound toxicants or their metabolites secreted

$$\mathrm{H\!-\!C(OH)_2\!-\!CCl_3}$$

Chloral hydrate (pear odor)

$$\mathrm{H_3C\!-\!C(=O)\!-\!CH_3}$$

Acetone (acetone odor)

$$\mathrm{C_6H_5\!-\!NO_2}$$

Nitrobenzene (shoe polish)

$$\mathrm{C_6H_4(OH)\!-\!C(=O)\!-\!O\!-\!CH_3}$$

Methyl salicylate (wintergreen)

$$\mathrm{H_3C\!-\!Se\!-\!CH_3}$$

Dimethyl selenide (garlic)

Fig. 1.10. Some toxicants and the odors they produce in exposed subjects.

through the skin, exhaled through the lungs, or present in tissue samples. In addition to the odors, others symptomatic of poisoning include aromatic odors from hydrocarbons and the odor of violets arising from the ingestion of turpentine. Alert pathologists have uncovered evidence of poisoning murders by noting the bitter almond odor of hydrogen cyanide (HCN) in tissues of victims of criminal cyanide poisoning. A characteristic rotten-egg odor is evidence of hydrogen sulfide (H_2S) poisoning. The same odor has been reported at autopsies of carbon disulfide poisoning victims. Even very slight exposures to some selenium compounds cause an extremely potent garlic breath odor.

Eyes

Careful examination of the eyes can reveal evidence of poisoning. The response, both in size and reactivity, of the pupils to light may indicate response to toxicants. Both voluntary and involuntary movement of the eyes can be significant. The appearance of eye structures, including optic disc, conjunctiva, and blood vessels, can be significant. Eye *miosis*, defined as excessive or prolonged contraction of the eye pupil, is a toxic response to a number of substances, including alcohols, carbamates, organophosphates, and phenycyclidine. The opposite response of excessive pupil dilation, *mydriasis*, is caused by amphetamines, belladonna alkaloids, glutethimide, and tricyclic antidepressants, among others. *Conjunctivitis* is a condition marked by inflammation of the conjunctiva, the mucus membrane that covers the front part of the eyeball and the inner lining of the eyelids. Corrosive acids and bases (alkalies) cause conjunctivitis, as do exposures to nitrogen dioxide, hydrogen sulfide, methanol, and formaldehyde. *Nystagmus*, the involuntary movement of the eyeballs, usually in a side-to-side motion, occurs in poisonings by some toxicants, including barbiturates, phenycyclidine, phentoin, and ethychlorovynol.

Mouth

Examination of the mouth provides evidence of exposure to some toxicants. Caustic acids and bases cause a moist condition of the mouth. Other toxicants that cause the mouth to be moister than normal include mercury, arsenic, thallium, carbamates, and organophosphates. A dry mouth is symptomatic of poisoning by tricyclic antidepressants, amphetamines, antihistamines, and glutethimide.

Gastrointestinal Tract

The gastrointestinal tract responds to a number of toxic substances, usually by pain, vomiting, or paralytic ileus. Severe gastrointestinal pain is symptomatic of poisoning by arsenic or iron. Both of these substances can cause vomiting, as can acids, bases, fluorides, salicylates, and theophyllin. Paralytic ileus can result from ingestion of narcotic analgesics, tricyclic antidepressants, and clonidine.

Central Nervous System

The central nervous system responds to poisoning by exhibiting symptoms such as *convulsions*, *paralysis*, *hallucinations*, and *ataxia* (lack of coordination of voluntary movements of the body). Other behavioral symptoms of poisoning include agitation, hyperactivity, disorientation, and delirium.

Among the many toxicants that cause convulsions are chlorinated hydrocarbons, amphetamines, lead, organophosphates, and strychnine. There are several levels of *coma*, the term used to describe a lowered level of consciousness. At level 0, the subject may be awakened and will respond to questions. At level 1, withdrawal from painful stimuli is observed and all reflexes function. A subject at level 2 does not withdraw from painful stimuli, although most reflexes still function. Levels 3 and 4 are characterized by the absence of reflexes; at level 4, respiratory action is depressed and the cardiovascular system fails. Among the many toxicants that cause coma are narcotic analgesics, alcohols, organophosphates, carbamates, lead, hydrocarbons, hydrogen sulfide, benzodiazepines, tricyclic antidepressants, isoniazid, phenothiazines, and opiates.

Reproductive and Developmental Effects

Some of the more serious effects of toxic substances are those that affect the reproduction of organisms and their development to adulthood. Because of the serious nature of these effects, they are commonly examined in animal studies of pharmaceuticals, pesticides, and other chemicals.

Developmental toxic effects are those that adversely influence the growth and development of an organism to adulthood. These may occur from exposure of either parent of the organism to toxic substances even before conception. They may be the result of exposure of the embryo or fetus before birth. And they include effects resulting from exposure during the growth of the juvenile organism from birth to adulthood.

Teratology refers specifically to adverse effects of substances on an organism after conception up until birth. The teratogenic effects of thalidomide that resulted when women took this tranquilizing drug during early stages of pregnancy stand as one of the most distressing examples of teratogenic substances. Teratogens are most likely to cause harmful effects during the first trimester of pregnancy, when organs are becoming differentiated.

The reproductive systems of both males and females are suceptible to adverse effects of toxic substances. The study of these effects is called *reproductive toxicology*.

The chemical alteration of cell DNA that results in effects passed on through cell division is known as *mutagenesis*. Mutagenesis may occur in germ cells (female egg cells, male sperm cells) and cause mutations that appear in offspring. Mutagenesis may also occur in somatic cells, which are any body cells that are not sexual reproductive cells. Somatic cell mutagens are of particular concern because of the possibility that they will result in uncontrolled cell reproduction leading to cancer. Somatic cell mutations are easier to detect than germ cell mutations through observation of chromsomal aberrations and other effects.

2

FORENSIC TOXICANTS

Toxicological chemistry is the chemistry of toxic substances, with emphasis on their interactions with biologic tissue and living systems. This chapter expands on this definition to define toxicological chemistry in more detail. In order to comprehend this topic, it is first necessary to have an appreciation of the chemical nature of inorganic and organic chemicals. An understanding of biochemistry, is required to comprehend the ways in which xenobiotic substances in the body undergo biochemical processes and, in turn, affect these processes. Additional perspective is provided by the discussion of metabolic processes. Finally, an understanding of the environmental biochemistry of toxicants requires an appreciation of environmental chemistry.

CHEMICAL NATURE OF TOXICANTS

It is not possible to exactly define a set of chemical characteristics that make a chemical species toxic. This is because of the large variety of ways in which a substance can interact with substances, tissues, and organs to cause a toxic response. Because of subtle differences in their chemistry and biochemistry, similar substances may vary enormously in the degrees to which they cause a toxic response. For example, consider the toxic effects of carbon tetrachloride, CCl_4, and a chemically closely related chlorofluorocarbon, dichlorodifluoromethane, CCl_2F_2. Both of these compounds are completely halogenated derivatives of methane possessing very strong carbon–halogen bonds. Carbon tetrachloride is considered to be dangerous enough to have been banned from consumer products in 1970. It causes a large variety of toxic effects in humans, with chronic liver injury being the most prominent. Dichlorodifluoromethane, a Freon compound, is regarded as nontoxic, except for its action as a simple asphyxiant and lung irritant at high concentrations.

An increasingly useful branch of toxicological chemistry is the one dealing with *quantitative structure-activity relationships* (QSARs). By relating the chemical structure and physical characteristics of various compounds to their toxic effects, it is possible to predict the toxicological effects of other compounds and classes of compounds.

With the qualification that there are exceptions to the scheme, it is possible to place toxic substances into several main categories. These are listed below:

1. Substances that exhibit *extremes of acidity*, *basicity*, *dehydrating ability*, or *oxidizing power*. Examples include concentrated sulfuric acid (a strong acid with a tendency to dehydrate tissue), strongly basic sodium hydroxide, and oxidant elemental fluorine, F_2. Such species tend to be nonkinetic poisons and corrosive substances that destroy tissue by massively damaging it at the site of exposure.
2. *Reactive substances* that contain bonds or functional groups that are particularly prone to react with biomolecules in a damaging way. One reason that diethyl ether, $(C_2H_5)-O-(C_2H_5)$, is relatively nontoxic is because of its lack of reactivity resulting from the very strong C–H bonds in the ethyl groups and the very stable C–O–C ether linkage. A comparison of allyl alcohol with 1-propanol shows that the former is a relatively toxic irritant to the skin, eyes, and respiratory tract that also damages liver and kidneys, whereas 1-propanol is one of the less toxic organic chemicals with an LD_{50} about 100 times that of allyl alcohol. As shown by the structures, allyl alcohol differs from 1-propanol in having the relatively reactive alkenyl group C=C.

```
     H H             H  H  H
H    | |             |  |  |
 \C=C—C—OH         H—C——C——C—OH
 /     |             |  |  |
H      H             H  H  H
 Allyl alcohol     Propyl alcohol
```

3. *Heavy metals*, broadly defined, contain a number of members that are toxic by virtue of their interaction with enzymes, tendency to bond strongly with sulfhydryl (–SH) groups on proteins, and other effects.
4. *Binding species* are those that bond to biomolecules, altering their function in a detrimental way. This binding may be reversible, as is the case with the binding of carbon monoxide with hemoglobin,

which deprives hemoglobin of its ability to attach molecular O_2 and carry it from the lungs to body tissues. The binding may be irreversible. An example is that which occurs when an electron-deficient carbonium ion, such as H_3C^+(an electrophile), binds to a nucleophile, such as an N atom on guanine attached to deoxyribonucleic acid (DNA).

5. *Lipid-soluble compounds* are frequently toxic because of their ability to traverse cell membranes and similar barriers in the body. Lipid-soluble species frequently accumulate to toxic levels through biouptake and biomagnification processes.
6. Chemical species that induce a toxic response based largely on their *chemical structures*. Such toxicants often produce an allergic reaction as the body's immune system recognizes the foreign agent, causing an immune system response. Lower-molecular-mass substances that act in this way usually must become bound to endogenous proteins to form a large enough species to induce an allergic response.

Biochemical Transformations

The toxicological chemistry of toxicants is strongly tied to their metabolic reactions and fates in the body. Systemic poisons in the body undergo (i) biochemical reactions through which they have a toxic effect, and (ii) biochemical processes that increase or reduce their toxicities, or change toxicants to forms that are readily eliminated from the body. In dealing with xenobiotic compounds, the body metabolizes them in ways that usually reduce toxicity and facilitate removal of the substance from the body, a process generally called *detoxication*. The opposite process by which nontoxic substances are metabolized to toxic ones or by which toxicities are increased by biochemical reactions is called *toxication* or *activation*.

Metabolic Reactions of Xenobiotic Compounds

Toxicants or their metabolic precursors (*protoxicants*) may undergo absorption, metabolism, temporary storage, distribution, or excretion. The modeling and mathematical description of these aspects as a function of time is called *toxicokinetics*. Here are discussed the metabolic processes that toxicants undergo. Emphasis is placed on xenobiotic compounds, on chemical aspects, and on processes that lead to products that can be eliminated from the organism. Of particular importance is *intermediary xenobiotic metabolism*, which results in the formation of somewhat transient species that are different from both

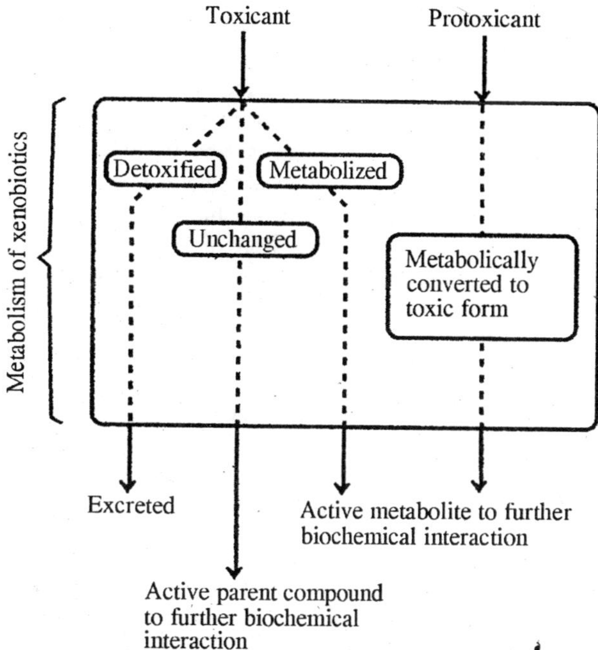

Fig. 2.1. Pathways of xenobiotic species prior to their undergoing any biochemical interactions that could lead to toxic effects.

those ingested and the ultimate product that is excreted. These species may have significant toxicological effects. Xenobiotic compounds in general are acted on by enzymes that function on an *endogenous substrate* that is in the body naturally. For example, flavin-containing monooxygenase enzyme acts on endogenous cysteamine to convert it to cystamine, but also functions to oxidize xenobiotic nitrogen and sulfur compounds.

Biotransformation refers to changes in xenobiotic compounds as a result of enzyme action. Reactions not mediated by enzymes may also be important. As examples of nonenzymatic transformations, some xenobiotic compounds bond with endogenous biochemical species without an enzyme catalyst, undergo hydrolysis in body fluid media, or undergo oxidation–reduction processes. However, the metabolic phase I and phase II reactions of xenobiotics discussed here are enzymatic.

The likelihood that a xenobiotic species will undergo enzymatic metabolism in the body depends on the chemical nature of the species. Compounds with a high degree of polarity, such as relatively ionizable carboxylic acids, are less likely to enter the body system and, when they do, tend to be quickly excreted. Therefore, such compounds are unavailable, or available for only a short time, for enzymatic metabolism. Volatile compounds, such as dichloromethane or diethylether, are expelled so quickly from the lungs that enzymatic metabolism is less likely. This leaves as the most likely candidates for enzymatic metabolic reactions *nonpolar lipophilic compounds*, those that are relatively less soluble in aqueous biological fluids and more attracted to lipid species. Of these, the ones that are resistant to enzymatic attack (polychlorinated biphenyls (PCBs), for example) tend to bioaccumlate in lipid tissue.

Xenobiotic species may be metabolized in a wide variety of body tissues and organs. As part of the body's defense against the entry of xenobiotic species, the most prominent sites of xenobiotic metabolism are those associated with entry into the body. The skin is one such organ, as is the lung. The gut wall through which xenobiotic species enter the body from the gastrointestinal tract is also a site of significant xenobiotic compound metabolism. The liver is of particular significance because materials entering systemic circulation from the gastrointestinal tract must first traverse the liver.

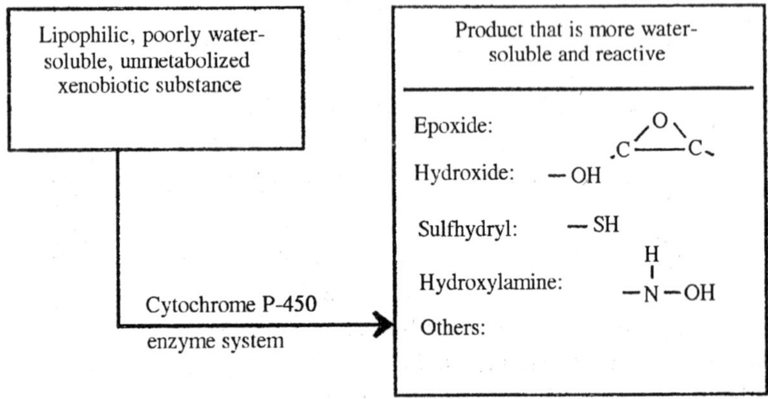

Fig. 2.2. Overall process of phase I reactions.

Phase I and Phase II Reactions

The processes that most xenobiotics undergo in the body can be divided into two categories: phase I reactions and phase II reactions. A *phase I reaction* introduces reactive, polar functional groups onto lipophilic (fat-seeking) toxicant molecules. In their unmodified forms, such toxicant molecules tend to pass through lipid-containing cell membranes and may be bound to lipoproteins, in which form they are transported through the body. Because of the functional group attached, the product of a phase I reaction is usually more water soluble than the parent xenobiotic species, and more importantly, it possesses a "*chemical handle*" to which a substrate material in the body may become attached so that the toxicant can be eliminated from the body. The binding of such a substrate is a *phase II reaction*, and it produces a *conjugation product* that normally (but not always) is less toxic than the parent xenobiotic compound or its phase I metabolite and more readily excreted from the body.

In general, the changes in structure and properties of a compound that result from a phase I reaction are relatively mild. Phase II processes, however, usually produce species that are much different from the parent compounds. It should be emphasized that not all xenobiotic compounds undergo both phase I and phase II reactions. Such a compound may undergo only a phase I reaction and be excreted directly from the body. Or a compound that already possesses an appropriate functional group capable of conjugation may undergo a phase II reaction without a preceding phase I reaction.

Phase I and phase II reactions are obviously important in mitigating the effects of toxic sustances. Some toxic substances act by inhibiting the enzymes that carry out phase I and phase II reactions, leading to toxic effects of other substances that normally would be detoxified.

Phase I Reactions

Normally a phase I reaction adds a functional group to a hydrocarbon chain or ring or modifies one that is already present.[4] The product is a chemical species that readily undergoes conjugation with some other species naturally present in the body to form a substance that can be readily excreted. Phase I reactions are of several types, of which oxidation of C, N, S, and P is most important. Reduction may occur on reducible functionalities by addition of H or removal of O. Phase I reactions may also consist of hydrolysis processes, which require that the xenobiotic compound have a hydrolyzable group.

Oxidation Reactions

The most important phase I reactions are oxidation reactions, particularly those classified as microsomal monooxygenation reactions, formerly called mixed-function oxidations. Microsomes refer to a fraction collected from the centrifugation at about 100,000 × *g* of cell homogenates and consisting of pellets. These pellets contain rough and smooth *endoplasmic reticulum* (extensive networks of membranes in cells) and Golgi bodies, which store newly synthesized molecules.

Monooxidations occur with O_2 as the oxidizing agent, one atom of which is incorporated into the substrate, and the other going to form water:

$$\text{Substrate} + O_2 \xrightarrow{\text{Monooxidation}} \begin{cases} \text{Product-OH} \\ H_2O \end{cases}$$

The key enzymes of the system are the cytochrome P-450 enzymes, which have active sites that contain an iron atom that cycles between the +2 and +3 oxidation states. These enzymes bind to the substrate and molecular O_2 as part of the substrate oxidation process. Cytochrome P-450 is found most abundantly in the livers of vertebrates, reflecting the liver's role as the body's primary defender against systemic poisons. Cytochrome P-450 occurs in many other parts of the body, such as the kidney, ovaries, testes, and blood. The presence of this enzyme in the lungs, skin, and gastrointestinal tract may reflect their defensive roles against toxicants.

Epoxidation consists of adding an oxygen atom between two C atoms in an unsaturated system. It is a particularly important means of metabolic attack on aromatic rings that abound in many xenobiotic compounds. Cytochrome P-450 is involved in epoxidation reactions. Both of the epoxidation reactions shown below have the effect of increasing the toxicities of the parent compounds, a process called *intoxication*. Some epoxides are unstable, tending to undergo further reactions, usually hydroxylation. A well-known example of the formation of a stable epoxide is the conversion to aldrin of the insecticide dieldrin.

$$Cl_2C{=}CHCl \xrightarrow[\text{epoxidation}]{O_2,\text{ enzyme-mediated}} Cl{-}C(Cl)(O)C(H){-}Cl$$

Trichloroethylene

↓

Trichloroacetaldehyde $Cl{-}C(Cl)_2{-}C({=}O){-}H$

$$C_6H_6 \xrightarrow[\text{epoxidation}]{O_2,\text{ enzyme-mediated}} C_6H_6O$$

Hydroxylation

Hydroxylation is the attachment of –OH groups to hydrocarbon chains or rings. *Aliphatic hydroxylation* of alkane chains can occur on the terminal carbon atom (–CH_3 group or ω-carbon) or on the C atom next to the last one (ω-1-carbon) by the insertion of an O atom between C and H, as shown below for the hydroxylation of the side chain on a substituted aromatic compound:

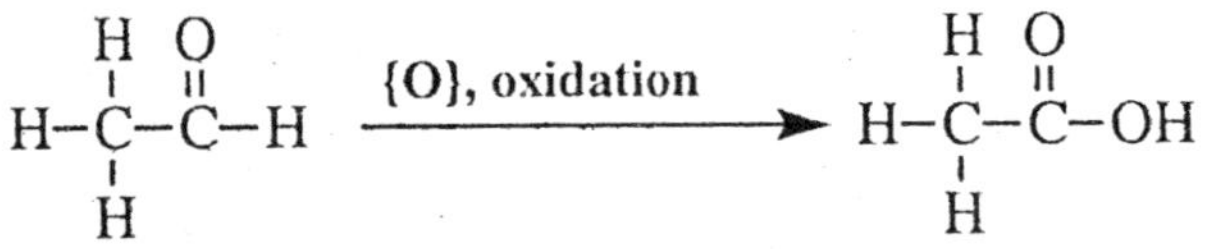

H O
| ||
H–C–C–H —{O}, oxidation→ H–C–C–OH
|
H

Aldehyde **Carboxylic acid**

Hydroxylation can follow epoxidation, as shown by the following rearrangement reaction for benzene epoxide:

Benzene epoxide **Phenol**

Epoxide Hydration

The addition of H_2O to epoxide rings, a process called *epoxide hydration*, is important in the metabolism of some xenobiotic materials. This reaction can occur, for example, with benzo(a)pyrene 7,8-epoxide,

Benzo(a)pyrene —{O}, epoxidation→ Benzo(a)pyrene 7,8-epoxide

+ H_2O, epoxide hydrolase

Benzo(a)pyrene 7,8-diol —{O}, epoxidation→ benzo(a)pyrene 7,8-diol-9,10-epoxide

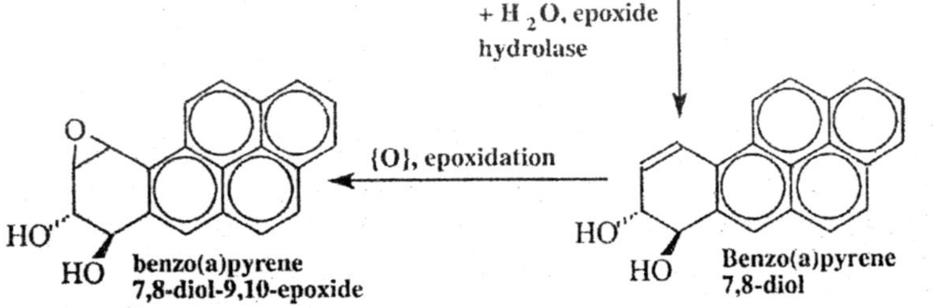

Fig. 2.3. Epoxidation and hydroxylation of benzo(a)pyrene (left) to form carcinogenic benzo(a)pyrene 7,8-diol-9, 10-epoxide.

formed by the metabolic oxidation of benzo(a)pyrene. Hydration of an epoxide group on a ring leads to the *trans* dihydrodiols in which the –OH groups are on opposite sides of the ring.

Formation of a dihydrodiol by hydration of epoxide groups can be an important detoxication process in that the product is often much less reactive to potential receptors than is the epoxide. However, this is not invariably the case because some dihydrodiols may undergo further epoxidation to form even more reactive metabolites. This can happen with benzo(a)pyrene 7,8-epoxide, which becomes oxidized to carcinogenic benzo(a)pyrene 7,8-diol-9,10-epoxide. The parent polycyclic aromatic hydrocarbon benzo(a)pyrene is classified as a procarcinogen, or precarcinogen, in that metabolic action is required to convert it to a species, in this case benzo(a)pyrene 7,8-diol-9,10-epoxide, which is carcinogenic as such.

Oxidation of Noncarbon Elements

The oxidation of nitrogen, sulfur, and phosphorus is an important type of metabolic reaction in xenobiotic compounds. It can be an important intoxication mechanism by which compounds are made more toxic. For example, the oxidation of nitrogen in 2-acetylaminofluorene yields potently carcinogenic N-hydroxy-2-acetylaminofluorene. Two major steps in the metabolism of the plant systemic insecticide aldicarb are oxidation to the sulfoxide and oxidation to the sulfone. The oxidation of phosphorus in parathion (replacement of S by O, oxidative desulfurization) yields insecticidal paraoxon, which is much more effective than the parent compound in inhibiting acetylcholinesterase enzyme.

In addition to cytochrome P-450 enzymes, another enzyme that mediates phase I oxidations is *flavin-containing monooxygenase* (FMO), likewise contained in the endoplasmic reticulum. It is especially effective in oxidizing primary, secondary, and tertiary amines. Additionally, it catalyzes oxidation of other nitrogen-containing xenobiotic compounds, as well as those that contain sulfur and phosphorus, but does not bring about hydroxylation of carbon atoms.

Alcohol Dehydrogenation

A common step in the metabolism of alcohols is carried out by *alcohol dehydrogenase* enzymes that produce aldehydes from primary alcohols that have the –OH group on an end carbon and produce ketones from secondary alcohols that have the –OH group on a middle carbon. As indicated by the double arrows in these reactions, the reactions are reversible and the aldehydes and ketones can be converted back to

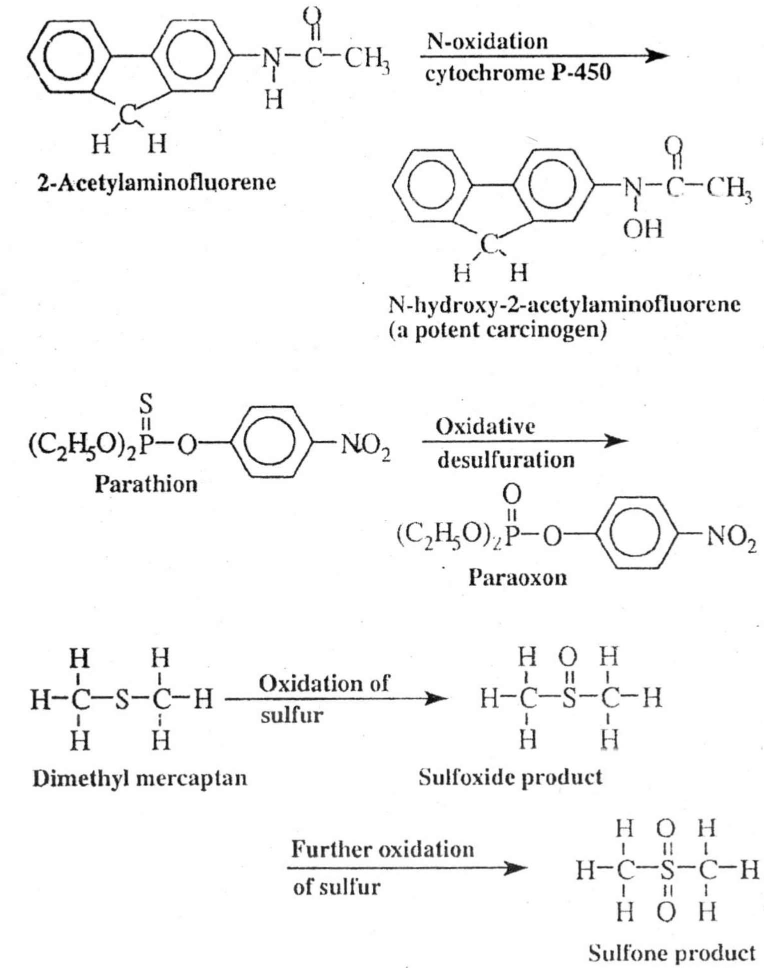

2-Acetylaminofluorene → (N-oxidation, cytochrome P-450) → N-hydroxy-2-acetylaminofluorene (a potent carcinogen)

$(C_2H_5O)_2P(=S)-O-C_6H_4-NO_2$
Parathion

→ (Oxidative desulfuration) →

$(C_2H_5O)_2P(=O)-O-C_6H_4-NO_2$
Paraoxon

$H_3C-S-CH_3$
Dimethyl mercaptan

→ (Oxidation of sulfur) →

$H_3C-S(=O)-CH_3$
Sulfoxide product

→ (Further oxidation of sulfur) →

$H_3C-S(=O)_2-CH_3$
Sulfone product

Fig. 2.4. Metabolic oxidation of nitrogen, phosphorus, and sulfur in xenobiotic compounds.

alcohols. The oxidation of aldehydes to carboxylic acids occurs readily. This is an important detoxication process because aldehydes are lipid soluble and relatively toxic, whereas carboxylic acids are more water soluble and undergo phase II reactions leading to their elimination.

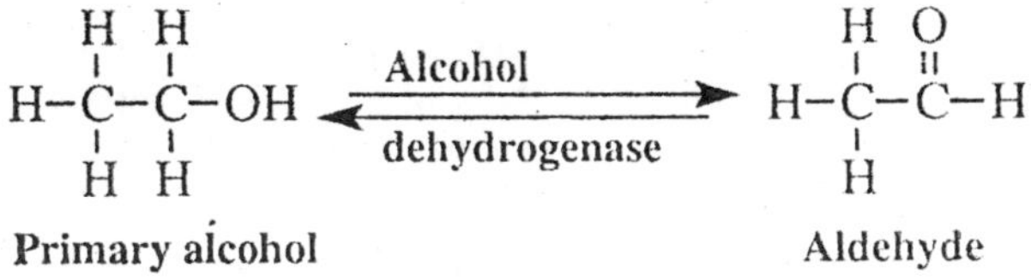

$$H_3C-CH_2-OH \underset{\text{dehydrogenase}}{\overset{\text{Alcohol}}{\rightleftharpoons}} H_3C-C(=O)-H$$

Primary alcohol — Aldehyde

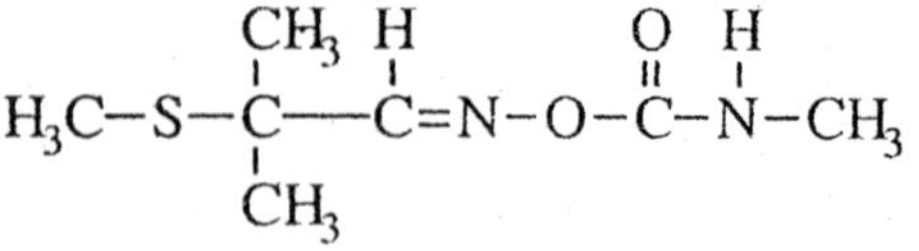

$$H_3C-S-\underset{CH_3}{\overset{CH_3}{C}}-\overset{H}{C}=N-O-\overset{O}{\overset{\|}{C}}-\overset{H}{N}-CH_3$$ Temik (aldicarb)

Fig. 2.5. Structure of the plant systemic insecticide temik. The sulfur is metabolically oxidizable.

Metabolic Reductions

Reductions are carried out by *reductase enzymes*; for example, nitroreductase enzyme catalyzes the reduction of the nitro group. Reductase enzymes are found largely in the liver and to a certain extent in other organs, such as the kidneys and lungs. Most reductions of xenobiotic compounds are mediated by bacteria in the intestines, the *gut flora*. The contents of the lower bowel may contain a huge concentration of anaerobic bacteria. The compounds reduced by these bacteria may enter the lower bowel by either oral ingestion (without having been absorbed through the intestinal wall) or secretion with bile. In the latter case, the compounds may be parent materials or metabolic products of substances absorbed in upper regions of the gastrointestinal tract. Intestinal flora are known to mediate the reduction of organic xenobiotic sulfones and sulfoxides to sulfides.

Metabolic Hydrolysis Reactions

Many xenobiotic compounds, such as pesticides, are esters, amides, or organophosphate esters, and hydrolysis is a very important aspect of their metabolic fates. *Hydrolysis* involves the addition of H_2O to a molecule accompanied by cleavage of the molecule into two species. The types of enzymes that bring about hydrolysis are *hydrolase enzymes*. Like most enzymes involved in the metabolism of xenobiotic compounds, hydrolase enzymes occur prominently in the liver. They also occur in tissue lining the intestines, nervous tissue, blood plasma, the kidney, and muscle tissue. Enzymes that enable the hydrolysis of esters are called *esterases*, and those that hydrolyze amides are *amidases*. Aromatic esters are hydrolyzed by the action of aryl esterases and alkyl esters by aliphatic esterases. Hydrolysis products of xenobiotic compounds may be either more or less toxic than the parent compounds.

Metabolic Dealkylation

Many xenobiotics contain alkyl groups, such as the methyl ($-CH_3$) group, attached to atoms of O, N, and S. These reactions are carried out by mixed-function oxidase enzyme systems. Examples of these kinds of reactions with xenobiotics include O-dealkylation of methoxychlor insecticides, N-dealkylation of carbaryl insecticide, and S-dealkylation

$$R-NH-CH_3 \xrightarrow{\text{N-dealkylation}} R-NH_2$$

$$R-O-CH_3 \xrightarrow{\text{O-dealkylation}} R-OH \quad + \; H-\overset{O}{\overset{\|}{C}}-H$$

$$R-S-CH_3 \xrightarrow{\text{S-dealkylation}} R-SH$$

Fig. 2.6. Metabolic dealkylation reactions shows for the removal of CH_3 from N, O, and S atoms in organic compounds.

of dimethyl mercaptan. Organophosphate esters also undergo hydrolysis, for the plant systemic insecticide demeton.

Removal of Halogen

An important step in the metabolism of the many xenobiotic compounds that contain covalently bound halogens (F, Cl, Br, I) is the removal of halogen atoms, a process called *dehalogenation*. This may occur by *reductive dehalogenation*, in which the halogen atom is replaced by hydrogen, or two atoms are lost from adjacent carbon atoms, leaving a carbon–carbon double bond. These processes are illustrated by the following:

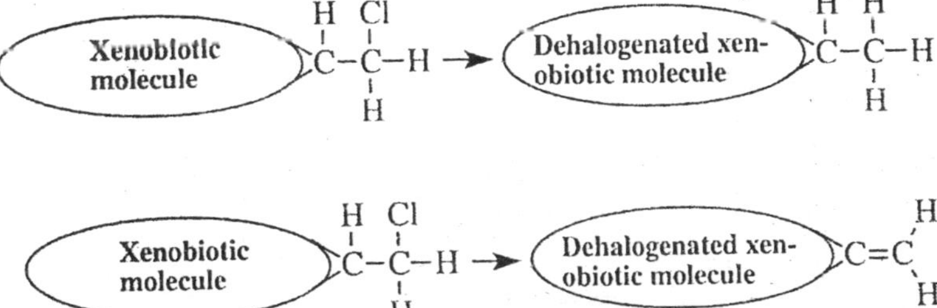

Oxidative dehalogenation occurs when oxygen is added in place of a halogen atom, as shown by the following reaction:

Xenobiotic molecule $\rangle C(H)-C(H)(Cl)-H \xrightarrow{O_2}$ Dehalogenated xenobiotic molecule $\rangle C(H)-C(=O)-OH$

Phase II Reactions of Toxicants

Phase II reactions are also known as *conjugation reactions* because they involve the joining together of a substrate compound with another species that occurs normally in (is endogenous to) the organism. This can occur with unmodified xenobiotic compounds, xenobiotic compounds that have undergone phase I reactions, and compounds that are not xenobiotic species. The substance that binds to these species is called an *endogenous* (present in and produced by the body) *conjugating agent*. Activation of the conjugating agent usually provides the energy needed for conjugation, although conjugation by glutathione or amino acids is provided by activation of the species undergoing conjugation preceding the reaction. Such a compound contains functional groups, often added as the consequence of a phase I reaction, that serve as "*chemical handles*" for the attachment of the conjugating agent. The conjugation product is usually less lipid soluble, more water soluble, less toxic, and more easily eliminated than the parent compound.

The conjugating agents that are attached as part of phase II reactions include glucuronide, sulfate, acetyl group, methyl group, glutathione, and some amino acids. Conjugation with glutathione is also a step in mercapturic acid synthesis. Glycine, glutamic acid, and

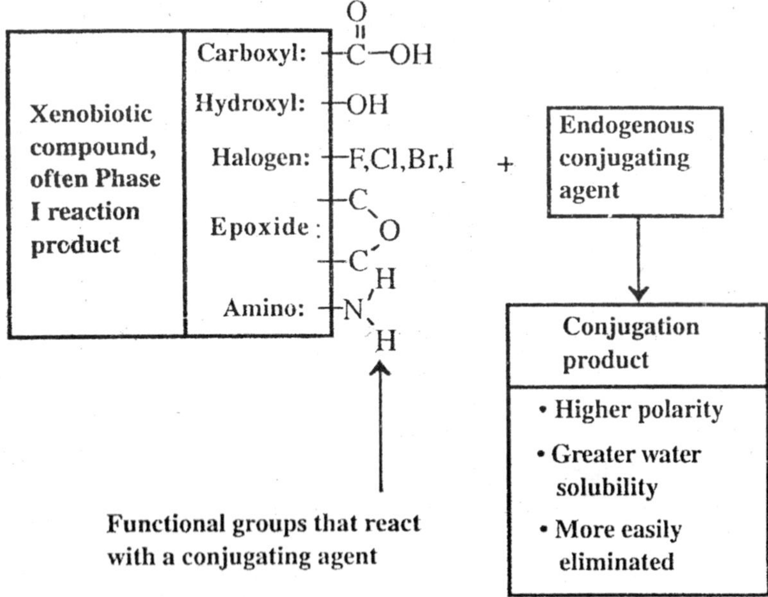

Fig. 2.7. Overall process of conjugation that occurs in phase II reactions.

taurine are common amino acids that act as conjugating agents. Most of the conjugates formed by these agents are more hydrophilic than the compounds conjugated, so the conjugates are more readily excreted. The exceptions are methylated and acetylated conjugates. Phase II conjugation reactions are usually rapid, and if they are performed on phase I reaction products, the rates of the latter are rate limiting for the overall process.

Conjugation by Glucuronides

Glucuronides are the most common endogenous conjugating agents in the body. They react with xenobiotics through the action of uridine diphosphate glucuronic acid (UDPGA). This transfer is mediated by glucuronyl transferase enzymes. These enzymes occur in the endoplasmic reticulum, where hydroxylated phase I metabolites of lipophilic xenobiotic compounds are produced. As a result, the lifetime of the phase I metabolites is often quite brief because the conjugating agent is present where they are produed. In this reaction HX–R represents the xenobiotic species in which HX is a functional group (such as -OH) and R is an organic moiety, such as the phenyl group (benzene ring less a hydrogen atom). The kind of enzyme that mediates this type of reaction is UDP glucuronyl-transferase.

Glucuronide conjugation products may be classified according to the element to which the glucuronide is bound. The atoms to which the glucuronide most readily attaches are electron rich, usually O, N, or S (nucleophilic heteroatoms in the parlance of organic chemistry). When the functional group through which conjugation occurs is a hydroxyl group, -OH, an ether glucuronide is formed. A carboxylic acid group for HX gives an ester glucuronide. Glucuronides may be attached directly to N as the linking atom, or through an intermediate O atom.

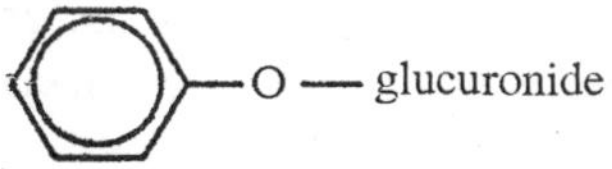

O — glucuronide

Phenylglucuronide, an O-glucuronide

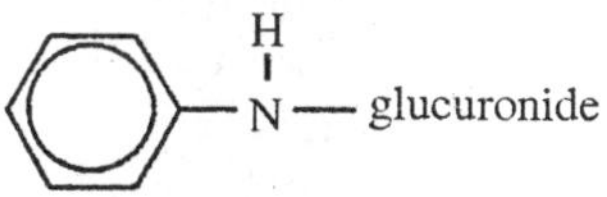

H
N — glucuronide

Anline glucuronide, an N-glucuronide

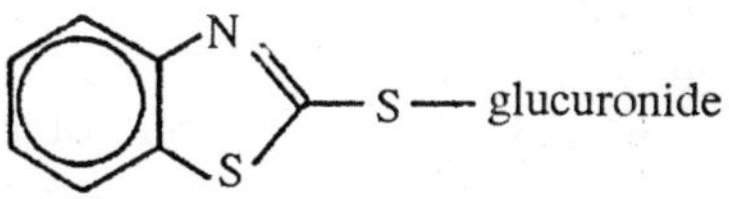

N
S — glucuronide
S

2-Mercaptothiazole-S-glucuronide, an S-glucuronide

Fig. 2.8. Examples of O-, N-, and S-glucuronides.

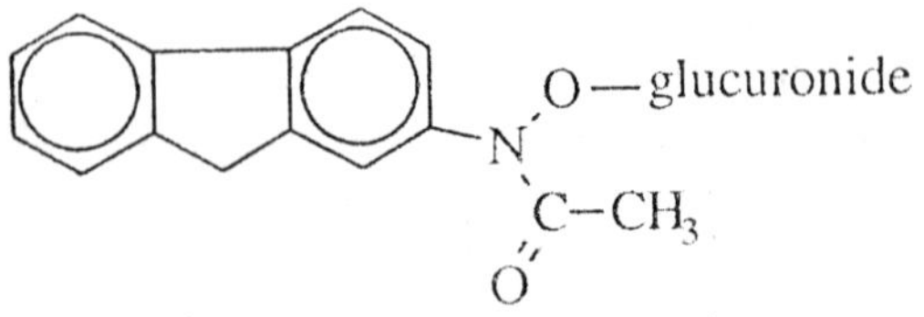

Fig. 2.9. N-hydroxyacetylaminofluorene glucuronide, a more potent carcinogen than its parent compound, N-hydroxyacetylaminofluorene.

This species is of interest because it is a stronger carcinogen than its parent xenobiotic compound, N-hydroxyacetylaminofluorene, contrary to the decrease in toxicity that usually results from glucuronide conjugation.

The carboxylic acid ($-CO_2H$ group) in glucuronides is normally ionized at the pH of physiological media, which is a major reason for the water solubility of the conjugates. When the compound conjugated (called the aglycone) is of relatively low molecular mass, the conjugate tends to be eliminated through urine. For heavier aglycones, elimination occurs through bile. *Enterohepatic circulation* provides a mechanism by which the metabolic effects of some glucuronide conjugates are amplified. This phenomenon is essentially a recycling process in which a glucuronide conjugate released to the intestine with bile becomes deconjugated and reabsorbed in the intestine.

Conjugation by Glutathione

Glutathione (commonly abbreviated GSH) is a crucial conjugating agent in the body. This compound is a tripeptide, meaning that it is composed of three amino acids linked together. These amino acids and their abbreviations are glutamic acid (Glu), cysteine (Cys), and glycine (Gly). It may be represented with the abbreviations of its constituent amino acids, where SH is shown specifically because of its crucial role in forming the covalent link to a xenobiotic compound. A glutathione conjugate may be excreted directly, although this is rare. More commonly, the GSH conjugate undergoes further biochemical reactions that produce mercapturic acids (compounds with N-acetylcysteine attached) or other species.

There are numerous variations on the general mechanism. Glutathione forms conjugates with a wide variety of xenobiotic species, including alkenes, alkyl epoxides (1,2-epoxyethylbenzene), arylepoxides (1,2-epoxynaphthalene), aromatic hydrocarbons, aromatic halides, alkyl halides (methyl iodide), and aromatic nitro compounds. The glutathione transferase enzymes required for the initial conjugation are widespread in the body.

The importance of glutathione in reducing levels of toxic substances can be understood by considering that loss of H^+ from –SH on glutathione leaves an electron-rich $-S^-$ group (nucleophile) that is highly attractive to electrophiles. Electrophiles are important toxic substances because of their tendencies to bind to nucleophilic biomolecules, including nucleic acids and proteins. Such binding can cause mutations (potentially cancer) and result in cell damage. Included among the toxic substances bound by glutathione are reactive intermediates produced in the metabolism of xenobiotic substances, including epoxides and free radicals (species with unpaired electrons).

Conjugation by Sulfate

Although conjugation by sulfate requires the input of substantial amounts of energy, it is very efficient in eliminating xenobiotic species through urine because the sulfate conjugates are completely ionized and therefore highly water soluble. The enzymes that enable sulfate conjugation are sulfotransferases, which act with the 3'-phosphoadenosine-5'-phosphosulfate (PAPS) cofactor:

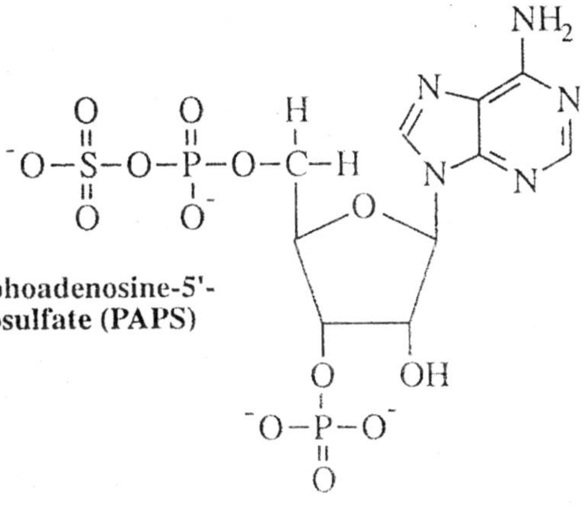

3'-phosphoadenosine-5'-phosphosulfate (PAPS)

Although sulfation is normally an effective means of reducing toxicities of xenobiotic substances, there are cases in which the sulfate conjugate is reactive and toxic. An interesting example of such a substance is produced by the sulfate conjugation of 1´-hydroxysafrole, which is a phase I hydroxylation product of safrole, an ingredient of sassafras, used as a flavoring ingredient until its carcinogenic nature was revealed. Figure shows the transformation of safrole through a sulfate conjugate intermediate to a positively charged electrophilic carbonium ion species that can bind with DNA and lead to tumor formation.

Acetylation

Acetylation reactions catalyzed by acetyltransferase enzymes involve the attachment of the acetyl moiety, shown as the final step in glutathione conjugation. The cofactor upon which the acetyltransferase enzyme acts in acetylation is acetyl coenzyme A:

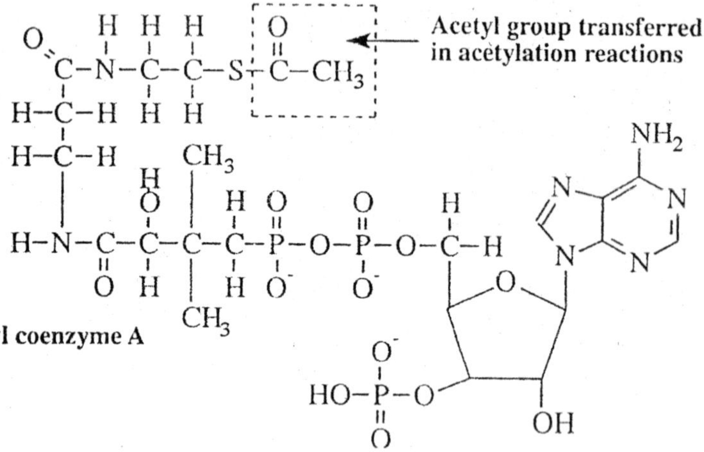

Acetyl group transferred in acetylation reactions

Acetyl coenzyme A

The acetyl transferase enzyme acts to acetylate aniline:

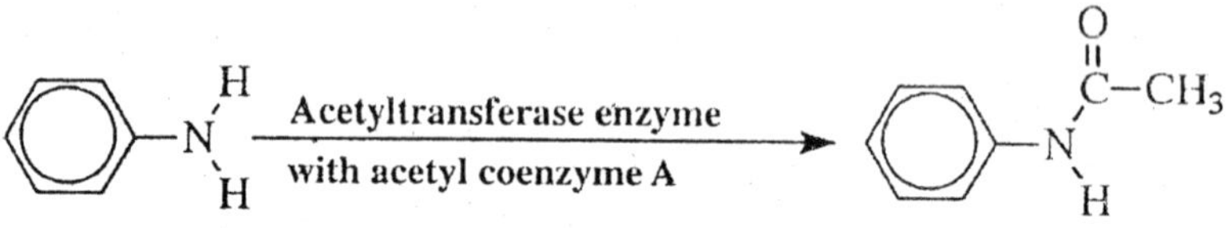

Acetyltransferase enzyme with acetyl coenzyme A

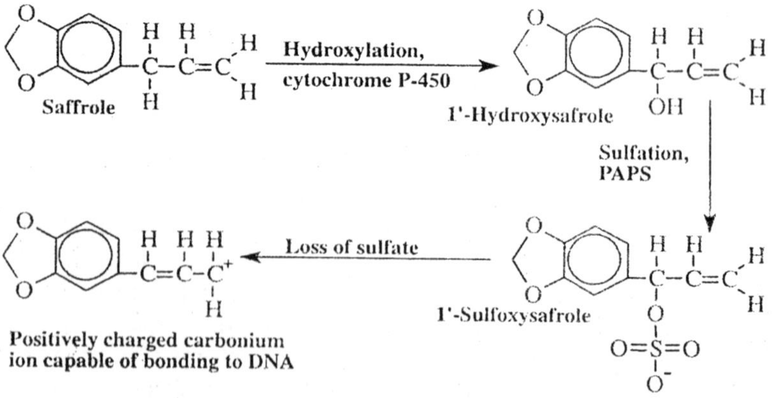

Saffrole

Hydroxylation, cytochrome P-450

1'-Hydroxysafrole

Sulfation, PAPS

1'-Sulfoxysafrole

Loss of sulfate

Positively charged carbonium ion capable of bonding to DNA

Fig. 2.10. Formation of a positively charged carbonium ion capable of binding to DNA and causing cancer formed by the phase I hydroxylation of saffrole, followed by sulfation and loss of sulfate.

The most important kind of acetylation reaction is the acetylation of aromatic amines. This converts the ionizable amine group to a nonionizable group, to which the acetyl group is attached. As a consequence, some acetylated products are not as soluble in water as the parent compounds. In some cases, acetylation of aromatic amines makes them less active as toxicants, particularly in binding with DNA, whereas in other cases, they are made more active. In the latter case, activity can be due to a cytochrome P-450 catalyzed attachment of an -OH group to the acetylated nitrogen, leading to a positively charged electrophilic species capable of binding with DNA.

Conjugation by Amino Acids

Common amino acids that conjugate xenobiotics are glycine, glutamine, taurine, and serine, the anionic forms of which are shown below:

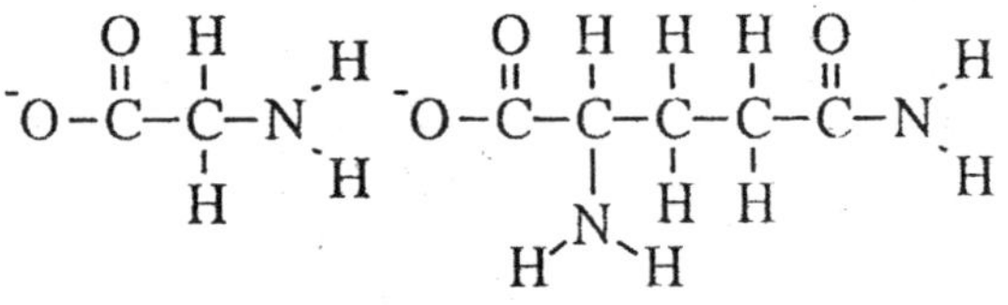

```
    O H     H     O H H H O      H
    ‖ |    /      ‖ | | | ‖     /
 ⁻O-C-C-N      ⁻O-C-C-C-C-C-N
      |    \        |  | |      \
      H     H       |  H H       H
                    N
                   / \
                  H   H
```

Glycine **Glutamine**

```
    O H H       H      O H       H
    ‖ | |      /       ‖ |      /
 ⁻O-S-C-C-N        ⁻O-C-C-N
    ‖ | |      \         |      \
    O H H       H      H-C-H     H
                         |
                         O
                         H
```

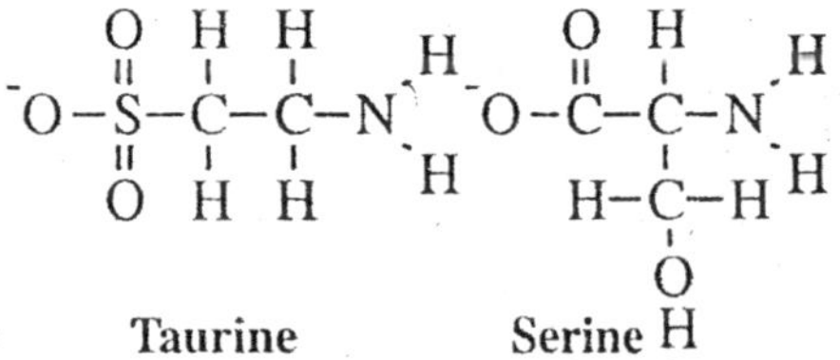

Taurine **Serine**

In addition to single amino acids, dipeptides consisting of two amino acids connected by a peptide linkage, such as glycylglycine and glycyltaurine, may conjugate xenobiotics to produce *peptide conjugates*. Amino acids have both an acid group and an amino (-NH2) group at which conjugation to a xenobiotic may occur. Both types of binding are involved in amino acid conjugation.

The classic example of amino acid conjugation to a carboxylic acid group is the production of hippuric acid from benzoic acid and glycine given below:

This is the oldest known biosynthesis, having been discovered in 1842. Before concerns over possible health effects ended the practice, it used to be performed by students of organic chemistry, who ingested

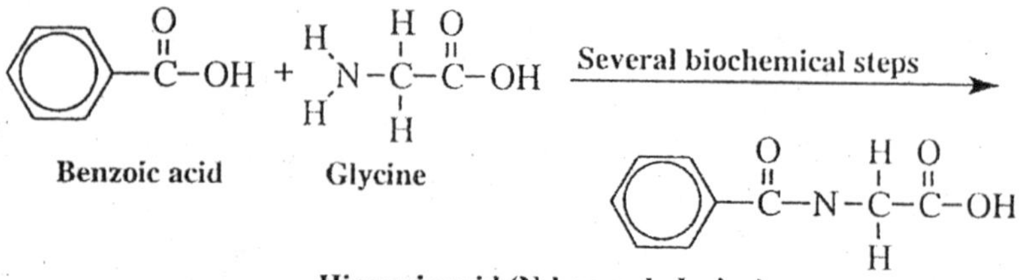

Several biochemical steps

Benzoic acid

Glycine

Hippuric acid (N-benzoyl glycine)

benzoic acid and then isolated hippuric acid from their urine. Conjugation of a xenobiotic substance containing a carboxylic acid group with the $-NH_2$ group of an amino acid is generally a detoxication mechanism.

Binding of an amino acid through its carboxylic acid group can occur with hydroxylamines generated by phase I hydroxylation of aromatic amino compounds. The N-esters formed by reactions such as the one above can react to form electrophilic cations (carbonium and nitrenium) that can bind with nucleophilic biomolecules to produce toxic responses. Therefore, binding of the carboxylic acid group of an amino acid with the hydroxylamino group of a xenobiotic material should be considered an intoxication pathway rather than detoxication.

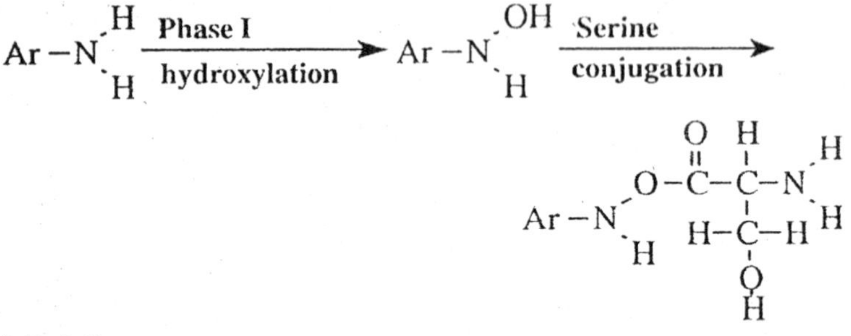

Phase I hydroxylation

Serine conjugation

Methylation

Phase II *methylation* occurs with the S-adenosylmethionine (SAM) cofactor acting as a methylating agent:

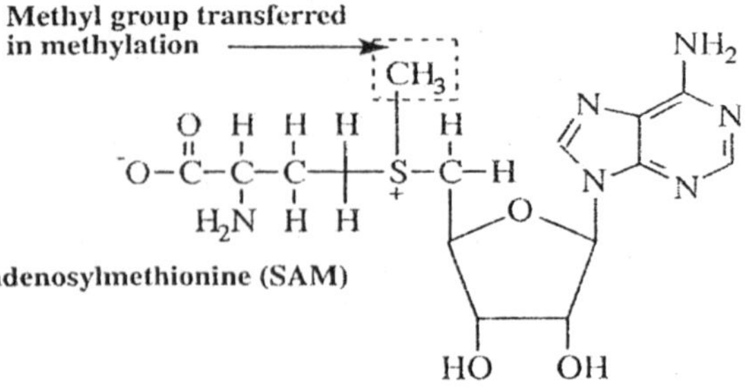

Methyl group transferred in methylation

S-adenosylmethionine (SAM)

The methyl group on SAM behaves as an electrophilic $^{+}CH_3$ positively charged carbocation that is attracted to electron-rich nucleophilic O, N, and S atoms on a xenobiotic compound; methylation of carbon is rare. Therefore, the kinds of compounds commonly methylated include amines, heterocyclic nitrogen compounds, phenols, and compounds containing the –SH group. A typical methylation reaction is that of nicotine:

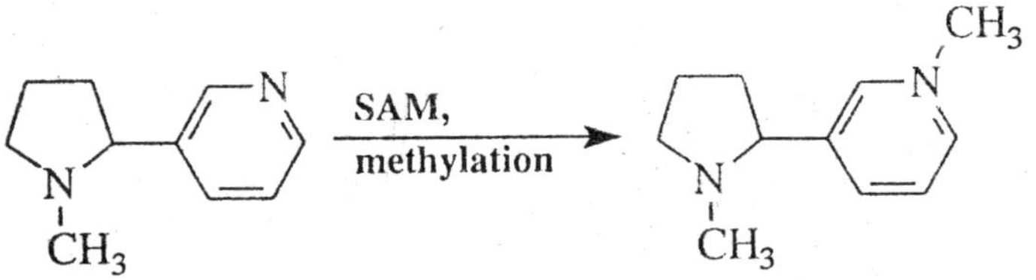

CH_3 N N SAM, methylation N N CH_3 CH_3

Nicotine N-methylnicotinium ion

Because of the hydrocarbon nature of the methyl group, it generally makes xenobiotic substrates less hydrophilic, which is the opposite of most other conjugation processes.

Biochemical Mechanisms of Toxicity

A critical aspect of toxicological chemistry is that which deals with the biochemical mechanisms and reactions by which xenobiotic compounds and their metabolites interact with biomolecules to cause an adverse toxicological effect.

As discussed earlier in this chapter, metabolic processes make toxic agents from nontoxic ones or make toxic substances more toxic. In order to cause a toxic response, substances are often quite reactive and, if introduced into an organism directly, would react before reaching a target at which they could cause a toxic response. However, when reactive substances are produced metabolically, it may be in a location where they can rapidly interact with a biomolecule, membrane, or tissue to cause a toxic response. Such agents generally fall into the following four categories:

1. *Electrophilic species* that are positively charged or have a partial positive charge and therefore a tendency to bond to electron-rich atoms and functional groups, particularly N, O, and S, that abound on nucleic acids and proteins (including proteinaceous enzymes), which are commonly affected by toxic substances.
2. *Nucleophilic species* that are negatively charged or partially so and have a tendency to bind with electron-deficient targets. These are much less common toxicants than electrophilic species, but

include agents such as CO, formed metabolically by loss of halogen and oxidation of dihalomethane compounds or cyanide, CN^-, produced by the metabolic breakdown of acrylonitrile, a biochemically reactive organic compound containing both a –CN group and a reactive C=C bond. Carbon monoxide bonds with Fe^{2+} in hemoglobin, depriving it of its ability to carry oxygen to tissues, and nucleophilic CN^- ion bonds with Fe^{3+} in *ferricytochrome oxidase* enzyme, preventing the utilization of oxygen in respiration.

3. *Free radicals* that consist of neutral or ionic species that have unpaired electrons. Free radicals include the superoxide anion radical, O_2^-, produced by adding an electron to O_2, and the hydroxyl radical, HO·, produced by splitting (homolytic cleavage) of the H_2O_2 molecule. These species can react with larger molecules to generate other free radical species. Electron transfer from cytochrome P-450 enzyme to xenobiotic carbon tetrachloride, CCl_4, can produce the reactive, damaging Cl_3C radical.
4. *Redox-reactive* reagents that bring about harmful oxidation–reduction reactions. An example is the generation from nitrite esters of nitrite ion, NO_2^-, which causes oxidation of Fe^{2+} in hemoglobin to Fe^{3+}, producing methemoglobin, which does not transport oxygen in blood.

In understanding the kinds of processes by which toxic substances harm an organism, it is important to understand the concept of receptors. Here a *receptor* is taken to mean a biochemical entity that interacts with a toxicant to produce some sort of toxic effect. Generally receptors are macromolecules, such as proteins, nucleic acids, or phospholipids of cell membranes, inside or on the surface of cells. In the context of toxicant–receptor interactions, the substance that interacts with a receptor is called a *ligand*. Ligands are normally relatively small molecules. They may be endogenous, such as hormone molecules, but in discussions of toxicity are normally regarded as xenobiotic materials.

The function of a receptor depends on its high specificity for particular ligands. This often involves the stereochemical fit between a ligand and a receptor, the idea of a "lock and key," similar to the interaction of enzymes with various substrates. It should be noted, however, that toxicant–receptor interactions are often around 100 times as strong as enzyme–substrate interactions. Furthermore, whereas an enzyme generally alters a substrate chemically (such as by hydrolysis), a toxicant does not usually change the chemical nature of a receptor other than binding to it. In many cases, the identity of a receptor is not known, as is the case, for example, with pyrethroid insecticides. In such a case, for toxicant X, reference may be made to the X receptor.

Several major categories of toxicant–receptor interactions occur. What is known about these kinds of interactions is largely based on studies of pharmaceuticals, which act by binding with various receptors. This information is now being applied to reactions of toxicants with receptors. In considering such interactions, it may be assumed that the receptor normally binds to some endogenous substance, causing a normal effect, such as a nerve impulse. In some cases, the toxicant may activate the receptor, causing an effect similar to that of the endogenous ligand, but different enough in degree that some adverse effect results. Another possibility is that the toxicant binds to a receptor site, preventing an endogenous ligand from binding; this is known as an *antagonist action*. Yet another possibility is for the toxicant to bind to a site different from, but close enough to, the normal binding site to interfere with the binding of an endogenous substance. As a final possibility, the receptor may not have any endogenous ligands, but being bound by a toxicant nevertheless has some sort of effect.

Advantage is taken of antagonist action to treat poisoning. A simple example is provided by treatment for carbon monoxide poisoning, in which blood hemoglobin, which normally carries molecular O_2 to tissues, is the receptor that is bound strongly by CO. By treating the subject with pure oxygen or even pressurized oxygen, the oxygen competes with the receptor sites, driving off carbon monoxide and reversing the effects of this toxic substance.

Interference with Enzyme Action

Enzymes are extremely important because they must function properly to enable essential metabolic processes to occur in cells. Substances that interfere with the proper action of enzymes obviously have the potential to be toxic. Many xenobiotics that adversely affect enzymes are *enzyme inhibitors*, which slow down or stop enzymes from performing their normal functions as biochemical catalysts. Stimulation of the body to make enzymes that serve particular purposes, a process called *enzyme induction*, is also important in toxicology.

The body contains numerous endogenous enzyme inhibitors that serve to control enzyme-catalyzed processes. When a toxicant acts as an enzyme inhibitor, however, an adverse effect usually results. An important example of this is the action of ions of heavy metals, such

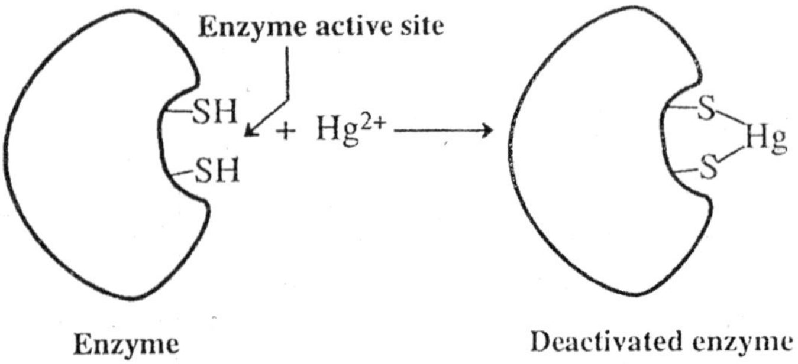

Enzyme active site

$-SH$ + Hg^{2+} ⟶ $-S-Hg-S-$

Enzyme Deactivated enzyme

Fig. 2.11. Binding of a heavy metal to an enzyme active site.

as mercury (Hg^{2+}), lead (Pb^{2+}), and cadmium (Cd^{2+}), which have strong tendencies to bind to sulfur-containing functional groups, especially –SS–, –SH, and –S–CH_3. These functional groups are often present on the active sites of enzymes, which, because of their specific three-dimensional structures, bind with high selectivity to the substrate species upon which the enzymes act. Toxic metal ions may bind strongly to sulfur-containing functional groups in enzyme active sites, thereby inhibiting the action of the enzyme.

Inhibition of Metalloenzymes

Substitution of foreign metals for the metals in metalloenzymes (those that contain metals as part of their structures) is an important mode of toxic action by metals. A common mechanism for cadmium toxicity is the substitution of this metal for zinc, a metal that is present in many metalloenzymes. This substitution occurs readily because of the chemical similarities between the two metals (for example, Cd^{2+} and Zn^{2+} behave alike in solution). Despite their chemical similarities, however, cadmium does not fulfill the biochemical function of zinc and a toxic effect results. Some enzymes that are affected adversely by the substitution of cadmium for zinc are adenosine triphosphate, alcohol dehydrogenase, and carbonic anhydrase.

Inhibition by Organic Compounds

The covalent bonding of organic xenobiotic compounds to enzymes, can cause enzyme inhibition. Such bonding occurs most commonly through hydroxyl (–OH) groups on enzyme active sites. Covalent bonding of xenobiotic compounds is one of the major ways in which acetylcholinesterase (an enzyme crucial to the function of nerve impulses) can be inhibited. An organophosphate compound, such as the nerve gas compound diisopropylphosphorfluoridate, may bind to acetylcholinesterase, thereby inhibiting the enzyme.

Biochemistry of Mutagenesis

Mutagenesis is the phenomenon in which inheritable traits result from alterations of DNA. Although mutation is a normally occurring process that gives rise to diversity in species, most mutations are harmful. The toxicants that cause mutations are known as *mutagens*. These toxicants, often the same as those that cause cancer or birth defects, are a major toxicological concern.

To understand the biochemistry of mutagenesis, it is important to DNA contains the nitrogenous bases adenine, guanine, cytosine, and thymine. The order in which these bases occur in DNA determines the nature and structure of newly produced ribonucleic acid (RNA), a substance produced as a step in the synthesis of new proteins and enzymes in cells. Exchange, addition, or deletion of any of the nitrogenous bases in DNA alters the nature of RNA produced and can change vital life processes, such as the synthesis of an important enzyme. This phenomenon, which can be caused by xenobiotic compounds, is a mutation that can be passed on to progeny, usually with detrimental results.

There are several ways in which xenobiotic species may cause mutations. It is beyond the scope of this work to discuss these mechanisms in detail. For the most part, however, mutations due to xenobiotic substances are the result of chemical alterations of DNA, such as those discussed in the following two examples.

Nitrous acid, HNO_2, is an example of a chemical mutagen that is often used to cause mutations in bacteria. To understand the mutagenic activity of nitrous acid, it should be noted that three of the nitrogenous bases—adenine, guanine, and cytosine—contain the amino group $-NH_2$. Nitrous acid acts to replace amino groups with doubly bonded oxygen atoms, thereby placing keto groups (C=O) in the rings of the nitrogenous bases and converting them to other compounds. When this occurs, the DNA may not function in the intended manner, and a mutation may occur.

Alkylation consisting of the attachment of a small alkyl group, such as $^{-}CH_3$ or $^{-}C_2H_5$, to an N atom on one of the nitrogenous bases in DNA is one of the most common mechanisms leading to mutation. O-alkylation may also occur by attachment of a methyl or other alkyl group to the oxygen atom in guanine. A number of mutagenic substances act as alkylating agents.

Alkylation occurs by way of generation of positively charged electrophilic species that bond to electron-rich nitrogen or oxygen atoms

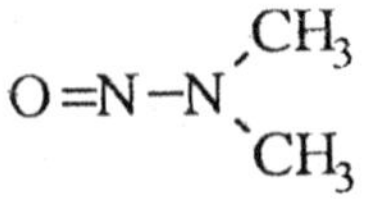

$$O{=}N{-}N(CH_3)_2$$

Dimethylnitrosamine

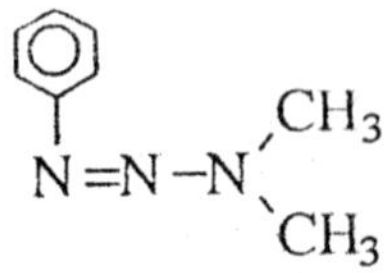

$$C_6H_5{-}N{=}N{-}N(CH_3)_2$$

3,3-Dimethyl-1-phenyltriazine

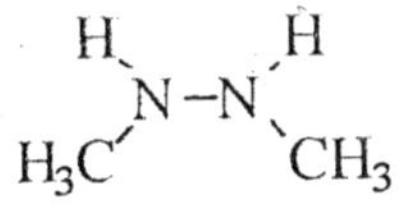

$$H_3C(H)N{-}N(H)CH_3$$

1,2-Dimethylhydrazine

$$H_3CO{-}S(=O)_2{-}CH_3$$

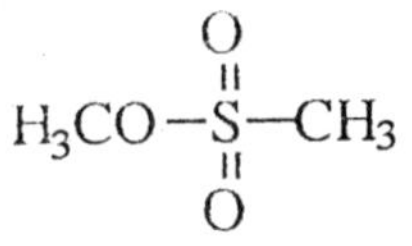

Methylmethanesulfonate

Fig. 2.12. Examples of simple alkylating agents capable of causing mutations.

on the nitrogenous bases in DNA. The generation of such species usually occurs by way of biochemical and chemical processes. For example, dimethylnitrosamine is activated by oxidation through cellular NADPH to produce the following highly reactive intermediate:

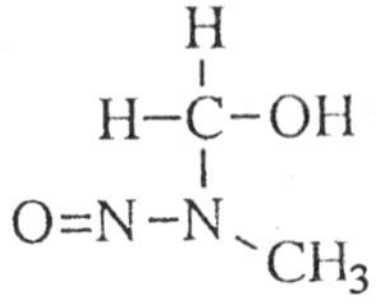

$$O{=}N{-}N(CH_3){-}CH_2OH$$

This product undergoes several nonenzymatic transitions, losing formaldehyde and generating a carbonium ion, $^+CH_3$, that can methylate nitrogenous bases on DNA:

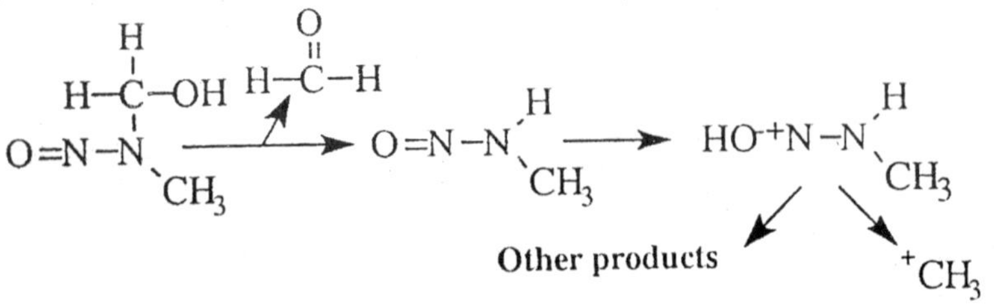

$$O{=}N{-}N(CH_3){-}CH_2OH \xrightarrow{-\,HCHO} O{=}N{-}N(H)CH_3 \longrightarrow HO{-}{}^+N{-}N(H)CH_3 \longrightarrow \text{Other products} + {}^+CH_3$$

One of the more notable mutagens is tris(2,3-dibromopropyl) phosphate, commonly called *tris*, which was used as a flame retardant in children's sleepwear. Tris was found to be mutagenic in experimental animals, and metabolites of it were found in children wearing the treated sleepwear. This strongly suggested that tris is absorbed through the skin, and its use was discontinued.

Biochemistry of Carcinogenesis

Cancer is a condition characterized by the uncontrolled replication and growth of the body's own cells (somatic cells). *Carcinogenic agents* may be categorized as follows:

1. Chemical agents, such as nitrosamines and polycyclic aromatic hydrocarbons
2. Biological agents, such as hepadna viruses or retroviruses
3. Ionizing radiation, such as x-rays
4. Genetic factors, such as selective breeding

Clearly, in some cases, cancer is the result of the action of synthetic and naturally occurring chemicals. The role of xenobiotic chemicals in causing cancer is called *chemical carcinogenesis*. It is often regarded as the single most important facet of toxicology and clearly the one that receives the most publicity.

Chemical carcinogenesis has a long history. In 1775, Sir Percivall Pott, surgeon general serving under King George III of England, observed that chimney sweeps in London had a very high incidence of cancer of the scrotum, which he related to their exposure to soot and tar from the burning of bituminous coal. (This occupational health hazard was exacerbated by their aversion to bathing and changing underwear.) A German surgeon, Ludwig Rehn, reported elevated incidences of bladder cancer in dye workers exposed to chemicals extracted from coal tar; 2-naphthylamine was shown to be largely responsible. Other historical examples of carcinogenesis include observations of cancer from tobacco juice (1915), oral exposure to radium from painting luminescent watch dials (1929), tobacco smoke (1939), and asbestos (1960).

Large expenditures of time and money on the subject in recent years have yielded a much better understanding of the biochemical bases of chemical carcinogenesis. The overall processes for the induction of cancer may be quite complex, involving numerous steps. However, it is generally recognized that there are two major steps in carcinogenesis: an initiation stage followed by a promotional stage.

Initiation of carcinogenesis may occur by reaction of a *DNA-reactive species* with DNA or by the action of an *epigenetic carcinogen* that does not react with DNA and is carcinogenic by some other mechanism. Most DNA-reactive species are *genotoxic carcinogens* because they are also mutagens. These substances react irreversibly with DNA. They are either electrophilic or, more commonly, metabolically activated to form electrophilic species, as is the case

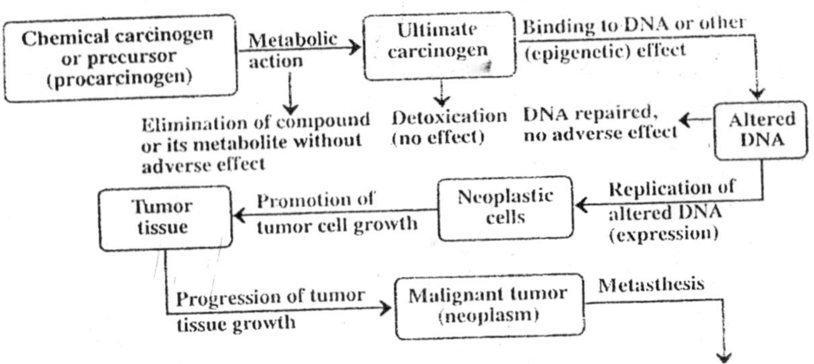

Fig. 2.13. Outline of the carcinogenic process.

with electrophilic $^{+}CH_3$' generated from dimethylnitrosamine, as discussed under mutagenesis above. Cancer-causing substances that require metabolic activation are called *precarcinogens* or *procarcinogens*. The metabolic species actually responsible for carcinogenesis is termed an *ultimate carcinogen*. Some species that are intermediate metabolites between precarcinogens and ultimate carcinogens are called *proximate carcinogens*. These definitions can be illustrated by the species, in which benzo(a)pyrene is a procarcinogen, benzo(a)pyrene 7,8-epoxide is the proximate carcinogen, and benzo(a)pyrene 7,8-diol-9,10-epoxide is the ultimate carcinogen. Carcinogens that do not require biochemical activation are categorized as *primary* or *direct-acting carcinogens*.

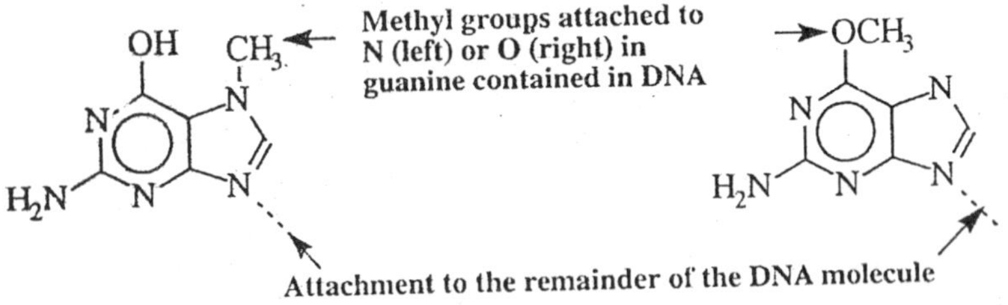

Methyl groups attached to N (left) or O (right) in guanine contained in DNA

Attachment to the remainder of the DNA molecule

Most substances classified as epigenetic carcinogens are *promoters* that act after initiation. Manifestations of promotion include increased numbers of tumor cells and decreased length of time for tumors to develop. Promoters do not initiate cancer, are not electrophilic, and do not bind with DNA. The classic example of a promotor is a substance known chemically as decanoyl phorbol acetate or phorbol myristate acetate, a substance extracted from croton oil.

Alkylating Agents in Carcinogenesis

Chemical carcinogens usually have the ability to form covalent bonds with macromolecular life molecules. Such covalent bonds can form with proteins, peptides, RNA, and DNA. Although most binding is with other kinds of molecules, which are more abundant, the DNA adducts are the significant ones in initiating cancer. Prominent among the species that bond to DNA in carcino-genesis are the alkylating agents that attach alkyl groups — such as methyl (CH_3) or ethyl (C_2H_5) — to DNA. A similar type of compound, *arylating agents*, act to attach aryl moieties, such as the phenyl group, to DNA. The alkyl and aryl groups become attached to N and O atoms in the nitrogenous bases that compose DNA. This alteration in the DNA can initiate the sequence of events that results in the growth and replication of neoplastic (cancerous) cells. The reactive species that donate alkyl groups in alkylation are usually formed by metabolic activation, as shown for dimethylnitrosamine in the discussion of mutagenesis above.

Testing for Carcinogens

In some cases, chemicals are known to be carcinogens from epidemiological studies of exposed humans. Animals are used to test for carcinogenicity, and the results can be extrapolated with some uncertainty to humans. The most broadly applicable test for potential carcinogens is the *Bruce Ames* procedure, which actually reveals mutagenicity. The principle of this method is the reversion of mutant histidine-requiring *Salmonella* bacteria back to a form that can synthesize their own histidine.

Ionizing Radiation

Although not a chemical agent as such, ionizing radiation, such as x-rays or alpha particles from ingested alpha emitters, causes chemical reactions that have toxic, even fatal, effects. The toxicologic effects of radiation have to do with its physical and chemical interactions with matter and the biological consequences that result. Ionizing radiation alters chemical species in tissue and can lead to significant and harmful alterations in the tissue and in the cells that make up the tissue.

There is not room here to discuss the detailed mechanisms by which exposure to radiation causes adverse responses. Much of the effects of radiation result from its interaction with water to produce active species that include superoxide (O_2^-), hydroxyl radical (HO·), hydroperoxyl radical (HOO·), and hydrogen peroxide (H_2O_2). These species oxidize cellular macromolecules. When DNA is so affected, mutagenesis and carcinogenesis may result. Ionizing radiation can also interact with organic substances to produce a carbonium ion, such as $^+CH_3$, that can alkylate nitrogenous bases on DNA.

3

FORENSIC INORGANIC TOXICANTS

In previous study, elements were discussed that as a rule tend to be toxic in their various forms. This chapter covers toxic inorganic compounds of elements that are not themselves generally regarded as toxic. These elements include for the most part the lighter nonmetals located in the upper right of the periodic table and exclude the heavy metals. Most of the elements involved in the inorganic compounds discussed in this chapter are those that are essential for life processes. Any division between "*toxic*" and "*nontoxic*" elements is by nature artificial in that most of the heavy metals have compounds of relatively low toxicity, and there are deadly compounds that contain elements essential for life.

In general, this chapter is organized in the order of increasing atomic number of the elements that are covered. Inorganic compounds of carbon, atomic number 6, are discussed first, followed by toxic inorganic compounds of nitrogen, atomic number 7. The next element, oxygen, occurs in so many different inorganic compounds that it is not discussed in a separate category. The halogens — fluorine, chlorine, bromine, and iodine — are discussed as a group because of their chemical similarities. The other major elements whose toxic inorganic compounds are discussed are silicon, phosphorus, and sulfur.

TOXIC INORGANIC CARBON COMPOUNDS

Cyanide

Cyanide, in the form of either gaseous *hydrogen cyanide* (HCN) or *cyanide ion* (CN^-) (present in cyanide salts such as KCN), is a notably toxic substance. Cyanide is a rapidly acting poison, and the fatal oral dose to humans is believed to be only 60 to 90 mg. Hydrogen cyanide and cyanide salts have numerous uses; examples are as ingredients of pest poisons, fumigants, metal (silver) polishes, and photographic chemical solutions. Therefore, exposure to cyanide is certainly possible. Hydrogen cyanide is used as a fumigant to kill pests such as rodents in warehouses, grain storage bins, greenhouses, and holds of ships, where its high toxicity and ability to penetrate obscure spaces are advantageous. Cyanide salt solutions are used to extract some metals such as gold from ores, in metal refining, in metal plating, and for salvaging silver from exposed photographic and x-ray film. Cyanide is used in various chemical syntheses. Polyacrylic polymers may evolve HCN during combustion, adding to the toxic gases that are usually responsible for deaths in fires. Sodium nitroprusside, $Na_2Fe(NO)(CN)_5$, used intravenously in humans to control hypertension, can hydrolyze in the body to release cyanide and cause cyanide poisoning.

Some plants contain cyanogenic glycosides, saccharidal substances that contain the –CN group and that may hydrolyze to release cyanide. Such substances, called *cyanogens*, include amygdalin, linamarin, and linseed cyanogens consisting of mixtures of linustatin and neolinustatin.[1] The release of cyanide by the enzymatic or acidic hydrolysis of amygdalin in the digestive tract is shown below:

Glucose units

$$C_6H_5\text{–}CH(C{\equiv}N)\text{–}O\text{–}C_6H_{10}O_4\text{–}O\text{–}C_6H_{11}O_5 + 2H_2O \rightarrow HCN + 2C_6H_{12}O_6 + C_6H_5\text{–}CHO$$

Benzaldehyde

The Romans used cyanide from natural seed sources, such as apple seeds, for executions and suicides. The seeds of apples, apricots, cherries, peaches, plums, and some other fruits contain sources of cyanide. Other natural sources of cyanide include arrowgrass, sorghum, flax, velvet grass, and white clover.

A potential source of cyanide poisoning is cassava, a starch from the root of *Manihot esculenta*, used as food in much of Africa. The root contains cyanogenic linamarin, which is normally removed in processing the root for food. Widespread cases of a spinal cord disorder called konzo and characterized by spastic paralysis have been attributed to ingestion of linamarin from inadequately processed cassava root.

Biochemical action of cyanide

Cyanide deprives the body of oxygen by acting as a *chemical asphyxiant* (in contrast to simple asphyxiants that simply displace oxygen in respired air). In acting as an asphyxiant, cyanide inhibits an enzyme involved in a key step in the oxidative phosphorylation pathway, by which the body utilizes oxygen in cell mitochondria. The inhibited enzyme is ferricytochrome oxidase (Fe(III)-oxid), an iron-containing metalloprotein that acts as an acceptor of electrons and is converted to ferrouscytochrome oxidase (Fe(II)-oxid) during the oxidation of glucose. The ferrouscytochrome oxidase that is formed transfers the electrons to molecular oxygen and produces energetic adenosine triphosphate (ATP) from adenosine diphosphate (ADP), regenerating Fe(III)-oxid that can repeat the cycle. The overall process is represented as follows:

$$\text{Fe(III)-oxid} + \text{Reducing agent} \rightarrow \text{Fe(II)-oxid} + \text{Oxidized reducing agent}$$

$$\text{Fe(II)-oxid} + 2H^+ + \tfrac{1}{2}O_2 \xrightarrow{\text{ADP} \quad \text{ATP}} \text{Fe(II)-oxid} + H_2O$$

Cyanide bonds to the iron(III) of the ferricytochrome enzyme, preventing its reduction to iron(II) in the first of the two reactions above. The result is that ferrouscytochrome oxidase, which is required to react with O_2, is not formed and utilization of oxygen in cells is prevented, leading to rapid cessation of metabolic processes. The decreased utilization of oxygen in tissue results in a buildup of oxyhemoglobin in venous blood, which gives the skin and mucous membranes a characteristic red color (flush).

The metabolic pathway for the detoxification of cyanide involves conversion to the less toxic thiocyanate by a reaction requiring thiosulfate or colloidal sulfur as a substrate:

$$CN^- + S_2O_2^{3-} \xrightarrow[\text{Rhodanse}]{} SCN^- + SO_3^{2-}$$

This reaction is catalyzed by *rhodanase* enzyme, also called *mitochondrial sulfur transferase*. Although not found in the blood, this enzyme does occur abundantly in liver and kidney tissue. Because of this reaction, thiosulfate can be administered as an antidote for cyanide poisoning.

Nitrite, NO_2^-, administered intravenously as sodium nitrite solution or inhaled as amyl nitrite, $C_5H_{11}NO_2$, an ester which hydrolyzes to NO_2^- in the blood, functions as an antidote to cyanide poisoning. This occurs because nitrite oxidizes iron(II) in blood hemoglobin (HbFe(II)) to methemoglobin (HbFe(III)), a brown substance that is ineffective in carrying oxygen to tissues. (This reaction is the mechanism of nitrite toxicity; excessive formation of methemoglobin causes oxygen deprivation that can be fatal.) Methemoblogin in the blood, however, has a high affinity for cyanide and removes it from ferricytochrome oxidase enzyme that has been inhibited by binding of cyanide (Fe(III)-oxid–CN),

$$HbFe(III) + Fe(III)\text{-}oxid\text{–}CN \rightarrow HbFe(III)\text{–}CN + Fe(III)\text{-}oxid$$

freeing the ferricytochrome oxidase enzyme so that it can participate in its normal metabolic functions. Additional treatment with thiosulfate results in elimination of the cyanide:

$$HbFe(III)\text{-}CN + S_2O_3^{2-} \rightarrow SCN^- + HbFe(III) + SO_3^{2-}$$

Carbon Monoxide

Carbon monoxide, CO, is a toxic industrial gas produced by the incomplete combustion of carbonaceous fuels. It is used as a reductant for metal ores, for chemical synthesis, and as a fuel. As an environmental toxicant, it is responsible for a significant number of accidental poisonings annually. Observable acute effects of carbon monoxide exposure in humans cover a wide range of symptoms and severity. These include impairment of judgment and visual perception at CO levels of 10 ppm in air; dizziness, headache, and weariness (100 ppm); loss of consciousness (250 ppm); and rapid death (1000 ppm). Chronic effects of long-term low-level exposure to carbon monoxide include disorders of the respiratory system and the heart. As evidence of the latter, cardiac dys-functions, including arrhythmia and myocardia ischemia (blood deficiency in the heart muscles), have been reported in victims of carbon monoxide poisoning. Autopsies of such victims have shown scattered hemorrhages throughout the heart.

Biochemical action of carbon monoxide

Carbon monoxide enters the bloodstream through the lungs and reacts with oxyhemoglobin (O_2Hb) to produce carboxyhemoglobin (COHb):

$$O_2Hb + CO \rightarrow COHb + O_2$$

Carboxyhemoglobin is several times more stable than oxyhemoglobin and ties up the hemoglobin so that it cannot carry oxygen to body tissues.

Cyanogen, Cyanamide, and Cyanates

Cyanogen, NCCN, is a colorless, violently flammable gas with a pungent odor. It may cause permanent injury or even death in exposed individuals. Fumes produced by the reaction of cyanogen with water or acids are highly toxic.

Cyanamide, H_2NCN, and calcium cyanamide, CaNCN, are used as fertilizers and raw materials. Calcium cyanamide is employed for the desulfurization and nitridation of steel. Inhalation or oral ingestion of cyanamide causes dizziness, lowers blood pressure, and increases rates of pulse and respiration. Calcium cyanamide acts as a primary irritant to the skin and to nose and throat tissues. The major metabolic product of cyanimide is N-acetylcyanamide, which is found in the urine of subjects exposed to cyanamide.

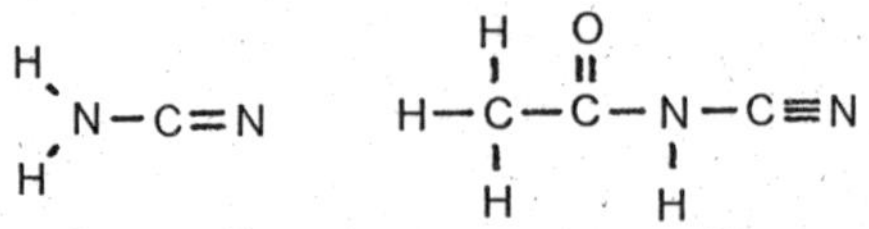

$$H_2N{-}C{\equiv}N \qquad\qquad H{-}\underset{H}{\overset{H}{C}}{-}\overset{O}{\overset{\|}{C}}{-}\underset{H}{N}{-}C{\equiv}N$$

Cyanamide N-acetylcyanamide

Cyanic acid, HOCN (boiling point (bp), 23.3°C; melting point (mp), –86°C), is a dangerously explosive liquid with an acrid odor. The acid forms cyanate salts, such as NaOCN and KOCN. During decomposition from heat or contact with strong acid, cyanic acid evolves very toxic fumes.

Toxic Inorganic Nitrogen Compounds

Ammonia

Ammonia, NH_3, is widely used as a gas for chemical synthesis, fertilizer, and other applications. It is also used as a solution of concentrated NH_3 in water as a chemical reagent and as a fertilizer. Tanks of liquified anhydrous ammonia are common targets for the operators of "meth labs" in rural areas, who steal this dangerous chemical to make illicit amphetamines. Undoubtedly, some of the thieves suffer injury in the process, though such injuries are rarely reported.

The evaporation of liquid ammonia in contact with flesh can cause frostbite. Ammonia is a potent skin corrosive and can damage eye tissue. When inhaled, ammonia causes constriction of the bronchioles. Because of its high water solubility, ammonia is absorbed by the moist tissues of the upper respiratory tract. Irritant damage to the lungs from ammonia can cause edema and changes in lung permeability.

Hydrazine

Hydrazine is a common inorganic nitrogen compound. Hydrazine is hepatotoxic, causing accumulation of triglycerides in the liver, a condition commonly called fatty liver. These effects may be related to hydrazine's ability to increase the activity of enzymes required to produce diglycerides, depletion of ATP, or inhibition of protein

$$\begin{array}{ccc} H & & H \\ & N-N & \\ H & & H \end{array} \quad \text{Hydrazine}$$

synthesis. Hydrazine acting in the liver induces hydrolysis of glycogen (animal starch) to release glucose, causing excessive blood glucose levels, a condition called *hyperglycemia*. This can result in depletion of glycogen, leading to the opposite effect, hypoglycemia. Hydrazine inhibits some enzymes, including phosphoenol pyruvatecarboxykinase and some transaminases that are involved in intermediary metabolism. Swelling of cell mitochondria has been observed after exposure to hydrazine, and prolonged exposure can result in formation of large megamitochondria.

The most serious toxicologic effect of hydrazine is its ability to indirectly cause methylation of DNA, leading to cancer. Inhalation of hydrazine has been linked to lung cancer.

Nitrogen Oxides

The two most common oxides of nitrogen are *nitric oxide* (NO) and *nitrogen dioxide* (NO_2), designated collectively as NO_x. Nitric oxide is produced in combustion processes from organically bound nitrogen endogenous to fossil fuels (particularly coal, heavy fuel oil, and shale oil) and from atmospheric nitrogen under the conditions that exist in an internal combustion engine, as shown by the two following reactions:

$$2N(\textit{fossil fuel}) + O_2 \rightarrow 2NO$$

$$N_2 + O_2 \xrightarrow{\text{Internal combustion engine}} 2NO$$

Under the conditions of photochemical smog formation, nitric oxide is converted to nitrogen dioxide by the following overall reaction:

$$2NO + O_2 \xrightarrow{\text{Organics, photochemical processes}} 2NO_2$$

This conversion consists of complex chain reactions involving light energy and unstable reactive intermediate species. The conditions required are stagnant air, low humidity, intense sunlight, and the presence of reactive hydrocarbons, particularly those from automobile exhausts. Of the NO_x constituents, NO_2 is generally regarded as the more toxic, although all nitrogen oxides and potential sources thereof (such as nitric acid in the presence of oxidizable organic matter) should be accorded the same respect as nitrogen dioxide.

Effects of NO_2 Poisoning

The toxic effects of NO_2 have been summarized. Inhalation of NO_2 causes severe irritation of the innermost parts of the lungs, resulting in pulmonary edema and fatal bronchiolitis fibrosa obliterans. Inhalation, for even very brief periods, of air containing 200 to 700 ppm of NO_2 can be fatal. The biochemical action of NO_2 includes disruption of some enzyme systems, such as lactic dehydrogenase. Nitrogen dioxide probably acts as an oxidizing agent similar to, though weaker than, ozone, which is discussed previously. Included is the formation of free radicals, particularly the hydroxyl radical HO·. Like ozone, it is likely that NO_2 causes *lipid peroxidation*. This is a process in which the C=C double bonds in unsaturated lipids are attacked by free radicals and undergo chain reactions in the presence of O_2, resulting in their oxidative destruction.

Nitrous Oxide

Nitrous oxide, once commonly known as laughing gas, is used as an oxidant gas and in dental surgery as a general anesthetic. It is a central nervous system depressant and can act as an asphyxiant.

Hydrogen Halides

Hydrogen halides are compounds with the general formula HX, where X is F, Cl, Br, or I. They are all gases, and all are relatively toxic. Because of their abundance and industrial uses, HF and HCl have the greatest toxicological significance of these gases.

Hydrogen Fluoride

Hydrogen fluoride, HF (mp, –83.1°C; bp, 19.5°C), may be in the form of either a clear, colorless liquid or gas. It forms corrosive fumes when exposed to the atmosphere. The major commercial application of hydrogen fluoride is as an alkylating catalyst in petroleum refining. Pot room workers in the primary aluminum industry are exposed to levels up to 5 mg/m^3 in the workplace atmosphere and exhibit elevated levels of F^- ion in their blood plasma. Hydrogen fluoride in aqueous solution is called *hydrofluoric acid*, which contains 30 to 60% HF by mass. Hydrofluoric acid must be kept in plastic containers because it vigorously attacks glass and other materials containing silica (SiO_2), producing gaseous silicon tetrafluoride, SiF_4. Hydrofluoric acid is used to etch glass and clean stone.

Both hydrogen fluoride and hydrofluoric acid, referred to collectively as HF, are extreme irritants to any tissue they contact. Exposed areas heal poorly, gangrene may develop, and ulcers can occur in affected areas of the upper respiratory tract.

The toxic nature of fluoride ion, F^-, is not confined to its presence in HF. It is toxic in soluble fluoride salts, such as NaF. At relatively low levels, such as about 1 ppm, used in some drinking water supplies, fluoride prevents tooth decay. At excessive levels, fluoride causes *fluorosis*, a condition characterized by bone abnormalities and mottled, soft teeth. Livestock are especially susceptible to poisoning from fluoride fallout on grazing land as a result of industrial pollution. In severe cases, the animals become lame and even die.

Hydrogen Chloride

Hydrogen chloride, HCl (mp, -114°C; bp, -84.8°C), may be encountered as a gas, pressurized liquid, or aqueous solution called *hydrochloric acid*, commonly denoted simply as HCl. This compound is colorless in the pure state and in aqueous solution. As a saturated solution containing 36% HCl, hydrochloric acid is a major industrial chemical, with U.S. production of about 2.3 million tons per year. It is used for chemical and food manufacture, acid treatment of oil wells to increase crude oil flow, and metal processing.

Hydrogen chloride is not nearly as toxic as HF, although inhalation can cause spasms of the larynx as well as pulmonary edema and even death at high levels. Because of its high affinity for water, HCl vapor tends to dehydrate tissue of the eyes and respiratory tract. Hydrochloric acid is a natural physiological fluid found as a dilute solution in the stomachs of humans and other animals.

Hydrogen Bromide and Hydrogen Iodide

Hydrogen bromide, HBr (mp, -87°C; bp, -66.5°C), and *hydrogen iodide*, HI (mp, -50.8°C; bp, -35.4°C), are both pale yellow or colorless gases, although contamination by their respective elements tends to impart some color to these compounds. Both are very dense gases, 3.5 g/l for HBr and 5.7 g/l for HI at 0°C and atmospheric pressure. These compounds are used much less than HCl. Both are irritants to the skin and eyes and to the oral and respiratory mucous membranes.

Interhalogen Compounds and Halogen Oxides

Halogens form compounds among themselves and with oxygen. Some of these compounds are important in industry and toxicologically. Some of the more important such compounds are discussed below.

Interhalogen Compounds

Fluorine is a sufficiently strong oxidant to oxidize chlorine, bromine, and iodine, whereas chlorine can oxidize bromine and iodine. The compounds thus formed are called *interhalogen compounds*.

The liquid interhalogen compounds are usually described as "fuming" liquids. For the most part, interhalogen compounds exhibit extreme reactivity. They react with water or steam to produce hydrohalic acid solutions (HF, HCl) and nascent oxygen {O}. They tend to be potent oxidizing agents for organic matter and oxidizable inorganic compounds. These chemical properties are reflected in the toxicities of the interhalogen compounds. Too reactive to enter biological systems in their original chemical state, they tend to be powerful corrosive irritants that acidify, oxidize, and dehydrate tissue. The skin, eyes, and mucous membranes of the mouth, throat, and pulmonary systems are susceptible to attack by interhalogen compounds. In some respects, the toxicities of the interhalogen compounds resemble the toxic properties of the elemental forms of the elements from which they are composed. The by-products of chemical reactions of the interhalogen compounds — such as HF from fluorine compounds — pose additional toxicological hazards.

Halogen Oxides

The oxides of the halogens tend to be unstable and reactive. Although these compounds are called oxides, it is permissible to call the ones containing fluorine fluorides because fluorine is more electronegative than oxygen. Commercially, the most important of the halogen oxides is chlorine dioxide, which offers some advantages over chlorine as a water disinfectant. It is also employed for odor control and bleaching wood pulp. Because of its extreme instability, chlorine dioxide is manufactured on the site where it is used.

Investigations on human blood and on rodents suggest that ClO_2 and its metabolic product ClO_2^- cause formation of methemoglobin, decrease the activities of glucose-6-phosphate dehydrogenase and glutathione peroxidase enzymes, reduce levels of reduced glutathione (a protective agent against oxidative stress), increase levels of hydrogen peroxide, and cause breakdown of red blood cells releasing hemoglobin (hemolysis). These effects would suggest an overall hematotoxicity of chlorine dioxide.

For the most part, the halogen oxides are highly reactive toxic substances. Their toxicity and hazard characteristics are similar to those of the interhalogen compounds, described previously in this section.

Hypochlorous Acid and Hypochlorites

The halogens form several oxyacids and their corresponding salts. Of these, the most important is hypochlorous acid (HOCl), formed by the following reaction:

$$Cl_2 + H_2O \rightleftarrows HCl + HOCl$$

Hypochlorous acid and hypochlorites are used for bleaching and disinfection. They produce active (nascent) oxygen, {O}, as shown by the reaction below, and the resulting oxidizing action is largely responsible for the toxicity of hypochlorous acid and hypochlorites as irritants to eye, skin, and mucous membrane tissue.

$$HClO \rightarrow H^+ + Cl^- + \{O\}$$

Perchlorates

Perchlorates are the most oxidized of the salts of the chlorooxyacids. Although perchlorates are not particularly toxic, ammonium perchlorate (NH_4ClO_4) should be mentioned because it is a powerful oxidizer and reactive chemical produced in large quantities as a fuel oxidizer in solid rocket fuels. Each of the U.S. space shuttle booster rockets contains about 350,000 kg of ammonium perchlorate in its propellant mixture. By 1988, U.S. consumption of ammonium perchlorate for rocket fuel uses was of the order of 24 million kg/year. In May 1988, a series of massive explosions in Henderson, Nevada, demolished one of only two plants producing ammonium perchlorate for the U.S. space shuttle, MX missile, and other applications, so that supplies were severely curtailed. The plant has since been rebuilt.

The toxicological hazard of perchlorate salts may depend on the cation in the compound. In general, the salts should be considered as skin irritants and treated as such. Perchlorate ion, ClO_4^-, may compete physiologically with iodide ion, I^-. This can occur in the uptake of iodide by the thyroid, leading to the biosynthesis of thyroid hormones. As a consequence, perchlorate can cause symptoms of iodine deficiency.

Nitrogen Compounds of the Halogens

Nitrogen Halides

The general formula of the nitrogen halides is N_nX_x, where X is F, Cl, Br, or I. The nitrogen halides are considered to be very toxic, largely as irritants to eyes, skin, and mucous membranes. Direct exposure to nitrogen halide compounds tends to be limited because of their reactivity, which may destroy the compound before exposure. Nitrogen triiodide is so reactive that even a "puff" of air can detonate it.

Azides

Halogen azides are compounds with the general formula XN_3, where X is one of the halogens. These compounds are extremely reactive and can be spontaneously explosive. Their reactions with water can produce toxic fumes of the elemental halogen, acid (e.g., HCl), and NO_X. The compound vapors are irritants.

Monochloramine and Dichloramine

The substitution of Cl for H on ammonia can be viewed as a means of forming nitrogen trichloride, monochloramine, and dichloramine. The formation of the last two compounds from ammonium ion in water is shown by the following reactions:

$$NH_4^+ + HOCl \rightarrow H^+ + H_2O + \underset{\text{Monochloramine}}{NH_2Cl}$$

$$NH_2Cl + HOCl \rightarrow H_2O + \underset{\text{Dichloramine}}{NHCl_2}$$

The chloramines are disinfectants in water and are formed deliberately in the purification of drinking water to provide *combined available chlorine*. Although combined available chlorine is a weaker disinfectant than water, containing Cl_2, HOCl, and OCl^-, it is retained longer in the water distribution system, affording longer-lasting disinfection.

Since they work as disinfectants, the chloramines have to have some toxic effects. They have been shown to inhibit acetylcholinesterase activity.

Inorganic Compounds of Silicon

Because of its use in semiconductors, silicon has emerged as a key element in modern technology. Concurrent with this phenomenon has been an awareness of the toxicity of silicon compounds, many of which, fortunately, have relatively low toxicities. This section covers the toxicological aspects of inorganic silicon compounds.

Silica

The silicon compound that has probably caused the most illness in humans is *silica*, SiO_2. Silica is a hard mineral substance known as quartz in the pure form and occurring in a variety of minerals, such as sand, sandstone, and diatomaceous earth. Because of silica's occurrence in a large number of common materials that are widely used in construction, sand blasting, refractories manufacture, and many other industrial applications, human exposure to silica dust is widespread. Such exposure causes a condition called *silicosis*, a type of pulmonary fibrosis, one of the most common disabling conditions that result from industrial exposure to hazardous substances. Silicosis causes fibrosis and nodules in the lung, lowering lung capacity and making the subject more liable to pulmonary diseases, such as pneumonia. A lung condition called *silicotuberculosis* may develop. Severe cases of silicosis can cause death from insufficient oxygen or from heart failure.

Silica exposure has been associated with increased incidences of *scleroderma*, a condition manifested by hardened, rigid connective tissue. In this respect, it is believed that silica acts by an adjuvant mechanism in which it enhances the autoimmune response caused by other agents, such as silicones or paraffin.

Asbestos

Asbestos describes a group of silicate minerals, such as those of the serpentine group, approximate formula $Mg_3P(Si_2O_5)(OH)_4$, which occur as mineral fibers. Asbestos has many properties, such as insulating abilities and heat resistance, that have given it numerous uses. It has been used in structural materials, brake linings, insulation, and pipe manufacture. Unfortunately, inhalation of asbestos damages the lungs and results in a characteristic type of lung cancer in some exposed subjects. The toxic effects of asbestos are initiated when asbestos fibers in the lung act as local irritants and become phagocytosed by macrophages (large white blood cells). The bodies of phagocytosed asbestos are taken up by cellular lysosomes, which secrete hydrolytic enzymes, digesting the matter surrounding the asbestos particles and releasing them to start the process over. This process causes lymphoid tissue to aggregate in the vicinity of the insult, forming fibrotic lesions from the synthesis of excess collagen.

The three major pathological conditions caused by the inhalation of asbestos are asbestosis (a pneumonia condition), mesothelioma (tumor of the mesothelial tissue lining the chest cavity adjacent to the lungs), and bronchogenic carcinoma (cancer originating with the air passages in the lungs). Because of these health effects, uses of asbestos have been severely curtailed and widespread programs have been undertaken to remove asbestos from buildings.

Lung cancer from asbestos exposure has a strong synergistic relationship with exposure to cigarette smoke. Long-term exposure to asbestos, alone, increases the incidence of lung cancer about 5-fold, cigarette smoking roughly 10-fold, but the two together more than 50-fold.

Silanes

Compounds of silicon with hydrogen are called *silanes*. The simplest of these is silane, SiH_4. Disilane is H_3SiSiH_3. Numerous organic silanes exist in which alkyl moieties are substituted for H.

In addition to SiH_4, the inorganic silanes produced for commercial use are dichloro- and trichlorosilane, SiH_2Cl_2 and $SiHCl_3$, respectively. These compounds are used as intermediates in the synthesis of organosilicon compounds and in the production of high-purity silicon for semiconductors. Several kinds of inorganic compounds derived from silanes have potential uses in the manufacture of photovoltaic devices for the direct conversion of solar energy to electricity. In general, not much is known about the toxicities of silanes. Silane itself burns readily in air. Chlorosilanes are irritants to eye, nasal, and lung tissue. The toxicities of silane, dichlorosilane, and tetraethoxysilane, $Si(OC_2H_5)$, have been reviewed for their relevance in the semiconductor industry. The major effects of silane and tetraethoxysilane appeared to be nephrotoxicity (kidney damage).

Silicon Halides and Halohydrides

Four *silicon tetrahalides*, with the general formula SiX_4, are known to exist. Of these, only silicon tetrachloride, $SiCl_4$, is produced in significant quantities. It is used to manufacture fumed silica (finely divided SiO_2). In addition, numerous *silicon halohydrides*, with the general formula $H_{4-X}SiX_X$, have been synthesized. The commercially important compound of this type is trichlorosilane, $HSiCl_3$, which is used to manufacture organotrichlorosilanes and elemental silicon for semiconductors.

Both silicon tetrachloride and trichlorosilane are fuming liquids with suffocating odors. They both react with water to give off HCl vapor.

Inorganic Phosphorus Compounds

Phosphine

Phosphine, PH_3 (mp, −132°C; bp, −88°C), is a colorless gas that undergoes autoignition at 100°C. It is used for the synthesis of organophosphorus compounds. Its inadvertent production in chemical syntheses involving other phosphorus compounds is a potential hazard in industrial processes and in the laboratory. Phosphine gas is a pulmonary tract irritant and central nervous system depressant that is very toxic when inhaled and can be fatal. Symptoms of acute exposure include headache, dizziness, burning pain below the sternum, nausea, vomiting, difficult, painful breathing, pulmonary irritation and edema, cough with fluorescent green sputum, tremors, and fatigue. Convulsions have appeared in some victims after they have apparently recovered from phosphine poisoning. Workers chronically exposed to phosphine have exhibited inflammation of the nasal cavity and throat, nausea, dizziness, weakness, and adverse gastrointestinal, cardiorespiratory, and central nervous system effects. Chronic effects have also included hepatotoxic symptoms, jaundice, nervous system abnormalities, and increased bone density.

Arsine gas, AsH_3, is mentioned here because of the position of arsenic directly below phosphorus in the periodic table, and hence the similarity between arsine and phosphine. Arsine may be generated by chemically reductive processes in the refining of various metals. It is a highly toxic substance that can cause fatal instances of poisoning. Its major effect is on the blood, and it may cause breakdown of red blood cells with liberation of hemoglobin (hemolysis). Symptomatic of this effect is the presence of hemoglobin in urine (hemoglobinuria). Acute symptoms of arsine poisoning include headache, shortness of breath, nausea, and vomiting. Jaundice and anemia may also accompany arsine poisoning.

Phosphorus Pentoxide

The oxide most commonly formed by the combustion of elemental white phosphorus and many phosphorus compounds is P_4O_{10}. As an item of commerce, this compound is usually misnamed *phosphorus pentoxide*. When produced from the combustion of elemental phosphorus, it is a fluffy white powder that removes water from air to form syrupy orthophosphoric acid:

$$P_4O_{10} + 6H_2O \rightarrow 4H_3PO_4$$

Because of its dehydrating action and formation of acid, phosphorus pentoxide is a corrosive irritant to skin, eyes, and mucous membranes.

Phosphorus Halides

Phosphorus forms halides with the general formulas PX_3 and PX_5. Typical of such compounds are phosphorus trifluoride (PF_3), a colorless gas (mp, −152°C; bp, −102°C), and phosphorus pentabromide (PBr_5), a yellow solid that decomposes at approximately 100°C. Of these compounds, the most important commercially is phosphorus pentachloride, used as a catalyst in organic synthesis, as a chlorinating agent, and as a raw material to make phosphorus oxychloride ($POCl_3$). Phosphorus halides react violently with water to produce the corresponding hydrogen halides and oxophosphorus acids, as shown by the following reaction of phosphorus pentachloride:

$$PCl_5 + 4H_2O \rightarrow H_3PO_4 + 5HCl$$

Largely because of their acid-forming tendencies, the phosphorus halides are strong irritants to eyes, skin, and mucous membranes, and should be regarded as very toxic.

Phosphorus Oxyhalides

Phosphorus oxyhalides, with the general formula POX_3, are known for fluoride, chloride, and bromide. Of these, the one with commercial uses is phosphorus oxychloride ($POCl_3$). Its uses are similar to those of phosphorus trichloride, acting in chemical synthesis as a chlorinating agent and for the production of organic chemical intermediates. It is a faintly yellow fuming liquid (mp, 1°C; bp, 105°C). It reacts with water to form hydrochloric acid and phosphonic acid (H_3PO_3). The liquid evolves toxic vapors, and it is a strong irritant to the eyes, skin, and mucous membranes. Phosphorus oxychloride is metabolized to phosphorodichloridic acid, a phosphorylating agent that phosphorylates acetylcholinesterase at the active site to form enzymically inactive (O-phosphoserine)acetylcholinesterase.

Inorganic Compounds of Sulfur

One of the elements essential for life, sulfur is a constituent of several of the more important toxic inorganic compounds. The common elemental form of yellow crystalline or powdered sulfur, S_8, has a low toxicity, although chronic inhalation of it can irritate mucous membranes.

Hydrogen Sulfide

Hydrogen sulfide (H_2S) is a colorless gas (mp, –86°C; bp, –6 1°C) with a foul, rotten-egg odor. It is produced in large quantities as a by-product of coal coking and petroleum refining, and massive quantities are removed in the cleansing of sour natural gas. Hydrogen sulfide is released in large quantities from volcanoes and hydrothermal vents. Indeed, if Yellowstone National Park in the U.S. were an industrial enterprise, parts of it would be shut down because of release of hydrogen sulfide from geothermal sources. Hydrogen sulfide is a major source of elemental sulfur by a process that involves oxidation of part of the H_2S to SO_2, followed by the Claus reaction:

$$2H_2S(g) + SO_2(g) \rightarrow 2H_2O(l) + 3S(s)$$

Hydrogen sulfide is a very toxic substance, which in some cases can cause a fatal response more rapidly even than hydrogen cyanide, the toxic effects of which it greatly resembles. Like cyanide, hydrogen sulfide inhibits the cytochrome oxidase system essential for respiration. Hydrogen sulfide affects the central nervous system, causing symptoms that include headache, dizziness, and excitement. Rapid death occurs at exposures to air containing more than about 1000 ppm of H_2S, and somewhat lower exposures for about 30 min can be lethal. Death results from asphyxiation as a consequence of respiratory system paralysis. Sulfide can also cause localized toxic effects at the point of contact, one of which is pulmonary edema. Another localized effect is eye conjunctivitis, a condition called "gas eye," perhaps named after conditions suffered by gas works employees formerly exposed to hydrogen sulfide produced in the gasification of high-sulfur coal in the production of synthetic gas, once widely used for cooking and lighting.

Accidental poisonings by hydrogen sulfide are not uncommon. In the most notorious such case, 22 people (by some accounts many more) were killed in 1950 in Poza Rica, Mexico, when a flare used to "dispose" of hydrogen sulfide from natural gas by burning it to sulfur dioxide became extinguished, releasing large quantities of H_2S and asphyxiating victims as they slept. In 1975, at Denver City, Texas, nine people were killed from hydrogen sulfide blown out of a secondary petroleum recovery well. There are numerous effects of chronic H_2S poisoning, including general debility.

Hydrogen sulfide is acted on in the body by methylation with thiol S-methyl transferase. The initial product is methanethiol, $HSCH_3$, which is also quite toxic. A second methylation produces dimethylsulfide, H_3CSCH_3. (Of some interest is the fact that dimethylsulfide is the major volatile sulfur compound released to the atmosphere from oceans, where it is produced by the action of marine microorganisms.)

Bacteria acting anaerobically in the colon produce large quantities of hydrogen sulfide and methanethiol. There is evidence to suggest that the mucous membranes of the colon have enzymes that convert hydrogen sulfide and methanethiol to nontoxic thiosulfate, $S_2O_3^{2-}$.

The nitrite-induced formation of blood methemoglobin has been used successfully to treat hydrogen sulfide poisoning. Like cyanide, hydrogen sulfide bonds to iron(III) in methemoglobin so that it is not available to inhibit cytochrome oxidase.

Sulfur Dioxide and Sulfites

Sulfur dioxide (SO_2) is an intermediate in the production of sulfuric acid. It is a common air pollutant produced by the combustion of pyrite (FeS_2) in coal and organically bound sulfur in coal and fuel oil, as shown by the two following reactions:

$$4FeS_2 + 11O_2 \rightarrow 2Fe_2O_3 + 8SO_2$$

$$S(\textit{organic, in fuel}) + O_2 \rightarrow SO_2$$

These sources add millions of tons of sulfur dioxide to the global atmosphere annually and are largely responsible for acid rain.

Sulfur dioxide is an irritant to the eyes, skin, mucous membranes, and respiratory system. As a water-soluble gas, it is largely removed in the upper respiratory tract. Its major effect is as a respiratory tract irritant, where it irritates the upper airways and causes bronchio-constriction, resulting in increased airflow resistance. Subjects who are hyperresponsive to sulfur dioxide are especially at risk from it. Asthmatics may suffer bronchioconstriction after only a few breaths of sulfur dioxide-contaminated air. The degree of response of asthma sufferers to sulfur dioxide is highly variable.

Dissolved in water, sulfur dioxide produces *sulfurous acid* (H_2SO_3), *hydrogen sulfite ion* (HSO_3^-), and *sulfite ion* (SO_3^{2-}). Sodium sulfite (Na_2SO_3) has been used as a chemical food preservative, although some individuals are hypersensitive to it.

Sulfuric Acid

Sulfuric acid is number one in synthetic chemical production. It is used to produce phosphate fertilizer, high octane gasoline, and a wide variety of inorganic and organic chemicals. Large quantities are consumed to pickle steel (cleaning and removal of surface oxides); disposal of spent pickling liquor can be a problem.

Sulfuric acid is of particular concern as an atmospheric pollutant. In times past, air polluted with unquestionably toxic levels of sulfuric acid aerosols, such as in the severe air pollution that occurred in London and around various smelters in the 1950s and early 1960s, produced toxic effects and even fatalities. At present, sulfuric acid is a major contributor to acid precipitation, and it may well be the most intense common irritant occurring in air polluted with acid substances. Most of the pollutant sulfur that becomes atmospheric H_2SO_4 is emitted to the atmosphere as SO_2 from the burning of sulfur-containing fuels (particularly coal). Sulfur dioxide emissions are almost always accompanied by emissions of particulate matter, which often contains metals, such as vanadium, iron, and manganese. These metals can catalyze the oxidation of SO_2 to H_2SO_4, either on particle surfaces or leached into aqueous solution in aerosol droplets:

$$SO_2 + {}^1/_2O_2 + H_2O \rightarrow H_2SO_4(aq)$$

The result can be formation of an aerosol mist of droplets containing intensely irritating sulfuric acid.

Sulfuric acid is a severely corrosive poison and dehydrating agent in the concentrated liquid form. It readily penetrates skin to reach subcutaneous tissue and causes tissue necrosis, with effects resembling those of severe thermal burns. Sulfuric acid fumes and mists can act as irritants to eye and respiratory tract tissue. Industrial exposure has caused tooth erosion in workers.

At lower levels, inhalation of sulfuric acid from sources such as atmospheric precipitation is damaging to the pulmonary tract. Compared to sulfur dioxide, sulfuric acid is the much more potent lung tissue irritant. Animal studies and limited data from exposed humans indicate that inhalation of H_2SO_4 aerosol increases airway resistance and inhibits bronchial clearance of inhaled particles. Asthmatic subjects are sensitive to sulfuric acid inhalation, and the effect may be synergistic with sulfur dioxide. Therefore, particularly for sensitive individuals, exposure to air containing sulfuric acid, sulfur dioxide, and particles — all of which tend to occur together when one is present in a polluted atmosphere — may be particularly damaging to the lungs.

Carbon Disulfide

Carbon disulfide, CS_2, is a toxicologically important compound because of its widespread use in making rayon and cellophane from cellulose and its well-established toxic effects. Skin contact with carbon disulfide has caused skin disorders, including blisters in rayon plant workers. Very high levels of atmospheric carbon disulfide vapor in the workplace of the order of 10 ppt can cause life-threatening effects on the central nervous system. Epidemiologic studies of viscose rayon workers exposed to carbon disulfide have shown increased mortalities, including cardiovascular mortality. Vascular atherosclerotic changes have been observed in workers exposed to carbon disulfide for long periods of time.

The most notable toxicological effects of carbon disulfide are on the nervous system, including damage to the peripheral nervous system. Individuals exposed to carbon disulfide have lost consciousness. Decreased nerve conduction velocities have been observed in workers exposed to 10 to 20 ppm of carbon disulfide in the workplace over periods of 10 to 20 years. Brain abnormalities suggesting toxic encephalopathy have been observed in exposed workers. Some studies have suggested the possibility of mental performance and personality disorders in workers exposed to carbon disulfide, including heightened levels of anxiety, introversion, and depression.

4

FORENSIC ORGANIC TOXICANTS

The present chapter discuss the toxicological chemistry of organic compounds that are largely of synthetic origin. Since the vast majority of the several million known chemical compounds are organic—most of them toxic to a greater or lesser degree—the toxicological chemistry of organic compounds covers an enormous area. Specifically, this chapter discusses hydrocarbons, which are organic compounds composed only of carbon and hydrogen and are in a sense the simplest of the organic compounds. Hydrocarbons occur naturally in petroleum, natural gas, and tar sands, and they can be produced by pyrolysis of coal and oil shale or by chemical synthesis from H_2 and CO.

CLASSIFICATION OF HYDROCARBONS

For purposes of discussion of hydrocarbon toxicities in this chapter, hydrocarbons will be grouped into the five categories: (1) *alkanes*, (2) *unsaturated nonaromatic* hydrocarbons, (3) *aromatic* hydrocarbons (understood to have only one or two linked aromatic rings in their structures), (4) *polycyclic* aromatic hydrocarbons with multiple rings, and (5) *mixed* hydrocarbons containing combinations of two or more of the preceding types.

Alkanes

Alkanes, also called *paraffins* or *aliphatic hydrocarbons*, are hydrocarbons in which the C atoms are joined by single covalent bonds (sigma bonds) consisting of two shared electrons. As shown by the examples, alkanes may exist as straight chains or branched chains. They may also exist as cyclic structures, for example, as in cyclohexane (C_6H_{12}). Each cyclohexane molecule consists of six carbon atoms (each

Alkanes

Methane 2,2,3-Trimethylbutane

Unsaturated nonaromatic

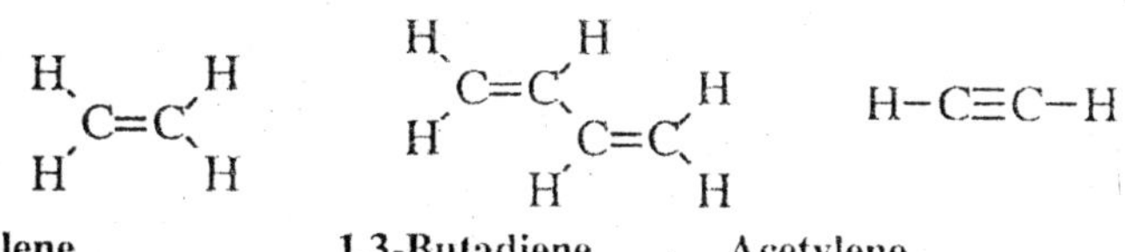

One/two-ring aromatic ***Polycyclic aromatic***

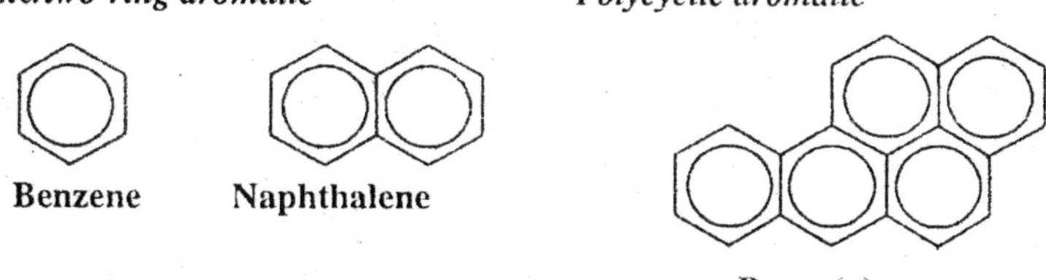

Mixed hydrocarbons

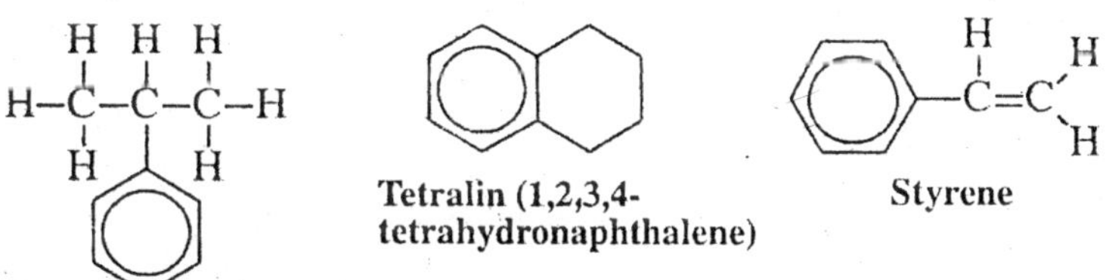

Cumene (benzene, (1-methylethyl))

Fig. 4.1. Hydrocarbons classified for discussion of their toxicological chemistry.

with two H atoms attached) in a ring. The general molecular formula for straight- and branched-chain alkanes is C_nH_{2n+2}, and that of a cyclic alkane is C_nH_{2n}. The names of alkanes having from one to ten carbon atoms per molecule are respectively (1) methane, (2) ethane, (3) propane, (4) butane, (5) pentane, (6) hexane, (7) heptane, (8) octane, (9) nonane, and (10) decane. These names may be prefixed by *n*- to denote a straight-chain alkane. The same base names are used to designate substituent groups on molecules; for example, a straight-chain four-carbon alkane group (derived from butane) attached by an end carbon to a molecule is designated as an *n*-butyl group.

Alkanes undergo a number of chemical reactions, two classes of which should be mentioned here. The first of these is *oxidation* with molecular oxygen in air, as shown for the following combustion reaction of propane:

$$C_3H_8 + 5O_2 \rightarrow 3CO_2 + 4H_2O + \text{heat}$$

Such reactions can pose flammability and explosion hazards. Another hazard occurs during combustion in an oxygen-deficient atmosphere or in an automobile engine, in which significant quantities of toxic carbon monoxide (CO) are produced.

The second major type of alkane reaction that should be considered here consists of *substitution reactions*, in which one or more H atoms on an alkane are replaced by atoms of another element. Most commonly, the H is replaced by a halogen, usually chlorine, to yield *organohalide* compounds; when chlorine is the substituent, the product is called an *organochlorine* compound. An example of this kind of reaction is that of methane with chlorine to give carbon tetrachloride, given below.

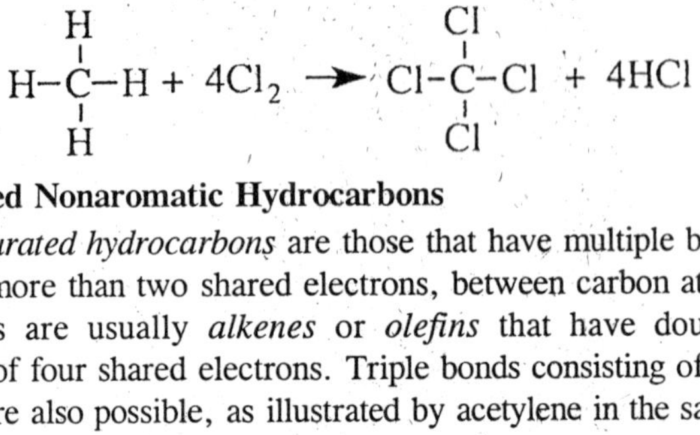

$$\mathrm{H{-}\underset{\underset{H}{|}}{\overset{\overset{H}{|}}{C}}{-}H} + 4Cl_2 \rightarrow \mathrm{Cl{-}\underset{\underset{Cl}{|}}{\overset{\overset{Cl}{|}}{C}}{-}Cl} + 4HCl$$

Unsaturated Nonaromatic Hydrocarbons

Unsaturated hydrocarbons are those that have multiple bonds, each involving more than two shared electrons, between carbon atoms. Such compounds are usually *alkenes* or *olefins* that have double bonds consisting of four shared electrons. Triple bonds consisting of six shared electrons are also possible, as illustrated by acetylene in the same figure.

Alkenes may undergo *addition reactions*, in which pairs of atoms are added across unsaturated bonds, as shown in the following reaction of ethylene with hydrogen to give ethane:

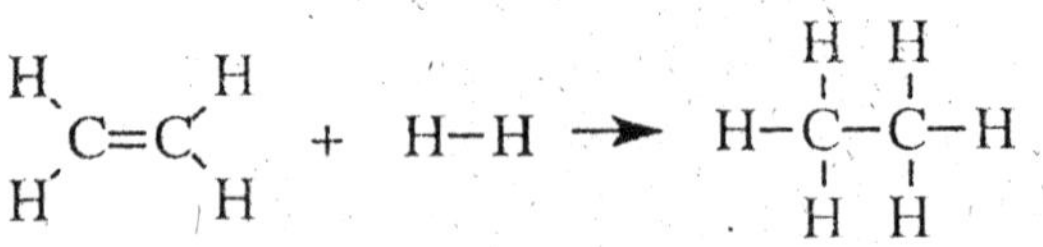

$$\mathrm{H_2C{=}CH_2} + \mathrm{H{-}H} \rightarrow \mathrm{H{-}\underset{\underset{H}{|}}{\overset{\overset{H}{|}}{C}}{-}\underset{\underset{H}{|}}{\overset{\overset{H}{|}}{C}}{-}H}$$

This kind of reaction, which is not possible with alkanes, adds to the chemical and metabolic, as well as toxicological, versatility of compounds containing unsaturated bonds.

Another example of an addition reaction is that of a molecule of HCl gas to one of acetylene to yield vinyl chloride:

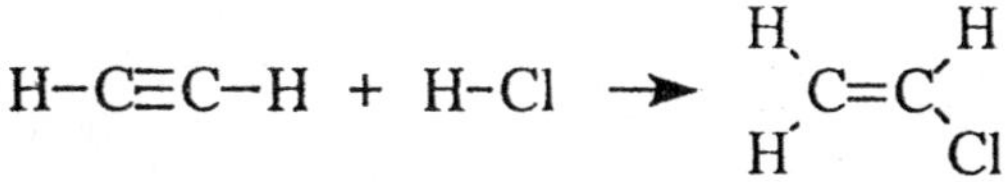

$$H{-}C{\equiv}C{-}H + H{-}Cl \rightarrow H_2C{=}CHCl$$

The vinyl chloride product is the monomer used to manufacture polyvinylchloride plastic and is a carcinogen known to cause a rare form of liver cancer among exposed workers.

As discussed already, compounds with double bonds can exist as geometrical isomers exemplified by the two isomers of 1,2-dichloroethylene. Although both of these compounds have the molecular formula $C_2H_2Cl_2$, the orientations of their H and Cl atoms relative to each other are different, and their properties, such as melting and boiling points, are not the same. Their toxicities are both relatively low, but significantly different. The *cis*- isomer is an irritant and narcotic known to damage the liver and kidneys of experimental animals. The *trans*- isomer causes weakness, tremor, and cramps due to its effects on the central nervous system, as well as nausea and vomiting, resulting from adverse effects on the gastrointestinal tract.

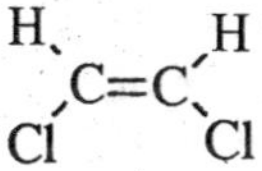

Cis -1,2-dichloroethylene, mp -80.5°C, bp 59°C

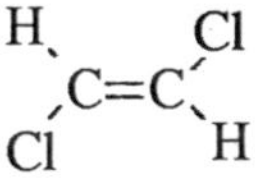

Trans -1,2-dichloroethylene, mp -50°C, bp 48°C

Fig. 4.2. The two geometrical isomers of 1,2-dichloroethane

Aromatic Hydrocarbons

The characteristics of *aromaticity* of organic compounds are numerous and are discussed at length in works on organic chemistry. These characteristics include a low hydrogen:carbon atomic ratio, C–C bonds that are quite strong and of intermediate length between such bonds in alkanes and those in alkenes, a tendency to undergo substitution reactions rather than the addition reactions characteristic of alkenes,

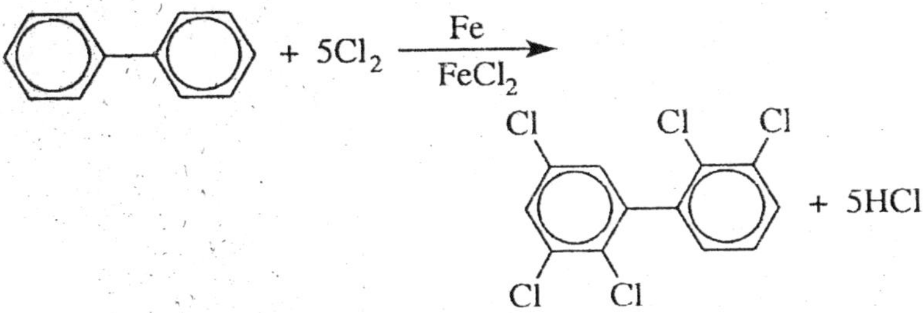

$$C_{12}H_{10} + 5Cl_2 \xrightarrow[FeCl_2]{Fe} C_{12}H_5Cl_5 + 5HCl$$

Fig. 4.3. An example of a substitution reaction of an aromatic hydrocarbon compound to produce an organochlorine product.

and delocalization of π-electrons over several carbon atoms, resulting in resonance stabilization of the molecule. For purposes of discussion here, most of the aromatic compounds discussed are those that contain single benzene rings or fused benzene rings, such as those in naphthalene or benzo(a)pyrene.

An example reaction of aromatic compounds with considerable environmental and toxicological significance is the chlorination of biphenyl. Biphenyl gets its name from the fact that it consists of two *phenyl* groups (where a phenyl group is a benzene molecule less a hydrogen atom) joined by a single covalent bond. In the presence of an iron(II) chloride catalyst, this compound reacts with chlorine to form a number of different molecules of polychlorinated biphenyls (PCBs).

Toxicology of Alkanes

Worker exposure to alkanes, especially the lower-molecular-mass compounds, is most likely to come from inhalation. In an effort to set reasonable values for the exposure by inhalation of vapors of solvents, hydrocarbons, and other volatile organic liquids, the American Conference of Governmental Industrial Hygienists sets *threshold limit values* (TLVs) for airborne toxicants. The *time-weighted average exposure* (E) is calculated by the formula

$$E = \frac{C_a T_a + C_b T_b + \cdots + C_n T_n}{8}$$

where C is the concentration of the substance in the air for a particular time T (hours), such as a level of 3.1 ppm by volume for 1.25 h. The 8 in the denominator is for an 8-h day. In addition to exposures calculated by this equation, there are short-term exposure limits (STELs) and ceiling (C) recommendations applicable to higher exposure levels for brief periods of time, such as 10 min once each day.

"Safe" levels of air contaminants are difficult to set based on systemic toxicologic effects. Therefore, TLVs often reflect nonsystemic effects of odor, narcosis, eye irritation, and skin irritation. Because of this, comparison of TLVs is often not useful in comparing systemic toxicological effects of chemicals in the workplace.

Methane and Ethane

Methane and ethane are *simple asphyxiants*, which means that air containing high levels of these gases does not contain sufficient oxygen to support respiration. Simple asphyxiant gases are not known to have major systemic toxicological effects, although subtle effects that are hard to detect should be considered as possibilities.

Propane and Butane

Propane has the formula C_3H_8 and butane C_4H_8. There are two isomers of butane, *n*-butane and isobutane (2-methylpropane). Propane and the butane isomers are gases at room temperature and atmospheric pressure; like methane and ethane, all three are asphyxiants. A high concentration of propane affects the central nervous system. There are essentially no known systemic toxicological effects of the two butane isomers; behavior similar to that of propane might be expected.

Pentane through Octane

The alkanes with five to eight carbon atoms consist of *n*-alkanes, and there is an increasing number of branched-chain isomers with higher numbers of C atoms per molecule. For example, there are nine isomers of heptane C_7H_{16}. These compounds are all volatile liquids under ambient conditions; the boiling points for the straight-chain isomers range from 36.1°C for *n*-pentane to 125.8°C for *n*-octane. In addition to their uses in fuels, such as in gasoline, these compounds are employed as solvents in formulations for a number of commercial products, including varnishes, glues, and inks. They are also used for the extraction of fats.

Once regarded as toxicologically almost harmless, the C_5–C_8 aliphatic hydrocarbons are now recognized as having some significant toxic effects. Exposure to the C_5–C_8 hydrocarbons is primarily via the pulmonary route, and high levels in air have killed experimental animals. Humans inhaling high levels of these hydrocarbons have become dizzy and have lost coordination as a result of central nervous system depression.

Of the C_5–C_8 alkanes, the one most commonly used for nonfuel purposes is *n* -hexane. It acts as a solvent for the extraction of oils from seeds, such as cottonseed and sunflower seed. This alkane serves as a solvent medium for several important polymerization processes and in mixtures with more polar solvents, such as furfural,

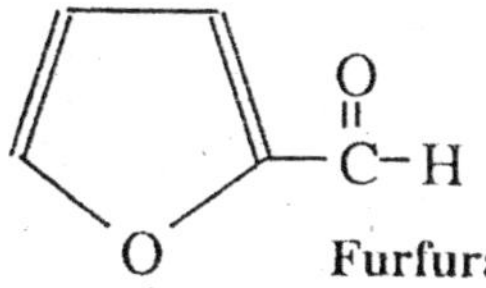

Furfural

for the separation of fatty acids. *Polyneuropathy* (multiple disorders of the nervous system) has been reported in several cases of human exposure to *n*-hexane, such as Japanese workers involved in home production of sandals using glue with *n*-hexane solvent. The workers suffered from muscle weakness and impaired sensory function of the hands and feet. Biopsy examination of nerves in leg muscles of the exposed workers showed loss of myelin (a fatty substance constituting a sheath around certain nerve fibers) and degeneration of axons (part of a nerve cell through which nerve impulses are transferred out of the cell). The symptoms of polyneuropathy were reversible, with recovery taking several years after exposure was ended.

Exposure of the skin to C_5–C_8 liquids causes dermatitis. This is the most common toxicological occupational problem associated with the use of hydrocarbon liquids in the workplace, and is a consequence of the dissolution of the fat portions of the skin. In addition to becoming inflamed, the skin becomes dry and scaly.

Alkanes above Octane

Alkanes higher than C_8 are contained in kerosene, jet fuel, diesel fuel, mineral oil, and fuel oil distilled from crude oil as middle distillate fuels with a boiling range of approximately 175 to 370°C. Kerosene, also called fuel oil no. 1, is a mixture of primarily C_8–C_{16} hydrocarbons, predominantly alkanes. Diesel fuel is called fuel oil no. 2. The heavier fuel oils, no. 3 to 6, are characterized by increasing viscosity, darker color, and higher boiling temperatures with increasing fuel oil number. Mineral oil is a carefully selected fraction of petroleum hydrocarbons with density ranges of 0.83 to 0.86 g/ml for light mineral oil and 0.875 to 0.905 g/ml for heavy mineral oil.

The higher alkanes are not regarded as very toxic, although there are some reservations about their toxicities. Inhalation is the most common route of occupational exposure and can result in dizziness, headache, and stupor. In cases of extreme exposure, coma and death have occurred. Inhalation of mists or aspiration of vomitus containing higher alkane liquids has caused a condition known as aspiration pneumonia. They are not regarded as carcinogenic, although experimental mice have shown weak tumorigenic responses with long latency periods upon prolonged skin exposure to middle distillate fuels. The observed effects have been attrributed to chronic skin irritation, and these substances do not produce tumors in the absence of skin irritation. Middle distillate fuels can be effective carriers of known carcinogens, especially polycyclic aromatic hydrocarbons.

Solid and Semisolid Alkanes

Semisolid petroleum jelly is a highly refined product commonly known as vaseline, a mixture of predominantly C_{16}–C_{19} alkanes. Carefully controlled refining processes are used to remove nitrogen and sulfur compounds, resins, and unsaturated hydrocarbons. Paraffin wax is a similar product, behaving as a solid. Neither petroleum jelly nor paraffin is digested or absorbed by the body.

Cyclohexane

Cyclohexane, the six-carbon ring hydrocarbon with the molecular formula C_6H_{12}, is the most significant of the cyclic alkanes. Under ambient conditions it is a clear, volatile, highly flammable liquid. It is manufactured by the hydrogenation of benzene and is used primarily as a raw material for the synthesis of cyclohexanol and cyclohexanone through a liquid-phase oxidation with air in the presence of a dissolved cobalt catalyst.

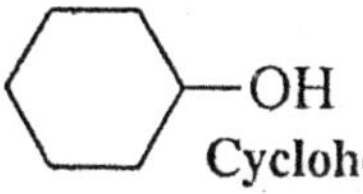

—OH
Cyclohexanol

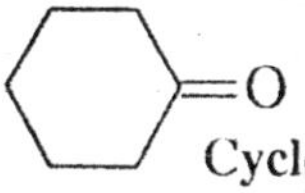

=O
Cyclohexanone

Like *n*-hexane, cyclohexane has a toxicity rating of 3, moderately toxic. Cyclohexane acts as a weak anesthetic similar to, but more potent than, *n*-hexane. Systemic effects have not been shown in humans.

Toxicology of Unsaturated Nonaromatic Hydrocarbons

Ethylene is the most widely used organic chemical. Almost all of it is consumed as a chemical feedstock for the manufacture of other organic chemicals. In addition to polyethylene, other polymeric plastics, elastomers, fibers, and resins are manufactured with ethylene as one of the ingredients. Ethylene is also the raw material for the manufacture of ethylene glycol antifreeze, solvents, plasticizers, surfactants, and coatings.

The boiling point (bp) of ethylene is –105°C, and under ambient conditions it is a colorless gas. It has a somewhat sweet odor, is highly flammable, and forms explosive mixtures with air. Because of its double bond (unsaturation), ethylene is much more active than the

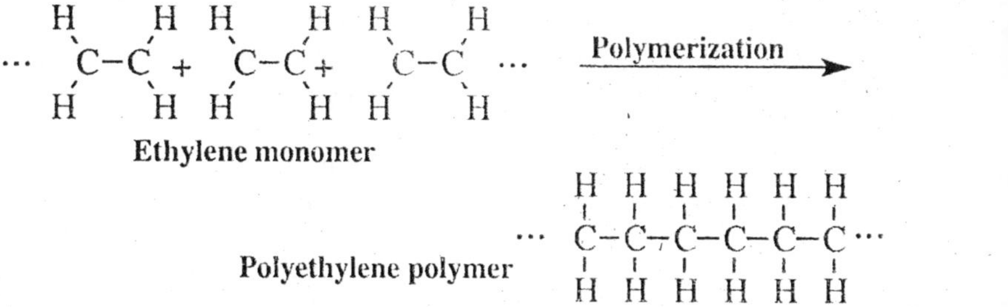

$$\cdots \mathrm{H_2C{=}CH_2} + \mathrm{H_2C{=}CH_2} + \mathrm{H_2C{=}CH_2} \cdots \xrightarrow{\text{Polymerization}}$$

Ethylene monomer

$$\cdots -\mathrm{CH_2-CH_2-CH_2-CH_2-CH_2-CH_2}- \cdots$$

Polyethylene polymer

Fig. 4.4. Polymerization of ethylene to produce polyethylene.

alkanes. It undergoes addition reactions, as shown in the following examples, to form a number of important products:

$$\mathrm{H_2C{=}CH_2 + O_2 \xrightarrow{Catalyst} H_2C{-}CH_2\ (\text{with bridging } O)}$$

Ethylene oxide

$$\xrightarrow{\text{Hydrolysis}} \mathrm{H{-}CH(OH){-}CH(OH){-}H}$$

Ethylene glycol

$$\mathrm{H_2C{=}CH_2 + Br_2 \rightarrow Br{-}CH_2{-}CH_2{-}Br}$$

1,2-dibromoethane (ethylene dibromide)

$$\mathrm{H_2C{=}CH_2 + Cl_2 \rightarrow Cl{-}CH_2{-}CH_2{-}Cl}$$

1,2-dichloroethane (ethylene dichloride)

$$\mathrm{H_2C{=}CH_2 + HCl \rightarrow H{-}CH_2{-}CH_2{-}Cl}$$

Chloroethane (ethyl chloride)

The products of the addition reactions shown above are all commercially, toxicologically, and environmentally important. Ethylene oxide is a highly reactive colorless gas used as a sterilizing agent, fumigant, and intermediate in the manufacture of ethylene glycol and surfactants. It is an irritant to eyes and pulmonary tract mucous membrane tissue; inhalation of it can cause pulmonary edema. Ethylene glycol is a colorless, somewhat viscous liquid used in mixtures with water as a high-boiling, low-freezing-temperature liquid (antifreeze and antiboil) in cooling systems. Ingestion of this compound causes central nervous system effects characterized by initial stimulation, followed by depression. Higher doses can cause poisoning due to metabolic oxidation of ethylene glycol to glycolic acid, glyoxylic acid, and oxalic acid.

Ethylene dibromide has been used as an insecticidal fumigant and additive to scavenge lead from leaded gasoline combustion. During the early 1980s, there was considerable concern about residues of this compound in food products, and it was suspected of being a carcinogen, mutagen, and teratogen. Ethylene dichloride (bp, 83.5°C) is a colorless, volatile liquid with a pleasant odor that is used as a soil and foodstuff fumigant. It has a number of toxicological effects, including adverse effects on the eye, liver, and kidneys, and a narcotic effect on the central nervous system. Ethyl chloride seems to have similar, but much less severe, toxic effects.

A highly flammable compound, ethylene forms dangerously explosive mixtures with air. It is phytotoxic (toxic to plants). Ethylene, itself, is not very toxic to animals, but it is a simple asphyxiant. At high concentrations, it acts as an anesthetic to induce unconsciousness. The only significant pathway of human exposure to ethylene is through inhalation. This exposure is limited by the low blood–gas solubility ratio of ethylene, which applies at levels below saturation of blood with the gas. This ratio for ethylene is only 0.14, compared, for example, with the very high value of 15 for chloroform.

Propylene

Propylene (C_3H_6) is a gas with chemical, physical, and toxicological properties very similar to those of ethylene. It, too, is a simple asphyxiant. Its major use is in the manufacture of polypropylene polymer, a hard, strong plastic from which are made injection-molded bottles, as well as pipes, valves, battery cases, automobile body parts, and rot-resistant indoor–outdoor carpet.

1,3-Butadiene

The dialkene 1,3-butadiene is widely used in the manufacture of polymers, particularly synthetic rubber. The first synthetic rubber to be manufactured on a large scale and used as a substitute for unavailable natural rubber during World War II was a styrene–butadiene polymer:

$$C_6H_5{-}CH{=}CH_2 \; + \; H_2C{=}CH{-}CH{=}CH_2 \xrightarrow{\text{Polymerization}} \cdots{-}CH(C_6H_5){-}CH_2{-}CH_2{-}CH{=}CH{-}CH_2{-}\cdots$$

Styrene **Butadiene** **Buna-S synthetic rubber**

Butadiene is a colorless gas under ambient conditions with a mild, somewhat aromatic odor. At lower levels, the vapor is an irritant to eyes and respiratory system mucous membranes, and at higher levels, it can cause unconsciousness and even death. Symptoms of human exposure include, initially, blurred vision, nausea, and paresthesia, accompanied by dryness of the mouth, nose, and throat. In cases of severe exposure, fatigue, headache, vertigo, and decreased pulse rate and blood pressure may be followed by unconsciousness. Fatal exposures have occurred only as the result of catastrophic releases of 1,3-butadiene

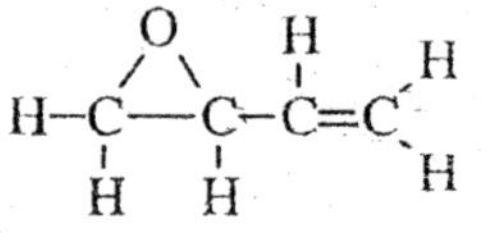

1,2-Epoxybutene-3

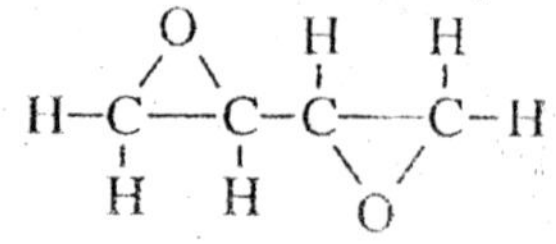

Diepoxybutane

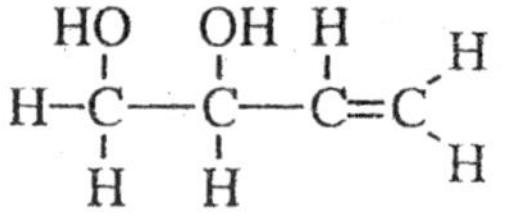

3-Butene-1,2-diol

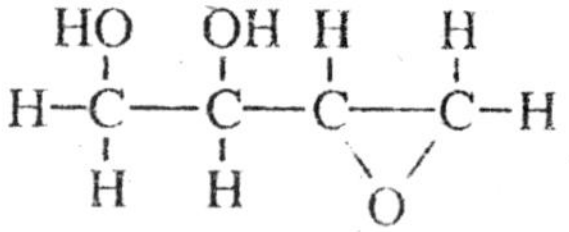

3,4-Epoxy-1,2-butane diol

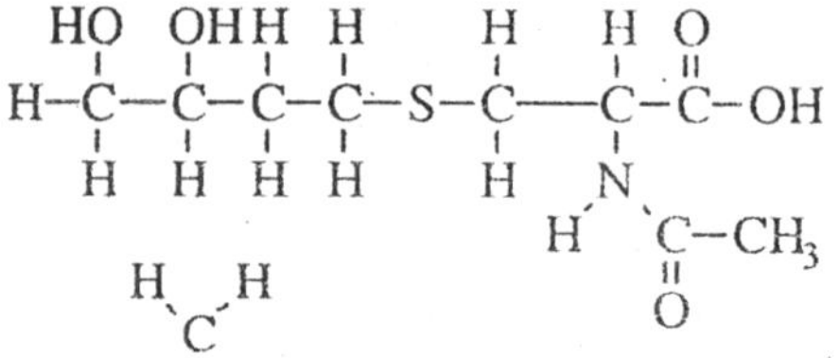

L-Cysteine, N-acetyl-S-(3,4-dihydroxybutyl) mercapturic acid conjugate

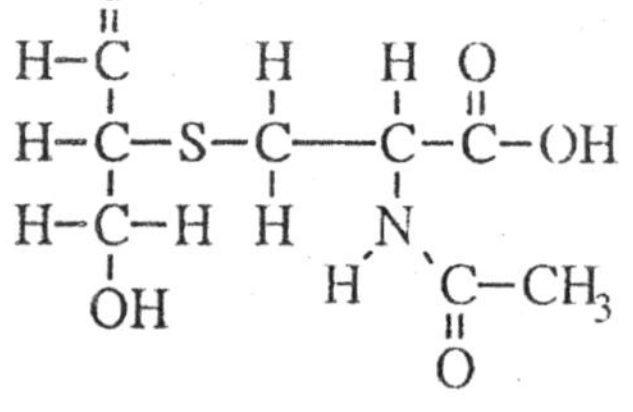

L-Cysteine, N-acetyl-S-[1-(hydroxymethyl)-2-propenyl] mercapturic acid conjugate

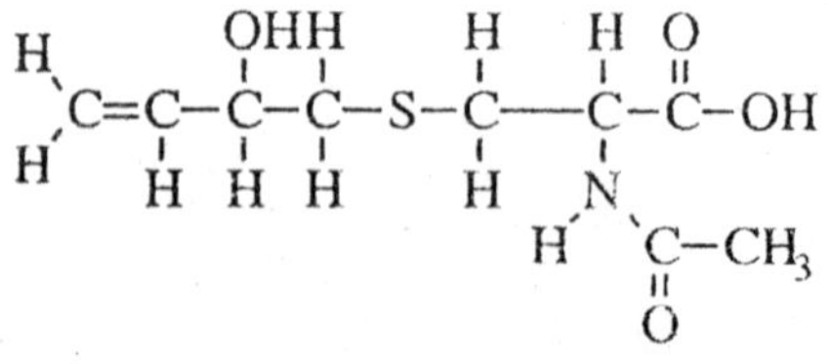

L-Cysteine, N-acetyl-S-(2-hydroxy-3-butenyl) mercapturic acid conjugate

Fig. 4.5. Common metabolites of 1,3-butadiene.

gas. The compound boils at –4.5°C and is readily stored and handled as a liquid. Release of the liquid can cause frostbite-like burns on exposed flesh.

The aspect of 1,3-butadiene of greatest toxicological concern is its potential carcinogenicity. Butadiene is a known carcinogen to rats and mice and is more likely to cause cancer in the latter. Although it is a suspected carcinogen to humans, epidemiological studies of exposed workers in the synthetic rubber and plastics industries suggest that normal worker exposures are insufficient to cause cancer. Butadiene is acted on by P-450 isoenzymes to produce genotoxic metabolites, most prominently epoxybutene and diepoxybutene. In addition, microsomal metabolic processes in rats produce the two possible stereoisomers of diepoxybutane, 3-butene-1,2-diol, and the two stereoisomers of 3,4-epoxy-1,2-butanediol. The production of mercapturic acid derivatives of the oxidation products of 1,3-butadiene results in detoxication of this compound and serves as a biomarker of exposure to it. Other useful biomarkers consist of the hemoglobin adducts 1- and 2-hydroxy-3-butenylvaline.

Butylenes

All gases under ambient conditions, these compounds have boiling points ranging from –6.9°C for isobutylene to 3.8°C for *cis*-2-butene. The butylenes readily undergo isomerization (change to other isomers). They participate in addition reactions and form polymers. Their major hazard is extreme flammability. Though not regarded as particularly toxic, they are asphyxiants and have a narcotic effect when inhaled.

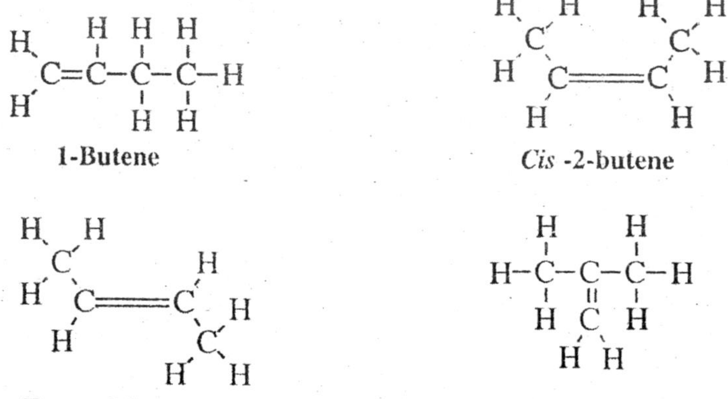

Fig. 4.6. The four butylene compounds, formula C_4H_6.

Alpha-Olefins

Alpha-olefins are linear alkenes with double bonds between carbons 1 and 2 in the general range of carbon chain length C_6 through about $C_{18.}$ They are used for numerous purposes. The C_6-C_8 compounds are used as comonomers to manufacture modified polyethylene polymer, and the C_{12}–C_{18} alpha-olefins are used as raw materials in the manufacture of detergents. The compounds are also used to manufacture lubricants and plasticizers. Worldwide consumption of the alpha-olefins was around 1 million metric tons. With such large quantities involved, due consideration needs to be given to the toxicological and occupational health aspects of these compounds.

Cyclopentadiene and Dicyclopentadiene

The cyclic dialkene cyclopentadiene has the structural formula shown below:

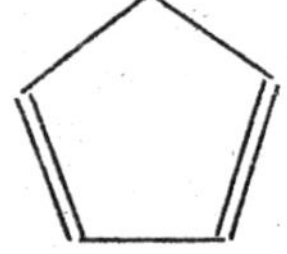

Cyclopentadiene

Two molecules of cyclopentadiene readily and spontaneously join together to produce dicyclopentadiene, widely used to produce polymeric elastomers, polyhalogenated flame retardants, and polychlorinated pesticides. Dicyclopentadiene mp, 32.9°C; bp, 166.6°C) exists as colorless crystals. It is an irritant and has narcotic effects. It is considered to have a high oral toxicity and to be moderately toxic through dermal absorption.

Acetylene

Acetylene is widely used as a chemical raw material and fuel for oxyacetylene torches. It was once the principal raw material for the manufacture of vinyl chloride, but other synthetic routes are now used. Acetylene is a colorless gas with an odor resembling garlic. Though not notably toxic, it acts as an asphyxiant and narcotic and has been used for anesthesia.

Exposure can cause headache, dizziness, and gastric disturbances. Some adverse effects from exposure to acetylene may be due to the presence of impurities in the commercial product.

Benzene and its Derivatives

These compounds are very significant in chemical synthesis, as solvents, and in unleaded gasoline formulations.

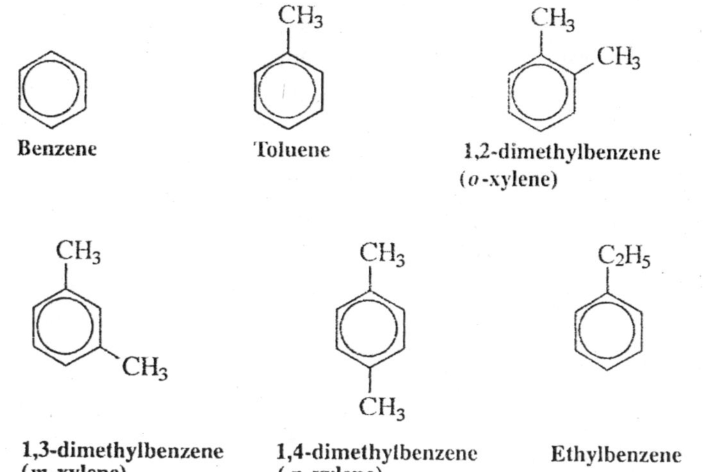

Fig. 4.7. Benzene and its most common methyl-substitution hydrocarbon derivatives.

Benzene

Benzene (C_6H_6) is chemically the single most significant hydrocarbon. It is used as a starting material for the manufacture of numerous products, including phenolic and polyester resins, polystyrene plastics and elastomers, alkylbenzene surfactants, chlorobenzene compounds, insecticides, and dyes. Benzene (bp, 80.1°C) is a volatile, colorless, highly flammable liquid with a characteristic odor.

Acute toxic effects of benzene

Benzene has been in commercial use for over a century, and toxic effects of it have been suspected since about 1900. Benzene has both acute and chronic toxicological effects. It is usually absorbed as a vapor through the respiratory tract, although absorption of liquid through the skin and intake through the gastrointestinal tract are also possible. Benzene is a skin irritant, and progressively higher local exposures can cause skin redness (erythema), burning sensations, fluid accumulation (edema), and blistering. Inhalation of air containing about 64 g/m^3 of benzene can be fatal within a few minutes; about one tenth that level of benzene causes acute poisoning within an hour, including a narcotic effect on the central nervous system manifested progressively by excitation, depression, respiratory system failure, and death.

Chronic toxic effects of benzene

Of greater overall concern than the acute effects of benzene exposure are chronic effects, which are still subject to intense study.

As with many other toxicants, subjects suffering from chronic benzene exposure suffer nonspecific symptoms, including fatigue, headache, and appetite loss. More specifically, blood abnormalities appear in people suffering chronic benzene poisoning. The most common of these is a lowered white cell count. More detailed examination may show an abnormal increase in blood lymphocytes (colorless corpuscles introduced to the blood from the lymph glands), anemia, and decrease in the number of blood platelets required for clotting (thrombocytopenia). Some of the observed blood abnormalities may result from damage by benzene to bone marrow. Epidemiological studies suggest that benzene may cause acute melogenous (from bone marrow) leukemia. Because of concerns that long-term exposure to benzene may cause preleukemia, leukemia, or cancer, the allowable levels of benzene in the workplace have been greatly reduced, and substitutes such as toluene and xylene are used wherever possible.

Metabolism of benzene

For a hydrocarbon, the water solubility of benzene is a moderately high 1.80 g/l at 25°C. The vapor is readily absorbed by blood, from which it is strongly taken up by fatty tissues. For nonmetabolized benzene, the process is reversible and benzene is excreted through the lungs. Benzene metabolism occurs largely in the liver. Initially, benzene is oxidized by the action of cytochrome P-450 enzymes to benzene oxepin and benzene oxide, which are interchangeable through the action of cytochrome P-450 enzymes:

Cytochrome P-450 → O ← Cytochrome P-450 → O

Benzene oxepin **Benzene oxide**

Benzene oxide may be hydrated through the action of epoxide hydrolase enzyme,

O + H_2O —Epoxide hydrolase→ H, OH, OH, H

Benzene *trans*-1,2-dihydrodiol

to produce benzene *trans*-1,2-dihydrodiol. This product is acted on by dihydrodiol dehydrogenase enzyme,

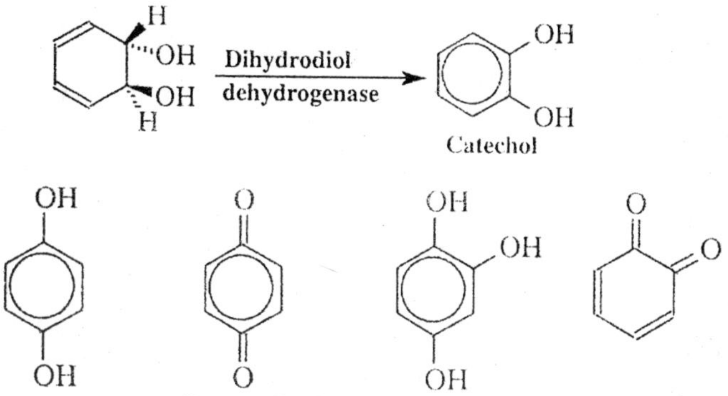

Dihydrodiol dehydrogenase

Catechol

Hydroquinone

p-Benzoquinone

1,2,4-trihydroxybenzene

o-Benzoquinone

Fig. 4.8. Products of phenol and catechol produced by the metabolic oxidation of benzene.

to produce catechol. Benzene oxepin or oxide may also react to produce muconaldehyde and muconic acid:

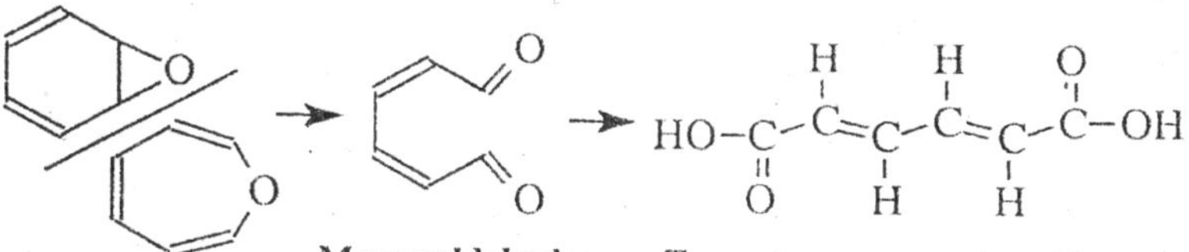

Muconaldehyde *Trans, trans*-muconic acid

Benzene oxepin or oxide may form a glutathione conjugate or undergo nonenzymatic rearrangement to produce phenol.

Phase 1 oxidation products of benzene, including phenol, hydroquinone, catechol, 1,2,4-trihydroxybenzene, and *trans,trans*-muconic acid in urine, are evidence of exposure to benzene. Another substance observed in urine of individuals exposed to benzene is S-phenyl-mercapturic acid,

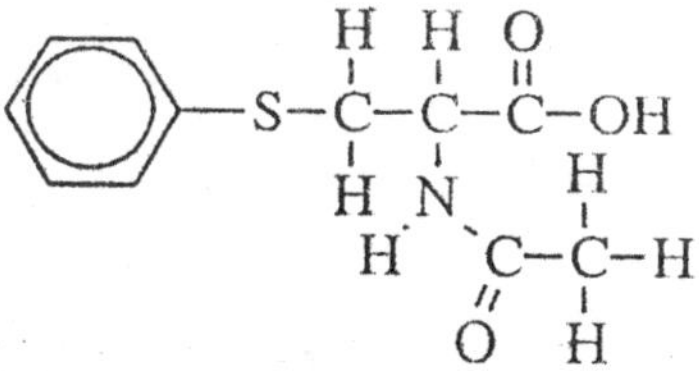

S-phenylmercapturic acid (L-cysteine, N-acetyl-S-phenyl-)

which is formed as a result of the phase 2 conjugation of benzene oxide by glutathione and subsequent reactions. Hemoglobin and albumin adducts of benzene oxide are commonly detected in the blood of workers exposed to benzene.

The oxidized metabolites of benzene, including reactive benzene oxide intermediate, are known to bind with DNA, RNA, and proteins.

This can result in cell destruction, alteration of cell growth, and inhibition of enzymes involved in the processes of forming blood cells. This phenomenon is probably responsible for the bone marrow damage, aplastic anemia (lowered production of blood cells due to damage to bone marrow), and, in severe cases, leukemia associated with benzene exposure.

Toluene, Xylenes, and Ethylbenzene

Toluene is a colorless liquid boiling at 101.4°C. Gasoline is 5 to 7% toluene and is the most common source of human exposure to toluene. Toluene is one of the most common solvents inhaled by solvent abusers. It is classified as moderately toxic through inhalation or ingestion and has a low toxicity by dermal exposure. Concentrations in ambient air up to 200 ppm usually do not result in significant symptoms, but exposure to 500 ppm may cause headache, nausea, lassitude, and impaired coordination without detectable physiological effects. At massive exposure levels, toluene acts as a narcotic, which can lead to coma.

Toluene tends to enter brain tissue, which it affects, and accumulates in adipose tissue. Unlike benzene, toluene possesses an aliphatic side chain that can be oxidized enzymatically, leading to products that are readily excreted from the body.

Xylenes and ethylbenzene are common gasoline constituents, industrial solvents, and reagents, so human exposure to these materials

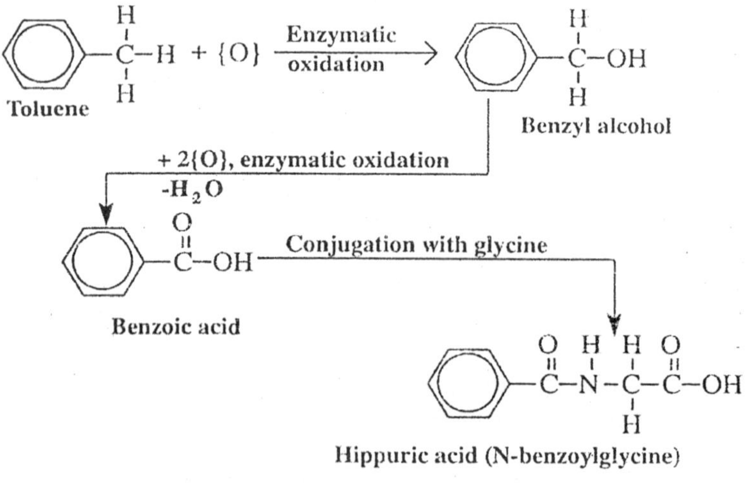

Toluene + {O} → (Enzymatic oxidation) → Benzyl alcohol

Benzyl alcohol + 2{O}, enzymatic oxidation, $-H_2O$ → Benzoic acid

Benzoic acid → (Conjugation with glycine) → Hippuric acid (N-benzoylglycine)

Fig. 4.9. Metabolic oxidation of toluene with conjugation to hippuric acid, which is excreted with urine.

is common. The absorption (primarily through inhalation), metabolism, and effects of these solvents are generally similar to those of toluene. Effects are largely on the central nervous system. Effects of xylenes and ethylbenzene on organs other than the central nervous system appear to be limited.

Styrene

Styrene is widely used to make various kinds of rubber, polystyrene plastics, resins, and insulators. As a consequence, human exposure to

$C_6H_5-CH=CH_2$ **Styrene**

this substance in the workplace has been quite high. As with the other volatile aromatic hydrocarbons discussed in this section, styrene is readily absorbed by inhalation, is lipid soluble, and is readily metabolized in the liver. The presence of the C=C group in styrene provides an active site for biochemical attack, and styrene is readily oxidized metabolically to styrene oxide:

Styrene-7,8-oxide

The major toxicological concern with styrene has to do with its potential role as a procarcinogen in producing carcinogenic styrene oxide, itself an industrial chemical to which workers may be exposed. Styrene oxide that is inhaled directly is distributed in the body by systemic circulation. However, styrene oxide that is produced by the metabolic oxidation of styrene in the liver is rapidly hydrolyzed in the liver by the action of epoxide hydrolase, leading to the formation of mandelic acid and phenylgloxylic acid, probably making the carcinogenicity hazard of styrene much lower than that of styrene oxide:

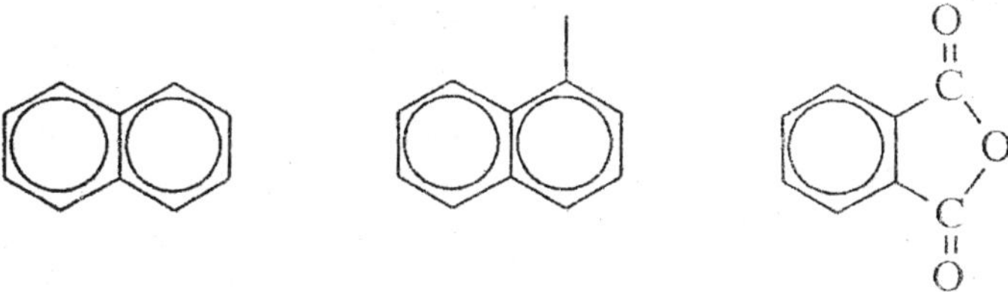

Naphthalene **1-(2-propyl)naphthalene** **Phthalic anhydride**

Fig. 4.10. Naphthalene and two of its derivatives.

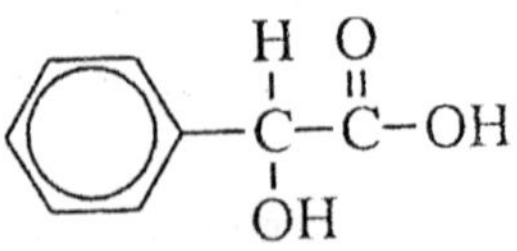

Mandelic acid 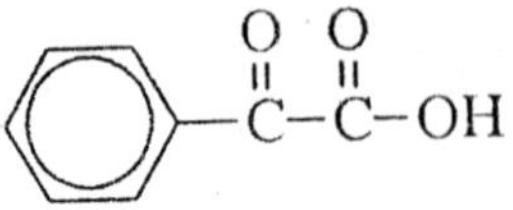 Glyoxylic acid

The albumin adduct of styrene oxide, S-(2-hydroxyl-1-phenylethyl) cysteine,

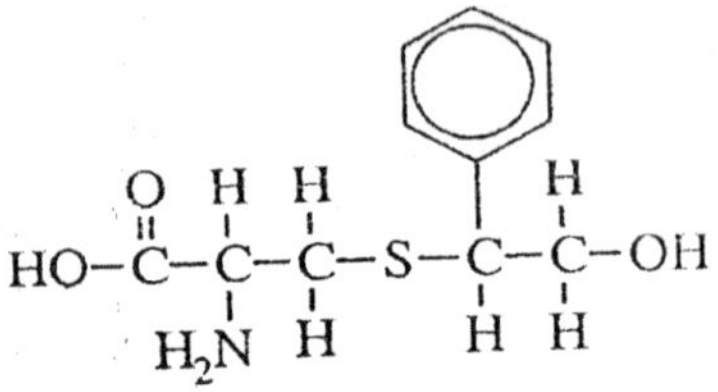

S-(2-hydroxy-1-phenylethyl)cysteine

has been monitored in blood as a biomarker of exposure to styrene and styrene oxide. Exposures to styrene oxide gave levels of the adduct approximately 2000 times that of comparable exposure to styrene. Since the production of S-(2-hydroxyl-1-phenylethyl)cysteine is a measure of tendency toward adduct formation, and by inference the formation of nucleic acid adducts leading to cancer, these findings are strong evidence that exposure to styrene poses a much lower risk of carcinogenicity than does direct exposure to styrene oxide.

Naphthalene

Naphthalene, also known as tar camphor, and its alkyl derivatives, such as 1-(2-propyl)naphthalene, are important industrial chemicals. Used to make mothballs, naphthalene is a volatile white crystalline solid with a characteristic odor. Coal tar and petroleum are the major sources of naphthalene. Numerous industrial chemical derivatives are manufactured from it.

Metabolism of Naphthalene

The metabolism of naphthalene is similar to that of benzene, starting with an enzymatic epoxidation of the aromatic ring:

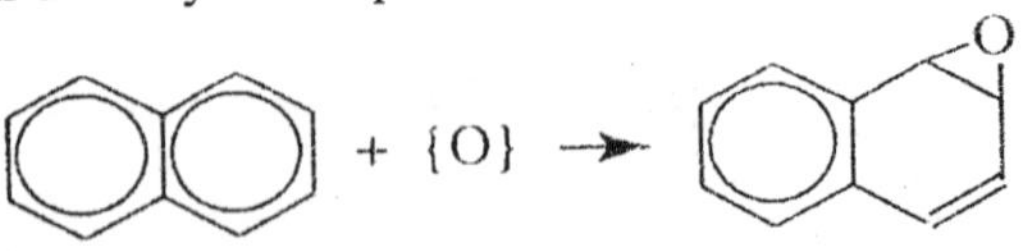

+ {O} →

followed by a nonenzymatic rearrangement to 1-naphthol:

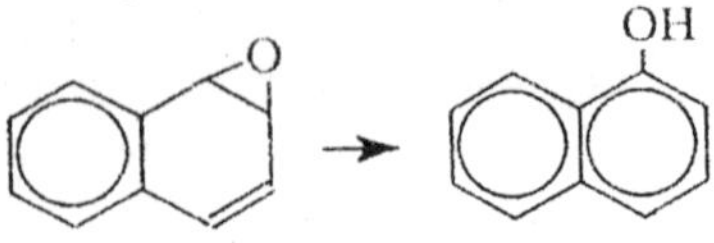

→

or addition of water to produce naphthalene-1,2-dihydrodiol through the action of epoxide hydrase enzyme:

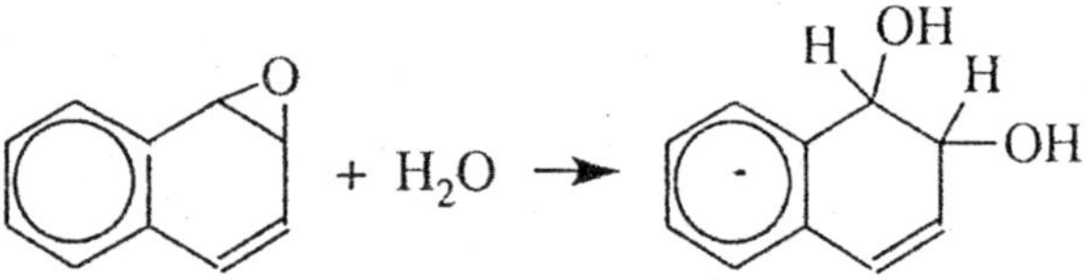

$$\text{(naphthalene 1,2-epoxide)} + H_2O \rightarrow \text{(naphthalene-1,2-dihydrodiol)}$$

Elimination of the metabolized naphthalene from the body may occur as a mercapturic acid, preceded by the glutathione S-transferase-catalyzed formation of a glutathione conjugate.

Toxic Effects of Naphthalene

Exposure to naphthalene can cause a severe hemolytic crisis in some individuals with a genetically linked metabolic defect associated with insufficient activity of the glucose-6-phosphate dehydrogenase enzyme in red blood cells. Effects include anemia and marked reductions in red cell count, hemoglobin, and hematocrit. Contact of naphthalene with skin can result in skin irritation or severe dermatitis in sensitized individuals. In addition to the hemolytic effects just noted, both inhalation and ingestion of naphthalene can cause headaches, confusion, and vomiting. Kidney failure is usually the ultimate cause of death in cases of fatal poisonings.

Naphthalene may adversely affect the eye, causing cortical cataracts and retinal degeneration. These affects are attributed to the naphthalene dihydrodiol metabolite.

Polycyclic Aromatic Hydrocarbons

Benzo(a)pyrene is the most studied of the polycyclic aromatic hydrocarbons (PAHs). These compounds are formed by the incomplete combustion of other hydrocarbons so that hydrogen is consumed in the preferential formation of H_2O. The condensed aromatic ring system of the PAH compounds produced is the thermodynamically favored form of the hydrogen-deficient, carbon-rich residue. To cite an extreme example, the H:C ratio in methane (CH_4) is 4:1, whereas in benzo(a)pyrene ($C_{20}H_{12}$) it is only 3:5.

There are many conditions of partial combustion and pyrolysis that favor production of PAH compounds, and they are encountered abundantly in the atmosphere, soil, and elsewhere in the environment. Sources of PAH compounds include engine exhausts, wood stove smoke, cigarette smoke, and charbroiled food. Coal tars and petroleum residues have high levels of PAHs.

PAH Metabolism

The metabolism of PAH compounds is mentioned here with benzo(a)pyrene as an example. Several steps lead to the formation of the carcinogenic metabolite product of benzo(a)pyrene. After an initial oxidation to form the 7,8-epoxide, the 7,8-diol is produced through the action of epoxide hydrase enzyme, as shown by the following reaction:

$+ H_2O \rightarrow$

7,8-Epoxide **7,8-Diol**

The microsomal mixed-function oxidase enzyme system further oxidizes the diol to the carcinogenic 7,8-diol-9,10-epoxide:

$+ \{O\} \rightarrow$

7,8-Diol

7,8-Diol-9,10-epoxide, carcinogenic (+)anti-isomer

Several isomers of the 7,8-diol-9,10-epoxide are formed, depending on the orientations of the epoxide and OH groups relative to the plane of the molecule. The (+)antiisomer is the one that is regarded as carcinogenic based on its demonstrated mutagenicity, ability to bind with DNA, and extreme pulmonary carcinogenicity to newborn mice.

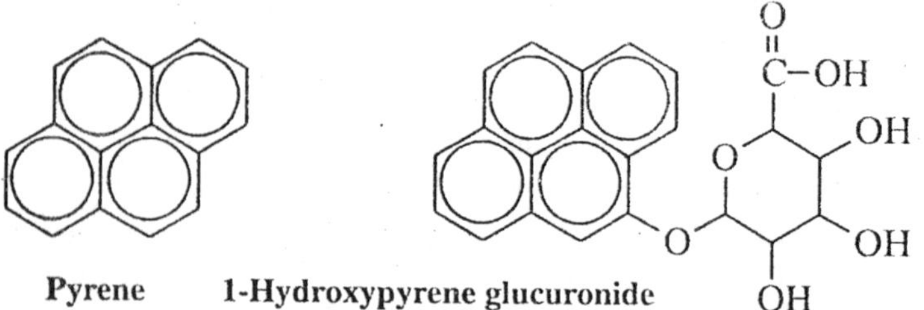

Fig. 4.11. Pyrene, a common PAH compound, and the 1-hydroxypyrene glucuronide conjugate that may serve as a biomarker of exposure to pyrene.

Because of inhalation of smoke, especially tobacco smoke, the lungs are the most likely sites of cancer from exposure to PAH compounds. However, these compounds are also found in foods cooked under direct exposure to pyrolysis conditions and are suspected of causing cancer in the alimentary canal. Extraordinarily high rates of esophageal cancer have been observed in Linxian, China, and may be attributable to PAHs from unvented cookstoves. In this study, the glucuronide conjugate of 1-hydroxypyrene was monitored as a biomarker of exposure to PAH compounds.

5

Organic Acids and Steroids in Forensic Science

Organic acids are a heterogeneous class of low-mol-wt metabolites that contain at least one carboxylic acid group. Several hundred compounds may be included, depending on how expansive a definition is used. Normally, amino acids are not included, although some organic acids contain nitrogen. The wealth of clinical information obtained by analysis of organic acids has tended to be ignored for a number of reasons. The primary clinical application has been limited to the diagnosis of inborn errors of metabolism. Also, traditional analysis has been performed using gas chromatographymass spectrometry (GC-MS), which is expensive and technically demanding. With the advent of less expensive methods of analysis such as capillary electrophoresis (CE), organic-acid analysis is finding many previously underutilized and unrecognized clinical applications. The current state of the art still requires organic acid profiling for inborn errors of metabolism by GC-MS analysis, however, this is unlikely to remain the case much longer. Already CE methods for the short-chain organic acids have been published and more comprehensive profiling methods are certain to be developed. The real promise of CE for organic acids, however, lies in fast and inexpensive assays for newer applications, several of which are discussed here.

Many of the CE applications for organic acids share a number of features to improve separation and detection. These include: (i) Flow reversal of the *electroosmotic flow* (EOF), (ii) the use of indirect photometric detection or direct detection at short wavelengths, and

(iii) the need for specimen preparation, particularly at low concentrations of analyte.

Flow Reversal

In the standard configuration, cations pass the detector first, followed by neutral compounds and then anions. Reversal of the EOF produces much faster separations for anions such as organic acids. Although not all assays for organic acids use flow reversal, the majority do. Flow reversal is achieved by two basic methods, use of coated capillaries or uncoated fused silica capillaries with a cationic surfactant added to the electrolyte. In general, coated capillaries require less conditioning and give more stable performance characteristics.

Detection Methods

Because commercially available instruments are equipped with photometric detection, many of the applications for organic acids use direct photometric detection at short wavelengths (185–200 nm) or indirect photometric methods. These detection methods are adequate and can be used for virtually any compound. One limitation is that identification depends entirely on the compound's characteristic migration time. Direct detection at longer wavelengths (>200 nm) offers more positive identification, but is limited to those organic acids that absorb strongly at these wavelengths. Other detection methods, such as fluorescence, have found fewer applications, mainly due to the limited number of organic acids that fluoresce or can be efficiently conjugated to a fluorogenic reagent, in addition to the cost of the detector. Electrochemical methods are just beginning to be applied to organic acids, and promise to provide good quality, sensitive, yet inexpensive detection methods in the future.

Specimen Preparation

Like many low-mol-wt compounds, organic acids may require specimen preparation to achieve adequate assay reproducibility. This may be critical when detection of levels on the order of μmol/L is needed. To account for variation in sample recovery, addition of an internal standard is highly desirable. Internal standards also allow for the calculation of a relative migration index, increasing the precision of the assay. Currently specimen preparation for organic acids remains relatively unsophisticated, often relying on dilution, filtration, and simple forms of extraction prior to injection onto the capillary. More efficient methods such as on-line analyte concentration will undoubtedly prove useful in the future.

Applications for the Clinical Laboratory

The applications discussed here, start with methylmalonic acid, since this is the one with which the authors have the most experience. An assay for urine methylmalonic acid has been operating on a routine basis in the first author's clinical laboratory since 1994. Several other applications share many characteristics with methylmalonic acid, and are discussed next, including succinic acid, oxalic and citric acids, and the simple short-chain organic acids. Most of these assays use either indirect detection or direct detection at short wavelengths. In contrast are the applications for orotic acid and xanthurenic acid, which rely on direct detection at longer wavelengths. Positive identification of these compounds can be enhanced by the use of diode array detection and spectral matching.

Methylmalonic Acid

Measurement of methylmalonic acid levels in urine or serum is an excellent way to assess vitamin B_{12} (cobalamin) status. Vitamin B_{12} in the form of 5-deoxyadenosylcobalamin is an essential cofactor in the enzymatic conversion of methylmalonyl-CoA into succinyl-CoA. In vitamin B_{12} deficiency, methylmalonic acid rises early, often reaching 10–100 times the levels seen in normal individuals. In contrast, anemia and macrocytosis and even serum vitamin B_{12} immunoassays are relatively insensitive markers. Because of cost and availability of automation, immunoassays are routinely used as the preferred screening method, although it is well-established that low normal vitamin B_{12} levels do not exclude vitamin B_{12} deficiency. In contrast, assays for methylmalonic acid, the most sensitive marker for vitamin B_{12} deficiency, is many times more expensive, particularly when using GC-MS. Because vitamin B_{12} deficiency is now recognized as being more common than previously thought, an efficient and economic method for methylmalonic acid analysis is becoming increasingly important.

Methylmalonic acid is a deceptively simple dicarboxcylic acid ($HOOC\text{-}CH\text{-}CH_3\text{-}COOH$), but the analysis is challenging due to the number of closely related organic acids. Methylmalonic acid contains no strongly absorbing constituents, therefore, analysis by CE is currently based on two approaches, derivatization or indirect detection. Derivatization offers two advantages: (i) less specimen is required, and (ii) the limit of detection is superior. Alternatively, indirect detection is faster and less expensive. Direct detection at ≤ 200 nm without derivatization is discussed further. This method does not have adequate sensitivity to detect levels found in normal individuals. Its use, therefore, is limited to the detection of inborn errors of metabolism.

Methylmalonic acid derivatization

Schneede and Ueland described a method using CE to quantitate levels of methlymalonic acid in serum. The assay used 1-pyrenyldiazomethane to react with acids present in serum producing a fluorescent 1-pyrenylmethyl monoester. After separation the products are detected by *laser-induced fluorescence* (LIF). Serum preparation requires addition of ethylmalonic acid as an internal standard, deproteinization with methanol, followed by a 12-h reaction with the derivatizing agent. Extensive dilution, needed to reduce matrix effects, is possible because of the sensitivity of the LIF method. Separation is based on a capillary (ID 75 μm) coated with a linear polyacrylamide to eliminate the EOF. The electrolyte consists of 30 mmol/L Tris-citrate buffer, pH 6.4. An organic modifier (50% dimethylformamide) and 0.1% hydroxypropyl methylcellulose are added to inhance separation and to suppress residual EOF. The specimen is introduced onto the capillary by pressure injection with a run time of about 26 min. The assay has a throughput of about 50 specimens per day. Reproducibility of the assay is acceptable with a *coefficient of variation* (CV) of 12% at 0.13 μmol/L and 5% at 4.3 μmol/L.

This method is adequate for routine analysis and the authors report having analyzed several thousand specimens at the time of publication. Although it represents a significant improvement over traditional GC-MS, the method requires a relatively lengthy specimen preparation and derivatization, in addition to an expensive method of detection. The HeCd laser is reported to be a major contributor to the cost. Use of ethylmalonic acid as an internal standard can also be problematic, since it can be found in some routine clinical specimens, although this is less of a problem for serum than for urine.

Methylmalonic acid by indirect detection

Methods for the indirect detection of methylmalonic acid have been described in assays for urine, and serum. These assays are similar, employing phthalic acid as the indirect detection agent, electrolyte, and buffer. Because the serum and urine assays use the same basic technology, only the serum assay will be described in the following paragraph.

Specimen (0.5 mL) preparation begins with addition of a dimethylsuccinic acid as the internal standard, acidification, and extraction with ethylacetate. The solvent is then evaporated, reconstituted in water, filtered, and injected electrokinetically (5 kV for 25 s). Separation employs an uncoated fused silica capillary (ID 75 μm). Flow reversal is accomplished by addition of cetyltrimethylammonium bromide (CTAB), a cationic surfactant. The electrolyte is composed of 3.3 mmol/L phthalic acid at pH 6.0, 0.46 mmol/L CTAB, and 35% acetonitrile (v/v). The organic modifier, acetonitrile, is added to improve resolution. The phthalic acid background signal is monitored by a diode array detector at 210 nm against a reference signal at 320 nm. Run time is about 6–7 min, and a batch of 15 specimens can be prepared and run in about 4 h. The *limit of detection* (LOD) is 0.2 μmol/L with a CV of $<10\%$ at 0.3 μmol/L.

The LOD of 0.2 μmol/L using indirect detection and phthalic acid is close to the reference limit of 0.4 μmol/L, the upper limit seen in normal individuals. Because methylmalonic acid rises dramatically (10–100 times normal levels) in vitamin B_{12} deficiency, the assay is adequate for clinical purposes. Indirect detection, however, depends entirely on migration time for identification. There is always the possibility that a coeluting compound could be hidden in the methylmalonic acid peak, falsely elevating the value. When methylmalonic acid is elevated, dilution should be used to reduce the possibility of interference by

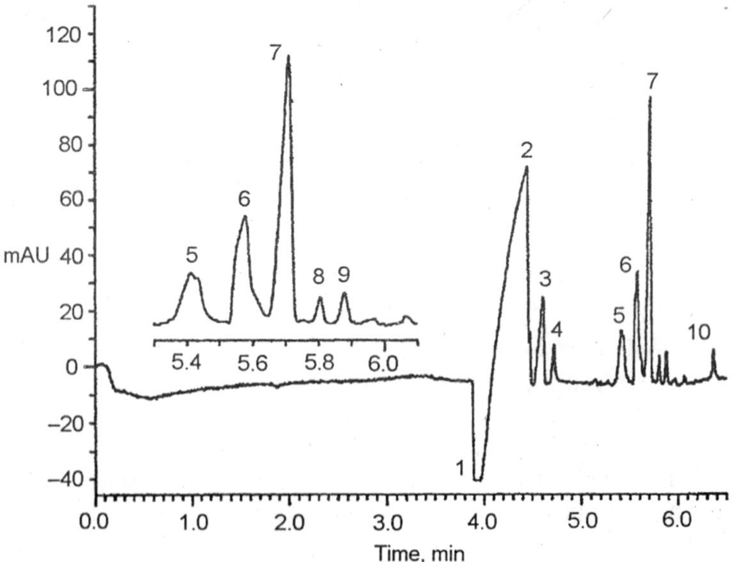

Fig. 5.1. Indirect photometric detection of serum methylmalonic acid using phthalic acid at pH 6.0 and monitored at 210 nm; the signal has been reversed to make decreased phthalic acid absorbance appear as peaks.

coeluting compounds. Also plasma specimens collected with citric acid as the anticoagulant cannot be analyzed with this assay. The massive peak due to citric acid will overwhelm all other peaks in the vicinity, including the one for methylmalonic acid. EDTA plasma does not cause a similar problem. Specimen preparation is based on an organic phase extraction, representing a significant amount of the total assay time. Although the extraction method is acceptable, a more efficient method of specimen preparation would be a considerable improvement.

Indirect methylmalonic acid assay improvements

The assay of Franke et al. has undergone a number of improvements to make it more robust for routine operation. These include: (i) use of an amine-coated capillary rather than the combination of an uncoated capillary with surfactant, and (ii) use of an electrolyte at pH 2.5 rather than the combination of an electrolyte at pH 6.0 with an organic modifier consisting of 35% acetonitrile. The reasons for these changes are discussed later, as are the advantages of using an instrument with a diode array detector and one with fluid-type cooling.

Diode array for indirect detection

Most often indirect detection is used with a simple single-wavelength detector. This type of detector tends to be more sensitive in absolute terms than a diode array detector, in addition to being less expensive. However, it is the experience of the authors that a diode array produces better results when using indirect detection. In the assay described earlier, a single-wavelength detector (210 nm) produced a baseline that was relatively noisy giving a LOD of 1 μmol/L. Using the same conditions, a diode-array detector (210 nm against a reference wavelength of 300 nm), gave a baseline that was relatively flat with a LOD of 0.1 μmol/L. Because indirect detection operates in the setting of high background absorbance, noise may become the limiting factor for assay sensitivity as it is here.

Capillary thermostating

Capillary thermostating to remove heat generated by the high voltage (Joule heating) used in CE is provided by two basic methods, air or fluid cooling. Air cooling is adequate for many purposes but it is not as efficient at removing heat as fluid cooling. It might be assumed that in a relatively low ionic-strength buffer, such as that used in the present assay (3.3 mmol/L phthalic acid), air cooling would be adequate. Direct comparison between commercially available air- and fluid-cooled instruments is difficult because instruments are configured differently. However, when this method was run in a fluid-cooled instrument, better overall assay performance was found. The clearest example of this was that larger samples could be introduced onto the capillary before broadening of the analyte peaks occurred. Presumably, this was due to inadequate heat-induced dispersion in the air-cooled instrument.

Coated capillaries

Replacing the uncoated capillaries with an amine-coated capillary and removing the surfactant from the electrolyte improved migration time stability considerably. It is known that surfactants are excellent at coating surfaces. However, they can also be difficult to keep in solution. Thus the use of a surfactant inevitably gives an electrolyte that tends to change composition with time, causing stability problems with the migration time. Using an amine-coated capillary (ID 50 μm) improved the reproducibility and durability of the methylmalonic acid assay.

pH

When investigating methods to separate anions, it is known that lowering the pH reduces the number of compounds that are ionized. These unionized compounds will be swept along with the EOF, thus, fewer anions will be present to cause potential interferences. For this reason, separation in acidic environment has the potential to reduce interfering compounds to a minimum. Although this approach has obvious limitations, it works well with methylmalonic acid (pKa_1 3.07). At pH 2.5, methylmalonic acid showed an electropherogram with significantly fewer interferences. Succinic acid (pKa_1 4.60), for example, is found in the EOF at this pH. Phthalic acid (pKa_1 2.89), used as electrolyte and indirect detection agent, still retains significant buffering capacity at this pH.

Organic modifiers

In the original assay, an organic modifier consisting of 35% acetonitrile was added to the electrolyte to improve resolution between methylmalonic and succinic acids. Although organic modifiers can enhance resolution significantly, they can also cause unwanted side effects. One obvious problem is that the solution is prone to differential evaporation that can contribute to assay variability. When changing the pH from 6.0 to 2.5, succinic acid migrated with the EOF and an organic modifier was no longer required.

Succinic Acid

Succinic acid ($HOOC-CH_2-CH_2-COOH$) is a closely related isomer of methylmalonic acid, although clinically, the utility of these two organic acids is much different. Succinic acid is a major metabolite in the tricarboxylic acid cycle and can be used to monitor mitochondrial function. Interestingly, succinic acid is also formed stoichiometrically as a product of the enzymatic synthesis of peptidyl hydroxyproline and it can be used to monitor increased collagen biosynthesis. As with many of the organic acids, analysis has been performed with GC-MS and studies on the clinical significance has been limited by the relatively high cost and difficulty of the analysis.

As expected from the similarity of the assays, many of the applications developed for methylmalonic acid and other related short-chain organic acids can also be used to detect succinic acid. The assay of Franke et al. for methylmalonic acid required little modification for use for serum succinic acid. Because the concentrations normally present are higher, succinic acid is a less demanding analyte. With the availability of a relatively easy and less expensive assay, increased investigations of the clinical utility of succinic acid can be expected in the future.

Oxalic and Citric Acids

Oxalic and citric acids are important analytes for the evaluation and treatment of urinary-tract calculi. The prevention of further stone formation is a major goal in the treatment of these individuals requiring an evaluation of the risk factors for calculi formation. Elevated oxalic-acid excretion is a risk factor for the formation of calcium oxalate stones and treatment includes removing sources of oxalic acid from the diet. In contrast, elevated citric-acid excretion is a protective factor that tends to prevent urinary calcium from precipitating. Thus, recurrent stone formers with low urinary citric acid may benefit from treatments to increase urinary citric acid levels.

Holmes describes an indirect detection method for oxalic and citric acid in 24 h urine collections. These compounds are also present on the electropherograms of many related assays. Because oxalic and citric acids are present at relatively high concentrations in urine, specimen preparation is minimal, and consists of acidification, centrifugation, and dilution (100-fold). Dilution is required primarily to reduce the chloride concentration, which is also detected by the indirect method used for this assay. Separation employs an uncoated capillary (ID 75 μm), an electrolyte and indirect detection agent consisting of sodium chromate (10 mmol/L), and a flow reversal agent consisting of 0.5 mM tetradecylammonium bromide (TTAB). The detection limit was 7 mg/L for both oxalic and citric acids, which compares favorably to standard enzymatic assays. Although standard enzymatic methods test for oxalic and citric acids separately, the method of Holmes measures both simultaneously. In addition, the assay can also be used to detect a number of related anions in urine, including chloride, sulfate, nitrate, phosphate, glycolate, and urate. All these components are potentially useful for the evaluation of the risks of urinary stone formation.

Profiling Short-Chain Organic Acids

The analysis of organic acids in urine is a well-established procedure for the diagnosis of inherited errors of metabolism. The large number of organic acids and the complexity of the urine matrix makes separation and quantitation difficult. Currently, GC-MS is the most reliable technique for this purpose. However, GC-MS is also expensive, labor intensive, and generally limited to referral laboratories. On the other hand, CE can provide a simple and rapid alternative. The benefits of a method, such as CE, that is widely available and that provides rapid analysis, is apparent in such situations as the critically ill newborn presenting with coma and metabolic acidosis. In such cases, rapid diagnosis facilitates appropriate treatment. Although CE is limited at the present time to the analysis of the short-chain organic acids, this is changing rapidly.

The methods for the small short-chain organic acids, originally developed from applications in the food sciences, share many characteristics, such as detection of similar compounds and migration orders. Both direct and indirect detection methods have been used. Direct detection is generally based on wavelengths from 200 to 185 nm, and are generally less sensitive than indirect methods.

Indirect detection of short-chain organic acids

Chen et al. described an indirect detection assay for 14 short-chain organic acids in serum and urine. The migration order was oxalic, citric, malonic, tartaric, methylmalonic, ketoglutaric, succinic, ethylmalonic, methylsuccinic, glutaric, adipic, methylglutaric, lactic, and pyruvic acids. Serum (0.5 mL) preparation consisted of deproteinization with methanol, centrifugation, drying the supernatant, and redissolving in water (250 μL) to provide concentration. Urine preparation consisted of filtration to remove particulates and a fivefold dilution. Ethylmalonic acid was used as an internal standard in both specimen types. Of the capillaries evaluated, polyacrylamide-coated capillaries showed superior performance. Phthalic acid was used as the indirect detection agent in a carbonate buffer; however to avoid interferences seen at shorter wavelengths, 230 nm was selected as the monitoring wavelength. The limit of detection was between 6 and 28 μg/mL for citric, methylmalonic, succinic, glutaratic, and lactic acids.

Direct detection of short-chain organic acids

Shirao et al. described an assay for 12 short-chain organic acids in urine based on direct detection at 185 nm. The migration order was: oxalic, formic, malonic, fumaric, succinic, α-ketoglutaric, citric, acetic, pyruvic, lactic, isovaleric, and hippuric acids. The limits of detection were given as 5 μg/mL for all but hippuric acid, which was 100 ng/mL. Urine was centrifuged and passed through a C18 column prior to hydrostatic injection. Separation was based on an uncoated capillary (ID 75 μm), with an electrolyte and buffer of 50 mM borate at pH 10.0 with addition of a commercial flow-reversal agent.

Hiraoka et al. described a similar assay for cerebrospinal fluid based on direct detection at 185 nm. Compounds detected included (in migration order): oxalic, fumaric, acetic, pyruvic, lactic, and glutamic acids. However, unlike urine, ascorbic acid was also seen.

Jariego and Hernanz also described an assay for 10 short-chain organic acids in urine based on direct detection at 185 nm. The migration order was methylmalonic, glutaric, 3-methylglutaric, N-acetylaspartic, 2- aminoadipic, propionic, lactic, 2-oxoisovaleric, isovaleric, and homogentisic acids. The limits of detection were between 5–15 μmol/L. Urine was prepared by passing through a centrifuge-type filter, and diluted to a creatinine concentration of about 1 mmol/L prior to introduction of the sample onto the capillary by pressure. Separation was accomplished using a polyimide-coated capillary (ID 75 μm). The electrolyte consisted of sodium sulfate, calcium chloride, and a commercial additive for flow reversal.

Barbas et al. described an assay for 10 short-chain organic acids in urine employing direct detection at 200 nm. The migration order was: fumaric, malic, methylmalonic, citric, pyruvic, acetoacetic, propionic, lactic, butyric, and 3-hydroxybutyric acids. Urine preparation consisted of passing through a centrifuge-type filter, followed by introduction of the sample onto the capillary by pressure. Separation was achieved on a neutralsurface capillary (ID 75 μm) using an electrolyte of 200 mmol/L sodium phosphate buffer at pH 6.0 with 100 mL/L methanol. The organic modifier was added to resolve methylmalonic, propionic, and lactic acids.

Orotic acid

Orotic acid is an intermediate in the biosynthesis of pyrimidines and an important analyte in the examination of a number of inborn errors of metabolism. The disorder most associated with elevated orotic acid is ornithine transcarbamylase deficiency, an inborn error of the urea cycle. In contrast, orotic acid is normal in the urea-cycle defect consisting of carbamoyl-phosphate synthase deficiency. Orotic acid can also useful for the evaluation of a number of other conditions including hereditary orotic aciduria and lysinuric protein intolerance.

Orotic acid has a distinctive absorbance signal in the region of 200–320 nm that makes direct detection possible. Unlike indirect photometric detection (and direct detection at very short wavelengths), direct detection in the midrange UV offers the advantage of matching the obtained spectra with a spectral library for a more positive identification. Like fluorescence, this type of detection is obviously limited to compounds having a suitable absorbance.

Franke and Nuttall describe an assay for orotic acid based on direct detection at 278 nm. Use of a diode-array detector allowed for automated spectral matching to monitor the purity of the orotic acid and internal standard peaks. Separation was on a polyvinyl alcohol-coated capillary (ID 50 μm), and an electrolyte consisting of 100 mM phosphate buffer at pH 3.0. Migration time at 20 kV was about 10 min at 35°C and about 14 min at 25°C. Above 20 kV, the Ohm's law plot deviated from linearity, although this was probably owing to the limitations of an air-cooled instrument. The migration time showed a coefficient of variation <1%. Urine-based control material showed a coefficient of variation <8% at 17 μmol/L (normal control).

Specimen preparation

Specimen preparation consisted of adding an internal standard (2,4-dinitrobenzoic acid) and barbituric acid buffer at pH 4.4 to the urine specimen, passing it through a single-use C18 reversed-phase column, and injecting the eluate. Although relatively complex, without preparation of the urine specimen, the migration time and assay precision did not have adequate reproducibility. Poor reproducibility resulting from minimal specimen preparation has been reported in a variety of circumstances, particularly when the concentrations are in the μmol/L range.

Coated capillaries

A polyvinyl alcohol-coated capillary was used to provide flow reversal, and performed well in this application. The capillaries were easily conditioned in under 10 min, required no additional conditioning between specimen injections, and proved to be durable. It is worth emphasizing that the performance of coated capillaries far outstripped that of uncoated capillaries, which required lengthy pre-conditioning in addition to re-conditioning between specimens.

Xanthurenic acid

Xanthurenic acid is a metabolite that can be used to evaluate vitamin B_6 status, much as methylmalonic acid can be used as a sensitive indicator of vitamin B_{12} status. Xanthurenic acid is a metabolite of tryptophan via the kynurenine pathway. This is also referred to as the tryptophan-niacin pathway. Several enzymes in this pathway require vitamin B_6 as a cofactor. As a result, high levels of several tryptohan metabolites, including xanthurenic acid, accumulate when vitamin B_6 is deficient. Xanthurenic acid also has a strong absorbance signal making it suitable for direct photometric detection. Significantly, xanthurenic acid has limited solubility below pH 8.0. This requires operating at higher pH, increasing the potential for interfering anions. However, as with orotic acid, direct detection and spectral matching can be used for positive identification of the xanthurenic acid peak.

Separation of serum xanthurenic acid was based on a polyvinyl alcoholcoated capillary (ID 50 μm), similar to the orotic acid assay. Instead of an acidic electrolyte, however, 200 mM glycylglycine was used to provide buffer capacity at pH 8.2. Specimen preparation started with 0.5 mL serum, addition of Tris acetate buffer at pH 9.0 (including an internal standard of 3 nitrobenzoic acid), and addition of urea and ethanol to completely solubilize xanthurenic acid. After mixing, this mixture was passed through a centrifuge-type filter, and pressure injected. A diode array detector was used to monitor peaks at 243 nm, and automated spectral matching was employed to monitor peak purity. The limit of detection for xanthurenic acid was 1 μmol/ L with a coefficient of variation was $< 9\%$ at 10 μmol/L.

Other Applications

Many organic acid assays can be found in the literature. Many are useful for applications in the food sciences and for research purposes, but fewer have been developed with the specific needs of the clinical laboratory in mind. Reviews of biomedical applications are available, but are inevitably incomplete by the time of publication.

Ascorbic acid

Koh et al. (24) describe an assay for ascorbic acid (vitamin C) in fruit beverages using direct detection at 254 nm. Urine and plasma were also examined briefly.

Bile acids

Yarabe et al. describe an assay for the separation of 15 bile acids in serum based on indirect detection.

Electrochemical detection

DeBacker and Nagel describe a potentiometric method of detection for short-chain organic acids that may be useful for future studies.

Fatty acids

Assays for saturated and unsaturated fatty acids in food products use indirect detection.

Nicotinic acid and metabolites

Zarzycki et al. describe an assay for nicotinic acid and its metabolites in human plasma. Nicotinic acid is related to the tyrptophan pathway, and the assay shows some similarities with that of Weber et al. in that direct detection at 254 nm is used.

Phenylketonuria

Dolnik described the separation of the acids of phenylketonuria based on direct detection at 260 nm. The specific organic acids identified were phenylpyruvate, 2-hydroxyphenylacetate, phenylacetate, mandelate, 4-hydroxyphenylpyruvate, and phenylalanine.

Profiling organic anions

Schoots et al. described an assay based on direct detection at 254 nm for profiling organic anions in the serum of uremic patients. The quantitation of hippuric, p-hydroxyhippuric, and uric acids was emphasized. Specimen preparation consisted of deproteinization with centrifuge-type filtration, and dilution (10-fold). Separation was based on a Teflon capillary (ID 200 μm). Analysis required 8 min, which was a significant improvement over the 90 min required for similar HPLC methods. Petucci et al. described an assay for profiling organic anions in serum and hemodialysate fluid from uremic patients using direct detection at 210 nm. Compounds identified included hippuric acid, tryptophan and tryptophan metabolites (indican, kynurenic acid, nicotinic acid), tyrosine, purine, and pyrimidine metabolites. Specimen preparation consisted of passing through a centrifuge-type filter to remove proteins. The filtrate was then pressure-injected. Separation was based on an uncoated capillary (ID 50 μm) and an electrolyte of 150 mM borate buffer at pH 9.0. Run time was about 16 min and did not use flow reversal. A similar assay based on micellar electrokinetic CE (MEKC) has also been described.

Quinolinic acid and other tryptophan metabolites

Weber et al. described an assay for tryptophan and 10 of its metabolites in urine using direct detection at 254 nm. Tryptophan metabolites are an interesting group of compounds that have not been fully exploited for their diagnostic potentials, and include xanthurenic acid and quinolinic acid. Quinolinic acid appears to be toxic to neurons, and may have important implications for the development of some neurological diseases.

CE is a sensitive and versatile technique and represents an inexpensive and practical method for the determination of organic acids. Applications include far more than the traditional investigation of inborn errors of metabolism. From the applications discussed previously, several general conclusions can be drawn concerning organic-acid assays.

Given the complex nature of biological specimens and the stringent requirements of the clinical laboratory, significant specimen preparation prior to injection is often needed to achieve stable migration times and good analytic precision, particularly when low concentrations are involved. The use of more sophisticated specimen preparation will undoubtedly make many applications more practical.

The analysis of anions such as organic acids is faster when flow reversal is used. Flow reversal with coated capillaries performs better than uncoated fused silica capillaries in combination with cationic surfactants. Coated capillaries require less conditioning, and give more stable migration times. Relatively large-diameter capillaries (ID 75 μm) are being used in most applications, primarily to maximize the limits of detection. Air-cooled instruments are adequate for many applications, although fluid-cooled instruments dissipate heat more efficiently and may give better assay characteristics. This is particularly true when larger diameter capillaries are used to increase detection limits.

Assays for the organic acids also tend to be sensitive to small pH changes, and may therefore be more reproducible when there is adequate buffering. When possible, operating at an acidic pH tends to reduce the number of potentially interfering anions.

STEROIDS

Adrenal Gland

The adrenal glands are paired structures situated above the kidneys that are approx 2–3 cm wide and 6 cm long and weigh approx 5 g. The glands consists of a yellow, outer cortex that constitutes approx

80% of the adrenal gland and a gray, inner medulla. The adrenal cortex consists of three distinct layers or zones of cells. The outermost layer, the zona glomerulosa, is the site of aldosterone synthesis, the principal mineralocorticoid produced by the human adrenal cortex, and corticosterone synthesis. The wider, middle zone is the zona fasciculata, and the innermost layer is the zona reticularis. The two inner zones of the adrenal cortex can be considered a single functional unit, where cortisol, along with some corticosterone, and dehydroepiandrosterone (DHEA) are synthesized. The glucocorticoids have widespread effects on carbohydrate and protein metabolism. Androgens secreted by the adrenal cortex pay a less important role than the androgens, which are secreted by the gonads.

Steroid synthesis

The human adrenal cortex produces and secretes glucocorticoids (cortisol and corticosterone), a mineralocorticoid (aldosterone), biosynthetic precursors of three end products (progesterone, 11-deoxycorticosterone, and 11-deoxycortisol) and androgenic substances (DHEA and its sulfate ester). The synthesis of adrenal cortical steroids begins with cholesterol, which is converted to pregnenolone. A cholesterol hydroxylase and desmolase mediate this rate-limiting step. ACTH stimulates this conversion and also increases the uptake of lipoprotein, which is the major source of adrenal cholesterol, by the adrenal cortex and stimulates the hydrolysis of cholesterol esters to free cholesterol. Many of the intermediates of steroid synthesis are secreted to some extent, but the steroids that are found in physiologically significant amounts are aldosterone, cortisol, corticosterone, DHEA, and androstenedione.

Physiological Effects of Glucocorticoids

Of the naturally occurring steroids only cortisol, corticosterone, cortisone, and 11-dehydrocorticosterone have appreciable glucocorticoid activity. Cortisol, which is found in the highest concentration, accounts for most of this activity. About 75% of plasma cortisol is bound to cortisol binding globulin (CBG, an alpha globulin), 15% is bound to plasma albumin, and 10% is unbound (free), representing the physiologically active portion. CBG also has a high binding affinity for progesterone, deoxycorticosterone, and some synthetic analogs.

Anti-inflammatory effects

Glucocorticoids inhibit inflammatory and allergic reactions. They do this by stabilizing the lysosomal membranes, inhibiting the release of proteolytic enzymes, and by increasing capillary permeability. This in turn reduces diapedesis of leukocytes. Glucocorticoids also reduce the number of circulating lymphocytes, monocytes, eosinophils, and basophils. The decrease in the number of basophils accounts for the fall in blood histamine levels and the reduction of the allergic response. There is also an increase in the number of inflammatory cells (neutrophils) caused by a decrease in the migration from the capillaries and an accelerated release from bone marrow. Glucocorticoids also inhibit the ability of neutrophils to marginate to the vessel wall. In addition, they cause impairment of the lymph nodes, thymus, and spleen that directly leads to decreased antibody formation.

Antigrowth effects

Large doses of cortisol have been shown to antagonize the effect of active vitamin D metabolites on the absorption of Ca^{2+} from the gut, inhibit mitosis of fibroblasts, and cause degradation of collagen. All of these effects can lead to osteoporosis, which is a reduction in bone mass per unit volume. Glucocorticoids can also delay wound healing because of the reduction of fibroblast proliferation. Connective tissue is reduced in quality and strength. In addition, chronic supra-physiologic doses of glucocorticoids will suppress growth secretion and inhibit somatic growth.

Vascular effects

Cortisol in pharmacological doses will enhance the vasopressor action of catecholamines. Thus, corticosteroids have a role in maintenance of normal arterial systematic blood pressure and volume through their support of vascular responsiveness to vasoactive substances. Cortisol also enhances catecholamine synthesis via activation of the epinephrine-forming enzyme.

Other effects

Glucocorticoids, unlike mineraldocorticoids, restore *glomerular filtration rate* (GFR) and renal plasma flow to normal following adrenalectomy. They also facilitate free-water excretion (clearance) and uric-acid excretion. Of Glucocorticoids have also been found to have psychoneural effects following chronic hyper- or hypo-cortisol secretion. In these cases patients may initially become euphoric and then psychotic, paranoid, and finally depressed. In addition, cortisol increases gastric flow and gastric secretion, while it decreases gastric mucosal-cell proliferation. The latter two effects can lead to peptic ulceration following chronic cortisol treatment.

Metabolic effects

Carbohydrate metabolism

Cortisol, the main glucocorticoid present in circulation, is a carbohydratesparing hormone exerting an anti-insulin effect, which can lead to hypoglycemia and insulin-resistance. In addition, glucocorticoids maintain blood glucose and the glycogen content of the liver by promoting the conversion of amino acids to carbohydrates and the storage of carbohydrate as hepatic glycogen.

Protein metabolism

The most important gluconeogenic substrates are amino acids that are derived from proteolysis in skeletal muscle. Cortisol enhances the release of amino acids from proteins in skeletal muscles and other extra hepatic tissues including the protein matrix of bone. The amino acids released are transported to the liver and then converted to glucose. This increased in glucose production via gluconeogenesis causes an increased urea production because of the conversion of amino-acid nitrogen to urea, accounting for the increased urinary nitrogen excretion. The proteolysis in skeletal muscle brings about a negative protein balance since the amino acids taken up by the liver that would have been used in the synthesis of new protein are instead used to form glucose or glycogen. This anabolic effect is an important exception to the overall protein catabolic effect of cortisol.

Fat metabolism

Glucocorticoids enhance the lipolytic actions of other hormones, such as growth hormone, catecholamines, glucagon, and thyroid hormone. Glucocorticoids also help in the mobilization of fatty acids from adipose tissues to the liver, where the metabolism of fatty acids inhibits glycolytic enzymes and promote gluconeogenesis. As a result of increased fatty acids oxidation, glucocorticoids may lead to increased ketosis, especially in patients with diabetes mellitus.

Congenital Adrenal Hyperplasia

Congenital adrenal hyperplasia (CAH) also known as the "*adrenogenital syndrome*" can be considered as a family of inborn error of steroidogensis. All CAH variants are inherited as autosomal recessive traits. Each member of this family is characterized by a specific enzyme deficiency that impacts cortisol production by the adrenal cortex, and if severe enough can lead to sexual ambiguity in both males and females. The enzymes usually affected are 21-hydroxylase (types I and II), beta hydroxylase (type III), 3 beta-hydroxylase (type IV), 17 hydroxylase (type V) and cholesterol 20-alpha hydroxylase (type VI). The most common syndromes are types I and II, which are caused by a 21-hydroxylase enzyme deficiency. The identification of the specific enzyme deficiency relies heavily on laboratory findings since all variants affect the glucocorticoid (cortisol) pathway in some manner. Although formation of cortisone and cortisol are blocked in type I and II CAH, precursors are still being manufactured, causing elevations of 17-hydroxyprogesterone. Normal basal serum 17-hydroxyprogesterone levels, however, cannot exclude late-onset CAH. Response to adrenocorticotrophic stimulation, however, clearly distinguishes this disorder from carriers of the classical disease.

In addition to being precursors of cortisone, many of the early intermediates are also estrogenic compounds. In the presence of abnormally high production of androgens, secondary sexual characteristics are affected. If this condition is manifested in utero, pseudohermaphroditism (masculinzation) of external genitalia occur in girls and macrogentisomia praecox (accentuation of male genitalia) occurs in boys. If the condition is not manifested until after birth, virilism (masculinization) develops in girls and precocious puberty in boys. In CAH variants IV, V, and VI, there is also some degree of interruption of the adrenal pathway, so that the external appearance of the female genitalia is not significantly affected and subsequent virilization is minimal or absent.

In CAH, the adrenal glands themselves increase in size because of hyperplasia of the steroid-producing adrenal cortex. This is because the level of cortisone and hydrocortisone produced by the adrenal gland controls normal pituitary production of ACTH through a negative-feedback mechanism. In variants of congenital adrenal hyperplasia, cortisone production is partially or completely blocked, prompting the pituitary to produce more ACTH in an attempt to increase cortisone production. This continues until the adrenal cortex tissue becomes hyperplastic under the continual ACTH stimulation. Also when the mineralocorticoid pathway leading to aldosterone is blocked (CAH types II, IV, VI), salt losing crises similar to those of Addison's disease occur.

In CAH, the correct identification of the enzyme affected is achieved by observation of clinical symptoms reflecting distinct hormonal patterns leading to the measurement cortisol, which should be low, as well as increased levels of steroids proximal to the suspected blocked step.

Two rounds of *polymerase chain reaction* (PCR) and *amplification-created restriction sites* (ACRS) analysis may provide important information for genetic counseling, prenatal diagnosis, and management of families at risk for CAH. The data from one study suggest that the steroidogenic acute regulatory protein amino acid replacement mutants that cause lipoid CAH are inactive because of fairly the inability of the enzyme to fold properly, which may be caused by the loss of salt bridges that stabilize the tertiary structure.

Some governments have done studies to evaluate the benefits of neonatal screening for CAH. One such study was done in Sweden from January 1989 to December 1994. The study concluded that the main benefits of screening was avoidance of serious salt-losing crises, earlier correct gender assignment in virilized girls, and detection of patients who would otherwise have been missed in neonatal period. Screening also prevented deaths due the decreased steroid production in the neonatal period.

Use of Capillary Electrophoresis (CE) in the Separation and Detection of Steroids

Clinically the evaluation of steroid levels is of great interest. There are many disorders that have been identified as being caused either by under or over secretion of steroids, e.g., CAH, Cushing's syndrome, Addison's disease, acromegaly, hirsutism, and adenomas. The ability to simultaneously measure multiple steroids in the urine and/or serum of these patients would be helpful in making the diagnosis of their disorder. However, the structural similarity and low concentrations of steroids have made rapid, yet accurate, analysis a problem. Radioimmunoassay (RIA), although extremely sensitive, requires extraction and purification by *high-performance liquid chromatography* (HPLC) to provide the required specificity. Thus, to analyze multiple steroids by RIA requires the same number of RIAs as steroids, limiting this application to specialized laboratories and, increasing the turnaround time. Other analytical methodologies based on chromatographic separation, such as *gas chromatography* (GC), *gas chromatography mass spectrometry* (GC-MS), and HPLC, have also been used for steroid testing. These procedures also require extraction, concentration, and derivation to enhance sensitivity and specificity, limiting their routine use because they are time-consuming and expensive.

Ideally, methodologies suitable for determination of steroids in clinical samples should meet the following criteria to be clinically justified. The methodology should:

1. Not require large sample volumes (typically <1 mL of plasma or serum should be used);
2. Have high sensitivity with detection limits in the 0.1–10 nmol/L range;
3. Be highly specific but retain the ability to detect and quantitate multiple steroids in the presence of other structurally similar compounds;
4. Have minimal derivation and/or prior sample preparation;
5. Provide a high sample throughput with a reasonable turn-around time;
6. Be relatively inexpensive; and
7. Be automatable.

In many ways *capillary electrophoresis* (CE) fit these criteria since it has the unique features high resolution, high mass sensitivity, low sample volume requirements, and over all versatility.

Serum

Steroids are neutral compounds and therefore would not be mobilized or separated when subjected to electrophoretic conditions. To overcome this inherent problem of neutral compounds, micellar electrokinetic capillary chromatography (MEKC), which uses ionic micelles to effect separation, was developed by Terabe et al. The separation principle of MEKC is similar to that of chromatography, except that MEKC utilizes electrokinetic phenomena to perform the chromatography instead of a liquid-delivery pump.

Using this technique, Abubaker et al. succeeded in developing a method to separate rapidly steroids whose measurement gives clinically useful information. They found excellent resolution for eight steroids by using a buffer of *sodium dodecyl sulfate* (SDS) and acetonitrile with a neutral capillary. A similar resolution was achieved with a fused silica capillary using a dodecyl trimethylammonium bromide (DTAB) buffer, although the time required for separation was increased six- to seven-fold. The steroids separated were testosterone propionate, progesterone, 17-hydroxy progesterone, testosterone, 11-deoxycortisol, 21-deoxycortisol, hydrocortisone, and cortisone. Three of these hormones (11-deoxycortsol, 17-OH progesterone, and 21-deoxycortisol), are known to be important in helping to establish the diagnosis of CAH. Thus, using these methods to separate and quantitate these steroids could be very useful in screening newborns for CAH. However, the sensitivity was found to be inadequate without preconcentration.

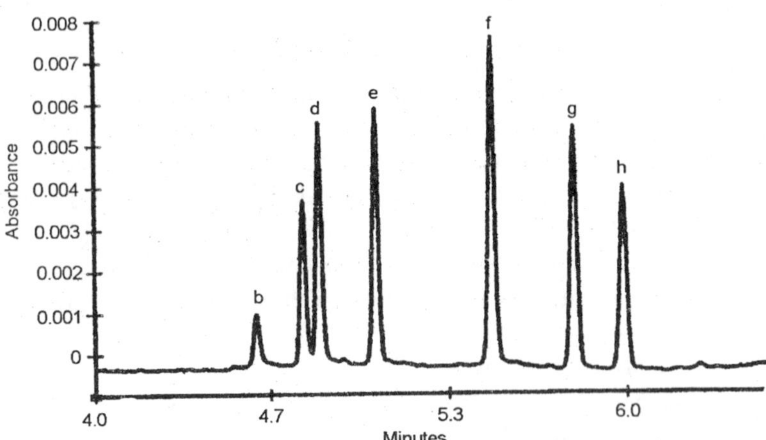

Fig. 5.2. Separation of testosterone propionate, progesterone, 17-hydroxyprogesterone, testosterone, 11-deoxycortisol, 21-deoxycortisol, cortisol, and cortisone (all at 10 μg/mL) from a serum ultrafiltrate.

The issue with sensitivity can potentially be overcome by using the on-line concentration techniques of stacking with reverse-migrating micelles or the field-enhanced sample injection with reverse migrating micelles developed by Quirino et al. Both techniques used the separation of ng/mL levels of testosterone and progesterone to demonstrate that this was a fast, effective, and easy way to concentrate neutral analytes inside the capillary. More work is still needed in this area to show its utility with serum.

Urinary-free cortisol

The total cortisol level in a 24-h urine represents the integrated or mean concentration of free cortisol in plasma over this 24-h period and provides an excellent diagnostic sensitivity and specificity for the detection of the increased secretion of cortisol by the adrenal glands (Cushing's syndrome). In contrast, total serum cortisol levels are not always an accurate measure of an overactive adrenocorticoid function and can be elevated in pregnancy, obesity, diabetes, or hyperthyroidism. *Urinary free cortisol* (UFC) measurement is therefore the most reliable single approach for screening patients for Cushing's syndrome. Currently the methods available for measuring UFC are associated with long turnaround times and interferences present in urine.

Lokinendi et al. used solid-phase extraction in conjunction with MEKC as a method for the separation and detection of UFC. The addition of an internal standard was found to be necessary for accurate and reliable quantitation of the free cortisol in urine. The internal

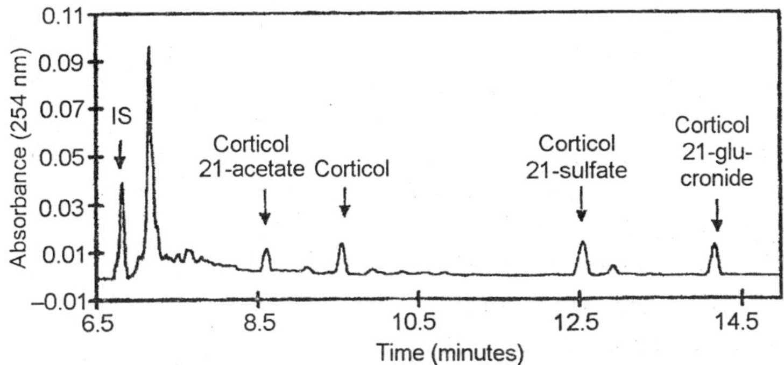

Fig. 5.3. Separation of internal standard (IS) (corticosterone) at 100 μg/dL and cortisol 21-acetate, cortisol, 21-sulfate, and cortisol 21-glucosidonate at 20 μg/dL in urine.

standard, corticosterone, was chosen because it did not coelute with the various compounds present in the extracted urine. The authors evaluated the overall performance and feasibility of the method. In addition, they also evaluated linearity, recovery, and lower limit of detection of free cortisol in human urine and compared the results with a commercially available immunoassay. They found an excellent correlation (R = 0.95 and slope = 0.934) with the immunoassay with little, if any, interference from endogenous urine substances.

Congenital adrenal hyperplasia

CAH as discussed earlier is a group of autosomal recessive disorders involving the adrenal glands, in which the primary defect is a deficiency of one or more enzymes involved in the biosynthesis. The main three steroids that are measured to help in making the differential diagnosis are 17-hydroxy progesterone, 21-deoxycortisol, and 11-deoxycortisol. In frank CAH the serum levels of these steroids can reach levels such that detection by CE is possible. The real challenge, however, is in the detection of normal levels in order to differentiate between patients who have a partial blockage and normals. The highest levels that these steroids are normally found in serum are 138 ng/dL and 155 ng/dL for 17-deoxyprogesterone and 11-deoxycortisol, respectively. MEKC can separate these structurally similar steroids rapidly, however, detection of normal serum levels is not currently possible with the conventional UV absorbance detectors available with most CE instruments. Using UV absorbance, the lower limit of detection for these steroids by MEKC is 0.05 mg/dL. Thus, a 3000-fold preconcentration is needed to detect normal levels, which may be achieved using field-enhanced sample injection methods.

It is possible to use CE to separate and detect steroids in body fluids (serum and urine). The p.oblems (limitation in sensitivity and the sample matrix) associated with CE are similar to those outlined in the other chapters in this book. Bodily fluids represent a complex matrix with high levels of proteins and salt that can bind to or precipitate inside a capillary. This can result in variable migration times as the result of change in the capillary surface or actual blockage of the capillary. In addition to the problems associated with migration times and capillary occlusion, CE has the additional problem of sensitivity. Thus, pre-concentration of samples, either by liquidliquid or solid phase extraction becomes very important in the development of a CE assay for determination of steroids.

6

Toxic Elements in Forensic Science

It is somewhat difficult to define what is meant by a toxic element. Some elements, such as white phosphorus, chlorine, and mercury, are quite toxic in the elemental state. Others, such as carbon, nitrogen, and oxygen, are harmless as usually encountered in their normal elemental forms. But, with the exception of those noble gases that do not combine chemically, all elements can form toxic compounds. A prime example is hydrogen cyanide. This extremely toxic compound is formed from three elements that are nontoxic in the uncombined form, and produce compounds that are essential constituents of living matter, but when bonded together in the simple HCN molecule constitute a deadly substance.

The following three categories of elements are considered here:

1. Those that are notable for the toxicities of most of their compounds
2. Those that form very toxic ions
3. Those that are very toxic in their elemental forms

Elements in these three classes are discussed in this chapter as *toxic elements*, with the qualification that this category is somewhat arbitrary. With a few exceptions, elements known to be essential to life processes in humans have not been included as toxic elements.

Toxic Elements and the Periodic Table

It is most convenient to consider elements from the perspective of the periodic table. Recall that the three main types of elements, based on their chemical and physical properties as determined by the electron configurations of their atoms, are metals, nonmetals, and metalloids. Metalloids (B, Si, Ge, As, Sb, Te, At) show some characteristics of both metals and nonmetals. The nonmetals consist of those few elements in groups 4A to 7A above and to the right of the metalloids. The noble gases, only some of which form a limited number of very unstable chemical compounds of no toxicological significance, are in group 8A. All the remaining elements, including the lanthanide and actinide series, are metals. Elements in the periodic table are broadly distinguished between representative elements in the A groups of the periodic table and transition metals constituting the B groups, the lanthanide series, and the actinide series.

Essential Elements

Some elements are essential to the composition or function of the body. Since the body is mostly water, hydrogen and oxygen are obviously essential elements. Carbon (C) is a component of all life molecules, including proteins, lipids, and carbohydrates. Nitrogen (N) is in all proteins. The other essential nonmetals are phosphorus (P), sulfur (S), chlorine (Cl), selenium (Se), fluorine (F), and iodine (I). The latter two are among the essential trace elements that are required in only small quantities, particularly as constituents of enzymes or as cofactors (nonprotein species essential for enzyme function). The metals present in macro amounts in the body are sodium (Na), potassium (K), and calcium (Ca). Essential trace elements are chromium (Cr), manganese (Mn), iron (Fe), cobalt (Co), copper (Cu), zinc (Zn), magnesium (Mg), molybdenum (Mo), nickel (Ni), and perhaps more elements that have not yet been established as essential.

Metals in an Organism

Metals are mobilized and distributed through environmental chemical processes that are strongly influenced by human activities. A striking example of this phenomenon is illustrated by the lead content of the Greenland ice pack. Starting at very low levels before significant industrialization had occurred, the lead content of the ice increased in parallel with the industrial revolution, showing a strongly accelerated upward trend beginning in the 1920s, with the introduction of lead into gasoline. With the curtailment of the use of leaded gasoline, some countries are now showing decreased lead levels, a trend that hopefully will extend globally within the next several decades.

Metals in the body are almost always in an oxidized or chemically combined form; mercury is a notable exception in that elemental mercury vapor readily enters the body through the pulmonary route.

The simplest form of a chemically bound metal in the body is the hydrated cation, of which $Na(H_2O)_6^+$ is the most abundant example. At pH values ranging upward from somewhat less than seven (neutrality), many metal ions tend to be bound to one or more hydroxide groups; an example is iron(II) in $Fe(OH)(H_2O)_5^+$. Some metal ions have such a strong tendency to lose H^+ that, except at very low pH values, they exist as the insoluble hydroxides. A common example of this phenomenon is iron(III), which is very stable as the insoluble hydrated iron(III) oxide, $Fe_2O_3 \cdot xH_2O$, or hydroxide, $Fe(OH)_3$. Metals can bond to some anions in body fluids. For example, in the strong hydrochloric acid medium of the stomach, some iron(III) may be present as $HFeCl_4$, where the acid in the stomach prevents formation of insoluble $Fe(OH)_3$ and a high concentration of chloride ion is available to bond to iron(III). Ion pairs may exist that consist of positively charged metal cations and negatively charged anions endogenous to body fluids. These do not involve covalent bonding between cations and anions, but rather an electrostatic attraction, such as in the ion pairs Ca^{2+} HCO_3^- or $Ca^{2+}Cl^-$.

Complex Ions and Chelates

With the exception of group 1A metals and the somewhat lesser exception of group 2A metals, there is a tendency for metals to form *complexes* with *electron donor* functional groups on *ligands* consisting of anionic or neutral inorganic or organic species. In such cases, covalent bonds are formed between the *central metal ion* and the ligands. Usually the resulting complex has a net charge and is called a complex ion; $FeCl_4^-$ is such an ion. In many cases, an organic ligand has two or more electron donor functional groups that may simultaneously bond to a metal ion to form a complex with one or more rings in its structure. A ligand with this capability is called a *chelating agent*,

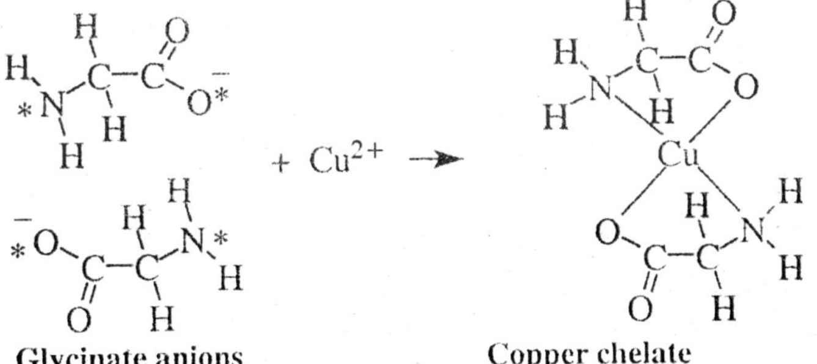

Fig. 6.1. Chelation of Cu^{2+} by glycinate anion ligands to form the glycinate chelate.

and the complex is a *metal chelate*. Copper(II) ion forms such a chelate with the anion of the amino acid glycine. This chelate is very stable.

Organometallic compounds constitute a large class of metal-containing species with properties quite different from those of the metal ions. These are compounds in which the metal is covalently bonded to carbon in an organic moiety, such as the methyl group, $-CH_3$. Unlike metal complexes, which can reversibly dissociate to the metal ions and ligands, the organic portions of organometallic compounds are not normally stable by themselves. However, it should be mentioned that neutral organometallic compounds tend to be lipid soluble, a property that enables their facile movement across biologic membranes. They often remain intact during movement through biological systems and so become distributed in these systems as lipid-soluble compounds.

A phenomenon not confined to metals, *methylation* is the attachment of a methyl group to an element and is a significant natural process responsible for much of the environmental mobility of some of the heavier elements. Among the elements for which methylated forms are found in the environment are cobalt, mercury, silicon, phosphorus, sulfur, the halogens, germanium, arsenic, selenium, tin, antimony, and lead.

Metal Toxicity

Inorganic forms of most metals tend to be strongly bound by protein and other biologic tissue. Such binding increases bioaccumulation and inhibits excretion. There is a significant amount of tissue selectivity in the binding of metals. For example, toxic lead and radioactive radium are accumulated in osseous (bone) tissue, whereas the kidneys accumulate cadmium and mercury. Metal ions most commonly bond with amino acids, which may be contained in proteins (including enzymes) or polypeptides. The electron-donor groups most available for binding to metal ions are amino and carboxyl groups. Binding is especially strong for many metals to thiol (sulfhydryl) groups; this is particularly significant because the –SH groups are common components of the active sites of many crucial enzymes, including those that are involved in cellular energy output and oxygen transport. The amino acid that usually provides –SH groups in enzyme active sites is cysteine. The imidazole group of the amino acid histidine is a common feature of enzyme active sites with strong metal-binding capabilities.

The absorption of metals is to a large extent a function of their chemical form and properties. Pulmonary intake results in the most

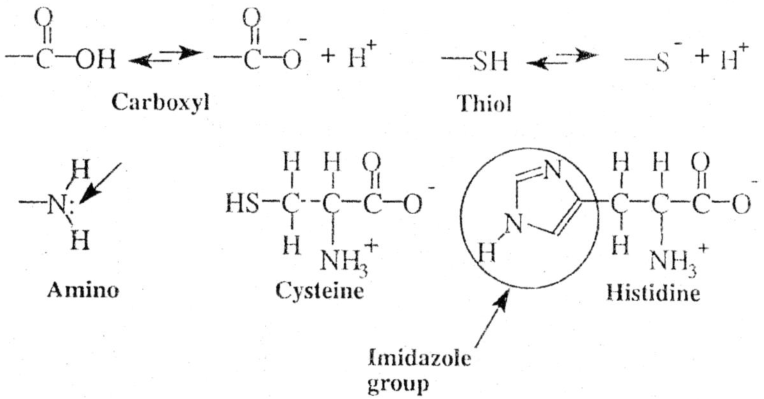

Fig. 6.2. Major binding groups for metal ions in biologic tissue (carboxyl, thiol, amino) and amino acids with strong metal-binding groups in enzyme active sites (cysteine, histidine).

facile absorption and rapid distribution through the circulatory system. Absorption through this route is often very efficient when the metal is in the form of respirable particles less than 100 μm in size, as volatile organometallic compounds or (in the case of mercury) as the elemental metal vapor. Absorption through the gastrointestinal tract is affected by pH, rate of movement through the tract, and presence of other materials. Particular combinations of these factors can make absorption very high or very low.

Metals tend to accumulate in target organs, and a toxic response is observed when the level of the metal in the organ reaches or exceeds a threshold level. Often the organs most affected are those involved with detoxication or elimination of the metal. Therefore, the liver and kidneys are often affected by metal poisoning. The form of the metal can determine which organ is adversely affected. For example, lipid-soluble elemental or organometallic mercury damages the brain and nervous system, whereas Hg^{2+} ion may attack the kidneys.

Because of the widespread opportunity for exposure, combined with especially high toxicity, some metals are particularly noted for their toxic effects. These are discussed separately in the following sections in the general order of their appearance in groups in the periodic table.

Lithium

Lithium, Li, atomic number 3, is the lightest group 1A metal that should be mentioned as a toxicant because of its widespread use as a therapeutic agent to treat manic-depressive disorders. It is also used in a number of industrial applications, where there is potential for exposure.

The greatest concern with lithium as a toxicant is its toxicity to kidneys, which has been observed in some cases in which lithium was ingested within therapeutic ranges of dose. Common symptoms of lithium toxicity include high levels of albumin and glucose in urine (albuminuria and glycosuria, respectively). Not surprisingly, given its uses to treat manic-depressive disorders, lithium can cause a variety of central nervous system symptoms. One symptom is psychosomatic retardation, that is, retardation of processes involving both mind and body. Slurred speech, blurred vision, and increased thirst may result. In severe cases, blackout spells, coma, epileptic seizures, and writhing, turning, and twisting choreoathetoid movements are observed. Neuromuscular changes may occur as irritable muscles, tremor, and ataxia (loss of coordination). Cardiovascular symptoms of lithium poisoning may include cardiac arrhythmia, hypertension, and, in severe cases, circulatory collapse. Victims of lithium poisoning may also experience an aversion to food (anorexia) accompanied by nausea and vomiting.

Lithium exists in the body as the Li^+ ion. Its toxic effects are likely due to its similarity to physiologically essential Na^+ and K^+ ions. Some effects may be due to the competion of Li^+ ion for receptor sites normally occupied by Na^+ or K^+ ions. Lithium toxicity may be involved in G protein expression and in modulating receptor–G protein coupling.

Beryllium

Beryllium (Be) is in group 2A and is the first metal in the periodic table to be notably toxic. When fluorescent lamps and neon lights were first introduced, they contained beryllium phosphor; a number of cases of beryllium poisoning resulted from the manufacture of these light sources and the handling of broken lamps. Modern uses of beryllium in ceramics, electronics, and alloys require special handling procedures to avoid industrial exposure.

Beryllium has a number of toxic effects. Of these, the most common involve the skin. Skin ulceration and granulomas have resulted from exposure to beryllium. Hypersensitization to beryllium can result in skin dermatitis, acute conjunctivitis, and corneal laceration.

Inhalation of beryllium compounds can cause *acute chemical pneumonitis*, a very rapidly progressing condition in which the entire respiratory tract, including nasal passages, pharynx, tracheobronchial airways, and alveoli, develops an inflammatory reaction. Beryllium fluoride is particularly effective in causing this condition, which has proven fatal in some cases.

Chronic berylliosis may occur with a long latent period of 5 to 20 years. The most damaging effect of chronic berylliosis is lung fibrosis and pneumonitis. In addition to coughing and chest pain, the subject suffers from fatigue, weakness, loss of weight, and dyspnea (difficult, painful breathing). The impaired lungs do not transfer oxygen well. Other organs that can be adversely affected are the liver, kidneys, heart, spleen, and striated muscles.

The chemistry of beryllium is atypical compared to that of the other group 1A and group 2A metals. Atoms of Be are the smallest of all metals, having an atomic radius of 111 pm. The beryllium ion, Be^{2+}, has an ionic radius of only 35 pm, which gives it a high polarizing ability, a tendency to form molecular compounds rather than ionic compounds, and a much greater tendency to form complex compounds than other group 1A or 2A ions. The ability of beryllium to form chelates is used to treat beryllium poisoning with ethylenediamine-tetraacetic acid (EDTA) and another chelating agent called Tiron:

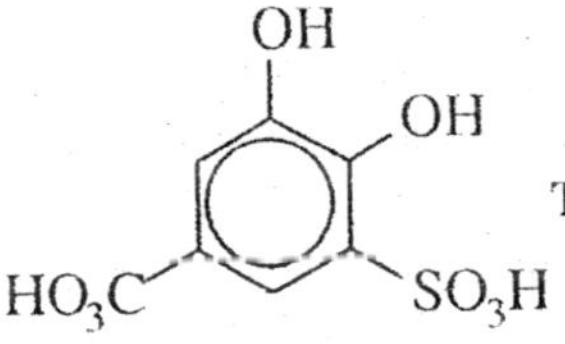

OH
OH
Tiron
HO_3C SO_3H

Vanadium

Vanadium (V) is a transition metal that in the combined form exists in the +3, +4, and +5 oxidation states, of which +5 is the most common. Vanadium is of concern as an environmental pollutant because of its high levels in residual fuel oils and subsequent emission as small particulate matter from the combustion of these oils in urban areas. Vanadium occurs as chelates of the porphyrin type in crude oil, and it concentrates in the higher boiling fractions during the refining process. A major industrial use of vanadium is in catalysts, particularly those in which sulfur dioxide is oxidized in the production of sulfuric acid. The other major industrial uses of vanadium are for hardening steel, as a pigment ingredient, in photography, and as an ingredient of some insecticides. In addition to environmental exposure from the combustion of vanadium-containing fuels, there is some potential for industrial exposure.

Probably the vanadium compound to which people are most likely to be exposed is vanadium pentoxide, V_2O_5. Exposure normally occurs via the respiratory route, and the pulmonary system is the most likely to suffer from vanadium toxicity. Bronchitis and bronchial pneumonia are the most common pathological effects of exposure; skin and eye irritation may also occur. Severe exposure can also adversely affect the gastrointestinal tract, kidneys, and nervous system.

Both V(IV) and V(V) have been found to have reproductive and developmental toxic effects in rodents. In addition to decreased fertility, lethal effects to embryos, toxicity to fetuses, and teratogenicity have been observed in mice, rats, and hamsters exposed to vanadium.

It has been observed that vanadium has insulin-like effects on the main organs targeted by insulin—skeletal muscles, adipose, and liver—and vanadium has been shown to reduce blood glucose to normal levels in rats that have diabetic conditions. In considering the potential of vanadium to treat diabetes in humans, the toxicity of vanadium is a definite consideration. Several organically chelated forms of vanadium have been found to be more effective in treating diabetes symptoms and less toxic than inorganic vanadium.

Chromium

Chromium (Cr) is a transition metal. In the chemically combined form, it exists in all oxidation states from +2 to +6, of which +3 and +6 are the more notable.

In strongly acidic aqueous solution, chromium(III) may be present as the hydrated cation $Cr(H_2O)_6{}^{3+}$. At pH values above approximately 4, this ion has a strong tendency to precipitate from solution the hydroxide:

$$Cr(H_2O)_6^{3+} \rightarrow Cr(OH)_3 + 3H^+ + 3H_2O$$

The two major forms of chromium(VI) in solution are yellow chromate, $CrO_4{}^{2-}$, and orange dichromate, $Cr_2O_7{}^{2-}$. The latter predominates in acidic solution, as shown by the following reaction, the equilibrium of which is forced to the left by higher levels of H^+:

$$Cr_2O_7^{2-} + H_2O \rightleftarrows 2HCrO_4^- \rightleftarrows 2H^+ + 2CrO_4^{2-}$$

Chromium in the +3 oxidation state is an essential trace element required for glucose and lipid metabolism in mammals, and a deficiency of it gives symptoms of diabetes mellitus. However, chromium must also be discussed as a toxicant because of its toxicity in the +6 oxidation state, commonly called *chromate*. Exposure to chromium(VI) usually involves chromate salts, such as Na_2CO_4. These salts tend to be water soluble and readily absorbed into the blood-stream through the lungs. The carcinogenicity of chromate has been demonstrated by studies of exposed workers. Exposure to atmospheric chromate may cause bronchogenic carcinoma with a latent period of 10 to 15 years. In the body, chromium(VI) is readily reduced to chromium(III); however, the reverse reaction does not occur in the body.

$$CrO_4^{2-} + 8H^+ + 3e^- \rightarrow Cr^{3+} + 4H_2O$$

An interesting finding regarding potentially toxic chromium (and cobalt) in the body is elevated blood and urine levels of these metals in patients who have undergone total hip replacement. The conclusion of the study was that devices such as prosthetic hips that involve metal-to-metal contact may result in potentially toxic levels of metals in biological fluids.

Cobalt

Cobalt is an essential element that is part of vitamin B_{12}, or cobalamin, a coenzyme that is essential in the formation of proteins, nucleic acids, and red blood cells. Although cobalt poisoning is not common, excessive levels can be harmful. Most cases of human exposure to toxic levels of cobalt have occurred through inhalation in the workplace. Many exposures have been suffered by workers working with hard metal alloys of cobalt and tungsten carbide, where very fine particles of the alloy produced from grinding it were inhaled. The adverse effects of cobalt inhalation have been on the lungs, including wheezing and pneumonia as well as allergic asthmatic reactions and skin rashes. Lung fibrosis has resulted from prolonged exposures. Human epidemiology and animal studies suggest an array of systemic toxic effects of cobalt, including, in addition to respiratory effects, cardiovascular, hematological hepatic, renal, ocular, and body weight effects.

Exposure to cobalt is also possible through food and drinking water. An interesting series of cobalt poisonings occurred in the 1960s when cobalt was added to beer at levels of 1 to 1.5 ppm to stabilize foam. Consumers who drank excessive amounts of the beer (4 to 12 liters per day) suffered from nausea and vomiting, and in several cases, heart failure and death resulted.

Nickel

Nickel, atomic number 28, is a transition metal with a variety of essential uses in alloys, catalysts, and other applications. It is strongly suspected of being an essential trace element for human nutrition, although definitive evidence has not yet established its essentiality to humans. A nickel-containing urease metalloenzyme has been found in the jack bean.

Toxicologically, nickel is important because it has been established as a cause of respiratory tract cancer among workers involved with nickel refining. The first definitive evidence of this was an epidemiological study of British nickel refinery workers published in 1958. Compared to the general population, these workers suffered a 150-fold increase in nasal cancers and a 5-fold increase in lung cancer. Other studies from Norway, Canada, and the former Soviet Union have shown similar increased cancer risk from exposure to nickel. Nickel subsulfide, Ni_3S_2, has been shown to cause cancer in rats at sites of injection and in lungs from inhalation of nickel subsulfide.

The other major toxic effect of nickel is nickel dermatitis, an allergic contact dermatitis arising from contact with nickel metal. About 5 to 10% of people are susceptible to this disorder. It almost always occurs as the result of wearing nickel jewelry in contact with skin. Nickel carbonyl, $Ni(CO)_4$, is an extremely toxic nickel compound.

Cadmium

Along with mercury and lead, cadmium (Cd) is one of the "big three" heavy metal poisons. Cadmium occurs as a constituent of lead and zinc ores, from which it can be extracted as a by-product. Cadmium is used to electroplate metals to prevent corrosion, as a pigment, as a constituent of alkali storage batteries, and in the manufacture of some plastics.

Cadmium is located at the end of the second row of transition elements. The +2 oxidation state of the element is the only one exhibited in its compounds. In its compounds, cadmium occurs as the Cd^{2+} ion. Cadmium is directly below zinc in the periodic table and behaves much like zinc. This may account in part for cadmium's toxicity; because zinc is an essential trace element, cadmium substituting for zinc could cause metabolic processes to go wrong.

The toxic nature of cadmium was revealed in the early 1900s as a result of workers inhaling cadmium fumes or dusts in ore processing and manufacturing operations. Welding or cutting metals plated with cadmium or containing cadmium in alloys, or the use of cadmium rods or wires for brazing or silver soldering, can be a particularly dangerous route to pulmonary exposure. In general, cadmium is poorly absorbed through the gastrointestinal tract. A mechanism exists for its active absorption in the small intestine through the action of the low-molecular-mass calcium-binding protein CaBP. The production of this protein is stimulated by a calcium-deficient diet, which may aggravate cadmium toxicity. Cadmium is transported in blood bound to red blood cells or to albumin or other high-molecular-mass proteins in blood plasma. Cadmium is excreted from the body in both urine and feces. The mechanisms of cadmium excretion are not well known.

Acute pulmonary symptoms of cadmium exposure are usually caused by the inhalation of cadmium oxide dusts and fumes, which results in cadmium pneumonitis, characterized by edema and pulmonary epithelium necrosis. Chronic exposure sometimes produces emphysema severe enough to be disabling. The kidney is generally regarded as the organ most sensitive to chronic cadmium poisoning. The function of renal tubules is impaired by cadmium, as manifested by excretion of both high-molecular-mass proteins (such as albumin) and low-molecular-mass proteins. Chronic toxic effects of cadmium exposure may also include damage to the skeletal system, hypertension (high blood pressure), and adverse cardiovascular effects. Based largely on studies of workers in the cadmium–nickel battery industry, cadmium is regarded as a human carcinogen, causing lung tumors and possibly cancer of the prostate.

Cadmium is a highly *cumulative* poison with a biologic half-life estimated at about 20 to 30 years in humans. About half of the body burden of cadmium is found in the liver and kidneys. The total body burden reaches a plateau in humans around age 50. Cigarette smoke is a source of cadmium, and the body burden of cadmium is about 1.5 to 2 times greater in smokers than in nonsmokers of the same age.

Cadmium in the body is known to affect several enzymes. It is believed that the renal damage that results in proteinuria is the result of cadmium adversely affecting enzymes responsible for reabsorption of proteins in kidney tubules. Cadmium also reduces the activity of delta-aminolevulinic acid synthetase, arylsulfatase, alcohol dehydrogenase, and lipoamide dehydrogenase, whereas it enhances the activity of delta-aminolevulinic acid dehydratase, pyruvate dehydrogenase, and pyruvate decarboxylase.

The most spectacular and publicized occurrence of cadmium poisoning resulted from dietary intake of cadmium by people in the Jintsu River Valley, near Fuchu, Japan. The victims were afflicted by *itai, itai* disease, which means "ouch, ouch" in Japanese. The symptoms are the result of painful osteomalacia (bone disease) combined with kidney malfunction. Cadmium poisoning in the Jintsu River Valley

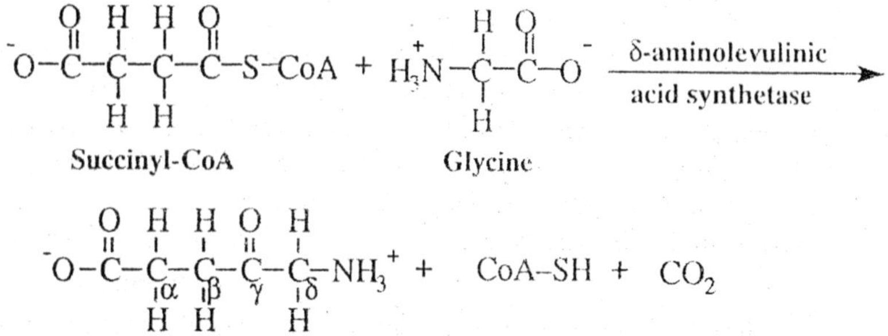

$$^{-}O-\overset{O}{\overset{\|}{C}}-\underset{H}{\overset{H}{C}}-\underset{H}{\overset{H}{C}}-\overset{O}{\overset{\|}{C}}-S-CoA + H_3\overset{+}{N}-\underset{H}{\overset{H}{C}}-\overset{O}{\overset{\|}{C}}-O^{-} \xrightarrow[\text{acid synthetase}]{\delta\text{-aminolevulinic}}$$

Succinyl-CoA **Glycine**

$$^{-}O-\overset{O}{\overset{\|}{C}}-\underset{H}{\overset{H}{C_{\alpha}}}-\underset{H}{\overset{H}{C_{\beta}}}-\overset{O}{\overset{\|}{C_{\gamma}}}-\underset{H}{\overset{H}{C_{\delta}}}-NH_3^{+} + CoA-SH + CO_2$$

δ-aminolevulinic acid

Fig. 6.3. Path of synthesis of delta-aminolevulinic acid.

was attributed to irrigated rice contaminated from an upstream mine producing lead, zinc, and cadmium.

Mercury

Mercury is directly below cadmium in the periodic table, but has a considerably more varied and interesting chemistry than cadmium or zinc. Elemental mercury is the only metal that is a liquid at room temperature, and its relatively high vapor pressure contributes to its toxicological hazard. Mercury metal is used in electric discharge tubes (mercury lamps), gauges, pressure-sensing devices, vacuum pumps, valves, and seals. It was formerly widely used as a cathode in the chloralkali process for the manufacture of NaOH and Cl_2, a process that has been largely discontinued, in part because of the mercury pollution that resulted from it.

In addition to the uses of mercury metal, mercury compounds have a number of applications. Mercury(II) oxide, HgO, is commonly used as a raw material for the manufacture of other mercury compounds. Mixed with graphite, it is a constituent of the Ruben–Mallory dry cell, for which the cell reaction is

$$Zn + HgO \rightarrow ZnO + Hg$$

Mercury(II) acetate, $Hg(C_2H_3O_2)_2$, is made by dissolving HgO in warm 20% acetic acid. This compound is soluble in a number of organic solvents. Mercury(II) chloride is quite toxic. The dangers of exposure to $HgCl_2$ are aggravated by its high water solubility and relatively high vapor pressure, compared to other salts. Mercury(II) fulminate, $Hg(ONC)_2$, has been used as a detonator for explosives. In addition to the +2 oxidation state, mercury can also exist in the +1 oxidation state as the dinuclear Hg_2^{2+} ion. The best-known mercury(I) compound is mercury(I) chloride, Hg_2Cl_2, commonly called calomel.

It is a constituent of calomel reference electrodes, such as the well-known saturated calomel electrode (SCE).

Absorption and transport of elemental and inorganic mercury

Monatomic elemental mercury in the vapor state, Hg(*g*), is absorbed from inhaled air by the pulmonary route to the extent of about 80%. Inorganic mercury compounds are absorbed through the intestinal tract and in solution through the skin.

Although elemental mercury is rapidly oxidized to mercury(II) in erythrocytes (red blood cells), which have a strong affinity for mercury, a large fraction of elemental mercury absorbed through the pulmonary route reaches the brain prior to oxidation and enters that organ because of the lipid solubility of mercury(0). This mercury is subsequently oxidized in the brain and remains there. Inorganic mercury(II) tends to accumulate in the kidney.

Metabolism, biologic effects, and excretion

Like cadmium, mercury(II) has a strong affinity for sulfhydryl groups in proteins, enzymes, hemoglobin, and serum albumin. Because of the abundance of sulfhydryl groups in active sites of many enzymes, it is difficult to establish exactly which enzymes are affected by mercury in biological systems.

The effect on the central nervous system following inhalation of elemental mercury is largely psychopathological. Among the most prominent symptoms are tremor (particularly of the hands) and emotional instability characterized by shyness, insomnia, depression, and irritability. These symptoms are probably the result of damage to the blood–brain barrier, which regulates the transfer of metabolites, such as amino acids, to and from the brain. Brain metabolic processes are probably disrupted by the effects of mercury. Historically, the three symptoms of increased excitability, tremors, and gum inflammation (gingivitis) have been recognized as symptoms of mercury poisoning from exposure to mercury vapor or mercury nitrate in the fur, hat, and felt trades.

The kidney is the primary target organ for Hg^{2+}. Chronic exposure to inorganic mercury(II) compounds causes proteinuria. In cases of mercury poisoning of any type, the kidney is the organ with the highest bioaccumulation of mercury.

Mercury(I) compounds are generally less toxic than mercury(II) compounds because of their lower solubilities. Calomel, a preparation containing Hg_2Cl_2, was once widely used in medicine. Its use as a teething powder for children has been known to cause a hypersensitivity response in children called "pink disease," manifested by a pink rash and swelling of the spleen and lymph nodes.

Excretion of inorganic mercury occurs through the urine and feces. The mechanisms by which excretion occurs are not well understood.

Minimata bay

The most notorious incident of widespread mercury poisoning in modern times occurred in the Minimata Bay region of Japan during the period of 1953 to 1960. Mercury waste from a chemical plant draining into the bay contaminated seafood consumed regularly by people in the area. Overall, 111 cases of poisoning with 43 deaths and 19 congenital birth defects were documented. The seafood was found to contain 5 to 20 ppm of mercury.

Lead

Lead (Pb) ranks fifth behind iron, copper, aluminum, and zinc in industrial production of metals. About half of the lead used in the U.S. goes for the manufacture of lead storage batteries. Other uses include solders, bearings, cable covers, ammunition, plumbing, pigments, and caulking.

Metals commonly alloyed with lead are antimony (in storage batteries), calcium and tin (in maintenance-free storage batteries), silver (for solder and anodes), strontium and tin (as anodes in electrowinning processes), tellurium (pipe and sheet in chemical installations and nuclear shielding), tin (solders), and antimony and tin (sleeve bearings, printing, high-detail castings).

Lead(II) compounds are predominantly ionic (for example, Pb^{2+} SO_4^{2-}), whereas lead(IV) compounds tend to be covalent (for example, tetraethyllead, $Pb(C_2H_5)_4$). Some lead(IV) compounds, such as PbO_2, are strong oxidants. Lead forms several basic lead salts, such as $Pb(OH)_2.2PbCO_3$, which was once the most widely used white paint pigment and the source of considerable chronic lead poisoning to children who ate peeling white paint. Many compounds of lead in the +2 oxidation state (lead(II)) and a few in the +4 oxidation state (lead(IV)) are useful. The two most common of these are lead dioxide and lead sulfate, which are participants in the following reversible reaction that occurs during the charge and discharge of a lead storage battery:

$$Pb + PbO_2 + 2H_2SO_4 \rightleftarrows 2PbSO_4 + 2H_2O$$
$$\text{Charge} \rightleftarrows \text{Discharge}$$

In addition to the inorganic compounds of lead, there are a number of organolead compounds, such as tetraethyllead.

Exposure and absorption of inorganic lead compounds

Although industrial lead poisoning used to be very common, it is relatively rare now because of previous experience with the toxic effects of lead and the protective actions that have been taken. Lead is a common atmospheric pollutant (though much less so now than when leaded gasoline was in general use), and absorption through the respiratory tract is the most common route of human exposure. The greatest danger of pulmonary exposure comes from inhalation of very small respirable particles of lead oxide (particularly from lead smelters and storage battery manufacturing) and lead carbonates, halides, phosphates, and sulfates. Lead that reaches the lung alveoli is readily absorbed into blood.

The other major route of lead absorption is the gastrointestinal tract. Dietary intake of lead reached average peak values of almost 0.5 mg per person per day in the U.S. around the 1940s. Much of this lead came from lead solder used in cans employed for canned goods and beverages. Currently, daily intake of dietary lead in the U.S. is probably only around 20 μg per person per day. Lead(II) may have much the same transport mechanism as calcium in the gastrointestinal tract. It is known that lead absorption decreases with increased levels of calcium in the diet and vice versa.

Transport and metabolism of lead

A striking aspect of lead in the body is its very rapid transport to bone and storage there. Lead tends to undergo bioaccumulation in bone throughout life, and about 90% of the body burden of lead is in bone after long-term exposure. The half-life of lead in human bones is estimated to be around 20 years. Some workers exposed to lead in an industrial setting have as much as 500 mg of lead in their bones. Of the soft tissues, the liver and kidney tend to have somewhat elevated lead levels.

About 90% of blood lead is associated with red blood cells. Measurement of the concentration of lead in the blood is the standard test for recent or ongoing exposure to lead. This test is used routinely to monitor industrial exposure to lead and in screening children for lead exposure.

The most common biochemical effect of lead is inhibition of the synthesis of heme, a complex of a substituted porphyrin and Fe^{2+} in

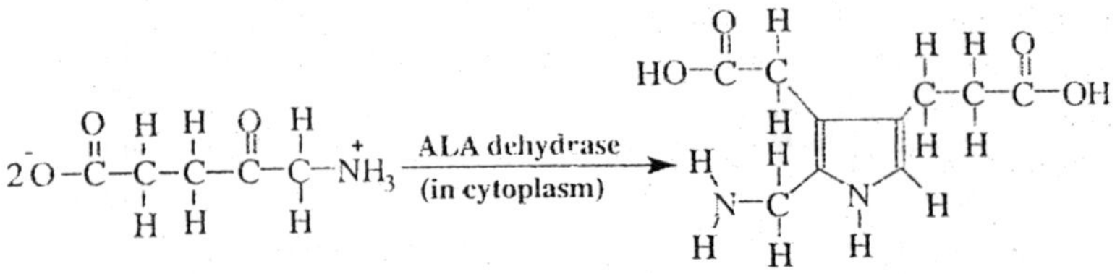

$$2\,{}^{-}O-\overset{O}{\overset{\|}{C}}-\underset{H}{\overset{H}{C}}-\underset{H}{\overset{H}{C}}-\overset{O}{\overset{\|}{C}}-\underset{H}{\overset{H}{C}}-\overset{+}{N}H_3 \xrightarrow[\text{(in cytoplasm)}]{\text{ALA dehydrase}} \text{Porphobilinogen}$$

δ-aminolevulinic acid — Porphobilinogen

Fig. 6.4. Synthesis of porphobilinogen from delta-aminolevulinic acid, a major step in the overall scheme of heme synthesis that is inhibited by lead in the body.

hemoglobin and cytochromes. Lead interferes with the conversion of delta-aminolevulinic acid to porphobilinogen, with a resulting accumulation of metabolic products. Hematological damage results. Lead inhibits enzymes that have sulfhydryl groups. However, the affinity of lead for the –SH group is not as great as that of cadmium or mercury.

Manifestations of lead poisoning

Lead adversely affects a number of systems in the body. The inhibition of the synthesis of hemoglobin by lead has just been noted. This effect, plus a shortening of the life span of erythrocytes, results in anemia, a major manifestation of lead poisoning.

The central nervous system is adversely affected by lead, leading to encephalopathy, including neuron degeneration, cerebral edema, and dea'h of cerebral cortex cells. Lead may interfere with the function of neurotransmitters, including dopamine and γ-butyric acid, and it may slow the rate of neurotransmission. Psychopathological symptoms of restlessness, dullness, irritability, and memory loss, as well as ataxia, headaches, and muscular tremor, may occur with lead poisoning. In extreme cases, convulsions followed by coma and death may occur. Lead affects the peripheral nervous system, causing peripheral neuropathy. Lead palsy used to be a commonly observed symptom in lead industry workers and miners suffering from lead poisoning.

Lead causes reversible damage to the kidney through its adverse effect on proximal tubules. This impairs the processes by which the kidney absorbs glucose, phosphates, and amino acids prior to secretion of urine. A longer-term effect of lead ingestion on the kidney is general degradation of the organ (chronic nephritis), including glomular atrophy, interstitial fibrosis, and sclerosis of vessels.

Reversal of lead poisoning and therapy

Some effects of lead poisoning, such as those on proximal tubules of the kidney and inhibition of heme synthesis, are reversible upon

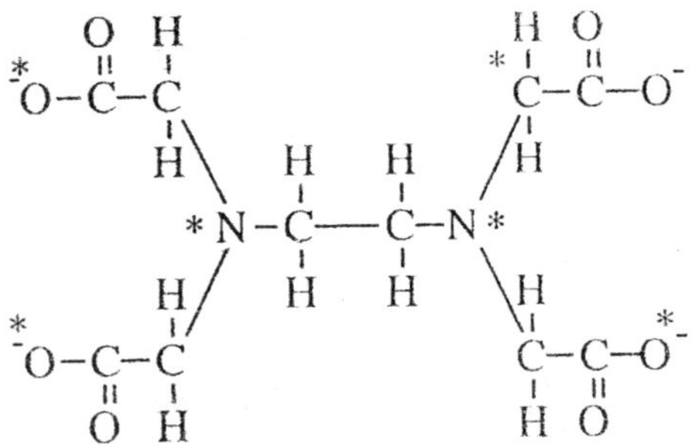

Anion of ethylenediaminetetraacetic acid, EDTA

Fig. 6.5. The ionized form of EDTA. Asterisks denote binding sites.

removal of the source of lead exposure. Lead poisoning can be treated by chelation therapy, in which the lead is solubilized and removed by a chelating agent. One such chelating agent is ethylenediaminetetraacetic acid, which binds strongly to most +2 and +3 cations. It is administered for lead poisoning therapy in the form of the calcium chelate. The ionized Y^{4-} form chelates metal ions by bonding at one, two, three, or all four carboxylate groups ($-CO_3^{2-}$) and one or both of the two N atoms. EDTA is administered as the calcium chelate for the treatment of lead poisoning to avoid any net loss of calcium by solubilization and excretion. Another compound used to treat lead poisoning is British anti-Lewisite, originally developed to treat arsenic-containing poison gas Lewisite. BAL chelates lead through its sulfhydryl groups, and the chelate is excreted through the kidney and bile.

Defenses Against Heavy Metal Poisoning

Organisms have some natural defenses against heavy metal poisoning. Several factors are involved in regulating the uptake and physiological concentrations of heavy metals. For example, higher levels of calcium in water tend to lower the bioavailability of metals such as cadmium, copper, lead, mercury, and zinc by fish, and the presence of chelating agents affects the uptake of such metals. Some evidence suggests that mechanisms developed to maintain optimum levels of essential metals, such as zinc and copper, are utilized to minimize the effects of chemically somewhat similar toxic heavy metals, of which cadmium, lead, and mercury are prime examples.

An interesting feature of heavy metal metabolism is the role of intracellular *metallothionein*, which consists of two similar proteins with a low molecular mass of about 6500. As a consequence of a high content of the amino acid cysteine,

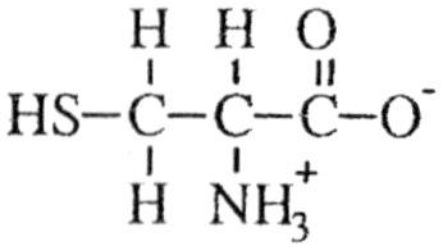

$$HS-\underset{H}{\overset{H}{C}}-\underset{NH_3^+}{\overset{H}{C}}-\overset{O}{\overset{\|}{C}}-O^- \quad \textbf{Cysteine}$$

metallothionein contains a large number of thiol (sulfhydryl, –SH) groups. These groups bind very strongly to other heavy metals, particularly mercury, silver, zinc, and tin. The metal most investigated for its interaction with metallothionein is cadmium. The general reaction of metallothionein with cadmium ion is the following:

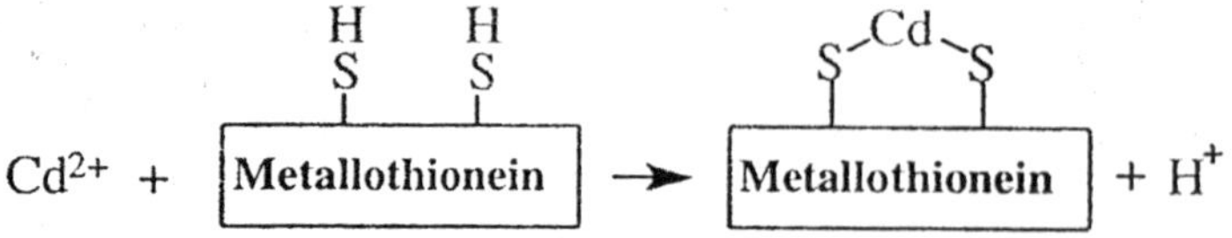

$$Cd^{2+} + \text{Metallothionein}(SH)_2 \rightarrow \text{Metallothionein}(S_2Cd) + H^+$$

By binding with metallothionein, the mobility of metals by diffusion is greatly reduced and the metals are prevented from binding to enzymes or other proteins essential to normal metabolic function.

Metallothionein has been isolated from virtually all of the major mammal organs, including liver, kidney, brain, heart, intestine, lung, skin, and spleen. Nonlethal doses of cadmium, mercury, and lead induce synthesis of metallothionein. In test animals, nonlethal doses of cadmium followed by an increased level of metallothionein in the body have allowed later administration of doses of cadmium at a level fatal to nonacclimated animals, but without fatalities in the test subjects.

Endogenous substances other than metallothionein may be involved in minimizing the effects of heavy metals and excreting them from the body. Hepatic (liver) glutathione, discussed as a phase II conjugating agent, plays a role in the excretion of several metals in bile. These include the essential metals copper and zinc; toxic cadmium, mercury(II), and lead(II) ions; and organometallic methyl mercury.

Some plants have particularly high tolerances for cadmium and some other heavy metals by virtue of their content of cysteine-rich peptides, known as *phytochelatins*, sulfur-rich peptides that perform in plants much like metallothionein acts in animals.

Plants that resist the effects of heavy metals through the action of phytochelatins require a high activity of cysteine synthase enzyme that makes the sulfur-containing cysteine amino acid from hydrogen sulfide and O-acetylserine. Cadmium-resistant transgenic tobacco plants have been bred that have a high activity of cysteine synthase from genes taken from rice.

METALLOIDS: ARSENIC

Sources and Uses

Arsenopyrite and loellingite are both arsenic minerals that can be smelted to produce elemental arsenic. Both elemental arsenic and arsenic trioxide (As_2O_3) are produced commercially; the latter is the raw material for the production of numerous arsenic compounds. Elemental arsenic is used to make alloys with lead and copper. Arsenic compounds have a number of uses, including applications in catalysts, bactericides, herbicides, fungicides, animal feed additives, corrosion inhibitors, pharmaceuticals, veterinary medicines, tanning agents, and wood preservatives. Arsenicals were the first drugs to be effective against syphilis, and they are still used to treat amebic dysentery. Arsobal, or Mel B, an organoarsenical, is the most effective drug for the treatment of the neurological stage of African trypanosomiasis, for which the infectious agents are *Trypanosoma gambiense* or *T. rhodesiense*.

Exposure and Absorption of Arsenic

Arsenic can be absorbed through both the gastrointestinal and pulmonary routes. Although the major concern with arsenic is its effect as a systemic poison, arsenic trichloride ($AsCl_3$) and the organic arsenic compound Lewisite (used as a poison gas in World War I) can penetrate skin; both of these compounds are very damaging at the point of exposure and are strong vesicants (causes of blisters). The common arsenic compound As_2O_3 is absorbed through the lungs and intestines. The degree of coarseness of the solid is a major factor in how well it is absorbed. Coarse particles of this compound tend to pass through the gastrointestinal tract and to be eliminated with the feces.

The chemistry of arsenic is so varied that it is difficult to regard as a single element. Arsenic occurs in the +3 and +5 oxidation states; inorganic compounds in the +3 oxidation state (arsenite) are generally more toxic. The conversion to arsenic(V) is normally favored in the environment, which somewhat reduces the overall hazard of this element.

Arsenic is a natural constituent of most soils. It is found in a number of foods, particularly shellfish. The average adult ingests somewhat less than 1 mg of arsenic per day through natural sources. Drinking water is a source of arsenic in some parts of the world. This was tragically illustrated in Bangladesh, where a United Nations program to develop water wells as a source of pathogen-free drinking water later resulted in perhaps millions of cases of arsenic poisoning from arsenic-containing well water. A directive by the U.S. Environmental Protection Agency in 2000 to lower the long-standing (since 1942) arsenic drinking water standard in the U.S. was overturned, pending further review by the newly elected administration in early 2001, causing a great deal of controversy.

Metabolism, Transport, and Toxic Effects of Arsenic

Biochemically, arsenic acts to coagulate proteins, forms complexes with coenzymes, and inhibits the production of adenosine triphosphate (ATP). Like cadmium and mercury, arsenic is a sulfur-seeking element. Arsenic has some chemical similarities to phosphorus, and it substitutes for phosphorus in some biochemical processes, with adverse metabolic effects. The reaction enzyme-catalyzed synthesis of 1,3-diphosphoglycerate from glyceraldehyde 3-phosphate. The product undergoes additional reactions to produce ATP, an essential energy-yielding substance in body metabolism. When arsenite AsO_3^{3-} is present, it bonds to glyceraldehyde 3-phosphate to yield a product that undergoes nonenzymatic spontaneous hydrolysis, thereby preventing ATP formation.

Symptoms of acute arsenic poisoning are many and may be severe — fatal at high doses. Fatal cases of arsenic poisoning have exhibited symptoms of fever, aversion to food, abnormal liver enlargement (hepatomegaly), cardiac arrhythmia, development of dark patches on skin and other tissue (melanosis), peripheral neuropathy, including sensory loss in the peripheral nervous system, gastrointestinal disorders, cardiovascular effects, and adverse effects on red blood cell formation, which can result in anemia. Mucous membranes may be irritated, form blisters, or slough off.

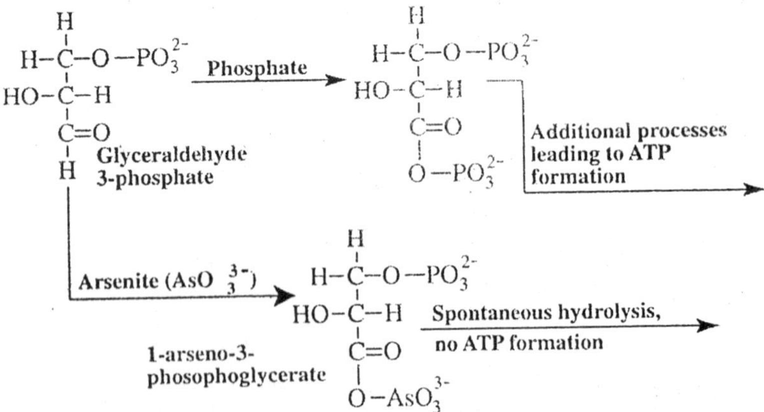

Fig. 6.6. Interference of arsenic(III) with ATP production by phosphorylation.

Chronic effects of arsenic poisoning include neurotoxic effects to the central and peripheral nervous systems. Symptoms include sensory changes, muscle sensitivity, prickling and tingling sensations (paresthesia), and muscle weakness. Liver injury is a common symptom of chronic arsenic poisoning. Studies of victims of chronic arsenic poisoning from contaminated drinking water in Taiwan and Chile have exhibited blueness of the skin in extremities, a condition called acrocyanosis, the result of periphereal vascular disease. In extreme cases, this may progress to gangrene in the lower extremities, a condition called blackfoot disease.

There is now sufficient epidemiological evidence to classify arsenic as a human carcinogen and a cause of skin cancer. In people chronically exposed to toxic doses of arsenic, such cancers may be preceded by discolored skin (hyperpigmentation) and development of horny skin surfaces (hyperkeratosis). These areas may progress to locally invasive basal cell carcinomas or to squamous cell carcinomas capable of metastasis. Unlike skin cancers that develop on skin exposed to ultraviolet solar radiation, arsenic-induced skin cancer frequently develops in areas not commonly exposed to sunlight, such as the palms of hands or soles of feet.

Analysis of hair, fingernails, and toenails can serve as evidence of arsenic ingestion. Such analyses are complicated by the possible presence of arsenic contamination, particularly in a work environment in which the air and surroundings may be contaminated with arsenic. Levels of arsenic may be correlated with the growth of nails and hair so that careful analysis of segments of these materials can indicate time frames of exposure.

Antidotes to arsenic poisoning take advantage of the element's sulfur-seeking tendencies and contain sulfhydryl groups. One such antidote is 2,3-mercaptopropanol (BAL), discussed in the preceding section as an antidote for lead poisoning.

Nonmetals

Oxygen and Ozone

Molecular oxygen, O_2, is essential for life processes in both humans and other aerobic organisms and is potentially damaging to tissue. Exposure to excessive levels of O_2 can cause toxic responses. This was tragically illustrated by the use of oxygen to assist the respiration of premature infants, a procedure that caused many to become blind. Even at normal levels of oxygen, some toxicants can cause this essential element to cause toxic lesions. To understand why this is so, consider that aerobic organisms, including humans, derive their energy by mediating the oxidation of nutrient molecules such as glucose:

$$C_6H_{12}O_6 + 6O_2 \rightarrow 6CO_2 + 6H_2O + \text{energy}$$

In this aerobic respiration process, molecular oxygen is the oxidizing agent or electron receptor and is reduced to the –2 oxidation state in the H_2O product. The process by which elemental oxygen accepts electrons is complex and multistepped. In this process, reactive intermediates are produced that can seriously damage the lipids in cell membranes, DNA in cell nuclei, and proteins. Under normal circumstances, these reactive oxidant species undergo further reactions before they can do much harm, or are scavenged by antioxidant molecules or by the action of enzymes designed to keep them at acceptable levels. However, under conditions of excessive exposure to oxidants and by the action of some kinds of toxicants, harmful levels of reactive intermediate oxidant species can build up to harmful levels.

The metabolic conversion of oxygen(0) in elemental oxygen to bound oxygen in the –2 oxidation state in H_2O can be viewed as the successive addition of electrons (e^-) and H^+ ions to O_2. The first step is addition of an electron to O_2 to produce reactive superoxide ion, O_2^- :

$$O_2 + e^- \rightarrow O_{\dot{2}}^-$$

In formulas such as that of superoxide, the dot represents an unpaired electron. Species that have unpaired electrons are very reactive *free radicals*. Addition of H^+ ion to superoxide produces reactive hydroperoxyl radical, HO_2:

$$O_{\dot{2}}^- + H^+ \rightarrow H_{\dot{2}}$$

Another electron and H^+ ion may be added to the hydroperoxyl radical, a process equivalent to adding an H atom, to produce hydrogen peroxide:

$$HO_{\dot{2}} + e^- + H^+ \rightarrow H_2O_2$$

Hydrogen peroxide may be produced from the superoxide radical anion by the action of superoxide dismutase enzyme. The catalase enzyme may act on hydrogen peroxide to produce O_2 and H_2O. Hydrogen peroxide may also be eliminated by the action of glutathione peroxidase, producing the oxidized form of glutathione. In the presence of appropriate metal ion catalysts, hydrogen peroxide may undergo the Haber–Weiss reaction,

$$O_{\dot{2}}^- + H_2O_2 + Fe^{2+} \rightarrow Fe^{3+} + O_2 + OH^- + HO\cdot$$

and the Fenton reaction,

$$H_2O_2 + Fe^{2+} \rightarrow Fe^{3+} + OH^- + HO\cdot$$

to produce hydroxyl radical, HO·.

Superoxide, hydroperoxyl, and especially reactive hydroxyl radicals along with hydrogen peroxide attack tissue and DNA either directly or through their reaction products. The damage done is sometimes referred to as oxidative lesions. It is now recognized that some toxicants have the ability to promote the formation of reactive oxidizing species to the extent that defensive mechanisms against oxidants are overwhelmed, a condition called *oxidative stress*. Under conditions of oxidative stress, lipids, nucleic acids, and proteins may be damaged by reactive oxidants. Another very damaging effect of oxidant reactive intermediates is *lipid peroxidation*, in which polyunsaturated fatty acids on lipids are attacked and oxidized, as shown. This can be especially damaging to lipid-rich cell membranes.

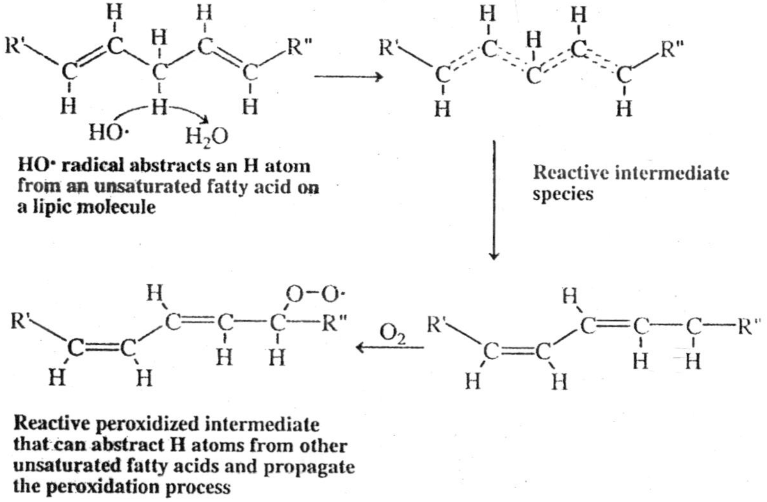

HO· H_2O

HO· radical abstracts an H atom from an unsaturated fatty acid on a lipic molecule

Reactive intermediate species

O_2

Reactive peroxidized intermediate that can abstract H atoms from other unsaturated fatty acids and propagate the peroxidation process

Fig. 6.7. Peroxidation of liquid molecules by reactive radical species such as the hydroxyl radical, HO·.

Superoxide radical anion, hydroxyl radical, and hydrogen peroxide are known as prooxidants, whereas substances that neutralize their effects are called antioxidants. Oxidative stress occurs when the prooxidant–antioxidant balance becomes too favorable to the prooxidants. The effects of prooxidants can be neutralized by their direct reaction with small-molecule antioxidants, including glutathione, ascorbate, and tocopherols. In addition, oxidizing radicals are scavenged from a living system by several enzymes, including peroxidase, superoxide dismutase, and catalase. Oxidative lesions on DNA may be repaired by DNA repair enzymes.

Probably the most important antioxidant molecule is glutathione, a tripeptide formed from glutamic acid, cysteine, and glycine amino acids:

```
    O  H  H  H  O  H  H  O  H  H  O
    ‖  |  |  |  ‖  |  |  ‖  |  |  ‖
 ⁻O–C––C––C––C––C––N––C––C––N––C––C–O⁻
       |  |  |        |        |
     H2N  H  H     H––C––H     H
                      |
                      S    Glutathione
                      H
```

This substance reacts with oxidant radicals to produce H_2O and the oxidized form of glutathione, consisting of two of the molecules of this substance joined by an SS bridge.

A potent oxidizing form of elemental oxygen is *ozone*, O_3. This species is arguably the most toxic environmental pollutant to which the general population is exposed because of its presence in polluted atmospheres, especially under conditions where photochemical smog is present. It can be a pollutant of the workplace in locations where electrical discharges or ultraviolet radiation pass through air (from sources such as laser printers).

A deep lung irritant, ozone causes pulmonary edema, which can be fatal. It is also strongly irritating to the upper respiratory system and eyes and is largely responsible for the unpleasantness of photochemical smog. A level of 1 ppm of ozone in air has a distinct odor, and inhalation of such air causes severe irritation and headache. The primary toxicological concern with ozone involves the lungs. Exposure to ozone increases the activity of free-radical-scavenging enzymes in the lung, indicative of ozone's ability to generate the reactive oxidant species responsible for oxidative stress. Arterial lesions leading to pulmonary edema have resulted from ozone exposure by inhalation. Animal studies of ozone inhalation have shown injury of epithelial (surface) cells throughout the respiratory tract.

Like nitrogen dioxide and ionizing radiation, ozone in the body produces free radicals that can be involved in destructive oxidation processes, such as lipid peroxidation or reaction with sulfhydryl (–SH) groups. Exposure to ozone can cause chromosomal damage. Ozone also appears to have adverse immunological effects. Radical-scavenging compounds, antioxidants, and compounds containing sulfhydryl groups can protect organisms from the effects of ozone.

Ozone is notable for being *phytotoxic* (toxic to plants). Loss of crop productivity from the phytotoxic action of ozone is a major concern in areas afflicted with photochemical smog, of which ozone is the single most characteristic manifestation.

Phosphorus

The most common elemental form of phosphorus, white phosphorus, is highly toxic. White phosphorus (melting point (mp), 44°C; boiling point (bp), 280°C) is a colorless waxy solid, sometimes with a yellow tint. It ignites spontaneously in air to yield a dense fog of finely divided, highly deliquescent P_4O_{10}:

$$P_4 + 5O_2 \rightarrow P_4O_{10}$$

White phosphorus can be absorbed into the body, particularly through inhalation, as well as through the oral and dermal routes. It has a number of systemic effects, including anemia, gastrointestinal system dysfunction, and bone brittleness. Acute exposure to relatively high levels results in gastrointestinal disturbances and weakness due to biochemical effects on the liver. Chronic poisoning occurs largely through the inhalation of low concentrations of white phosphorus and through direct contact with this toxicant. Severe eye damage can result from chronic exposure to elemental white phosphorus. A number of cases of white phosphorus poisoning have resulted from exposure in the fireworks industry. At least one case of fatal poisoning has occurred when a child accidentally ate a firecracker containing white phosphorus. White phosphorus used to be a common ingredient of rat poisons, and some suicidal individuals have been fatally poisoned from ingesting rat poison.

The most characteristic toxic effects of white phosphorus are musculoskeletal effects. Victims of phosphorus poisoning tend to develop necrosis of both bone and soft tissue in the oral cavity. As a result, the jawbone may deteriorate and become brittle, a condition called *phossy jaw*. Instances of this malady have been reported among workers handling white phosphorus, and it is believed that direct exposure of the mouth and oral cavity have occurred as the result of poor hygiene practices. Those afflicted with phossy jaw tend to develop abscessed teeth, and the sockets remaining from the extraction of teeth heal poorly. Infections of the jaw around teeth accompanied by severe pain are common symptoms of phossy jaw.

Halogens

The elemental *halogens*—fluorine, chlorine, bromine, and iodine—are all toxic. Both fluorine and chlorine are highly corrosive gases that are very damaging to exposed tissue. These elements are chemically and toxicologically similar to many of their compounds, such as the interhalogen compounds.

Fluorine

Fluorine, F_2 (mp, –218°C; bp, –187°C), is a pale yellow gas produced from calcium fluoride ore by first liberating hydrogen fluoride with sulfuric acid, then electrolyzing the HF in a 4:1 mixture with potassium fluoride, KF, as shown in the reaction

$$2HF(\text{molecule KF}) \xrightarrow[\text{current}]{\text{Direct}} H_2(\text{cathode}) + F_2(\text{anode})$$

Of all the elements, fluorine is the most reactive and the most electronegative (a measure of tendency to acquire electrons). In its chemically combined form, it always has an oxidation number of –1. Fluorine has numerous industrial uses, such as the manufacture of UF_6, a gas used to enrich uranium in its fissionable isotope, uranium-235. Fluorine is used to manufacture uranium hexafluoride, SF_6, a dielectric material contained in some electrical and electronic apparatus. A number of organic compounds contain fluorine, particularly the chlorofluorocarbons used as refrigerants and organofluorine polymers, such as DuPont's Teflon.

Given elemental fluorine's extreme chemical reactivity, it is not surprising that F_2 is quite toxic. It is classified as "a most toxic irritant." It strongly attacks skin and the mucous membranes of the nose and eyes.

Chlorine

Elemental chlorine, Cl_2 (mp, –101°C; bp, –34.5°C), is a greenish yellow gas that is produced industrially in large quantities for numerous uses, such as the production of organochlorine solvents and water disinfection. Liquified Cl_2 is shipped in large quantities in railway tank cars, and human exposure to chlorine from transportation accidents is not uncommon.

Chlorine was the original poison gas used in World War I. It is a strong oxidant and reacts with water to produce an acidic oxidizing solution by the following reactions:

$$Cl_2 + H_2O \rightleftarrows HCl + HOCl$$

$$Cl_2 + H_2O \rightleftarrows 2HCl + \{O\}$$

where HOCl is oxidant hypochlorous acid and {O} stands for nascent oxygen (in a chemical sense regarded as freshly generated, highly reactive oxygen atoms). When chlorine reacts in the moist tissue lining the respiratory tract, the effect is quite damaging to the tissue. Levels of 10 to 20 ppm of chlorine gas in air cause immediate irritation to the respiratory tract, and brief exposure to 1000 ppm of Cl_2 can be fatal. Because of its intensely irritating properties, chlorine is not an insidious poison, and exposed individuals will rapidly seek to get away from the source if they are not immediately overcome by the gas.

Bromine

Bromine, Br_2 (mp, –7.3°C; bp, 58.7°C), is a dark red liquid prepared commercially from elemental chlorine and bromide ion in bromide brines by the reaction

$$Cl_2 + 2Br^- \rightarrow 2Cl^- + Br_2$$

and the elemental bromine product is swept from the reaction mixture with steam. The major use of elemental bromine is for the production of organobromine compounds such as 1,1-dibromoethane, formerly widely used as a grain and soil fumigant for insect control and as a component of leaded gasoline for scavenging lead from engine cylinders.

Bromine is toxic when inhaled or ingested. Like chlorine and fluorine, it is an irritant to the respiratory tract and eyes because it attacks their mucous membranes. Pulmonary edema may result from severe bromine poisoning. The severely irritating nature of bromine causes a withdrawal response in its presence, thereby limiting exposure.

Iodine

Elemental iodine, I_2 (solid, sublimes at 184°C), consists of violet-black rhombic crystals with a lustrous metallic appearance. More irritating to the lungs than bromine or chlorine, its general effects are similar to the effects of these elements. Exposure to iodine is limited by its low vapor pressure, compared to liquid bromine or gaseous chlorine or fluorine.

Radionuclides

Radon

The toxicological effects of ionizing radiation are mentioned, and radon is cited as a source of such radiation. Radon can pose very distinct health risks. Radon's toxicity is not the result of its chemical properties, because it is a noble gas and does not enter into any normal chemical reactions. However, it is a radioactive element (radionuclide) that emits positively charged alpha particles, the largest and — when emitted inside the body — the most damaging form of radioactivity. Furthermore, the products of the radioactive decay of radon are also alpha emitters. Alpha particles emitted from a radionuclide in the lung cause damage to cells lining the lung bronchi and other tissues, resulting in processes that can cause cancer.

Radon is a decay product of radium, which in turn is produced by the radioactive decay of uranium. During its brief lifetime, radon may diffuse upward through soil and into dwellings through cracks in basement floors. Radioactive decay products of radon become attached to particles in indoor air, are inhaled, and lodge in the lungs until they undergo radioactive decay, damaging lung tissue. Synergistic effects between radon and smoking appear to be responsible for most of the cases of cancer associated with radon exposure.

Radium

A second radionuclide to which humans are likely to be exposed is *radium*, Ra. Occupational exposure to radium is known to have caused cancers in humans, most tragically in the cases of a number of young women who were exposed to radium because of their employment in painting luminescent radium-containing paint on the dials of watches, clocks, and instruments. These workers would touch their tongues with the very fine brushes used for the radioactive paint in order to "point" the brushes. Many eventually developed bone cancer and died from this malady.

The most likely route for human exposures to low doses of radium is through drinking water. Areas in the U.S. where significant radium contamination of water has been observed include the uranium-producing regions of the western U.S., Iowa, Illinois, Wisconsin, Missouri, Minnesota, Florida, North Carolina, Virginia, and the New England states.

The maximum contaminant level (MCL) for total radium (^{226}Ra plus ^{228}Ra) in drinking water is specified by the U.S. Environmental Protection Agency as 5 pCi/l, where a picocurie is 0.037 disintegrations per second. Perhaps as many as several hundred municipal water supplies in the U.S. exceed this level and require additional treatment to remove radium. Fortunately, conventional water-softening processes, which are designed to take out excessive levels of calcium, are relatively efficient in removing radium from water.

Fission products

The anthropogenic radionuclides of most concern are those produced as fission products from nuclear weapons and nuclear reactors. The most devastating release from the latter source to date resulted from the April 26, 1986, explosion, partial meltdown of the reactor core, and breach of confinement structures by a power reactor at Chernobyl in the Ukraine. This disaster released 5×10^7 Ci of radionuclides from the site, which contaminated large areas of Soviet Ukraine and Byelorussia, as well as areas of Scandinavia, Italy, France, Poland, Turkey, and Greece. Radioactive fission products that are the same or similar to elements involved in life processes can be particularly hazardous. One of these is radioactive iodine, which tends to accumulate in the thyroid gland, which may develop cancer or otherwise be damaged as a result. Radioactive cesium exists as the Cs^+ ion and is similar to sodium and potassium in its physiological behavior. Radioactive strontium forms the Sr^{2+} ion and substitutes for Ca^{2+}, especially in bone.

7

Natural Products Toxicity

Toxic natural products are poisons produced by organisms. They include an enormous variety of materials, including animal venoms and poisons, bacterial toxins, protozoal toxins, algal toxins, mycotoxins (from fungi), and plant toxins. These substances may affect a number of organs and tissues in humans, including the skin, heart, liver, kidney, neurological system, immune system, and gastrointestinal system. Some such substances may be hypnotic or psychotropic; others are carcinogenic.

Perhaps the most acutely toxic substance known is the botulism toxin, produced by the anaerobic bacterium *Clostridium botulinum* and responsible for many food poisoning deaths, especially from improperly canned food. Mycotoxins generated by fungi (molds) can cause a number of human maladies, and some of these materials, such as the aflatoxins, are carcinogenic to some animals. Venoms from wasps, spiders, scorpions, and reptiles—consisting of an exotic variety of biomolecules, including low-molecular-mass polypeptides, proteins, enzymes, steroids, lipids, 5-HT, and glycosides—can be fatal to humans. Each year, in the Orient, tetrodotoxin from improperly prepared puffer fish makes this dish the last delicacy consumed by some unfortunate diners. The stories of Socrates' execution from being forced to drink an extract of the deadly poisonous spotted hemlock plant and Cleopatra's suicide at the fangs of a venomous asp are rooted in antiquity. Many household poisonings result from children ingesting toxic plant leaves or berries. High on this list is philodendron. Other plants that may be involved in poisonings include diefenbachia, jade plant, wandering Jew, Swedish ivy, pokeweed, string of pearls, and yew. Pollen from plants causes widespread misery from allergies, and reactions to toxins from plants such as poison ivy can be severe.

Living organisms wage chemical warfare against their potential predators and prey with a fascinating variety of chemical substances. Some organisms produce toxic metabolic by-products that have no obvious use to the organisms that make them. This chapter briefly describes some of the toxic natural products from living organisms, with emphasis on those that are toxic to humans.

A few distinctions should be made at this point that apply particularly to animals. A *poisonous organism* is one that produces toxins. A *poisonous animal* may contain toxins in its tissues that act as poisons to other animals that eat its flesh. *Venoms* are poisons that can be delivered without the need for the organism to be eaten. *Venomous animals* can deliver poisons to another animal by means such as biting (usually striking with fangs) or stinging. The puffer fish—some tissues of which are deadly when ingested—is a poisonous animal, whereas the rattlesnake is a venomous one, although its flesh may be eaten safely. Some organisms—notoriously, the skunk—wage chemical warfare by emitting substances that are not notably toxic, but still effective in keeping predators away. Perhaps these organisms should be classified as noxious species.

Toxic Substances from Bacteria

Bacteria are sources of a number of toxic substances, including botulinus toxin, which is arguably the most deadly substance known. The two greatest concerns regarding toxic substances from bacteria are their roles in causing symptoms of bacterial disease and food poisoning. It is useful to consider as one class those bacteria that produce toxins that adversely affect a host in which the bacteria are growing, and as another class those bacteria that produce toxins to which another organism is subsequently exposed, such as by ingestion.

Bacteria are single-celled microorganisms that may grow in colonies and are shaped as spheres, rods, or spirals. They are usefully classified with respect to their need for oxygen, which accepts electrons during the metabolic oxidation of food substances, such as organic matter. *Aerobic bacteria* require molecular oxygen to survive, whereas *anaerobic bacteria* grow in the absence of oxygen, which may be toxic to them. *Facultative bacteria* can grow either aerobically or anaerobically. Anaerobic bacteria and facultative bacteria functioning anaerobically use substances other than molecular O_2 as electron acceptors (oxidants that take electrons away from other reactants in a chemical reaction). For example, sulfate takes the place of O_2 in the anaerobic degradation of organic matter (represented as $\{CH_2O\}$) by

Desulfovibrio, yielding toxic hydrogen sulfide (H_2S) as a product, as shown by the following overall reaction:

$$SO_4^{2-} + 2\{CH_2O\} + 2H^+ \rightarrow H_2S + 2CO_2 + 2H_2O$$

Toxicants such as H_2S produced by microorganisms are usually not called microbial toxins, a term that more properly refers to usually proteinaceous species of high molecular mass synthesized metabolically by microorganisms and capable of inducing a strong response in susceptible organisms at low concentrations. Bacteria and other microorganisms do produce a variety of poisonous substances, such as acetaldehyde, formaldehyde, and putrescine. The proteinaceous toxins produced by bacteria act in a number of ways, including effects on enzymes, detrimental interactions with cell surfaces, and food poisoning.

In Vivo Bacterial Toxins

Some important bacterial toxins are produced in the host and have a detrimental effect on the host. For example, such toxins are synthesized by *Clostridium tetani*, common soil bacteria that enter the body largely through puncture wounds.

The toxin from this bacterium interferes with neurotransmitters, such as acetylcholine, causing *tetanus*, commonly called lockjaw. Abnormal populations or strains of *Shigella dysenteriae* bacteria in the body can cause a severe form of dysentery, hemorrhagic colitis, and hemolytic uremic syndrome, releasing a toxin that causes intestinal hemorrhaging and gastrointestinal tract paralysis. These shiga toxins, which are also produced by some strains of the common intestinal bacteria *Escherichia coli*, possess structural groups that bind with cell surfaces and an enzymatically active component that enters the cell and inhibits protein synthesis. Toxin-releasing bacteria responsible for the most common form of food poisoning are those of the genus *Salmonella*. Victims are afflicted with flu-like symptoms and may even die from the effects of the toxin. Other bacteria that cause many cases of food poisoning include *Staphylococcus aureus* and *Clostridium perfringens*. Diphtheria is caused by a toxin generated by *Cornybacterium diphtheriae*. The toxin interferes with protein synthesis and is generally destructive to tissue.

Toxic shock syndrome

Toxic shock syndrome is a very damaging, often fatal condition caused by toxins from *Staphylococcus aureus* or *Streptococcus pyogenes*. First reported in children in 1978, it is manifested by high fever, erythroderma (a skin rash condition), and severe diarrhea. Patients may exhibit confusion, hypotension, and tachycardia, and they may go into shock with failure of several organs. Survivors often suffer from skin desquamation (flaky skin).

In 1980, toxic shock syndrome in menstruating women was linked to the use of a new superabsorbent tampon that altered the vaginal environment, including sequestration of magnesium ion, in a way that greatly increased susceptibility to the infection. The tampons were quickly withdrawn from the market, and now most cases occur in surgical patients infected by the bacteria that cause the syndrome.

The bacterial toxins responsible for toxic shock syndrome are proteins that are classified as superantigens. These proteins bypass some of the steps normally involved in antigen-mediated immune response, thereby activating 5 to 30% of the T cell population, compared to 0.01 to 0.1% activated by conventional antigens. The consequence of the huge numbers of activated T cells is release of cytokines that cause capillaries to leak, resulting in many of the symptoms of the syndrome.

Bacterial Toxins Produced Outside the Body

The most notorious toxin produced by bacteria outside the body is that of *Clostridium botulinum*. This kind of bacteria grows naturally in soil and on vegetable material. Under anaerobic or slightly aerobic conditions, it synthesizes an almost unbelievably toxic product. The conditions for generating this toxin most commonly occur as the result of the improper canning of food, particularly vegetables. Botulinum toxin binds irreversibly to nerve terminals, preventing the release of acetylcholine; the affected muscle acts as though the nerve were disconnected. The toxin actually consists of several polypeptides in the range of 200,000 to 400,000 molecular mass. Fortunately, these proteins are inactivated by heating for a sufficient time at 80 to 100°C. Botulinum poisoning symptoms appear within 12 to 36 h after ingestion, beginning with gastrointestinal tract disorders and progressing through neurologic symptoms, paralysis of the respiratory muscles, and death by respiratory failure.

MYCOTOXINS

Mycotoxins are toxic secondary metabolites from fungi that have a wide range of structures and a variety of toxic effects. Human and animal exposure to mycotoxins usually results from ingestion of food upon which fungal molds have grown. Among the many kinds of molds that produce mycotoxins are *Aspergillus flavus*, *Fusarium*, *Trichoderma*,

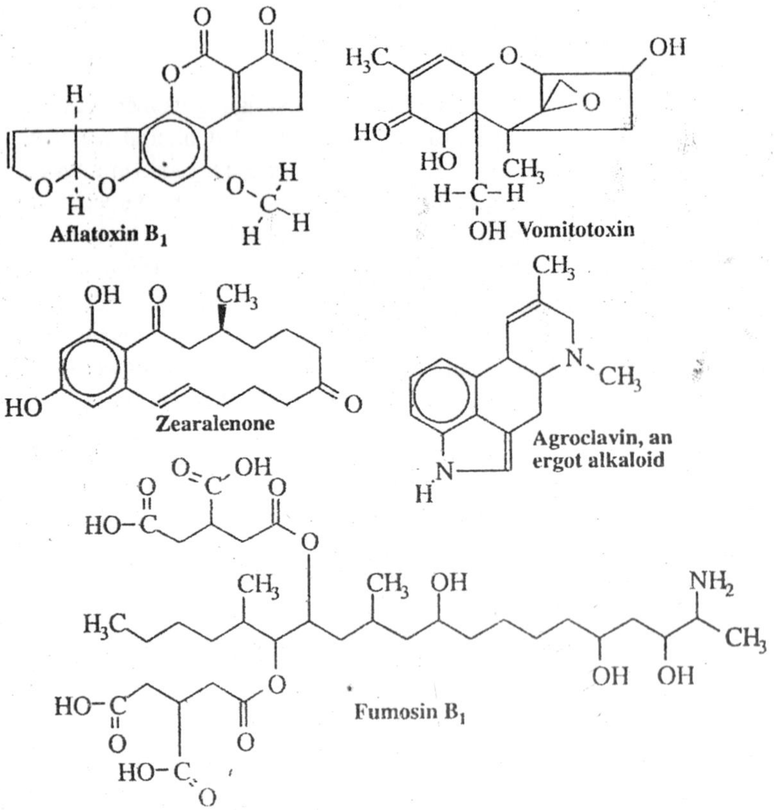

Fig. 7.1. Representative compounds of the large number of mycotoxins produced as secondary metabolites by fungi.

Aspergillus, and *Penicillium*. Perhaps the most well-known mycotoxins are the *aflatoxins* produced by *Aspergillus*. These molds grow on a variety of food products, including corn, cereal grains, rice, apples, peanuts, and milk. Other mycotoxins include ergot alkaloids, ochratoxins, fumonisins, trichothecenes, tremorgenic toxins, satratoxin, zearalenone, and vomitotoxin. Humans and other animals suffer from a variety of ill effects resulting from exposure to mycotoxins. Monogastric (single stomach) animals are relatively more susceptible to adverse effects from toxin ingestion, whereas the rumen microbiota (bacteria) in the digestive systems of ruminant animals tend to reduce the toxicity of mycotoxins to ruminants.

Adverse human health effects of mycotoxins have occurred during times of short food supply when substandard grain has been consumed for food. One such case occurred in the vicinity of Orenburg in Siberia in 1944 during World War II. Harvest delayed by the war resulted in contamination of barley, millet, and wheat by trichothecenes. Humans that later consumed the grain were afflicted with a number of disorders, including gastrointestinal maladies, internal hemorrhaging, and severe skin rash; about 10% of those afflicted died. Another major class of mycotoxins consists of the *ergot alkaloids* from *Claviceps*. Several genera of *fungi imperfecti* produce toxic tricothecenes.

Aflatoxins

The most common source of aflatoxins is moldy food, particularly nuts, some cereal grains, and oil seeds. The most notorious of the aflatoxins is aflatoxin B_1. Produced by *Aspergillus niger*, it is a potent liver toxin and liver carcinogen in some species. It is metabolized in the liver to an epoxide. The product is electrophilic with a strong tendency to bond covalently to protein, DNA, and RNA. Other common aflatoxins produced by molds are those designated by the letters B_2, G_1, G_2, and M_1.

Other Mycotoxins

The ergot alkaloids have been associated with a number of spectacular outbreaks of central nervous system disorders, sometimes called *ergotism*. St. Anthony's fire is an example of convulsive ergotism. From examination of historical records, it is now known that outbreaks of this malady resulted for the most part from ingestion of moldy grain products. Although ergotism is now virtually unknown in humans, it still occurs in livestock.

Trichothecenes are composed of 40 or more structurally related compounds produced by a variety of molds, including *Cephalosporium*, *Fusarium*, *Myrothecium*, and *Trichoderma*, which grow predominantly on grains. Much of the available information on human toxicity of trichothecenes was obtained from an outbreak of poisoning in Siberia in 1944, mentioned above.

Several species of *Fusarium* that commonly grow on barley, corn, wheat, and other grains produce zearalenone. This toxic substance binds with the estrogenic receptor in animals, causing a variety of adverse estrogenic effects. These include enlarged uteri, infertility, reabsorption of the fetus, and vaginal prolapse.

Mushroom Toxins

Mushrooms are spore-forming bodies of filamentous terrestrial fungi, some of which are considered to be food delicacies, whereas others, such as *Amanita phalloides*, *Amanita virosa*, and *Gyromita esculenta*, are very toxic, with reported worldwide deaths of the order of 100 per year. In extreme cases, one bite of one poisonous mushroom can be fatal. Accidental mushroom poisonings are often caused by the death's head mushroom, because it is easily mistaken for edible varieties.

Some toxins in mushrooms are alkaloids that cause central nervous system effects of narcosis and convulsions. Hallucinations occur in subjects who have eaten mushrooms that contain *psilocybin*. The toxic alkaloid *muscarine* is present in some mushrooms.

Another class of toxins produced by some mushrooms consists of polypeptides, particularly amanitin and phalloidin. These substances are stable to heating (cooking). They are systemic poisons that attack cells of various organs, including the heart and liver. In early 1988, an organ transplant was performed on a woman in the U.S. to replace her liver, which was badly damaged from the ingestion of wild mushrooms that she and a companion had mistakenly identified as edible varieties and consumed.

The symptoms of mushroom poisoning vary. Typical early symptoms involve the gastrointestinal tract and include stomach pains and cramps, nausea, vomiting, and diarrhea. Victims in the second phase of severe poisoning may suffer paralysis, delirium, and coma, along with often severe liver damage.

Edible *Coprinus atramentarius* mushrooms produce an interesting ethanol-sensitizing effect similar to that of disulfiram. Ingestion of alcohol can cause severe reactions in individuals up to several days after having eaten this kind of mushroom.

Toxins from Protozoa

Protozoa are microscopic animals consisting of single eukaryotic cells and classified on the bases of morphology, means of locomotion, presence or absence of chloroplasts, presence or absence of shells, and ability to form cysts. Several devastating human diseases, including malaria, sleeping sickness, and some kinds of dysentery, are caused by parasitic protozoa. Parasitic protozoa can cause debilitating, even fatal, diseases in livestock and wildlife.

Toxic substances from two of the major types of unicellular protista —bacteria and fungi—were discussed in the preceding sections. Protozoans are also notable for the production of toxic substances. Most of the protozoans that produce toxins belong to the order

Dinoflagellata, which predominantly consists of marine species. The cells of these organisms are enclosed in cellulose envelopes, which often have beautiful patterns on them. Among the effects caused by toxins from these organisms are gastrointestinal, respiratory, and skin disorders in humans; mass kills of various marine animals; and paralytic conditions caused by eating infested shellfish.

The marine growth of dinoflagellates is characterized by occasional incidents in which they multiply at such an explosive rate that they color the water yellow, olive green, or red by their vast numbers. In 1946, some sections of the Florida coast became so afflicted by "red tide" that the water became viscous, and for many miles the beaches were littered with the remains of dead fish, shellfish, turtles, and other marine organisms. The sea spray in these areas became so irritating that coastal schools and resorts were closed.

The greatest danger to humans from dinoflagellata toxins comes from the ingestion of shellfish, such as mussels and clams, that have accumulated the protozoa from sea water. In this form the toxic material is called paralytic shellfish poison. As little as 4 mg of this toxin, the amount found in several severely infested mussels or clams, can be fatal to a human. The toxin depresses respiration and affects the heart, resulting in complete cardiac arrest in extreme cases.

One of the most damaging dinoflagellates in recent years has been *Pfiestria piscicida*, an organism that thrives in polluted estuarine waters enriched in nutrients from fertilizers, feedlot runoff, and sewage. This organism has been responsible for massive fish kills in estuary regions of the Atlantic, especially North Carolina's Albermarle–Pamlico Estuary. It releases a toxin of unknown chemical structure in the presence of fish, disabling and killing fish and enabling their attack by *Pfiestria*. Humans studying this phenomenon were themselves afflicted by the toxin, through either contact with contaminated water or inhalation of spray from such water. The victims suffered acute eye and respiratory irritation with concurrent fatigue and headaches. They also suffered from nausea, stomach cramps, and vomiting characteristic of gastrointestinal disorders. *Pfiestria piscicida* is a remarkable organism that takes on numerous forms during its life cycle. It is highly opportunistic, and when fish are not available for food, it will even retain chloroplasts from ingested algae (kleptochloroplasts) within a large food vacuole in the *Pfiestria piscicida* cell, where the chloroplasts can function for several days, providing nutrients to their hosts.

Toxic Substances from Plants

Various plants produce a wide range of toxic substances, as reflected by plant names such as deadly nightshade and poison hemlock. Although the use of "*poison arrows*" having tips covered with plant-derived curare has declined as the tribes that employed them have acquired the sometimes dubious traits of modern civilization, poisoning by plants is still of concern in the grazing of ruminant animals, and houseplants such as philodendron and yew are responsible for poisoning some children. Taxol from the western yew tree is a neurotoxin, but

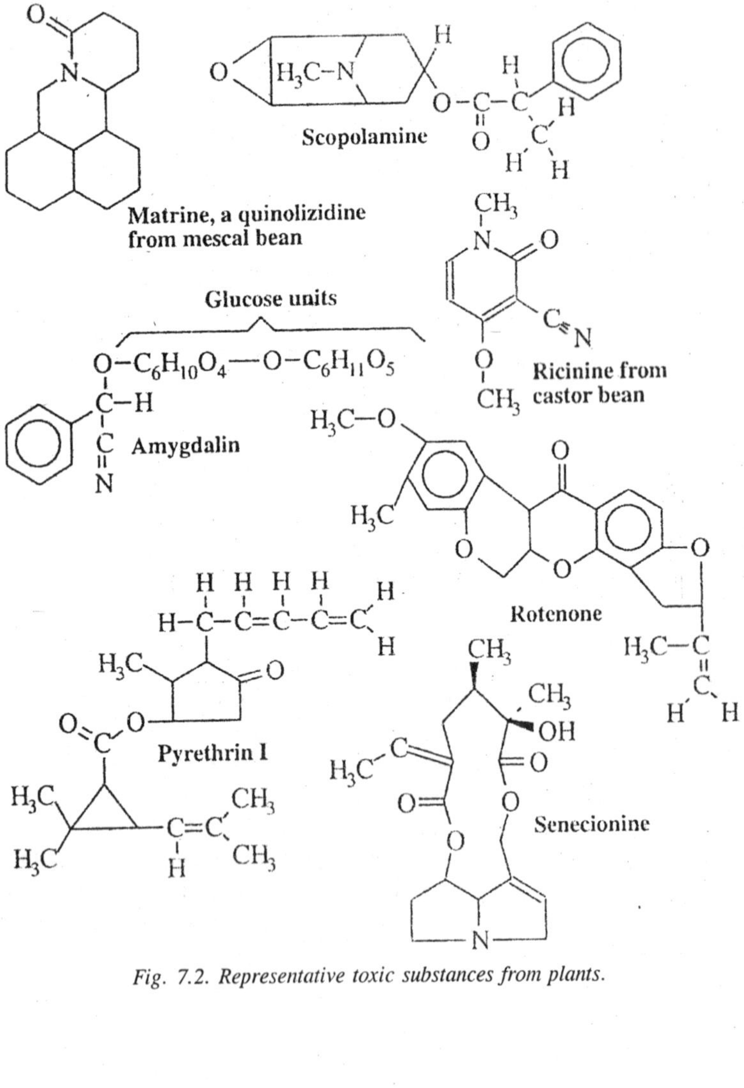

Fig. 7.2. Representative toxic substances from plants.

has proven to be a useful chemotherapeutic agent for the treatment of breast cancer. Plant-derived cocaine causes many deaths among those who use it or get into fatal disputes marketing it.

Toxic substances from plants are discussed here in five categories: nerve poisons, internal organ poisons, skin and eye irritants, allergens, and metal (mineral) accumulators. Plant toxins have a variety of chemical structures. Prominent among the chemical classes of toxicants synthesized by plants are nitrogen-containing alkaloids, which usually occur in plants as salts. Some harmful plant compounds undergo metabolic reactions to form toxic substances. For example, amygdalin, present in the meats of fruit seeds such as those of apples and peaches, undergoes acid hydrolysis in the stomach or enzymatic hydrolysis elsewhere in the body to yield toxic HCN.

Extracts from the castor bean can be used to isolate ricin, an extremely potent poison that is one of the leading candidates for use by terrorists. Ricin is a large-molecule, heterogeneous protein.

Pyrrolizidine alkaloids in the plant *Senecio vernalis* have been implicated in the poisoning of cattle. The toxic agents in this plant include three closely related alkaloids—senecionine, senkirkin, and seneciphyllin.

Nerve Toxins from Plants

Nerve toxins from plants cause a variety of central nervous and peripheral nervous system effects. Several examples are cited here.

Plant-derived *neurotoxic psychodysleptics* affect peripheral neural functions and motor coordination, sometimes accompanied by delirium, stupor, trance states, and vomiting. Prominent among these toxins are the pyrollizidines from peyote. Also included are erythriononones from the coral tree and quinolizidines from the mescal bean.

A plant neurotoxin that is receiving much current publicity because of its effectiveness in the chemotherapeutic treatment of at least one form of cancer is *taxol*, a complex molecule that belongs to the class of taxine alkaloids. Taxol occurs in most tissues of *Taxus breviofolia*, the western yew tree, and is isolated from the bark of that tree (once considered a nuisance tree in forestry, but in short supply following discovery of the therapeutic value of taxol until alternate sources were developed). Ingestion of taxol causes a number of neurotoxic effects, including sensory neuropathy, nausea and gastrointestinal disturbances, and impaired respiration and cardiac function. It also causes blood disorders (leukopenia and thrombocytopenia). The mechanism of taxol neurotoxicity involves binding to tubulin, a protein involved in the assembly of microtubules, which assemble and dissociate as part of cell function. This binding of tubulin in nerve cell microtubules stabilizes the microtubules and prevents their dissociation, which can be detrimental to normal nerve cell function.

Spotted hemlock contains the alkaloid nerve toxin coniine. Ingestion of this poison is followed within about 15 min by symptoms of nervousness, trembling, arrythmia, and bradycardia. Body temperature may decrease and fatal paralysis can occur. The nightshade family of plants contains edible potato, tomato, and eggplant. However, it also contains the deadly night-shade, or *Atropa Belladonna* (beautiful woman). This toxic plant contains scopolamine and atropine. Ingestion causes dizziness, mydriasis, speech loss, and delirium. Paralysis can occur. Fatally poisoned victims may expire within half an hour of ingesting the poison.

Several nerve toxins produced by plants are interesting because of their insecticidal properties. Insecticidal nicotine is extracted from tobacco. Rotenone is synthesized by almost 70 legumes. This insecticidal compound is safe for most mammals, with the notable exception of swine. The most significant insecticidal plant derivatives, however, are the pyrethrins, discussed below.

Tall larkspur, a plant of the genus *Delphinium* of the buttercup family growing in the mountain ranges of the western U.S., produces more than 40 alkaloids. The alkaloids in these plants are the largest source of plant poisonings of livestock on mountain rangelands in the western U.S.

Pyrethrins and pyrethroids

Pyrethrins and their synthetic analogs represent both the oldest and newest of insecticides. Extracts of dried chrysanthemum or pyrethrum flowers, which contain pyrethrin I and II, jasmolin I and II, and cinerin I and II, have been known for their insecticidal properties for a long time, and may have even been used as botanical insecticides in China almost 2000 years ago. The most important commerical sources of insecticidal pyrethrins are pyrethrum flowers (*Chrysanthemum cinerariaefolium*) grown in Kenya, which produces about 7000 tons of pyrethrin each year. Production does not meet demand, and research is actively under way to biosynthesize natural pyrethrins from plant cell cultures and with genetically engineered organisms. Pyrethrins have several advantages as insecticides, including facile enzymatic degradation, which makes them relatively safe for mammals, ability to rapidly paralyze (knock down) flying insects, and good biodegradability characteristics.

Synthetic analogs of the pyrethrins, *pyrethroids*, have been widely produced as insecticides during recent years. The first of these was allethrin. Three pyrethroids that are relatively safe and can be used on cereal crops are fluvalinate, zeta-cypermethrin, and deltametrin.

Pyrethroids act as neurotoxins that cause excitation of the nervous system. Organisms may become hypersensitive to stimuli and experience paresthesia (abnormal sensations of burning or prickling of

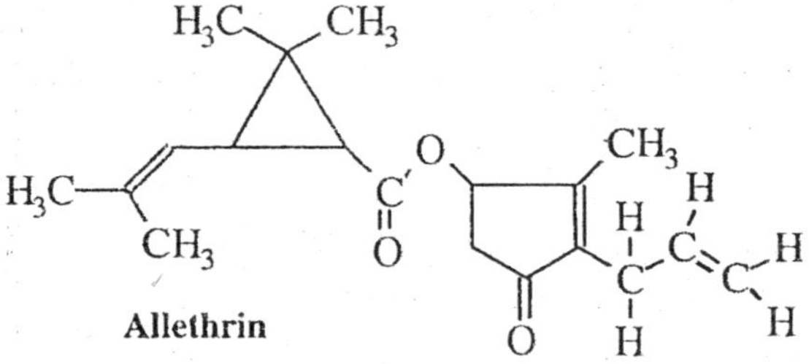

Allethrin

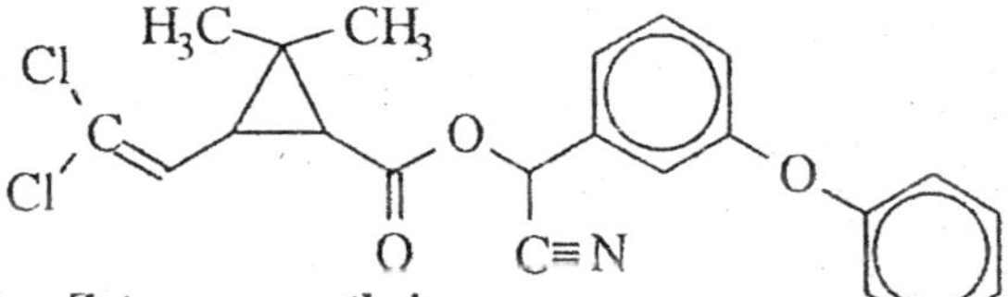

Zeta-cypermethrin

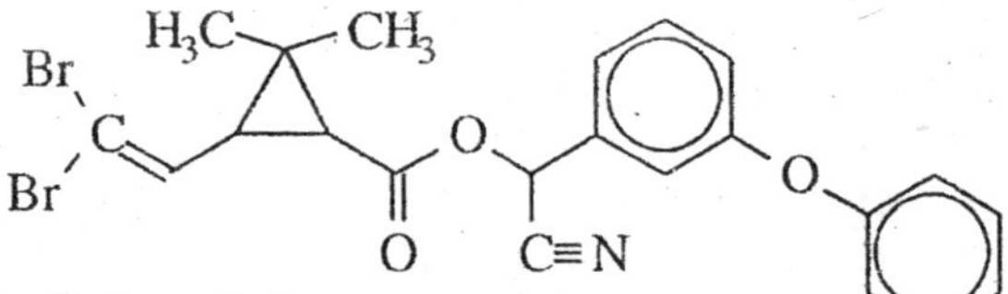

Deltamethrin

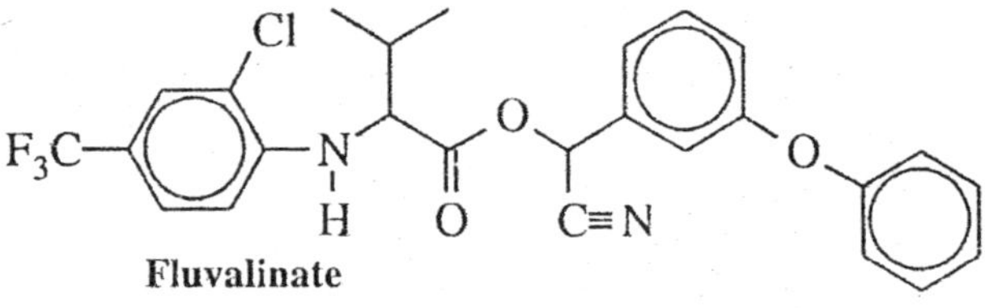

Fluvalinate

Fig. 7.3. Four synthetic pyrethroids with insecticidal properties similar to those of the natural pyrethrins.

the skin). Tremors and salivation are common symptoms of mammals exposed to toxic levels of pyrethroids.

Internal Organ Plant Toxins

Toxins from plants may affect internal organs, such as the heart, kidney, liver, and stomach. Because of their very different digestive systems involving multiple stomachs, ruminant animals may react differently to these toxins than do monogastric animals.

Eye and Skin Irritants

Anyone who has been afflicted by poison ivy, poison oak, or poison sumac appreciates the high potential that some plant toxins have to irritate skin and eyes. The toxic agents in the plants just mentioned are catechol compounds, such as urishikiol in poison ivy. Contact with the poison causes a characteristic skin rash that may be disabling and very persistent in heavily exposed, sensitive individuals. Lungs may be affected—often by inhalation of smoke from the burning plants—to the extent that hospitalization is required. Photosensitizers constitute a class of systemic plant poisons capable of affecting areas other than those exposed. These pigmented substances may pass through the liver without being conjugated and collect in skin capillaries. When these areas of the skin are subsequently exposed to light, the capillaries leak. (Since light is required, the phenomenon is called a photosensitized condition.) In severe cases, tissue and hair are sloughed off. St. John's wort or horsebrush causes this kind of condition in farm animals.

Allergens

Many plants are notorious for producing allergens that cause allergic reactions in sensitized individuals. The most common plant allergens consist of pollen. The process that leads to an allergic reaction starts when the allergen, acting as a hapten, combines with an endogenous protein in the body to form an antigen. Antibodies are generated that react with the antigen and produce histamine, resulting in an allergic reaction. The severity of the symptoms varies with the amount of histamine produced. These symptoms can include skin rash, watery eyes, and runny nose. In severe cases, victims suffer fatal anaphylactic shock. An example of an allergic reaction to a plant product—all too familiar to many of its victims—is hay fever induced by the pollen of ragweed or goldenrod.

Mineral Accumulators

Some plants classified as mineral accumulators become toxic because of the inorganic materials that they absorb from soil and water and retain in the plant biomass. An important example of such a plant is *Astragalus*, sometimes called *locoweed*. This plant causes serious problems in some western U.S. grazing areas because it accumulates selenium. Animals that eat too much of it get selenium poisoning, characterized by anemia and a condition known descriptively as "*blind staggers*."

Nitrate accumulation may occur in plants growing on soil fertilized with nitrate under moisture-deficient conditions. In the stomachs of ruminant animals, nitrate (NO_3^-) ingested with plant material is reduced to nitrite (NO_2^-). The nitrite product enters the bloodstream and oxidizes the iron(II) in hemoglobin to iron(III). Another toxicological problem that can result from excessive nitrate in plant material is the generation of toxic nitrogen dioxide gas during the fermentation of ensilage composed of chopped plant matter contaminated with nitrate. The toxic effect of NO_2 from this source has been called *silo-filler's disease*.

Toxic Algae

Photosynthetic algae that live in water can produce toxic substances. These are usually manifested during so-called algae blooms characterized by a rapid increase in the numbers of algae. Typical of such outbreaks was a February and March 2002 infestation of *Dinophysis acuminata* in the Potomac River and its Virginia tributaries. Toxic algae may accumulate in shellfish and cause diarrhetic shellfish poisoning in people who eat the contaminated shellfish. The toxins that cause this condition consist of fiendishly complicated molecules. They include okadaic acid ($C_{44}H_{68}O_{13}$), pectenotoxin ($C_{47}H_{68}O_{16}$), dinophysistoxin ($C_{45}H_{70}O_{13}$), and yessotoxin ($C_{55}H_{82}O_{21}S_2$).

Reef barrier fish, including barracuda, grouper, red snapper, and sea bass, may accumulate toxic levels of ciguatoxin produced by ciguetera algae. Problems from this toxin have occurred in the Caribbean and in some areas of the Indian and Pacific Oceans. The toxin is insidious and gives no warning by taste or odor. Cooking does not destroy it. Symptoms of ciguatoxin poisoning include gastrointestinal effects of diarrhea, vomiting, and abdominal pain; tingling sensation in the mouth; pain, tingling, and weakness in the legs; and hot–cold sensation reversal.

Insect Toxins

Although relatively few insect species produce enough toxin to endanger humans, insects cause more fatal poisonings in the U.S. each year than do all other venomous animals combined. Most venomous insects are from the order *Hymenoptera*, which includes ants, bees, hornets, wasps, and yellow jackets. These insects deliver their toxins by a stinging mechanism.

Chemically, the toxic substances produced by insects are variable and have been incompletely characterized. In general, hymenopteran venoms are composed of water-soluble, nitrogen-containing chemical species in concentrated mixtures. Although they contain chemical compounds in common, the compositions of insect venoms from different species are variable. The three major types of chemical species are biologically synthesized (biogenic) amines, peptides and small proteins, and enzymes. Of the biogenic amines, the most common is histamine, which is found in the venoms of bees, wasps, and hornets. Wasp and hornet venoms contain serotonin, and hornet venom contains the biogenic amine acetylcholine. Among the peptides and low-molecular-mass proteins in insect venoms are apamin, mellitin, and mast cell degranulating peptide in bee venom, and kinin in wasp and hornet venoms. Enzymes contained in bee, wasp, and hornet venoms are phospholipase A and hyaluronidase. Phospholipase B occurs in wasp and hornet venoms.

Bee Venom

Bee venom contains a greater variety of proteinaceous materials than do wasp and hornet venoms. Apamin in bee venom is a polypeptide containing 18 amino acids and having three disulfide (–SS–) bridges in its structure. Because of these bridges and its small size, the apamine molecule is able to traverse the blood–brain barrier and function as a central nervous system poison. Mellitin in bee venom consists of a chain of 27 amino acids. It can be a direct cause of erythrocyte hemolysis. Symptoms of bradycardia and arrythmia can be caused by mellitin. Mast cell degranulating peptide in bee venom acts on mast cells. These are a type of white blood cell believed to be involved in the production of heparin, a key participant in the blood-clotting process. The degranulating peptide causes mast cells to disperse, with an accompanying release of histamine into the system.

Wasp and Hornet Venoms

Wasp and hornet venoms are distinguished from bee venoms by their lower content of peptides. They contain kinin peptide, which may cause smooth muscle contraction and lowered blood pressure. Two biogenic amines in wasp and hornet venoms (serotonin and acetylcholine) lower blood pressure and cause pain. Acetylcholine may cause malfunction of heart and skeletal muscles.

Toxicities of Insect Venoms

The toxicities of insect venoms are low to most people. Despite this, relatively large numbers of fatalities occur each year from insect stings because of allergic reactions in sensitized individuals. These reactions can lead to potentially fatal anaphylactic shock, which affects the nervous system, cardiovascular function, and respiratory function. The agents in bee venom that are responsible for severe allergic reactions are mellitin and two enzymes of high molecular mass—hyaluronidase and phospholipase A-2.

Spider Toxins

There are about 30,000 species of spiders, virtually all of which produce venom. Fortunately, most lack dangerous quantities of venom or the means to deliver it. Nevertheless, about 200 species of spiders are significantly poisonous to humans. Many of these have colorful common names, such as tarantula, trap-door spider, black widow, giant crab spider, poison lady, and deadly spider.

Brown Recluse Spiders

Brown recluse spiders (*Loxosceles*) are of concern because of their common occurrence in households in temperate regions. Many people are bitten by this spider despite its nonaggressive nature. A brown spider bite can cause severe damage at the site of the injury. When this occurs, the tissue and underlying muscle around the bite undergo severe necrosis, leaving a gaping wound up to 10 cm across. Plastic surgery is often required in an attempt to repair the damage. In addition, *Loxosceles* venom may cause systemic effects, such as fever, vomiting, and nausea. In rare cases, death results. The venom of *Loxosceles* contains protein and includes enzymes. The mechanisms by which the venom produces lesions are not completely understood.

Widow Spiders

The widow spiders are *Latrodectus* species. Unlike the *Loxosceles* species described above, the bite sites from widow spiders show virtually no damage. The symptoms of widow spider poisoning are many and varied. They include pain, cramps, sweating, headache, dizziness, tremor, nausea, vomiting, and elevated blood pressure. The venom contains several proteins, including a proteinaceous neurotoxin with a molecular mass of about 130,000.

Other Spiders

Several other types of venomous spiders should be mentioned here. Running spiders (*Chiranthium* species) are noted for the tenacity with which they cling to the bite area, causing a sharply painful wound. The bites of cobweb spiders (*Steatoda* species) cause localized pain and tissue damage. Venomous jumping spiders (*Phidippus* species) produce a wheal (raised area) up to 5 cm across in the bite area.

Reptile Toxins

Snakes are the most notorious of the venomous animals. The names of venomous snakes suggest danger—Eastern diamondback rattlesnake, king cobra, black mamba, fer-de-lance, horned puff adder, *Crotalus horridus horridus*. About 10% of the approximately 3500 snake species are sufficiently venomous to be hazardous to humans. These may be divided among *Crotilidae* (including rattlesnakes, bushmaster, and fer-de-lance), *Elipidae* (including cobras, mambas, and coral snakes), *Hydrophidae* (true sea snakes), *Laticaudae* (sea kraits), and *Colubridae* (including the boomslang and Australian death adder). Although snake bites in the U.S. are generally regarded as more of a problem from former times in rural areas, they can be a very serious danger as human dwellings and activities intrude into the snakes' normal territories. In 2001, rattlesnake bites in Arizona approached record levels. Incidents were described in which victims had to be placed in intensive care, and one victim walking to the pool in his apartment complex was bitten on the foot by a baby rattlesnake.

Chemical Composition of Snake Venoms

Snake venoms are complex mixtures that may contain biogenic amines, carbohydrates, glycoproteins, lipids, and metal ions. The most important snake venom constituents, however, are proteins, including numerous enzymes. Approximately 25 different enzymes have been identified in various snake venoms.

The most prominent of the enzymes in snake venom are the proteolytic enzymes, which bring about the breakdown of proteins, thereby causing tissue to deteriorate. Some proteolytic enzymes are associated with hemorrhaging Collagen (connective tissue in tendons, skin, and bones) is broken down by collagenase enzyme contained in some snake venoms. Among the other kinds of enzymes that occur in snake venoms are hyaluronidase, arginine ester hydrolase, lactate dehydrogenase, DNase, L-amino acid oxidase, nucleotidase enzymes, RNase, phospholipase enzymes, phosphoesterase enzymes, and acetylcholinesterase.

Numerous nonenzyme polypeptides occur in snake venom. Some of these polypeptides, though by no means all, are neurotoxins.

Toxic Effects of Snake Venom

The effects of snake bite can range from relatively minor discomfort to almost instant death. The latter is often associated with drastically lowered blood pressure and shock. The predominant effects of snake venoms can be divided into two major categories: cardiotoxic and neurotoxic effects. Blood-clotting mechanisms may be affected by enzymes in snake venom, and blood vessels may be damaged as well. Almost all organs in the victims of poisoning by *Crotilidae* have exhibited adverse effects, many of which appear to be associated with changes in the blood and with alterations in the lung. Clumped blood cells and clots in blood vessels have been observed in the lungs of victims. These effects are caused in part by the action of thrombin-like enzymes, which are constituents of *Crotilidae* (e.g., copperheads, rattlesnakes, Chinese habu) and *Viperidae* (e.g., puff adders, European viper, Sahara sand viper) venoms. Thrombin-like enzymes cause the release of fibrinopeptides that result in fibrinogen clot formation. Agents in cobra toxin break down the blood–brain barrier by disrupting capillaries and cell membranes. So altered, the barrier loses its effectiveness in preventing the entry of other brain-damaging toxic agents.

Nonreptile Animal Toxins

Several major types of animals that produce poisonous substances have been considered so far in this chapter. With the exception of birds, all classes of the animal kingdom contain members that produce toxic substances. It has now been demonstrated that there are even birds that are "toxic." It is believed that such birds do not produce toxins but accumulate toxic alkaloids, including andromedotoxin, batrachotoxins, and cantheridin, from their diets and deposit these poisonous materials in their skin and feathers. Toxic animals not covered so far in this chapter are summarized here.

Numerous kinds of fish contain poisons in their organs and flesh. The most notorious of the poisonous fish are puffers and puffer-like fish that produce tetrodotoxin. This supertoxic substance is present in the liver and ovary of the fish. It acts on nerve cell membranes by affecting the passage of sodium ions, a process involved in generating nerve impulses. The fatality rate for persons developing clinical symptoms of tetrodotoxin poisoning is about 40%. Usually associated with Japan, puffer fish poisoning kills about 100 people per year globally. Some of these poisonings are self-inflicted by suicidal individuals.

Some fish are venomous and have means of delivering venom to other animals. This is accomplished, for example, by spines on weever fish. The infamous stingray has a serrated spine on its tail that can be used to inflict severe wounds, while depositing venom from specialized cells along the spine. The venom increases the pain from the wound and has systemic effects, especially on the cardiovascular system.

Numerous species of amphibia (frogs, toads, newts, salamanders) produce poisons, such as bufotenin, in specialized skin secretory glands. Most of these animals pose no hazard to humans. However, some of the toxins are extremely poisonous. For example, Central American Indian hunters have used hunting arrows tipped with poison from the golden arrow frog.

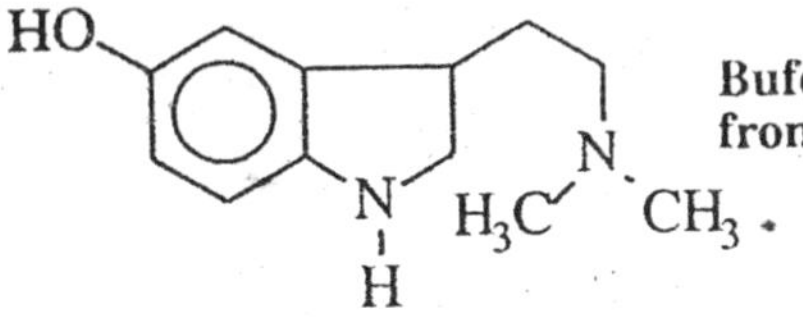

Bufotenin, a compound isolated from some amphibian toxins

In addition to the poisonous fish and sea snakes mentioned previously in this chapter, several other forms of marine life produce toxins. Among these are *Porifera*, or sponges, consisting of colonies of unicellular animals. The sponges release poisons to keep predators away. They may have sharp spicules that can injure human skin, while simultaneously exposing it to poison. Various species of the *Coelenterates*, including corals, jellyfish, and sea anenomes, are capable of delivering venom by stinging. Some of these venoms have highly neurotoxic effects. *Echinoderms*, exemplified by starfish, sea cucumbers, and sea urchins, may possess spines capable of delivering toxins. People injured by these spines often experience severe pain and other symptoms of poisoning. Various mollusks produce poisons, such as the poison contained in the liver of the abalone, *Haliotis*. Some mollusk poisons, such as those of the genus *Conus*, are delivered as venoms by a stinging mechanism.

Arthropods, which consist of a vast variety of invertebrate animals that have jointed legs and a segmented body, are notable for their production of toxins. Of the arthropods, insects and spiders were discussed earlier in this chapter. Some *scorpions*, arachnidal arthropods with nipper-equipped front claws and stinger-equipped long, curved, segmented tails, are notably venomous animals. The stings of scorpions, some of which reach a length of 8 in., are a very serious hazard, especially to children; most fatalities occur in children under age 3. In Mexico, the particularly dangerous scorpion *Centruroides suffusus* attains a length up to 9 cm. Mexico has had a particularly serious problem with fatal scorpion bites. During the two decades following 1940, it is estimated that over 20,000 deaths occurred from venomous scorpion stings. Some *centipedes* are capable of delivering venom by biting. The site becomes swollen, inflamed, and painful. Some millipedes secrete a toxic skin irritant when touched.

Although the greater hazard from ticks is their ability to carry human diseases, such as Rocky Mountain spotted fever or Lyme disease, some species discharge a venom that causes a condition called tick paralysis, characterized by weakness and lack of coordination. An infamous mite larva, the chigger, causes inflamed spots on the skin that itch badly. The chigger is so small that most people require a magnifying glass to see it, but a large number of chigger bites can cause intense misery in a victim.

8

Bio-Insecticides and Pesticides

Pesticides occupy a rather unique position among the many chemicals that man encounters daily, in that they are deliberately added to the environment for the purpose of killing or injuring some form of life. Ideally their injurious action would be highly specific for undesirable target organisms and noninjurious to desirable, nontarget organisms. In fact, however, most of he chemicals that are used as pesticides are not highly selective but are generally toxic to many nontarget species, including man, and other desirable forms of life that coinhabit the environment. Therefore, lacking highly selective pesticidal action, the application of pesticides must often be predicated on selecting quantities and manners of usage that will minimize the possibility of exposure of nontarget organisms to injurious quantities of these useful chemicals.

Toxicologic evaluations of the hazard of handling and use of pesticides have for many years focused primarily on preventing injury to man, and common laboratory animals have served as the experimental models for man's biochemical, physiologic, and pathologic responses to these chemicals. Problems of species differences in susceptibility have always left some doubt concerning assignment of safe dosages for man on the basis of studies on common laboratory animals, but this approach appears to have been reasonably successful in protecting the *general population* in that there has not emerged any clear association between increasing use of pesticides and incidence of chronic diseases. However, as discussed subsequently, occupational exposures have resulted in chronic or persistent neurologic disease states in the case of a few compounds.

Acute poisoning by pesticides do occur. They are usually the result of occupational exposures or of careless use, misuse, or mishandling the pesticides. The mortality rate attributed to poisoning by pesticides has been estimated at 0.65 per one million population in the United States, but it has also been estimated that there are 100 nonfatal poisonings for each fatal one. In spite of the fact that a clear association between chronic diseases and pesticide exposures is not apparent, new and sensitive toxicologic and analytic methods have raised many questions concerning the possibility to subtle effects that would be difficult to recognize unless one directed investigations specifically to reveal them. A review of the status of epidemiologic studies on pesticide toxicology pointed out design and interpretive pitfalls that give cause to question whether our knowledge is adequate to assess the degree of injury or lack of injury to man's health resulting from past or current uses of pesticides.

Furthermore, increased awareness and concern for ecologic implications of the use of pesticides have begun to direct the attention and research of toxicologists toward studies on wild species as well as on man and domestic animals and laboratory animals that are selected as test models to represent man. The toxicology of pesticides, therefore, must take into account problems relating to both their injurious effects directly upon man and their effects on other species of animals in the environment from which man derives pleasure as well as food or which are essential to maintain a proper ecologic balance.

It is not uncommon for people to equate *pesticides* with *insecticides*. This is erroneous since the term "pesticide" is a general classification and includes a variety of chemicals with different uses. Pesticides chemicals have in common the capability of destroying life of some forms and are classified as pesticides because the organisms against which they are directed are deemed to be undesirable by the person or society that applies them. Indeed, insecticides represent one group of pesticides that are used in large quantities and have a history of causing toxic effects in man, but among the other types of pesticides one can find several potent, injurious agents. In terms of quantities used, the *herbicides*, chemicals used to destroy unwanted plants, rival the insecticides. Another common misconception is that pesticides imply a unity of action, that they all act similarly. This of course is not true. There is as great a diversity in their types of action and primary target tissues as there is diversity in their chemistry and physicochemical properties. There are a large number of pesticides whose acute toxicity is manifested through functional or biochemical action in the central and peripheral nervous systems, but there are others in which nervous system involvement does not occur or is merely secondary to primary effects in other organ systems. The literature on pesticides reveals great disparities in the extent of knowledge concerning specific mechanisms of action. For some groups of compounds the mechanism of toxic action is well understood at the molecular level. For others there is essentially no information concerning mechanisms of toxicity. Similarly the full gamut of toxic dose-response ranges is represented by pesticide chemicals. Even within a similar chemical class, individual compounds ranging from extremely toxic to practically nontoxic may be found. Obviously, therefore, one cannot generalize either qualitatively or quantitatively concerning the toxicity of pesticides.

Economic and Public Health

As with the use of any potentially injurious chemical substance, the use of pesticides must take into consideration the balance of the benefits that maybe expected versus the possible risk of injury to human health or to degradation of environmental quality. It is indeed extremely difficult to quantify the risk-benefit equation relating to the use of pesticides. In some cases the prospect of mass starvation due to destruction of food crops by inserts and noxious weeds versus the question of possible injury to a few members of the population as a result of use of insecticides may clearly indicate an advantage of pesticide use in terms of numbers of people whose health and welfare are protected. Similarly where vector-borne diseases represent a major threat to the health of large populations of humans and where the use of chemical pesticides to destroy the vectors of these diseases is a successful procedure, the application of these chemicals seems to be clearly indicated On the other hand, widespread distribution of chemicals in the environment to control what may be primarily a nuisance situation raises questions as to whether the benefits to be achieved really justify any risk, however minimal, that human health may be jeopardized.

If one extends these considerations beyond purely a concern for human health and considers the question of ecologic balance, the risk-benefit equation takes on different proportions. In the first case, with the exception of possible exposures of the persons who handle the concentrated pesticides, the human population may not be exposed to any significant quantity of the chemical. However, when these chemicals are distributed over widespread areas of land and aquatic surfaces, there is a distinct possibility that desirable species in the environment, other than man, will receive potentially toxic doses of the chemicals. This may not appear to have any direct effect on man's health and welfare; however, if such effects lead to a serious ecologic imbalance, indirect effects on man are possible. Perhaps the best known of all pesticides, DDT, exemplifies a situation of a product that when introduced as an insecticide in 1942 appeared to hold immense promise of benefit to agricultural economics and protection of public health against vector-borne disease. It was hailed as the miracle insecticide and for two decades was used with little concern for injury, and indeed little evidence that injury was produced. However, during the third decade of its use, effects on the environment, effects in nontarget species other than man, began to arise serious doubts concerning its continued usefulness. Now three decades after its patent many countries of the world have critically restricted the use of DDT because of evidence of environmental damage.

Control of Vector-Borne Disease

Pesticides of various types are used in the control of insects, rodents, and other pests that are involved in the life-cycle of vector-borne disease such as malaria, filariasis, yellow fever, viral encephalitis, typhus, bubonic plague, Rocky Mountain spotted fever, rickettsialpox, etc. The success of DDT in reducing the incidence of malaria in many parts of the world has been dramatic. To cite one example, in the Latina province of Italy in 1944 there were 175 new cases of malaria; in 1945 a DDT spray control program was initiated and by 1947 there were only five new cases of malaria, and by 1949 no new cases of malaria appeared.

This is only one example of a success story for DDT. The story has been repeated and continues to be repeated in some areas. Worldwide estimates of the lives saved by using DDT to destroy insects that transmit malaria and other diseases are numbered in the millions and the illnesses prevented are numbered in the hundreds of millions.

Agricultural Productivity

In many parts of the world excessive loss of food crops to insects and other destructive pests contribute to an obvious health problem—starvation. In these countries use of chemicals for controlling these pests clearly seems to have a favourable cost-benefit relationship. In lands of plenty such a clear health benefit may be less obvious. Then, attempts to evaluate the cost-benefit ratios are often reduced to economic considerations. It has been estimated that in 1963 the use of pesticides in the United States resulted in an increase in the value of farm production of about 1.8 billion dollars. This was achieved with an expenditure of about 0.44 billion dollars for control chemicals and procedures. Thus, one can estimate that the net economic benefit was an approximate 1.4-billion-dollar contributed to the gross national product.

Urban Pest Control

Although the total usage of pesticides, in term of pounds applied, is largest in those applications related to agriculture or forestry, these toxic chemicals are also used in urban areas. In addition to the use of pesticides by government service agencies, as in mosquito and rodent control programs and weed control on highways and utility rights of way, there is a rather large use of pesticides by individual home owners and gardens. For example, during a one-year period in Salt Lake Country, Utah, of the total of 200,865 lb of pesticides used, 102,490 lb were used for domestic or household applications. The balance was used by farmers, commercial applicators, fruit growers, and government agencies, and for mosquito abatement, and on livestock. There are, however, great contrasts in these proportions, as illustrated by the statistics of Arizona. The domestic usage for the state accounted for only about 0.6 per cent of the total compared to over 50 per cent of the total in Salt Lake Country, Utah.

It is clear that the opportunities for exposure to pesticides are great. Because the use of pesticides is associated primarily with agricultural operations, major concern is usually for the food we eat. However, it is quite possible that less controlled and less regulated uses of pesticides may offer the greatest opportunity for exposure to toxicologically significant quantities.

Environmental Contamination

It is apparent that there are many sources of exposure of humans and other nontarget species to pesticides by direct contact with materials at the site of application. In recent years, however, it has become increasingly apparent that exposures to pesticides far remote from the source of application are also possible. This results from the translocation of the chemicals from their sites of application through the various media of the environment. The extent to which translocation within the environment occurs will depend to a large degree on the physicochemical properties of the pesticides. Perhaps one of the most important factors is the extent of and time required for degradation of chemicals to simpler nontoxic forms. Since several of the organochlorine insecticides and some of the heavy metals are the most persistent types of pesticides, these compounds have been the object of most concern for problems of translocation and biomagnification. For example DDT is only slowly metabolized by biologic systems. Some of the metabolites are extremely resistant to further degradation, but retain some of the biologic activities of the parent compound. In addition, the partition coefficient for DDT in fat-soluble substances, relative to aqueous media, is very high. Therefore, this chemical will be concentrated through a food chain since it tends to partition into lipoidal biologic materials in increasing concentrations until, at the top of the food chain pyramid, a potentially hazardous concentration may exist.

Other nonbiologic modes of translocation include vaporization and drift by airborne routes so that the materials are carried by prevailing wind patterns far remote from their site of application. Subsequently, they may be precipitated out by rainfall onto land and surface waters in areas in which the pesticides have not been applied directly. Application to the soil may result, ultimately, in suspension of the pesticides, adsorbed on soil particles, and airborne translocation as dust. The extent to which pesticides will remain in soil after application depends upon a number of factors; such as soil type, moisture, temperature, pH, microorganism content, degradability of the pesticide itself, and the extent of cultivation and cover crops. In general, the organochlorine insecticides are most persistent in soils (with the exception of heavy metals, which of course are not further degraded), followed by certain of the herbicides and with the phosphate insecticides and carbamate insecticides and herbicides being the least persistent. An understanding of the potential for persistence and translocation, therefore, must take into consideration not only the biologic aspects of pesticides but also an analysis of their behaviour under various physical and chemical characteristics of the environment. As will be pointed out subsequently, chemical changes of the parent insecticides that result from either physicochemical reactions in the environment or biologically catalyzed reactions may lead to products with either greater or lesser toxicity and with either greater or lesser potential for biotranslocation.

Production and Use Statistics

Before the mid-1940s the primary pesticides in use were botanical in origin and compounds of heavy metals. Subsequently, there has been a marked increase in total pesticide usage and a rapid proliferation of synthetic organic compounds. There are now approximately 900 chemicals that are registered for sale as pesticides against about 2,000 pest species. The U.S. production of pesticides in 1971 was approximately 1.2 billion lb.

Shifts in uses of major classes reflect not only developments in agricultural practice but also the effect of regulatory restrictions and the development of resistance by the pests to certain classes of chemicals.

Human Poisonings

As stated initially, pesticides have a relatively good record in the United States in terms of fatalities resulting from exposure. The United States escaped major incidents of mass acute fatal poisonings, but this is not the case when one considers the worldwide record. There have been several reports of various disease conditions or altered clinical test values resulting from chronic exposure to pesticides, but these conditions are generally reversible and thus cannot be classified as true chronic injury. The relatively small numbers of cases in which progressive chronic disease has been associated with pesticide exposure preclude establishment of cause-and-effect relationships and prevent the conclusion that the widespread use of pesticides has contributed to an increasing incidence of chronic disease. This is not to say there is room for complacency in this regard. As new methods of toxicologic evaluation reveal subtle effects previously unknown and as this information is applied to well-designed epidemiologic studies, it may be found that pesticides have produced currently undetected effects on health. In our present state of knowledge, however, we must deal with the evidence at hand and hope that increased awareness on the part of the medical profession and of the public will stimulate further exploration of any possible injurious effects.

Most of the epidemiologic studies that have been conducted to search for possible associations between disease and pesticide exposure have been done on sample populations that would be expected to be high-risk groups, such as persons occupationally exposed in the manufacturing, formulating, or application of the materials. This appears an obvious choice of study groups; however, failure to find effects in these groups need not preclude that effects occur. For example, persons who experience discomfort or mild illnesses may voluntarily remove themselves from occupations involving the use of pesticides. In addition, as will be discussed later, laboratory animal research has shown that certain types of adaptation occur with continuous and frequent exposures to pesticides. Whether or not this is a factor that can influence the detection of effects in workers with different durations of exposure remains to be demonstrated. As discussed below, however, there is ample evidence that exposure to pesticides has resulted in acute fatal poisonings and reversible illnesses.

Injuries from occupational exposures reported under the requirements of the State Workmen's Compensation Law in California have provided statistical compilations of the extent of injuries due to pesticides and other agricultural chemicals. The rate for all occupational disease reports in agricultural workers reports in agricultural workers in 1969 was 8.5 per 1,000 workers, more than three times the rate for all industry (2.6 per 1,000). There were 727 occupational disease reports attributed to agricultural chemicals in California in 1969. Thirty-two per cent of these involved organic phosphate insecticides, 10 per cent herbicides, 8 per cent halogenated hydrocarbon insecticides, 6 per cent fertilizers, and 44 per cent miscellaneous or unidentified chemicals. Of the 175 cases diagnosed as systemic poisonings, organophosphate insecticides were responsible for 80 per cent, and they were involved in 47 per cent of another 160 reports of digestive and other non-localized symptoms of illness. This high contribution of systemic poisonings due to organic phosphates continued the record of several years. Parathion was the agent most frequently involved. Clearly, workers involved in direct agricultural operations were a high-risk group, and clearly, organophosphorus insecticides were high-risk compounds. Although, as a class herbicides ranked second as a cause of occupational disease, less than 5 per cent of these reports involved systemic poisoning.

Routes of Exposure

Analysis of residues on masks or on pads placed on exposed skin surfaces of workers involved in pesticide applications indicated that the dermal route offers the greatest potential for occupational exposure. The type of pesticide formulation applied was also a factor in the relative contribution of the respiratory route of exposure. When aerosols were used, an average of 2.87 per cent of the total (dermal and respiratory) exposure was by the respiratory route, compared with 0.23 per cent for dilute sprays and 0.94 per cent for dusts. Different degrees of hazard were associated with different jobs. Thus, indoor house spraying was much more hazardous than outdoor spraying of several types. In an airplane spraying operation the relative hazard differed depending on the particular job. For example in the airplane spraying of a fruit orchard the loader received about three times as much as the pilot and $4^2/_3$ times as much as the flagman. Of course, the hazard to applicators is dependent not only on the extent and route of exposure, but on several other factors such as the relative rates of absorption from the skin and lungs, particle sizes of dust and aerosols, and the inherent toxicity of the materials. Wolfe and coworkers (1967) found, in their studies of a wide variety of spraying operations involving 11 different pesticides, that the highest means value for the percentage of toxic dose received per hour of work was 44.2 per cent for workers who loaded airplanes with 1 per cent TEPP (tetraethyl pyrophosphate) dust. Although there were several illnesses associated with this operation, these authors considered the incidence quite low in view of the relative hazard. They suggested that three factors might account for this: the number of hours per day (or week) that the worker is actually engaged in loading airplanes is low; knowledge of the high toxicity of TEPP may prompt more diligent use of protective clothing and respiratory protective devices; and only a small percentage of the dry dust impinging on exposed skin is likely to be absorbed.

Oral ingestion is the most frequent route of exposure in cases of nonoccupational poisonings. Dermal exposures have resulted in deaths of small children who come in contact with presumably empty containers for highly toxic pesticides. Respiratory exposure as well as dermal of the general population is possible as a result of drift from agricultural operations. Household use of pesticide aerosol "bombs," vaporizers, pest strips, and other aerosol or vapor-generating devices is a potential source of respiratory exposure in nonoccupational settings. Hayes (1969) reported that 19 different organophosphorus insecticides that have resulted in human poisonings there were 20 compounds in the organochlorine class, five different carbamates, four botanicals, three inorganic elements, and six miscellaneous compounds for a total of 57 different insecticides. Eight herbicides were responsible for human poisonings, seven fungicides, six rodenticides, one molluscicide, and one nematocide for a total 80 different compounds.

Insecticides

Only select examples of the various classes of insecticides will be discussed here. For additional discussion of their chemistry and metabolism the reader should consult the extensive report by Menzie (1969). Comprehensive complication of chemical and common names, structures, and LD 50 values in rats may be found in Gaines (1969) and Frear (1969). Acute toxicity data for fish and wildlife are available in several reports. Summaries of results of subacute and chronic feeding studies for many compounds have been made available in the monograph by Lehman (1965). Several books and monographs that are devoted exclusively to pesticides provide much more extensive coverage than is possible here. Handbooks prepared by Hayes (1963) and by Morgan (1976) provide information on clinical toxicology and emergency treatment for many pesticides.

Organophosphorus Insecticides

As discussed earlier, insecticides (of the several classes of pesticides) have most frequently been involved in human poisonings and organophosphorus compounds have most frequently been the offending agents.

Historic considerations

The first organophosphate insecticide was tetraethyl pyrophosphate (TEPP). It was developed in Germany as substitute for nicotine, which was in short supply in that country during World War II. Related extremely toxic compounds such as ethyl N-dimethyl phosphoroamidocyanidate (tabun) and isoprophyl methylphosphonofluoridate (sarin) were kept secrete by the German government as potential chemical warfare agents. These, and other extremely toxic compounds, are the so-called nerve gas chemical warfare agents.

TEPP, although an effective insecticide, was highly toxic to mammals and are rapidly hydrolyzed in the presence of moisture. Further efforts to find more stable compounds for use in agriculture led to the synthesis by Schrader in 1944 of parathion (E605; O,O-diethyl O-*p*-nitrophenyl phosphate). Because it exhibited a wide range of insecticidal activity and suitable physical and chemical properties such as low volatility and sufficient stability in water and mild alkali, parathion became one of the most widely used organophosphorus insecticides. It continues to be used extensively in agriculture, but because of its high mammalian toxicity, by all routes of exposure, other less hazardous compounds have begun to take its place. Parathion has the dubious distinction of being the pesticide most frequently involved in fatal poisonings. During the last two decades the agricultural chemistry industry has developed many other organic triesters of phosphoric acid and phosphorothioic acid that have been registered for use as insecticides.

Shortly after parathion became available for study, acute toxicity studies on experimental animals revealed signs of poisoning that resembled excessive of cholinergic nerves. These could be alleviated by atropine, a cholinergic blocking agent. This suggested inhibition of acetylcholinesterase of nerve tissues as the mechanism of toxic action, as had been demonstrated for related organophosphate triesters, and was confirmed by the finding that tissues of rats poisoned by parathion had markedly reduced cholinesterase activity and increased free acetylcholine in their brains. Thus, the biochemical basis for nerve tissue, became known soon after its introduction as an insecticide. Subsequent development and research on other organophosphate insecticides have revealed that they all, in sufficient doses, inhibit acetylcholine-esterase *in vivo* and thus share a common mechanism of acute toxic action. The chemical mechanism of cholinesterase inhibition is discussed in more detail later in this chapter and in several extensive reviews and monographs.

Signs and symptoms of acute poisoning

Signs and symptoms of acute systemic poisoning by organophosphate insecticides are predictable from their biochemical mechanism of action. Thus inhibition of acetylcholinesterase results in accumulation of endogenous acetylcholine in nerve tissue and effector organs with consequent signs and symptoms that mimic the muscarinic, nicotinic, and central nervous system actions of acetylcholine. Acetylcholine is the chemical transmitter of nerve impulses at endings of postganglionic parasympathetic nerve fibers, somatic motor nerves to skeletal muscle, preganglionic fibers of both parasympathetic and sympathetic nerves, and certain synapses in the central nervous system.

Muscarinic receptors for acetylcholine are found primarily in smooth muscles, the heart, and exocrine glands. Signs and symptoms of organophosphorus insecticide poisoning that results from stimulation of these receptors include tightness in the chest and wheezing expiration due to bronchoconstriction and increased bronchial secretions, increased salivation and lacrimation, increased sweating, increased gastrointestinal tone and peristalsis with consequent development of nausea, vomiting, abdominal cramps, diarrhea, tenesmus and involuntary defecation, bradycardia that can progress to heart block, frequent and involuntary urination due to contraction of smooth muscle of the bladder, and constriction of the pupils (miosis).

Nicotinic signs and symptoms result from accumulation of acetylcholine at the endings of motor nerves to skeletal muscle and autonomic ganglia. Muscular effects include easy fatigue and mild weakness followed by involuntary twitching, scattered fasciculations and cramps with progression to generalized fasciculations, and muscular weakness that affects the muscles of respiration and contributes to dyspnea and cyanosis. Nicotinic actions at autonomic ganglia may, in severe intoxication, mask some of the muscarinic effects. Thus tachycardia may result from stimulation of sympathetic ganglia to overcome the usual bradycardia to muscarinic action on the heart. Pallor, elevation of blood pressure, and hyperglycemia also reflect nicotinic action at sympathetic ganglia.

Accumulation of acetylcholine in the central nervous system is believed to be responsible for the tension, anxiety, restlessness, insomnia, headache, emotional instability and neurosis, excessive dreaming and nightmares, apathy, and confusion that have been described after organophosphate poisoning. Slurred speech, tremor, generalized weakness, ataxia, convulsions, depression of respiratory and circulatory centers, and coma are other central nervous system effects.

The immediate cause of death in fatal organophosphate poisoning is asphyxia resulting from respiratory failure. Contributing factors are the muscarinic actions of bronchoconstriction and increased bronchial secretions, nicotinic action leading to paralysis of the respiratory muscles and the central nervous system action of depression and paralysis of the respiratory center.

Localized effects

Localized effects at the site of exposure may be seen in the absence of obvious signs and symptoms of systemic absorption as described above. Exposure to vapours, dusts, or aerosols can exert local effects on the smooth muscles of the eyes and respiratory tact resulting in early miosis and blurred vision due to spasm of accommodation in the first case and bronchoconstriction in the case of respiratory exposure. Secretory glands of the respiratory tract, as well as smooth muscles, may be affected by minimal inhalation exposure to the organophosphates leading to watery nasal discharge, nasal hyperemia, sensation of tightness in the chest, and prolonged wheezing respiration. Local effects of dermal exposure include localized sweating and fasciculations at the site of contact. Gastrointestinal manifestations are usually the first to appear after oral ingestion and some of them may be due to local anticholinesterase action in the gastrointestinal tract.

Systemic effects

Systemic effect are, in general, similar irrespective of route of absorption, but the sequence and time may differ. Respiratory and ocular symptoms would be expected first after exposure to airborne organophosphates, while gastrointestinal symptoms and localized sweating would likely be first to appear after oral and dermal exposure, respectively. However, these generalizations may not hold for compounds that must be metabolically activated. The onset of symptoms after exposure to organophosphate compounds is usually rapid, within a few minutes to two or three hours. The duration of symptoms is generally from one to five days. In fatal untreated poisonings, deaths, usually occur within 24 hours. It should be recognized that, in addition to the usual factors of route or exposure, concentrations of active material, etc., the quality of sings and symptoms, their rate of onset, and their durations may differ markedly for different compounds by virtue of differences in rat of biotransformation, distribution, and affinities for acetylcholinesterase. For example, in five cases of attempted suicide by ingestion of dichlofenthion, severe cholinergic crises did not appear until 40 to 48 hours but they persisted for 5 to 48 days in the three survivors. This extremely prolonged course was associated with persistent residues of this insecticide in the blood and fat of the patients. Dichlofenthion has a higher octanol/water partition coefficient that most organophosphorus insecticides, and the prolonged course of the poisonings was due to a slow release of the insecticides from adipose tissue reservoirs.

Organophosphate insecticides in common use are rapidly metabolized and excreted, and subacute or chronic poisoning by virtue of accumulation of the compounds in the body does not occur. However, because several of the organophosphates produce slowly reversible inhibition of cholinesterase *accumulation of this effect* can occur. Signs and symptoms of poisoning that resemble those produced by a single high dose will occur when the accumulated inhibition of cholinesterase produced by smaller, repeated doses reaches a critical level. Cessation of exposure normally results in complete recovery. Chronic complaints associated with poisoning by organophosphates have been reported as due to sequelae of severe acute poisoning. A few compounds have produced delayed and persistent peripheral neuropathy, apparently unrelated to anticholinesterase action.

Delayed neurotoxic effects

These are produced by several phosphate triesters. Although this can result from a single toxic dose, the neuropathology is generally delayed in onset. Most notorious of the compounds that produce this effect is triorthocresyl phosphate (TOCP). This compound is not a potent anticholinesterase, and it is not used as an insecticide. However, a number of compounds that are used as insecticides can produce this effect and it is common practice to screen for this action in safety evaluation tests. The function disturbances associated with phosphate triester neuropathy begin in the distal parts of the lower limbs in both man and other sensitive animals. Mild sensory disturbances and motor weakness with ataxia occur, progressing in severity and extent to increased weakness and flaccidity of the legs and varying amounts of sensory disturbance. Upper limbs may also become involved. After several days to a few weeks the peak of the process is reached and thereafter improvement in the functional disturbance begins. Recovery is slow and not always complete.

Although hens and man seem to be the most sensitive species to the organic phosphate triester neuropathy, studies on various compounds have shown that dogs, cats, calves, monkeys, sheep, pigs, horses, pheasants, ducks, and rats will also sustain this effect. For screening for possible production of this effect by pesticides, hens are usually used as the experimental animal. Because of potent anticholinesterase actions of many pesticides, it is often impossible to administer sufficient doses to the animal to produce the neuropathic effect. To overcome this and to screen for the neuropathy, a common procedure is to administer atropine to protect against the acute cholinergic action. Using this procedure Gaines (1969) found that 22 to 30 organophosphorus pesticides tested and three out of nine carbamate insecticides produced leg weakness in atropinized hens under sufficient time and dosage conditions. With all but three of the compounds, however, the onset of leg weakness occurred within 24 hours, and for most compounds the hens recovered within a months. Aldridge and Johnson (1971) consider this rapid onset and relatively rapid recovery to result from a different mechanism than for TOCP and other long-acting neurotoxins.

Metabolism

Toxicity Relationship. Several biotransformation reactions that organophosphorus insecticides undergo have been discussed in several reviews and monographs. In this section selected biotransformation reactions are discussed as illustrations of the development of knowledge that has led to an understanding of factors that affect the susceptibility of animals to poisoning by these compounds.

Activation

The early organophosphorus anticholinesterases such as TEPP and DEP were phosphate triesters and were potent inhibitors of cholinesterase both *in vivo* and *in vitro*. The development of parathion introduced the phosphorothionates. The majority of compounds now in use as insecticides contain the (=S) thiono moiety and are either phosphorothionates (e.g., parathion, methyl parathion) or phosphorodithioates (e.g., azinphosmethyl, malathion). Early in research on parathion and its oxygen analog, paraoxon, it became apparent that in addition to conferring greater stability against nonenzymatic hydrolysis, substitution of =S for =O on the phosphorus compound altered its toxic properties. Parathion was less toxic to animals than paraoxon, and several factors that altered the toxicity of parathion in rats did not affect paraoxon's toxicity; although both compounds inhibited acetylcholinesterase and produced similar cholinergic signs of poisoning. Further studies showed that highly purified parathion did not inhibit cholinesterase *in vitro*, and that the inhibitory activity of less purified samples could be attributed to contamination with the S-ethyl and S-phenyl isomers of parathion or with its oxygen analog, paraoxon. Subsequently it was demonstrated that paraoxon was the active anticholinesterase formed from parathion in intact rats.

There are other activation reactions, involving a few compounds, in which parents insecticides are converted to more potent anticholinesterase agents. They include oxidation of phosphoroamidates and thioether oxidation by mixed function oxidases.

Inactivation

In addition to the requirement for an oxo (=O) group to be present for anticholinesterase activity, metabolic modification of the alkyl and

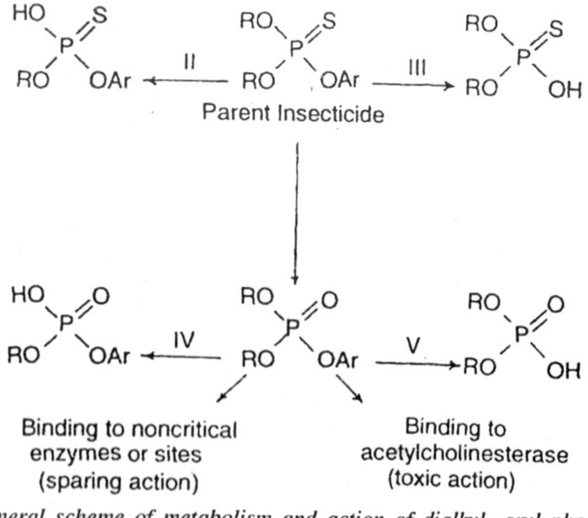

Parent Insecticide

Binding to noncritical enzymes or sites (sparing action)

Binding to acetylcholinesterase (toxic action)

Fig. 8.1. General scheme of metabolism and action of dialkyl, aryl phosphorothioate insecticides.

aryl substituents can also influence activity. Reactions II, III, IV, and V are enzymatic detoxification reactions that yield products that do not inhibit acetylcholinesterase. Largely as a result of *in vitro* studies, it was proposed that reaction V, catalyzed by paraoxonase (A-esterase), was the major pathway of detoxication of parathion. This enzyme is widely distributed among several tissues in rats and other mammals. It does not require addition of cofactors for measurements of activity *in vitro* and probably hydrolyzes several other organophosphates (P=O compounds), but apparently does not hydrolyze the P=S compounds directly. Thus, the proposed enzymatic mechanism of detoxification of parathion and other phosphorothionate insecticides was for many years, based on the concept that hydrolytic detoxication (reaction V) followed the formation of the oxygen analogs (reaction I). However, studies using ^{32}P-labeled parathion have shown that the arylphosphorus bond can be cleaved (reaction III) without prior oxidation to paraoxon.

Another detoxification pathway involves the hydrolysis of carboxyester or carboxyamide linkages in some insecticides by tissue or plasma carboxylesterases Malathion and dimethoate examples. Products or the hydrolysis of the carboxyester of the carboxyester or amide groups do not inhibit cholinesterase, and enzymatic formation of these products has been demonstrated *in vivo* and *in vitro* studies. In several species of mammals, this appears to be the major pathway of detoxification for these insecticides, and their selective insecticidal action is due to a relative lack of these hydrolytic enzymes in insects. The importance of this reaction in mammals as a detoxification pathway has been demonstrated in studies in which animals pretreated with other organophosphate compounds that strongly inhibit carboxylesterases become more susceptible to the acute toxicity and anticholinesterase action of malathion. Pretreatment with triorthocresyl phosphate (TOCP), a strong inhibitor of carboxylesterase but weak anticholinesterase, reduced the LD 50 of malathion in rats from 1100 to 10 mg/kg, a 110-fold potentiation.

It is apparent from the above discussion that the relationships between enzymatic metabolism and toxicity of organophosphorus insecticides is extremely complex. The toxicity depends upon the net availability of active compound to inhibit acetylcholinesterase at critical sites in nerve tissue, and this in turn is dependent upon the dynamic relationships between activation and inactivation reactions. There are not always predictable from results of measurements of relative of enzyme reactions under optimum conditions *in vitro*, particularly when both activation and inactivation reactions are catalyzed by enzyme systems with common cofactor requirements, tissue distributed, and intracellular location.

Acetylcholinesterase inhibition and reversal

There is abundant evidence that both the organophosphorus and carbamate insecticides (discussed subsequently) produce their acute toxic actions by inhibiting acetylcholinesterase. In addition to the fact that it has been demonstrated that many of these compounds are potent inhibitors *in vitro*, several lines of *in vivo* evidence support this mechanism. The consequence of acetylcholinesterase inhibition is accumulation of acetylcholine at effector sites, and the protection against acute poisoning offered by atropine and other cholinergic blocking agents supports the mechanism. Additionally, induced reversal of cholinesterase inhibition by chemical compounds, such as the oxime derivatives, results in alleviation of symptoms of poisoning. A combination of pharmacologic antidotes (atropine) and biochemical antidotes (oximes) is potentiative in its antidotal activity.

The rate of recovery of free and active acetylcholinesterase following poisoning by organophosphorus and carbamate insecticides varies with different compounds. In general, the carbamates are usually considered reversible inhibitors of cholinesterase, and their duration of action is relatively short. In addition, because of the reversal of inhibition by dilution of the enzyme (as would occur if one sampled a tissue and diluted it with buffer during preparation for assay), determination of acetylcholinesterase inhibition by carbamates *in vivo* poses some technical difficulties. Unless care is taken, it is quite possible to observe the typical signs of anticholinesterase poisoning following carbamates; but by the time tissues are removed and prepared for assay, decarbamylation or reversal of enzyme-carbamate complex may have occurred and inhibition is undetectable. Therefore, in suspected cases of poisoning, where the history and signs and symptoms suggest a carbamate exposure, but clinical tests show a normal or nearly normal blood cholinesterase value, one must be guided by the history before concluding that the poisoning was not the result of a carbamate insecticide.

The case for organophosphate poisoning is somewhat different in that the compounds are in general much more slowly reversible inhibitors. However, even within this class there are marked differences in the persistence of inhibition following toxic doses of the compound. Spontaneous reversal of enzyme inhibition by organophosphates as well

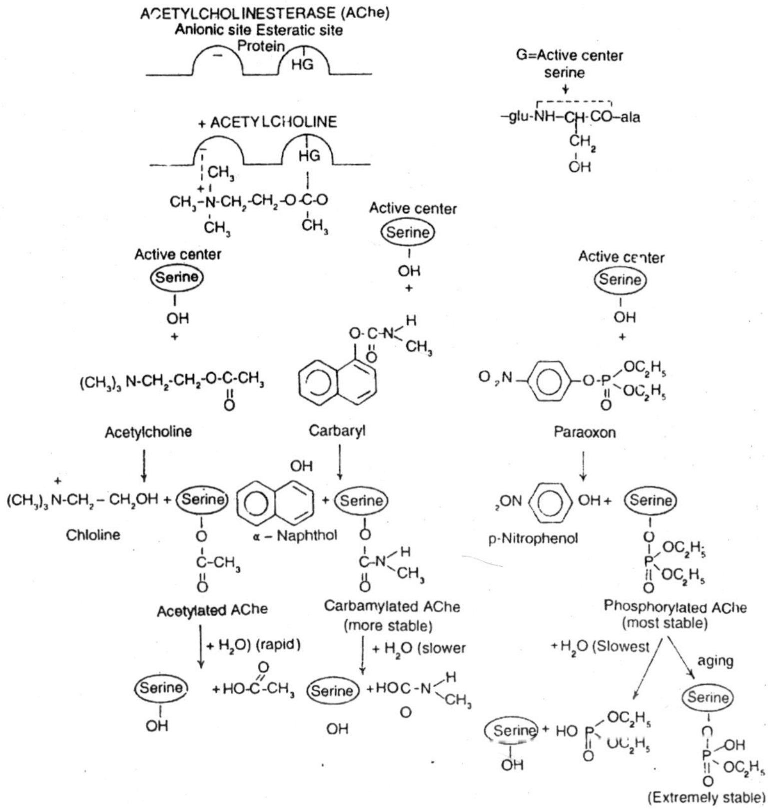

Fig. 8.2. Scheme of hydrolysis of acetylcholine by acetylcholinesterase and reactions of the anticholinesterase insecticides carbaryl and paraoxon.

as carbamates can occur at varying rates, depending upon the insecticide, by hydrolysis of the phosphorylated cholinesterase. The rate of reactivation *in vitro* of mouse brain and diaphragm acetylcholinesterase inhibited *in vivo* was five to ten times greater for azinphosmethyl and parathion-methyl than for azinphosmethyl and parathion-ethyl.

Fortunately, there are available chemicals that will accelerate the hydrolysis of the phosphorylated enzyme, and hence accelerate regeneration of active acetylcholinesterase. The most successful compounds are oxime derivatives, and the best known of these is 2-pyridine aldoxime methiodide which is now a standard part of the therapy of organophosphorus poisoning. In addition to the capacity of 2-PAM to accelerate the dephosphorylation of acetylcholinesterase it

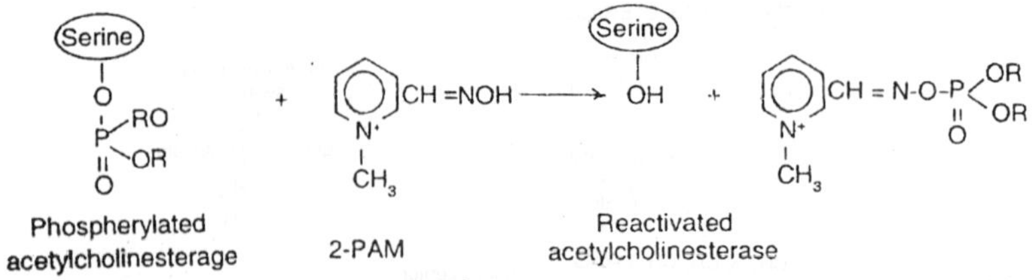

Serine — O — P(=O)(RO)(OR) + 2-PAM (CH=NOH, N·, CH_3) ⟶ Serine — OH + (CH = N-O-P(=O)(OR)(OR), N+, CH_3)

Phospherylated acetylcholinesterage 2-PAM Reactivated acetylcholinesterase

Fig. 8.3. Reactivation of phosphorylated acetylcholinesterase by pralidoxine (2-PAM).

can also enhance the direct hydrolysis of the active inhibitor at physiologic pH. The effectiveness of 2-PAM in reversing cholinesterase inhibition *in vivo* is dependent upon its early administration following poisoning, because the "aged" phosphorylated enzyme is not reversible by the oximes. The rate of reactivation by oximes appears to vary with the source of the cholinesterase and the substituents on the phosphorylation group. Diethyoxy-phosphorylated enzyme appears to be most readily reactivated as compared with diisopropoxy-phosphorylated and dimethoxy-phosphorylated enzymes. It is believed that the effectiveness of the oximes as dephosphorylating agents is inversely related to the rate of aging of the phosphorylated enzyme. Hence the dimethoxyphosphoryl enzyme and the diisopropoxy phosphoryl enzyme age more rapidly than the diethoxy phosphoryl enzyme.

Diagnosis and treatment of poisoning

As in any case of poisoning, careful taking of the history of vents that led to sings and symptoms is essential. However, the organophosphate insecticides frequently produce poisoning rapidly and if in sufficient doses, may have a rapid fatal outcome. It is important, therefore, to be guided by the characteristic signs and symptoms and take emergency action even though a complete history may not have been obtained.

In very severe case the treatment should include (1) artificial respiration, preferably by mechanical means, and (2) atropine sulfate, 2 to 4 mg intravenously as soon as cyanosis is overcome. This may be repeated at five to ten-minute intervals until signs of atropinization appear. Note that this dosage of atropine is greater than that usually used for other purposes, but because people poisoned by anticholinesterase compounds have increased tolerance for atropine, it is a safe dose, used carefully by an astute physician. (3) Following atropinization, treatment before time is spent in decontaminating the skin, stomach, or eyes as may be indicated; however, decontamination must be followed promptly. The skin should be washed with an alkaline soap, which will not only remove, but also help hydrolyze, the phosphate ester. Appropriate clinical procedures for evacuating the stomach and cleansing the eyes may be indicated. A case history of successful treatment of poisoning by dicrotophos, in which a total of 3911.5 mg of atropine and 92 g of pralidoxime chloride was given over a 23-day period, illustrates the importance of vigorous treatment in severe cases of poisoning.

In more usual and less severe cases the procedure should be as follow: Administer atropine SO_4, 1 to 2 mg, if symptoms appear. If excessive secretions occur, keep the patient fully atropinized by giving atropine sulfate every hour up to 25 to 50 mg in a day. Proceed with decontamination of the skin and removal of the poison from the stomach or eyes as the second step in this case. In these less severe poisonings 2-PAM administration should be instituted if the patient fails to respond satisfactorily to atropine, followed, of course, by symptomatic treatment. The doses indicated above are those suggested for adults. Anyone expecting to face the possibility of dealing with severe poisoning by organophosphate insecticides should consult more detailed descriptions of diagnosis and therapy.

Knowledge of the biochemical action of the organophosphate insecticides has provided a means for a relative specific clinical test for diagnosis of excessive exposure to these compounds Routine measurements of blood cholinesterase activity are frequently made in workers engaged in occupations where exposure to phosphate insecticides is a possibility. As discussed in several reports the inhibition of the activity of plasma or red cell cholinesterase is reasonably well correlated with the severity of exposure and poisoning. Measurement of the cholinesterase activity of the blood only indirectly reflects the extent of biochemical lesion at critical sites in nerve tissues or effector organs, however. Depending upon the compound, the relative inhibition of plasma pseudocholinesterase and erythrocyte acetylcholinesterase may differ. Since the red cell enzyme is apparently identical to that in nerve tissue, assays on red cells are usually considered more reflective of nerve tissue activity. Rather marked inhibition of red cell and plasma cholinesterase may be present in the absence of symptoms. Total inhibition of plasma and 60 to 70 per cent inhibition in red cell activity has been noted in the absence of overt signs of poisonings. However, the relationship between inhibition of blood cholinesterase activity and symptoms differs with different compounds and may reflect differences in distribution of the inhibitions. Relationships between blood and nerve tissue cholinesterase inhibition and signs of poisoning for various compounds in experimental animals have been reviewed by DuBois (1963) and Wills (1972).

Tolerance to acute, sublethal effects of some organophosphates

This has been demonstrated in experimental animals. In these experiments the phosphates were administered repeatedly or fed in the diet at sublethal doses for several days. Initially, acute cholinergic signs and symptoms were observed. In time, however, the animals no longer responded with obvious signs after each dose, and their general appearance, growth, and behaviour appeared normal. However at sacrifice, these apparently normal animals had markedly inhibited blood and nervous tissue cholinesterase activity and elevated levels of acetylcholine in their brains. Adaptation or compensation to central nervous system and behavioural effects of anticholinesterase insecticides also occur in rats in spite of continued brain acetylcholinesterase inhibition and elevated acetylcholine levels.

Experiments by Brodeur and DuBois (1964) suggest that the apparent tolerance involves development of a refractoriness of cholinergic receptor sites. Tolerant animals were resistant to the acute toxicity of carbachol, which has direct effect on cholinergic receptors. Adaptation to high concentrations of acetylcholine has been observed to occur at the neuromuscular junction and at ganglia within a few minutes to a few hours, in contrast to the several days required for adaptation in the subacute experiments cited above. There are also reports that tolerance to reduced cholinesterase activity also occurs in man. Stavinoha and associates (1969) found that two different strains of rats that had adapted to low acetylcholinesterase activity in the brain different with respect to the levels of acetylcholine in the brain; one strain had normal levels of acetylcholine during adaptation while the other had elevated concentrations. They concluded there was no apparent correlation between the concentration of brain acetylcholine and adaptation. Although the mechanism suggested by Brodeur and DuBois (1964) of a refractoriness of cholinergic receptor sites is attractive, other possibilities related to the rate of production, release and destruction of acetylcholine could be considered.

Carbamate Insecticides

The acute toxicities of the carbamate insecticides also vary through a wide range. Unlike the organophosphates, most of the aromatic carbamate-ester insecticides have low dermal toxicities. However, one cannot generalize that carbamates are without dermal toxicity as illustrated by the extreme toxicity of aldicarb by both the oral and dermal routes. This compound, because of its extreme toxicity, is recommended only for limited use in greenhouse operations. The carbamates are not broad-spectrum insecticides, and some of the common household insect pests such as the housefly and German cock, each are relatively immune; however, bees are extremely sensitive to these insecticides. For several of the compounds, the LD 50 values for houseflies and German cockroaches are, on a body weight basis, greater than the LD 50s for rats.

Action and mechanism

The mode of action of the carbamates, like the organophosphates, is inhibition of acetylcholinesterase and the signs and symptoms of poisoning are typically cholinergic with lacrimation, salivation, miosis convulsions, and death. As indicated previously, however, the carbamates are relatively rapidly reversible inhibitors of cholinesterase. Atropine sulfate is the recommended antidote for poisoning by carbamate insecticides. Administration of 2-PAM is not recommended and at least for some compounds, seems to be specifically contraindicated since there have been reports that it aggravates the toxicity of carbaryl. In addition to the typical cholinergic signs of poisoning, experiments in rats showed that some of the less toxic carbamate insecticides when administrated intravenously produced a pronounced anesthetic effect with respiratory failure as the most critical determinant of the intravenous toxicity. This anesthetic action was rapid in onset. However, if artificial respiration was applied for two to five minutes animals resumed spontaneous respiration. Cholinergic signs then gradually developed. No pronounced anesthetic effects were observed with the carbamate insecticides when they were administered by the intraperitoneal or oral routes. This anesthetic effect has also been noted with several organophosphate insecticides and also appears to be unrelated to their anticholinesterase action.

Metabolism-toxicity relationships

Studies of the correlation between toxicity and *in vitro* anticholinesterase activity of a series of monomethylcarbamates showed that there was good correlation between *in vitro* inhibition and intravenous LD50s in rats, but the *in vitro* anticholinesterase action was poorly correlated with oral LD50s. The carbamate insecticides are direct inhibitors of acetylcholinesterase (i.e. they do not require metabolic activation), and the lack of correlation between the oral toxicity and *in vitro* anticholinesterase activity appeared to reflect differing rates of detoxication of the compounds. Hydrolysis of the

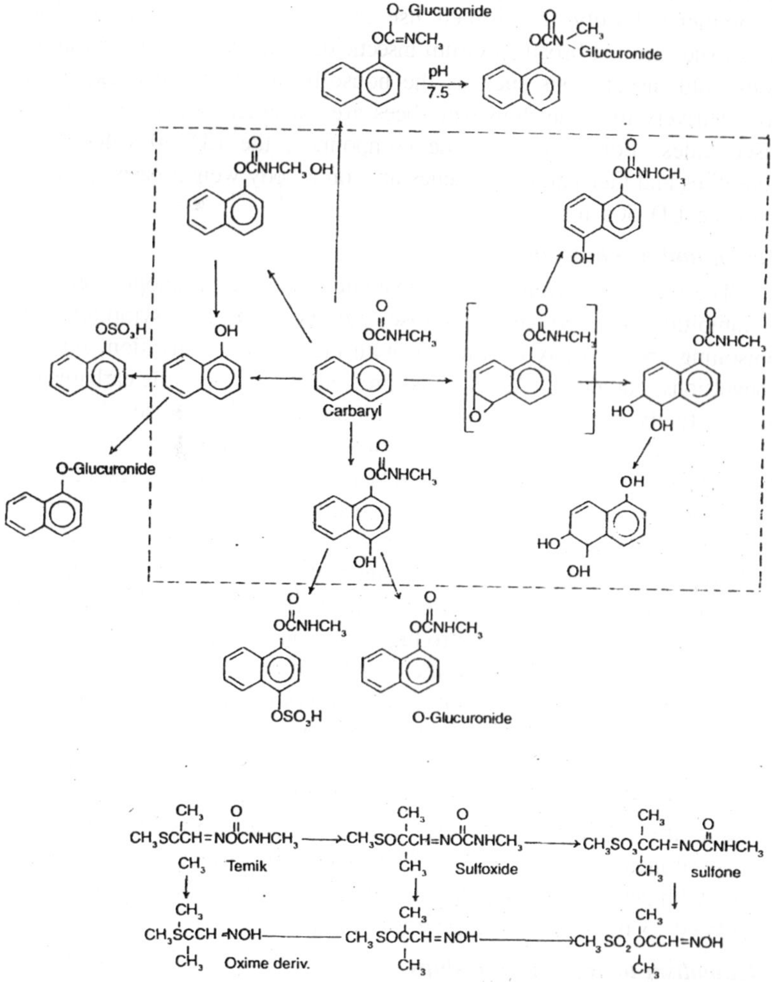

Fig. 8.4. Examples of metabolism of carbamate insecticides. A–Metabolism of carbaryl pathways within dashed rectangle demonstrated with liver microsomes in vitro. B–Metabolism of Temik.

carbamic acid ester linkage results in metabolites that lack anticholinesterase activity. The biotransformation pathways for typical carbamate insecticides are shown. Although hydrolysis occurs to some extent with all compounds, various oxidation steps that are catalyzed by mixed function oxidases also occur. The products formed by these reactions are not always less toxic than the parent compounds, but the parent compounds themselves, do have anticholinesterase action.

Cholinesterase inhibition and symptoms

Studies of the relationship between cholinesterase inhibition and signs and symptoms of poisoning in rats showed that with dosages that did not produce any noticeable symptoms (0.25 to 1.0 mg/kg, intramuscularly, of propoxur) the activity of both brain and plasma cholinesterase was reduced the brain and plasma cholinesterase activities to 50 per cent of normal level. At higher dosages (10 to 50 mg/kg) the degree of inhibition of both brain and plasma cholinesterase closely followed the severity of symptoms that were produced, with brain cholinesterase being slightly more inhibited than plasma. Studies on human volunteer were also conducted to determine the relationship between the inhibition of erythrocyte cholinesterase and onset of sings of poisoning. The lowest erythrocyte cholinesterase activity (27 per cent of normal) was observed at 15 minutes after ingestion of 1.5 mg/kg of propoxur in a 90 kg adult man. At this time no sings were observed, but moderate discomfort, that was described as pressure in the head was present. Blurred vision and nausea developed three minutes later, and 20 minutes after ingestion the man was pale and his face was sweating, pulse rate was 140 minutes compared to 76 before ingestion, and both systolic and diastolic blood pressures were increased. Following these symptoms, nausea, repeated vomiting, and profuse sweating developed. The symptoms lasted from about the thirtieth until the fortyfifth minute after ingestion, and during this period erythrocyte cholinesterase activity recovered from a level of 50 to 55 per cent of its normal value. Sixty minutes after ingestion the patient showed signs of improvement but felt nauseated and tired; pulse and blood pressure were normal. Two hours after ingestion the patient felt completely recovered. This rapid disappearance of symptoms was accompanied by further rapid recovery of erythrocyte cholinesterase activity. Studies on both rats and men indicated that the lethal dose of a carbamate insecticide is a considerably greater multiple of the dose causing the first signs of poisoning than for the organophosphorus insecticides. As a result, overexposure to carbamates might be expected to give early warning of poisoning in the form of appearance of slight symptoms, when, if heeded and exposure terminated, could prevent exposure to acutely dangerous quantities.

Other actions of carbamates

One of the least acutely toxic carbamate insecticides, carbaryl, has reportedly produced teratogenic effects in experimental animals. Although in most species the doses for effects on fetuses were near the maternal toxic doses, in beagle dogs the teratogenic dose was found to be only about a tenth of the toxic to the mother, hen given as single daily doses in gelatin capsules. Weil and coworkers (1972) reviewed the considerable literature on studies of reproductive and teratogenic action of carbaryl and concluded that the sensitivity of dogs to teratogenic action was related to the fact that dogs did not metabolize carbaryl to l-naphthol, a major metabolic pathway in most other species including man.

Cloudy swelling of cells in the proximal convoluted tubules of the kidneys was noted in rats and dogs fed 400 ppm of carbaryl in their diets for several months. Of related interest, it has been reported that the urinary amino acid-nitrogen: creatinine ratios were increased in a group of human volunteers who ingested daily of carbaryl of 0.12 mg/kg/day of several weeks. Although the exact relationships between the histologic changes in experimental animals and the biochemical changes in man is not established, they would seem to be related effects and the dosage relationships suggest that man may be much more sensitive to injurious effects of carbaryl on the kidney.

Organochlorine Insecticides

The organochlorine insecticides include the chlorinated ethane derivatives, of which DDT is the best known examples; the cyclodienes, which include chlordane, aldrin, dieldrin, hepatchlor, endrin, and toxaphene; and the hexachlorocyclohexanes, such as lindane. From the mid-1940s to the mid-1960s the organochlorine insecticides enjoyed wide use in agriculture, soil, and structure insect control, and in malaria control programs. However, they have, as a class, come into disfavour because they are very persistent in the environment and tend to accumulate in biologic as well as nonbiologic media. As a class the organochlorine insecticides are often considered to be less acutely toxic, but of greater potential for chronic toxicity, than the organophosphate and carbamate insecticides. However, there is a wide range of acute toxicities of individual compounds, from extremely toxic to slightly toxic. The organochlorine insecticides can also be classed as neuropoisons. However, their mechanism of action is not the same as that of the phosphates and carbamates. Indeed the precise mechanism is unknown for most of them.

DDT

DDT has been the best known, the cheapest, and probably one of the most effective of the synthetic insecticides. It was synthesized as early as 1874 but its insecticidal effectiveness was not discovered until 1939, and it was patented for this use in 1942. DDT was used extensively during World War II in control of lice and other insects by application directly to humans. There is no evidence that harm to these people resulted from this direct application. Indeed there seems to be no documented, unequivocal report of fatal human poisoning from DDT in spite of its widespread use and availability. Acute, nonfatal poisonings have occurred as a result of accidents or suicide attempts. Statistical associations between levels of storage of DDT and its metabolites and certain types of chronic disease in man have been reported however, causal relationships have not been established and other reports indicate no association between tissue DDT levels and chronic disease. There is no question, however, that the general population has sustained exposure to DDT and derivatives, and as a result practically everyone born since the mid-1940s, when DDT was introduced into commerce, has had a lifeline of exposure and storage of some quantity of this insecticide in fatty tissues. Thus chronic exposure to DDT has resulted in an accumulation of residues in man and other animals, but the health significance of these residues is not currently apparent and remain to be further evaluated.

On the other hand, there is convincing evidence that DDT and metabolites accumulate in natural food chains by a process of biologic concentration in ecosystems. As a result, organisms at the top of these natural food chains may sustain injury from DDT or its metabolites that are present as a result of gradual accumulations of residues in organisms that make up their food sources. Both field and laboratory studies have provided evidence that reproductive success in certain species of wild birds is adversely affected by exposure to DDT or its metabolites. Additionally, fish and some lower aquatic organisms are extremely sensitive to the acute toxicity of DDT.

The prospect of possible ecologic imbalance from continued use of DDT, the uncertainty as to the effect, if any, of continued prolonged exposure and storage of low levels of DDT in humans, and the development of resistant strains of insects have promoted the Environmental Protection Agency to markedly restrict the use of DDT in the U.S.A. Several other countries have taken similar actions. However, because of its relatively low cost, unavailability of substitutes that are both safe and effective, and its continuing presence as an environmental contaminant in spite of curtailed use, there continues to be interest in its toxicity.

Signs and symptoms of acute and subacute poisoning

Signs and symptoms of poisoning in man and animals resulting from high doses of DDT include paresthesia of the tongue, lips, and face; apprehension hypersusceptibility to stimuli; irritability; dizziness; disturbed equilibrium; tremor; and tonic and colonic convulsions. Motor unrest and fine tremors associated with voluntary movements progress to coarse tremors without interruption in moderate to severe poisoning. Symptoms appear several hours after large doses, and in animals poisoned with fatal doses death occurs in 24 to 72 hours. It has been estimated that a dose of 10 mg/kg will cause signs of poisoning in man. Although there are rather marked species differences in susceptibility to acute poisoning by oral ingestion, when the compound is given by intravenous administration, the dose and time required for poisoning are quite similar for a wide variety of species including insects. Unlike most of the organophosphate insecticides, DDT is poorly absorbed after dermal exposure, especially when applied in the powder form. This poor absorption from the skin probably accounts for the rather good safety record of DDT in spite of its wide and sometimes careless use by applications and formulators.

Although the functional injury produced by high doses of DDT is referable to effects in the central nervous system, there is little pathologic changes in the cells and tissues of the central nervous system in acute poisonings. Inhalation of the dust results in irritation in the lungs, but primary pathologic changes that result from exposure to high, but nonfatal, doses, or from subacute or chronic feeding, are observed in the liver. With large doses centrolobular narcosis of the liver has been reported. Smaller doses result in liver enlargement, which in rodents is somewhat characteristic in that the cells and mitochondria themselves are enlarged. Histologic changes in the livers of male rats fed diets containing 5 to 15 ppm or more for six months include hypertrophy, inclusion bodies, and cytoplasmic granulation of a characteristic type in which the granules orient themselves around the periphery of the cell. These changes were not seen in female rats fed less than 200 ppm in the diet, however, and liver necrosis was observed only at dietary levels of 1,000 ppm or more Severe, unremitting tremors were observed at levels of 1,000 ppm, and nervousness, hyperactivity, and occasional tremors were observed at 200 and 400 ppm. The histologic changes in the liver appeared to be characteristically restricted to rodents and were not seen in experiments on primates. These changes were reversible with cessation of exposure. Cockerels given subcutaneous injections of DDT daily for 90 days had reduced testicular size, and direct estrogenic effects have been observed in female rats given single doses of 50 mg/kg of DDT.

Site and mechanism of toxic action

The locus of primary toxic action of DDT is believed to be sensory and motor nerve fibers and the motor cortex. The mechanism of action is still incompletely known; however, recent evidence indicates that DDT is capable of altering the transport of sodium and potassium ions across the membranes of nerve axons. Studies on isolated neurons and nerve fibers have shown that DDT blocks potassium efflux across the membrane. This action results in an increased negative after potential. Narahashi (1969) studied the effect of DDT on giant nerve fibers of the squid and lobster by means of the voltage clamp technique. He concluded that DDT slows the turning-off process of sodium conductance across the nerve membrane and inhibits the turning-on process of the potassium conductance. The molecular mechanisms for these effects are uncertain, but two possibilities have been suggested. Matsumura and O'Brien (1966) suggested that a charged-transfer complex between DDT and constituents of nerve fibers might account for the altered nerve axon membrane permeabilities. This hypothesis was based upon the findings of specific DDT-binding components in cockroach nerves. It has also been shown that DDT inhibits Na^+, K^+, and Mg^{2+} adenosine triphosphatase activity in the nerve-ending fraction of rat brain *in vitro*. The degree of inhibition of this enzyme by various toxic and nontoxic analogs of DDT corresponded, in general, to their *in vivo* toxicities. This suggests a possible interference in energy metabolism required for ion transport across nerve membranes.

Distribution and storage

DDT and one of its major metabolic products, DDE, have high fat: water partition coefficients and, therefore, tend to accumulate in adipose tissue. Studies in both man and laboratory animals indicate there is a log-log relationship between the daily intake and the residues of DDT and DDT-derived material in adipose tissue. At a constant rate of intake, however, the concentration of the insecticide in adipose tissue reaches an equilibrium and remains relatively constant. Following cessation of exposure, DDT is slowly eliminated from the body. Elimination has been estimated at a rate of approximately 1 percent of stored DDT excreted per day. During the years of its most extensive use in the late 1950s and early 1960s, the average of DDT in fat was about 5 ppm. Total storage of DDT derived from material was about

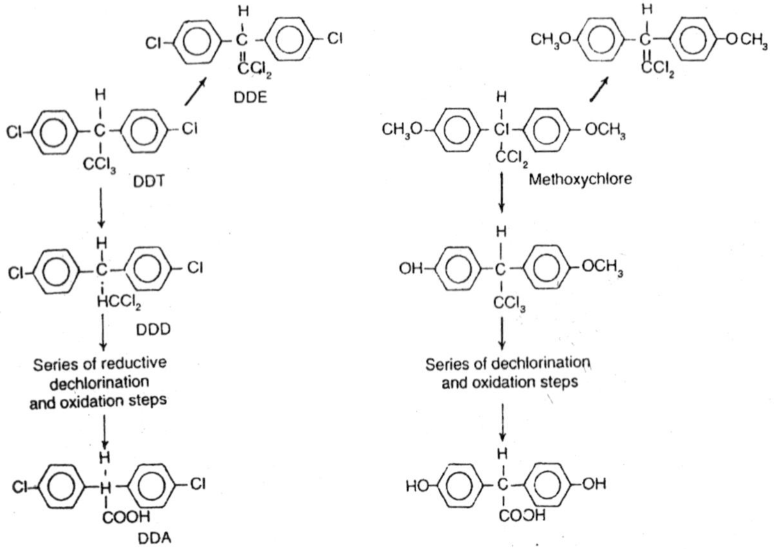

Fig. 8.5. Summary comparison of major metabolic pathways for DDT and methoxychlor.

15 ppm; this consisted primarily of DDT and its lipophilic metabolite; DDE. With declining use of DDT, there appears to have been a reduction in these levels so that the average adipose tissue level for man in the late 1960s was 1 to 2 ppm of DDT and a total of about 9 ppm of total DDT derived materials. Corresponding in time with these observations, analyses of whole meals indicated that the average amount of DDT that an adult in the United States obtained from food decreased from approximately 0.2 mg in 1958 to only about 0.04 mg per day in 1970.

Because lipid storage of DDT is, in a sense, a detoxication mechanism (it removes the compound from reactive sites of action) the insecticide can accumulate to relatively high concentration in adipose tissue when ingested by various species at low dosage rate over prolonged periods of time. This contributed to the so-called biomagnification of DDT in which a series of organisms in a food chain accumulate greater and greater quantities in their fat at each higher trophic level. Ultimately a species at the top of a food chain, e.g., carnivorous birds, may be a adversely affected. Because of the nature of reproduction in birds, they may be considered a more susceptible species. Eggshell thinning has been demonstrated both in the field and in laboratory studies to result from ingestion of DDT and related chlorinated hydrocarbon insecticides. Increased breakage of thin-shelled eggs probably has contributed to population declines of these fish-eating birds.

Another action of DDT that may contribute to effects on wild bird populations is the capacity of DDT and related materials to enhance the metabolism of estrogens. This could create an endocrine imbalance that affects the egg-laying and nesting cycle in such a way that total reproductive success and survival of young during the nesting season may be reduced.

An example of biomagnification related to human exposures was reported for nursing infants by Quimby and coworkers (1965). From an analysis of DDT content of typical meals, it was estimated 0.08 ppm of DDT. This would result in an infant dosage of 0.0112 mg/kg per day or approximately 20 times as much as the infants' mothers. Although this indicates the possibility of biomagnification involving humans there remains no evidence that infants have been harmed by these quantities.

Methoxychlor

Methoxychlor is a chlorinated ethane derivative that has enjoyed increasing use as an insecticide as the use of DDT has declined. The attractiveness of methoxychlor is that it is practically nontoxic to mammals and compared to DDT has relatively low persistence. Of course, it also has some less desirable insecticidal properties than DDT. Compared to oral LD50 values for rats in the range of 100 to 250 mg/kg for DDT, the LD50 for methoxychlor is 6,000 mg/kg. While DDT has been estimated to be stored in fat at an average of 10 to 20 times its chronic intake, and the half-life of stored methoxychlor in rats is one to two weeks compared with an estimated six months to a year for DDT. Although methoxychlor is slowly metabolized to a small extent by pathways similar to those for DDT the major and much more rapid pathway of metabolism is by O-demethylation and subsequent conjugation and excretion. These pathways are catalyzed by microsomal enzymes in mammals and by enzymes in soil organisms and other biota. Consequently, methoxychlor presents much reduced problems of persistence in the environment and biomagnification. Research by on other analogs of DDT suggests the possibility of development of rapidly degradable compounds that have as effective insecticidal properties as DDT but with reduced persistence in the environment.

Chlorinated cyclodiene insecticides

These compounds are also neuropoisons, and many of the signs and symptoms of poisoning resemble those produced by DDT. Unlike

DDT, however, these compounds tend to produce convulsions before other less serious signs of illness have appeared; Persons who have been poisoned by cyclodiene insecticides report headache and nausea, vomiting, dizziness, and mild chronic jerking. On the other hand, patients occasionally have convulsions with no warning symptoms. Unlike the situation with DDT there have been a number of fatalities resulting from acute poisoning by the cyclodiene insecticides.

Davies and Lewis (1956) reported 14 case histories of acute endrin poisoning resulting from an ancient in which at least 49 persons were made ill from eating bakery foods that had been prepared with endrin-contaminated flour. The source of the contamination was a railroad transport cart that had been used to transport bags of flour and that had, some two months previously, been used to transport a leaking container of a concentrated solution of endrin in xylene. The syndrome associated with these poisoning was referred to as fits and consisted of several, and in some cases sudden and unforewarned convulsions.

Several human fatalities have resulted from drinking emulsions or solutions of dieldrin. Garrestton and Curley (1969) described an incident in which a four-years-old boy and his two-year-old sister ingested a 5 per cent solution of dieldrin. Generalized convulsions began within 15 minutes after ingestion and the younger child died before medical assistance could be obtained. At autopsy there were no gross abnormalities apparent. The older child sustained convulsive seizures for 7.5 hours, but these were ultimately controlled with a high dose of anticonvulsants and he survived. Dieldrin distribution studies in this child showed that dieldrin strongly binds to serum proteins in a ratio of 440:1 (bound:unbound) plasma dieldrin. Dieldrin partitioned into fat as fat biopsies showed ratios of fat to serum concentrations of 174:1 at three days after poisoning and 2,200:1 at 179 days after poisoning. Liver function tests indicated some liver injury present for several months after the acute poisoning. Similar studies of a nonfatal case of acute chlordane poisoning in a child revealed signs of poisoning that were similar but the half-life of chlordane in the body appeared to be less than for dieldrin. Studies on persons exposed to dieldrin indicated that 20 mg/100 ml of blood is the approximate threshold at which symptoms of intoxication occur. Delayed and sudden appearance of symptoms of acute dieldrin poisoning several weeks or months after last exposure have been demonstrated in experimental animals and occupationally exposed men. Abnormal EEG recordings have been observed for months after exposure to dieldrin.

Increased incidence of liver tumors in mice fed dieldrin has been observed in chronic feeding studies. On the other hand, Deichmann and MacDonald (1971) found that overall tumor incidence in rats fed aldrin (20 to 50 ppm) or dieldrin (20 to 50 ppm) was lower than in controls and no different from controls in endrin-fed (2 to 12 ppm) rats. A panel review of several studies related to tumorigenicity of aldrin and dieldrin led to a conclusion that the available data did not meet criteria required to detect carcinogenic activity. Another panel, however, concluded that aldrin, dieldrin, and heptachlor (as well as DDT) could be judged "positive" for tumor induction on the basis of adequate tests in one more species of laboratory animal. A working group of the International Agency for Research on Cancer concluded that dieldrin was hepatocarcinogenic in mice, but that conflicting reports prevented conclusion of carcinogenicity of aldrin and heptachlor. To a large extent, because of suspicion of carcinogenicity, the manufacture and use of these compounds have been severely curtailed. No convincing evidence that these compounds or any other insecticide in use has contributed to increased incidence of tumor in man has emerged, and the subject of carcinogenic potential of the organochlorine insecticides remains an area of controversy and continued research.

Aldrin and dieldrin have been reported to produce various effects on reproduction in a variety of species, e.g., decreased fertility and decreased viability of the young, but the dietary concentrations required for these effects were as high as or higher than those that produced other effects such as histologic changes in livers of adult animals and were thought to be related to hormonal imbalance.

Action, metabolism, and storage

Acute poisoning by the chlorinated cyclodienes can also be classified as neurotoxicity. Generally they are considered central nervous system stimulants; however, their precise site and mechanism of action are incompletely known. Biochemical studies have shown that in animals poisoned with dieldrin and other cyclodienes there was an alteration of brain amino acid ratios and an increased level of ammonia in the brain. These actions might explain the central nervous system effects; however, other convulsive agents produce similar effects, and it is not clear whether the biochemical changes in the brain were the cause or the result of convulsions produced by the insecticides. It has been reported that in brains of rats poisoned with dieldrin, gamma butyrobetaine and related compounds were released from brain mitochondria. It was suggested that they might be responsible for the effects of dieldrin, because intracranial injections of the betaine esters caused violent and fetal convulsions. Other treatments that produce convulsions also led to a release of betainecoenzyme A esters These treatments include electroshock, ammonium chloride, and comphor. Although the release of betaine esters as a common underlying mechanism for the convulsive effects of a variety of agents may be attractive, it also may the result of postconvulsive action initiated by different mechanisms for different agents.

An important difference between DDT and the chlorinated cyclodienes that should be noted is that cyclodienes are absorbed from the intact skin. The difference between the oral dermal LD5 values for the cyclodienes is much less than the difference for DDT. Whereas the cyclodienes may not be pose any appreciably greater risk than DDT to the general population that might be exposed to small quantities of these materials in their food, from the standpoint of the occupational exposure, working the concentrated solutions of the cyclodienes would be more hazardous than working with concentrates of DDT.

Aldrin and heptachlor are metabolized by microsomal enzymes to their corresponding epoxides. Because the epoxides are equally or more toxic by acute dosage than the corresponding parent compounds, it has been suggested that epoxide formation represents an activation reaction. However, it is also felt that the parent compounds are toxic in their own. The epoxides of aldrin and heptachlor are lipid-soluble and it is the epoxides i.e., dieldrin and heptachlor epoxide, that are stored in the adipose tissue of man and other animals. Evidence that epoxidation occur readily in a variety of species is derived from the fact analysis of residues in animals that have been exposed to the parent compounds aldrin and heptachlor reveals only storage of the epoxide forms. The epoxides of these compounds may be further metabolized to more hydrophylic substances as the dihydrols, which can be conjugated and excreted in the urine. Biliary and fecal excretion of the cyclodiene insecticides also occur.

Toxaphene

In recent years this insecticides has ranked first in quantity used in the United States with estimated annual production of the order of 75 to 95 million lb. Toxaphene is described as the mixed isomers of chlorinated camphene containing 67 to 69 per cent chlorine. Thus, in spite of its commercial use as an insecticide for over 25 years, its exact chemical structure has been largely unknown, and it has been listed by the empiric formula $C_{10}H_{10}Cl_8$. Recently, the active ingredients of toxaphene have been the object of extensive investigation that has revealed that it includes more than 170 C_{10} compounds with six to ten chlorine atoms. Identified compounds include several endo-exo isomers of hexa-, hepta-, and nona- chlorobornanes and chlorobornenes of widely varying biologic activity. In view of the extremely high toxicity of the 8-octachlorobornane, it is obvious that the proportion of this (and other highly toxic isomers) present in technical toxaphene could greatly influence the toxicity to both target and nontarget species. Piperonyl butoxide, an insecticide synergist and mixed-function oxidase inhibitor, potentiated the toxicity of heptachlorobornane in both mice and houseflies. The other compounds were potentiated to a moderate degree in houseflies but not in mice. Heptachlorobornane undergoes reductive dechlorination by reduced microsomal cytochrome P-450 and *in vivo* in flies and rats. Enzymatic dehydrochlorination and oxidation of carbon substituents no doubt also help account for the extensive dechlorination that occur in rats. Such extensive metabolism probably also accounts for the relatively low persistence of toxaphene in comparison to other chlorinated hydrocarbon insecticides.

Chronic exposure of laboratory animals to toxaphene in their diet resulted in degenerative or other changes in liver and kidneys, generally at concentrations in excess of 25 ppm. Terpene polychlorinates closely related to toxaphene, increased the incidence of hepatomas in one strain of mice. Thus toxaphene, like most of the other related chlorinated insecticides, comes under suspicion of having potential for tumorigenic action.

Lindane

The gama isomer of hexachlorocyclohexane (HCH) sometimes called benzene hexachloride (HHC) products signs of poisonings that resemble those produced by DDT, i.e., tremors, ataxia, convulsions, and prostration, with stimulated respiration. Violent tonic and clinic convulsions occur in severe cases of acute poisoning. Fatty changes in the liver kidney tubule degeneration have been noted in fatal cases. Technical grades of HCH used in insecticidal preparations actually contain a mixture of isomers. The γ and α isomers are convulsant poisons, while the β and δ isomers are central nervous system depressants and the ε and η isomers appear to be inactive. The mechanism of neurotoxic action has been demonstrated. One interesting but unproven hypothesis reviewed by O'Brien (1967) suggested that the differing actions of the isomers could be related to their binding and goodness-of-fit into pores of a "hypothetic lattice in axonic membranes.

Technical HCH and several of the isomers contained therein have been found to produce liver cell tumors in mice when fed in the diet at high concentrations for most of the animal's lifetime.

Residues of HCH have been found in human fat and milk. Although the α, β, and γ isomers were all found as residues, the α and γ isomers are more rapidly metabolized and the β isomer accounted for 90 per cent of total HCH is isomer residue. Intraperitoneally administered HCH was eliminated in rats at a rate of 5 to 10 per cent of the dose per day. Gamma HCH was metabolized in rats by progressive dehydrochlorination, glutathione conjugation, and aromatic hydroxylation to yield 2,4-dichlorophenyl-mercapturic acid and conjugates of 2,3,5- and 2,4,5-trhchlorophenols that are excreted in the urine.

Mirex and kepone

Mirex has been used extensively in the southeastern United States for control of the fire ant. The acute toxicity of mirex to rats indicated that it was less toxic than DDT. However, the chronicity factor (defined as the single dose LD50 in mg/kg divided by 90-dose LD50 in mg/kg per day was much greater for mirex than for DDT. The respective chronicity factors for mirex, DDT, and dieldrin in rats were 60.8, 5.6, and 12.8. Rats fed mirex in the diet for 166 days had minimal pathologic changes in the liver with 5 ppm and definite enlargement of liver cells, cytoplasmic inclusions, and biliary stasis with 25 ppm. Female rats given 25 ppm of mirex in the diet gave birth to fewer and less viable offspring than control rats and one-third or more of the offspring of mirex-led rats developed cataracts (Gaines and Kimbrough, 1970). A total of 5 ppm in the diet had no effect on rats' reproduction. Mice given 1,000 mg/kg mirex subcutaneously in a single dose developed tumors of various types, and oral administration of 10 mg/kg/day for three weeks followed by feeding 26 ppm in the diet for 18 months resulted in a 40 per cent incidence of hepatomas. Rats fed 50 to 100 ppm of mirex in their diet had a dose-dependent, increased incidence of hepatic megalocytosis, cellular alterations, and neoplastic nodules, with a significantly increased incidence of hepatocellular carcinoma only in males at the high dietary level.

Mirex stimulates hepatic microsomal oxidative metabolism and causes proliferation of the smooth endoplasmic reticulum of the liver. No evidence of metabolism of mirex *in vivo* and *in vitro* has yet been found and it is stored in adipose tissue. Hence, the possibility that environmental contamination with mirex may lead to exposure to Kepone has increased concern about the adverse health and environmental effects of both these compounds. Both mirex and Kepone are highly persistent and have high lipid: water partition coefficients and have been shown to bioconcentrate several thousand fold in food chains.

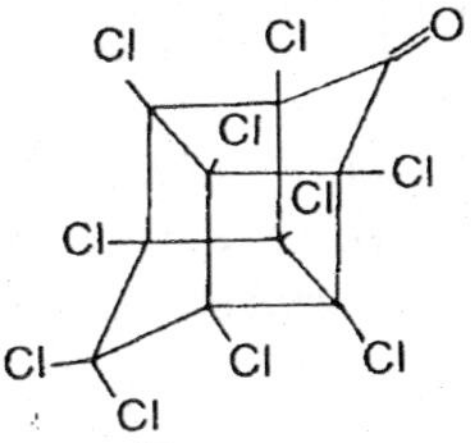

Kepone

The toxic effects of Kepone, as seen in humans, were described earlier in this chapter. It is encouraging that a means for hastening the excretion of stored Kepone has been developed. This involves the use of an anion-exchange resin, cholestyramine, which when given orally to patients, enhanced fecal excretion of Kepone by three- to eighteenfold, reduced the half-life of stored Kepone dramatically, and enhanced the rate of recovery from the toxic manifestations, as judged by recovery toward normal sperm counts. The rationale for the use of cholestyramine relates to the biliary-enterohepatic circulation, which cycles Kepone, hence cholestyramine, by binding the insecticide, interrupts the reabsorption phase and shifts the equilibrium from reabsorption and storage to fecal excretion.

The toxic effects of Kepone noted in excessively exposed workers, namely tremor, liver, injury, and altered reproductive potential, had been previously in laboratory animals. Studies at the National Cancer Institute revealed an increased incidence of hepatocellular carcinomas in mice and rats fed Kepone in the diet.

Treatment of organochlorine insecticide poisoning

Treatment of acute poisoning by all of the organochlorine insecticides is largely symptomatic. Phenobarbital has been recommended as an antidote to control convulsions produced by DDT and other compounds. However, intravenous diazepam, because of its lesser respiratory depression, is recommended to sedate and control convulsions associated with most of the organochlorine insecticides. Calcium gluconate has also been useful in controlling convulsions produced by DDT. As with, all exposure, attention should be given to removal of unabsorbed poison from the gastrointestinal tract and the skin. Oil-based cathartics should be avoided, however, as they may increase adsorption.

Botanical Insecticides

It is commonly felt that insecticides derived from natural products are less toxic to mammals than synthetic pesticides. The fallácy of this view, however, can be illustrated by the oral LD50s to rats of the three major products used as botanical insecticides: nicotine has an LD50 of 10 to 60 mg/kg, placing it amongst the most toxic insecticides; pyrethrum and rotenone have oral LD50s in the range of 100 to 300 mg/kg, comparable to several moderately toxic synthesis.

Nicotine

Nicotine acts to stimulate nicotinic receptors in automic ganglia, at the neuromuscular junction, and in some pathways of the central nervous system. Its action at these sites mimics the normal transmitter acetylcholine. Poisoning in vertebrates is followed by symptoms of salivation and vomiting (from ganglionic stimulation), muscular weakness and fibrillation by stimulation at the neuromuscular junction, and ultimately, clonic convulsions and cessation of respiration (effects in the central nervous system). Treatment for nicotine Poisoning is by use of anticonvulsants. Nicotine is oxidized and hydroxylated by microsomal oxidases, which yield less toxic metabolic products. Because it is the principal alkaloid in tobacco, nicotine has been studied extensively for its pharmacologic actions and detailed discussions of its pharmacology are available in textbooks of that science and in a comprehensive review on the effects of tobacco.

Rotenoids

A preparation extracted from tuber root, *Derris elliptica*, was used by primitive people to paralyze fish. It was from this use that its possibility for application as an insecticide developed. The active principle of the Derris species is the compound rotenone plus as many as 13 related derivatives. Poisoning by rotenone in man is rare, and it has been used by direct application for head lice, scabies, and other ectoparasites. Local effects include conjunctivitis, dermatitis, pharyngitis, and rhinitis. Orally, rotenone preparations produce gastrointestinal irritation, nausea, and vomiting. The estimated fatal oral dose for 70-kg man is from 10 to 100 g. Inhalation of the dust is more hazardous, and it can cause respiratory stimulation followed by depression with fits and convulsions. A biochemical mode of action for rotenone in insect tissues, which also occurs in mammalian tissues, is the inhibition of the oxidation of reduced NAD ($NADH_2$ to NAD). The consequence of this blockage is that oxidation of substrates via the NAD system, such as glutamate, alphaketoglutarate, and pyruvate, are blocked by rotenone.

Pyrethrum

Pyrethrum is one of the oldest insecticides known to man, and the active principle of pyrethrum flowers are pyrethrin I and II and cinerin I and II. Pyrethrum extract is used in many household insecticides because of its rapid knock-down action. The estimated fatal oral dose for man of pyrethrum is 50 g/70 kg; fatal poisoning of a child occurred as the result of eating 15 g of pyrethrum concentrate. Signs and symptoms of poisoning by pyrethrum may take several forms. Contact dermatitis is the most common. Cases of asthmatic-like reactions have been reported in some individuals who had a previous history of asthma with a broad allergic background. Severe anaphylactic reactions with peripheral vascular collapse and respiratory difficulty are considered a rare accompaniment of the dermatologic reactions. With massive doses ingested orally, nervous system symptoms may occur, which include excitation and convulsions leading to paralysis and accompanied by muscular fibrillation and diarrhea. Death is due to respiratory failure.

Preparations containing synthetic pyrethroids are less likely to result in allergic reactions. Allethrin one of the synthetic pyrethroids, inhibited both sodium potassium conductances in squid and cockroach giant axons. It exerts four actions on nerve membrane: slightly depolarizes the membrane, increases the negative afterpotential, induces repetitive after discharges, and eventually blocks the action potential.

HERBICIDES

The production and use of chemicals for destruction of noxious weeds have increased markedly during the last decade. Herbicides rival or exceed insecticides in quantity and value of sales. Because plants differ markedly from animals in their morphology and physiology, it might be expected that herbicides would present little hazard of chemical toxicity to vertebrates. Indeed some compounds have very low toxicity in mammals, but even among the herbicides there are highly toxic chemicals, and a number of these have caused fatal poisoning in man.

Chlorophenoxy Compounds

The compounds 2,4-dichlorophenoxyacetic acid (2,4-D) and (2,4,5-T) as their salts and esters are probably the most familiar chemicals used as herbicides. They are used in agriculture for control of broad-leaf weeds and in the control of woody plants along highways and utilities' rights of way. They exert their herbicidal action by acting as growth hormones in plants. They have no hormonal action in animals but their mechanism of toxic action is poorly understood. Animals killed by massive doses of 2,4-D are believed to die of ventricular fibrillation.

At lower doses, when death is delayed, various signs of muscular involvement are seen including stiffness of the extremities, ataxia, paralysis, and eventually coma. Sublethal doses, singly or repeated, lead to a general unkempt appearance without specific signs except a tenseness and muscular weakness. Feeding studies in animals indicate that repeated exposures to doses just slightly smaller than the single toxic dose are tolerated, indicating little cumulative effect. In a case of suicide, an oral dose of not less than 6500 mg led to death. It has been estimated that the oral dose required to produce symptoms in man is probably about 3 to 4 g. Profound muscular weakness was noted in a patient recovering from an episode of acute poisoning by 2,4-D. Peripheral neuritis was reported for three men who had recent heavy occupational exposure to 2,4-D. Pathologic changes in experimental animals killed by the chlorophenoxy compounds are generally nonspecific with irritation of the stomach and some liver and kidney injury.

The chlorophenoxy herbicides have produced contact dermatitis in man, and as mentioned earlier, a rather severe type of dermatitis, chloracne, has been observed in workmen involved in the manufacture 2,4,5-T. This effect appears to be due primarily to the action of a contaminant, 2,3,7,8-tetracholorodibenzo-ρ-dioxin.

Concern about the toxicology of 2,4,5-T and related compounds centers primarily on teratogenic action in experimental animals. The first studies to reveal this action were, it is now known, conducted with a sample of 2,4,5-T that contained a high level (about 30 ppm) of a contaminant 2,3,7,8-tetrachlorodibenzo-ρ-dioxin. This contaminant is formed during the synthesis of the trichlorophenol precursor as shown below.

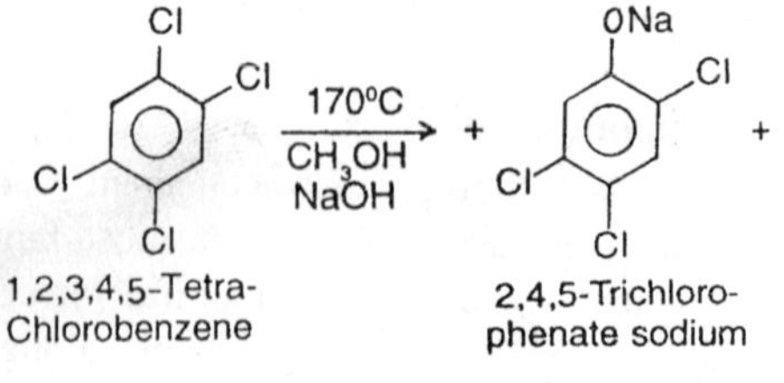

Cl Cl Cl Cl → (170°C, CH_3OH, NaOH) + ONa Cl Cl Cl +

1,2,3,4,5-Tetra-Chlorobenzene

2,4,5-Trichloro-phenate sodium

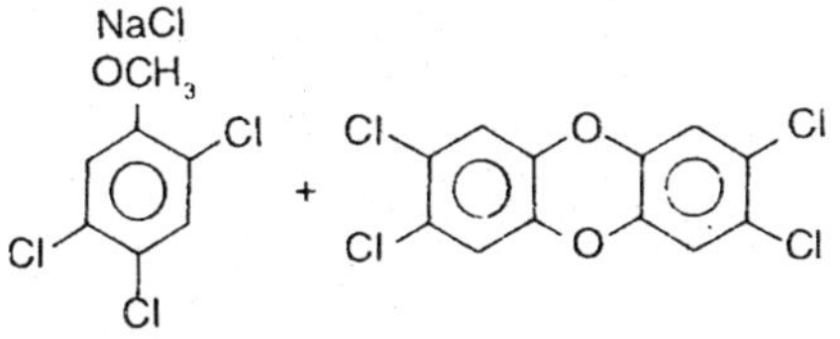

2,4,5 - Trichloroanisole   2, 3, 7, 8-Tetrachlorodibenzodioxin

Tetrachlorodioxin (TCDD) is an extremely toxic chemical with LD50s of 0.022 and 0.045 mg/kg for male and female rats and only 0.006% mg/kg for female guinea pig. For female guinea pig, the ratio of the LD50 of 2,4,5-T to the LD50 of the dioxin is 630,000. For female rats the acute oral LD50 for tetrachlorodioxin is about 10,000 times less than the oral LD50 for 2,4,5-T. The daily dose of the dioxin given to pregnant rats during the gestational period that resulted in fetal toxicity was only about 1/400 of the material LD50 of dioxin, or about 1/4,000,000 of the single oral LD50 of 2,4,5-T to female rats. It would appear, then, that the concentration of dioxin as a contaminant in 2,4,5-T is a major factor in determining its teratogenicity. In addition to its extreme acute toxicity and its teratogenic action. TCDD has recently been reported to induce tumor in laboratory rodents fed very low concentrations (5 ppt to 5 ppb) in the diet.

The 2,4,5-T teratogenesis experiments illustrate an important principle for evaluation of the safety of commercial products; that is, one must be concerned not only with major active component, but with minor contaminants that may be prevent as a result of their formation during the manufacture or as the recent of degradative reactions occurring in the development. Presently, the TCDD content is regulated in 2,4,5-T at 0.1 ppm or less.

The acute toxicities of chlorophenoxy herbicides and various enters and salts have been summarized by Rowe and Hymas (1954). The LD50s ranged from 300 to > 1,000 mg/kg in several experimental species tested, with the exception that dogs were relatively more sensitive (LD50 of 100 mg/kg for 2,4,5-T isopropylester).

Dinitrophenols

Several substituted dinitrophenols alone or as salts of aliphatic amines or alkalies are used in weed control. Human poisonings by dinitro orthocresol (DNOC) have been reported. Signs and symptoms of acute poisoning in man include nausea, gastric upset, restlessness, sensation of heat, flushed skin, sweating, rapid respiration, tachycardia, fever, cyanosis, and finally collapse and coma. The illness runs a rapid course with death or recovery generally within 24 to 48 hours. These signs and symptoms reflect an increased metabolic rate, which may exceed several times normal values and is dose-dependent. If heat production exceeds the capacity for heat loss, fatal hyperthermia may result. Chronic exposure to dinitro-orthocresol may also produce fatigue, restlessness, anxiety, excessive sweating, unusual thirst, and loss of weight. A yellow staining of the conjunctiva has been noted, and cataract formation is another possible sequela of chronic dinitro-orthocresol exposure. Blood levels of DNOC below 10 ppm are considered of trivial importance; levels of 11 to 20 ppm indicate appreciable absorption; and above these blood levels toxic manifestations are likely. Levels greater than 50 ppm are critically dangerous. After removal of the poison from the skin or gastrointestinal tract, treatment consists of ice baths to reduce fever and administration of oxygen to assure maximal oxygenation of the blood. Fluid and electrolyte therapy may be necessary to replace loss by sweating. Atropine sulfate is absolutely contraindicated in cases of poisoning by dinitrophenolic compounds, and therefore care should be taken to avoid a misdiagnosis of organophosphate poisoning. Symptoms of poisoning and their severity are enhanced when the environmental temperature is high. In very cool weather blood levels as high as 50 ppm have been tolerated without symptoms. The oral LD50 of DNOC in rats is approximately 30 mg/kg.

It will be noted that the nitrocresol compounds produce symptoms of toxicity similar to those produced by dinitrophenol and therefore probably act by uncoupling of oxidative phosphorylation as has been proposed for dinitrophenol. Compounds that produce uncoupling of oxidative phosphorylation also have the peculiar property of rapidly producing rigor mortis after death. Studies on the toxicology of substituted nitrophenols used in agriculture may be found in report by Spencer and coworkers (1948).

Bipyridyl Compounds

Paraquat is the best-known compound of this class of herbicides, which are increasing in use. Over 200 cases of accidental or suicidal fatalities resulted from paraquat poisoning have been reported during the past decade. Pathologic changes observed at autopsy in all of these

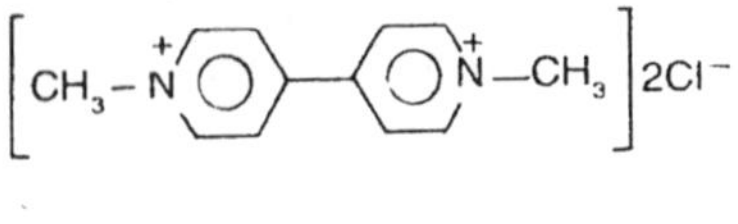

$$\left[CH_3-\overset{+}{N}C_5H_4-C_5H_4\overset{+}{N}-CH_3\right]2Cl^-$$

fatal human poisoning showed evidence of lung, liver, and kidney damage. Some cases had myocarditis, and one case showed transient neurologic signs. The most striking pathologic change was a widespread cellular proliferation in the lungs. This pathology was also evident in a suicide case in which the paraquat was injected subcutaneously. In this case the victim died in respiratory distress, and the main pathologic findings at autopsy were in the lungs. Hence, paraquat produces lung damage even when administered by routes in which exposure of the lung is secondary. Although ingestion of paraquat results in gastrointestinal upset within a few hours after exposure, the onset of respiratory symptoms and eventual death by respiratory distress may be delayed for several days. In a case involving a six-year-old child the concentration of paraquat present in the liver and kidney at necropsy was 208 mg per 100 g of kidney. One accidental case involved an individual who mistakenly took a mouthful of the herbicide from a "snout" bottle, and although he spat it out almost immediately, 14 days later cyanosis and severe dyspnea developed. The patient who administered paraquat by subcutaneous injection had chest radiograph changes three days after administration, but did not develop respiratory symptoms for an additional 11 days. Davies et al. (1977) suggest, on the basis of pharmacokinetic studies in dogs and humans, that because paraquat in the systemic circulation is rather rapidly cleared via the kidneys, accumulation of toxic amounts in the lung is secondary to kidney injury. They indicate that the presence of more than 0.2 μg/ml of paraquat in plasma, accompanied by impaired renal function in the first 24 hours after dosing, will usually result in fatal lung injury. On this basis, treatment of paraquat poisoning must be instituted early and involves (1) removal of paraquat from the alimentary tract by gastric lavage and use of cathartics; (2) prevention of further absorption by oral administration of Fuller's earth (30 per cent w/v); and (3) removal of absorbed paraquat by hemodialysis or hemoperfusion. A very similar course of treatment was recommended by Cavalli and Fletcher (1977) who evaluated 96 published cases of paraquat poisoning, 70 of them fatal. They indicate that treatment, in order to be effective, should be initiated within ten hours of ingestion. Ten to fifteen milliliter of commercially prepared concentrate of paraquat is estimated as a lethal oral dose for adults, and massive overdoses of the order of 50 ml are very difficult to treat.

A great deal of concern and public interest is the toxicology of paraquat was stimulated by revelation of its use in a herbicide spray program to control illicit production of marijuana and heroin. High residues of paraquat were found in marijuana cigarettes. It was estimated that 0.26 μg of paraquat could be inhaled by smoking a marijuana cigarette contaminated with 1,000 ppm. It was suggested that a slow buildup of lung "scarring" might occur in persons inhaling even these low quantities. There presently is little or no documentation to support these allegations, although direct inhalation of such a progressive lung toxin as paraquat is obviously to be avoided.

The toxicology of bipyridyl herbicides was initially reviewed by Conning and associates (1969) and recently by Smith and Heath (1976). In animal studies all species examined showed the same response after a single large dose of paraquat given by mouth or by subcutaneous or intraperitoneal injection. There was an early onset of hyperexcitability, which in some cases led to convulsions or incoordination. The animals died over a period of ten days after administration. Early deaths were not associated with any specific systemic pathology. Later death that occurred at two to five days after administration usually were accompanied by severe pulmonary congestion and edema with hyaline membrane formation and inflammatory infiltrates. Animals that survive the pulmonary edema associated with a single dose occasionally show progression of lung lesions of fibrosis and eventual death from respiratory failure. As in man, a single dose may produce pulmonary fibrosis in the dog. The feeding of 0.03 per cent or more of paraquat in the diet of experimental animals led to the production of pulmonary fibrosis in most of the animals. Studies of organ cultures of lungs treated with paraquat revealed extensive necrosis of alveolar cells. Inhalation of paraquat aerosols for several hours produces severe congestion, alveolar edema, and bronchial irritation two to three days after the exposure. However, it the animal survives during this period there is, surprisingly, no further chronic fibrosis produced.

The LD50 for paraquat in guinea pigs, cats, and cows is in the range of 30 to 50 mg/kg. Rats appear to be somewhat more resistant with an LD50 of about 125 mg/kg. The LD50 for man is estimated at about 40 mg/kg. Studies of several species indicate that absorption of paraquat from the gastrointestinal tract is relatively low, in no cases exceeding 20 per cent of the administered dose. There is a rapid disappearance from the blood with 90 to 100 per cent of the dose excreted in the urine within 48 hours. Since there is a long delay until onset of respiratory signs, this compound has been classified among the "hit-and-run" type of toxic agents. Exposure of the skin to solutions of dipyridyls results in erythemia and a mild reactive hyperkeratosis, which may be associated with pustule formation.

Diquat produces acute and chronic effects that differ from those produced by paraquat in that marked effects on the lung are not observed. This has been attributed to an energy-dependent system in the lung that selectively concentrates paraquat. Oral doses near the LD50 produce hyperexcitability leading to convulsions and distention of the gastrointestinal tract with discolouration of intestinal fluids. The only pathology associated with long-term feeding of diquat at levels of 0.05 per cent was the production of cataracts in about ten months. A related compound, chlormequat, has as its target organ the kidney. In both rats and dogs, kidney lesions were the only striking pathology noted in both acute and chronic studies.

It has been suggested that the mechanism of the herbicidal action of the dipyridyls is mediated by free radical reactions, and a similar mechanism has been proposed for the action in mammals. Gage (1968) showed that free radicals could be produced from paraquat and diquat incubated in the presence of reduced NADP and liver microsomes. Proposed biochemical mechanisms of paraquat toxicity are discussed in detail in a recent proceedings of a conference on this subject. The formation of free radicals via a cyclic single reduction-oxidation of paraquat predominates. Since initial reduction of oxidized paraquat uses NADPH, the possibility that paraquat competes for and deprives other systems (essential for cell integrity) of this biologic reducing agent is one aspect of the toxic mechanism. A more comprehensive mechanism that has been proposed involves the reoxidation of reduced paraquat by molecular oxygen with the concomitant production of superoxide radicals that dismulate nonenzymatically to single oxygen. These attack unsaturated lipids of cell membranes and produce lipid hydroperoxides, which may form lipid-free-radicals with consequent membrane damage or which may be reduced by GSH-dependent systems that depend on NADPH for GSH regeneration. The early event of paraquat-induced increased superoxide production is the underlying rationale for the proposal that administration of purified superoxide dismutase may be valuable in therapy of paraquat poisoning.

Carbamate Herbicides

This class of herbicides contains a large number of aromatic and aliphatic esters, which for the most part have relatively low acute toxicities. The compound propham is a typical example of this class of herbicides. Its LD50 by oral administration in rats and rabbits was of the order of 5,000 mg/kg. Feeding rats dietary concentrations of 1,000 ppm for three months produced no signs of effects on general condition and growth, fertility, or pathologic changes. Barban is somewhat more toxic than propham with an oral LD50 to 600 mg/kg for rats and rabbits and 24 mg/kg for guinea pigs. Daily oral administration of 75 mg/kg for 22 days produced some loss of weight, while half of this quantity produced on toxic action. Feeding experiments with rats showed no toxic action, of 150 ppm in the diet for 18 months. Barban, however, is a potent skin-sensitizing agent in man, and allergic reactions and rash may develop on subsequent contact.

Substituted Urea

Like the carbamate herbicides the substituted urea are, as a class, rather nontoxic by acute oral administration. Monuron and diuron are typical examples, with LD50 values in rats of over 3,000 mg/kg. Chronic toxicity studies suggest that monuron has carcinogenic potential. An increased incidence of lung tumors was observed in male mice of one of two strains tested by oral administration in one study. In another study an increased incidence of hepatomas was observed when mice were given 6 mg per animal weekly by gavage, but this study was subject to question as the survival of controls was not fully reported. In two separate studies, rats were fed monuron in their diets for 18 to 24 months. In one study no increased tumor rate over controls was observed, while in the second study 7 per cent of monuron-fed rats developed tumors at various sites while control rats were reported to be tumor free.

Triazines

Most member of this class of herbicides also have low oral scute toxicities ranging above 1,000 mg/kg. Simazine was nontoxic to a variety of animal species including mice, rats, rabbits, chickens, and pigeons. Rats survived daily doses of 2,500 mg/kg for four weeks. Simazine is, however, more toxic to sheep and cattle. Sheep were killed by three daily dose doses of 250 mg/kg, 14 daily doses of 100 mg/kg, or 31 daily doses of 50 mg/kg. Cattle were killed by three daily doses of 250 mg/kg. The acute toxicity of atrazine to rats is greater than for simazine; however, cattle and sheep appear to be more resistant to atrazine than to simazine.

The herbicide amitrole (3-amino-1H-1,2,4-triazole), although not classified as a triazine, is structurally somewhat similar. This compound also has a very low acute oral toxicity to rats and mice (ranging from 15,000 to 25,000 mg/kg). However, amitrole is a rather potential antithyroid agent, and feeding levels of 2 ppm in the diet resulted in significant effects on thyroid function. These functional changes occurred after only one week of feeding of amitrole and goiters can be induced by amitrole with long continuous administration. Amitrole given to rats in the diet at 100 ppm for two years resulted in the development of thyroid adenomas and adenocarcinomas. This has resulted in prohibition of this compound for use as a herbicide where residues might occur on food crops. Amitrole inhibits peroxidase activity in livers and thyroids, and the mode of action in producing thyroid tumors appears to be related to the goitrogenic effect of amitrole with resultant increased TSH (thyroid-stimulating hormone) since other antithyroid agents that result in TSH stimulation also can produce thyroid tumors experimentally. The amitrole case illustrates an important principle in toxicology, that is, the fallacy of assuming safety purely on the basis of low acute toxicity. As is illustrated by this compound, which is practically nontoxic acutely, rather profound functional changes can occur that directly or indirectly may lead to irreversible pathology, e.g., cancer.

Amide Herbicides

Several aniline derivatives esterified with organic acids are currently used as herbicides. These compounds also have relatively high oral LD50s for rats. A typical example is the herbicide propanil, which is used extensively to control noxious weeds in rice crops. The rice plant is selectively resistant to the herbicidal action of propanil because it contains an acylamidase that hydrolyzes propanil to 3,4-dichloroaniline and propionic acid. An interesting case of herbicide potentiation was observed in field studies in which propanil was applied to rice following the application of organophosphate insecticides. This procedure resulted in damage to rice plants and was subsequently explained on the basis that the organophosphates inhibited the hydrolysis of propanil, and thus the parent compound was preserved and exerted its herbicidal action in the rice. Williams and Jacobson (1966) demonstrated that mammalian livers also contained an amidase that hydrolyzed propanil, and they speculated that organophosphates and carbamates might potentiate the acute mammalian toxicity of this herbicide.

Studies of interactions did not reveal a significant potentiation, however. Further investigation demonstrated that inhibition of liver acylamidase by triorthocresyl phosphate (TOCP) prevented the cyanosis that was observed when mice were given toxic doses of propanil. The cyanosis was due to methemoglobin formation following hydrolysis to 3,4-dichloroaniline. Other signs of poisoning, i.e., CNS depression and death, were not prevented by inhibiting the hydrolysis of the herbicide. It appears, therefore, that aromatic amides that are hydrolyzed to aniline derivatives may produce methemoglobin, but that the acute lethal action is due to a different mechanism.

Much more extensive discussion of the toxicology of herbicides may be found in Dalgaard-Mikkelsen and Poulsen's review (1962) and comprehensive summaries of the toxicity and ecologic effects of herbicides are contained in the report by House and associates (1967).

Fungicides

Fungicides like other classes of pesticides comprise a heterogenous group of chemical compounds. With a few exceptions, the fungicides have not attracted the detailed toxicologic research as have insecticides. A detailed review of their action on the target organisms (fungi-toxicity) has appeared. Although many of the compounds used to control fungus diseases on plants, seeds, and produce are rather nontoxic activity, there are some notable exceptions. The mercury-containing fungicides comprise the group that has been of greatest concern for hazard to health, and they have been responsible for many deaths or permanent neurologic disability resulting from the misdirection of mercury fungicide-treated seed grains into human and animal food.

Captan and *Folpet* because of some structural similarities to thalidomide were suspected as being possible teratogens, and this effect was confirmed in the developing chick embryo. Robens (1970) reported teratogenic effects in hamsters wit!. doses of 500 mg/kg to pregnant females on days 7 and 8 of gestation. Other studies in rabbits, rats, and hamsters failed to reveal teratogenic effects from Folpet but in one study nine malformed offspring were observed out of 75 implantations in nine pregnant rabbits given, 75 mg/kg/day of captan orally on days 6 through 16 of gestation. Rats fed a low-protein diet were reported to be much sensitive to the acute oral toxicity (LD50, 480/mg/kg) of captan than rats receiving a normoprotein diet (LD50, 12,500 mg/kg).

Pentachlorophenol production and use are of the order of 50 million lb per year. It is used as an insecticide and herbicide as well as a fungicide, with major application as a wood preservative. Several cases of human poisonings have resulted in association with these uses. It acute toxic action in men and experimental animals resembles that produced by the nitrophenolic herbicides, i.e., marked increases in metabolic rate as the result of uncoupling of oxidative phosphorylation. It is readily absorbed through the skin. Two cases of fatal poisonings and several non-fatal cases occurred in a hospital nursery in which pentachlorophenol had been used as fungicide in the laundry room (against the labeled instructions) and ultimately contacted infants through their diapers. Several infants died before the cause and source of poisoning were identified. The fatal dose of pentachlorophenol for laboratory animals ranges from 30 to 100 mg/kg, and it is readily absorbed through the skin. In recent years it has become apparent that many commercial samples of pentachlorophenol with polychlorinated dibenzodioxins and dibenzofurans. These contaminants are generally hexachlorinated or octachlorinated dibenzodioxins or dibenzofurans, and they are less toxic than the tetrachlorodioxin contaminant in 2,4,5-T. Nevertheless, some isomers of hexachlorodibenzodioxin have LD50 values in guinea pigs of the order of 60 to 100 μg/kg, ranking them as extremely toxic chemicals. The octachlorodioxins are much less acutely toxic, in the order of 1 g/kg. Although pentachlorophenol is highly toxic in its own right, some studies suggest that contaminants may be responsible for some of the toxic effects of technical grade. A comparison of effects of technical versus purified pentachlorophenol indicated that only the technical produced grade produced chlorance, chick edema, hepatic porphyria, and increased relative liver weight. Technical grade was also much more active as a liver enzyme inducer.

Another fungicide, hezachlorobenezene (noted that this is distinct from hexachlorocyclohexane or lindane), produced more than 3,000 cases of acquired toxic porphyria autanea tarda, which was characterized by severe skin manifestation including photosensitivity, bulbae formation, deep scarring, permanent loss of hair and skin atrophy. The poisonings were traced to the consumption of wheat that had been prepared for planting by treating it with hexachlorobenzene for its fungicidal effects.

Dithiocarbamate fungicides have enjoyed rather widespread use in agriculture. They have a low order to acute toxicity, with oral LD50 values in rats ranging from several hundred milligrams to several grams per kilogram. There is little evidence of human injuries from exposure to the compounds; however, recently some of these compounds have been reported to have teratogenic and/or carcinogenic potential. Two groups of dithiocarbamates have been used, the dimethyldithiocarbamates and the ethylenebisdithiocarbamates. Their respective general structures are as follows:

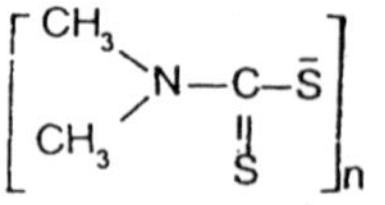

Dimethyldithiocarbamates

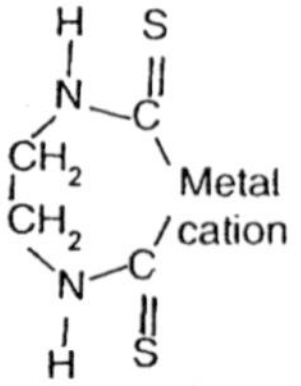

Diethydithiocarbamates

The names of the fungicides are derived from the metallic cations. For example, when the cation is zinc or iron, the respective dimethyldithiocarbamates are ziram or ferbam. With manganese, zinc, or sodium as the cation in the diethyldithiocarbamates, the respective fungicide is maneb, zineb, or nabam. Some dimethyl-dithiocarbamates are reported to be teratogenic in animals, and they can be nitrosated to form nitrosamines *in vitro* and *in vivo*. The ethylenebisdithiocarbamates maneb, nabam, and zineb are also reported to be teratogenic. Furthermore, this group of compounds breaks down to form ethylene thiourea (ETU) *in vivo*, in the environment,. and during cooking of food containing their residues ETU is carcinogenic, mutagenic, and teratogenic as well as antihyroid. A scheme for the degradation of maneb is as follows:

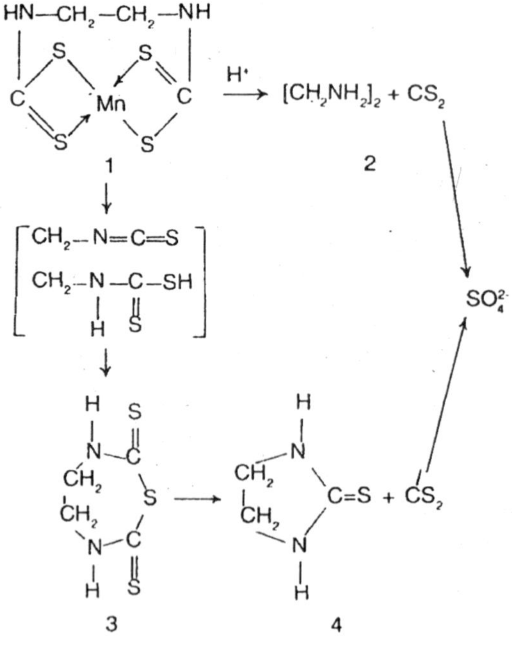

Maneb is hydrolysed by acids to ethylenediamine and carbon disulfide. Carbon disulfide is also produced when ethylene bisthiuram monosulfide is transformed into ETU. Maneb produced an increased incidence of lung tumors in only one of four strains of mice that have been tested and studies in rats were equivocal. However, because of its conversion to the much more active ETU, it and other fungicides of this class require further study and evaluation of hazard.

Rodenticides

A wide variety of chemicals, which defy classification, have been used in the control of rats and mice. Although they are used to kill mammals, which resemble man in their physiology and biochemistry, there are wide differences in degree of hazard to man. In some case the rodenticidal selectivity of these compounds is based on the peculiar physiology of rodents, which differs from that of primates and other desirable species, and in some cases it is merely a question of taking advantage of the habits of rodents as opposed to species that are to be protected. In addition to potential widespread destruction of food and fiber by rodents, another primary reason for attempting their control is to eliminate intermediate hosts in the transmission of various vectroborne diseases, e.g., bubonic plague. Since rodenticides can be used in baits and placed in inaccessible places their likelihood of becoming widespread contaminants of the environment is much less than that associated with the use of insecticides and herbicides. The toxicologic problem posed by rodenticides, therefore, is primarily acute accidental or suicidal ingestion.

Warfarin

Warfarin, 3-(alpha-acetonylbenzyl)-4-hydroxycoumarin, is one of the most widely used rodenticides. Its safe usage is based on the fact that it requires repeated dosing for toxicity to develop. Thus, placed in baits accessible to rodents, repeated ingestion results in fatalities to rodents with little likelihood that pets or children would be repeatedly exposed.

The mechanism of action of warfarin is as an anticoagulant. It is an antimetabolite of vitamin K, and hence it inhibits the synthesis of prothrombin. Multiple doses are usually required to maintain inhibition of synthesis until prothrombin levels are sufficiently depleted to result in hemorrhage throughout the whole body, which is the cause of death. In addition to its anticoagulant action, direct capillary damage has also been attributed to warfarin. Single fatal doses in common laboratory animals range between 200 and 400 mg/kg. Basing estimates of toxicity to man on values for single lethal doses for animals, it has been suggested that an adult man would have to eat 1.5 lb of a warfrain concentrate or about 30 lb of a strong rat bait to result in fatality. On the other hand, daily ingestion for six days of as little as 1 to 2 mg/kg has produced severe illness in an attempted suicide. Two members of a Korean family of 14 persons lived for 15 days on a diet of cornmeal containing warfarin that was intended as a rat bait. All became severely ill with hemorrhage. The estimated dosage was 1 to 2 mg/kg/day. Symptoms of poisoning, which begin after a few days or weeks of repeated ingestion, include epistaxis and bleeding gums, pallor, and sometimes petechial rash leading to hematomas around the joints and on the buttocks, ultimately blood in the urine and feces, and occasionally paralysis due to cerebral hemorrhage, and finally to hemorrhagic shock and death. The principal diagnostic test for excessive repeated exposure to warfarin is a markedly reduced prothrombin activity, and therapy is directed to correcting this by the administration of vitamin K. Additional details concerning the toxicity and treatment are given by Hayes (1963).

Related anticoagulants used as rodenticides are coumafuryl (3-[1-furyl-3-acetyl-ethyl]4-hydroxycoumarin), diphacinone (2-diphenylactetyl-1,3-indandione), and pindone (2-pivalyl-1,3-indandione). These have the advantage over warfarin of being more readily soluble in water.

Red Squill

The bulbs of red squill (Urginen maritima) have been used for many years as a relatively safe rodenticide. The active principles are glycosides scillaren-A and scillaren-B. These glycosides have cardiotonic actions like the digitalis glycosides. Crude red squill also contains a central-acting emetic, which causes vomiting in animals other than rodents. This emetic action is the main factor that contributes to the safety of the rodenticide to humans. Symptoms that are associated with ingestion of large doses of red squill include vomiting and abdominal pain, blurred vision, cardiac irregularity, convulsions, and death from ventricular-irregularities. Quinine sulfate is used in treatment of reduce mild cardioirritability. The selective rodenticidal usefulness of squill, then takes advantage of the physiologic peculiarity of the rat's inability to vomit.

Norbormide

Norbormide is another rodenticide that takes advantage of a physiologic peculiarity of the rat for its selective toxicity. This compound acts directly on the smooth muscle of peripheral vessels causing them to constrict irreversibly resulting in widespread ischemia leading to death. The receptor sites for norbormide in the vascular smooth muscle apparently are different from the vasoconstrictive receptors for epinephrine. Since the compound is lethal to rats in dosages of 5 to 15 mg/kg and is essentially nontoxic for cats, dogs, chicken, ducks, primates, sheep, or swine, it must be assumed that the norbormide receptors in smooth muscle of peripheral vessels exist uniquely in the rat.

Sodium Fluoroacetate and Fluoro-acetamide

These rodenticides, whose use is largely restricted to licensed pest control operators, are among the most potent rodenticides known and are also highly toxic to other animals.

Fluoroacetate produces its toxic action by inhibiting the citric acid cycle. The fluorine substituted acetate becomes incorporated, as a normal acetate, into fluoroacetyl coenzyme A, which condenses with oxaloacetate to form fluorocitrate. Fluorocitrate inhibits the enzyme aconitase and thereby inhibits the conversion of citrate to isocitrate. As a result there is an accumulation of large quantities of citrate in the tissue, and the cycle is blocked. As might be excepted, the heart and central nervous system are the most critical tissues involved in poisoning by a general inhibition of oxidative energy metabolism. Thus, the symptoms following fluoroacetate poisoning, in addition to nonspecific signs of nausea and vomiting, include cardiac irregularities, cyanosis, generalized convulsions, and death from ventricular fibrillation or respiratory failure.

Estimates of the means lethal dose of fluoroacetate in man range from 2 to 10 mg/kg, and there have been a number of human fatalities. There are apparent species differences in the quality of symptoms that lead to death. Dogs die of convulsions or respiratory paralysis, but in man, monkeys, horses, and rabbits central nervous system actions are usually incidental, and the dangerous fatal complication is ventricular fibrillation. Provision of large quantities of acetate appears to antagonize fluoroacetate poisoning in a competitive manner in that monkey have been successfully protected from fluoroacetate poisoning by the administration of glycerol monoacetate.

Alpha Naphthyl Thiourea (ANTU)

ANTU was developed as a rodenticide following the observation that phenylthiourea kills rats but is not toxic to man. The thiourea derivative ANTU provide to be effective as a rodenticide because it lacked the bitter taste associated with phenylthiourea. However, some species of rats are not sensitive to it, and others develop resistance. There is a wide range of susceptibility to the acute toxicity of ANTU among mammals. The LD50 to rats is a few milligrams, approximately 3 mg/kg. Dogs appear to be next most sensitive with LD50s of 10 ml/kg. Pigs, horses, and cows require 30 to 50 mg/kg for fatalities, and guinea pigs require 400 mg/kg. A mean lethal dose in monkeys was 4 g/kg, and it is assumed that man would be similarly resistant. ANTU produces its principal toxic action in susceptible species by causing massive pulmonary edema and pleural effusion, apparently due to action on pulmonary capillaries. Resistant animals do not show pulmonary edema. Biochemical changes occurred in poisoned rats that suggested effects of ANTU on carbohydrate metabolism may be secondary to adrenal stimulation since adrenal demedullation blocked these biochemical changes. Altered thyroid function also alters the toxicity of ANTU. Tolerance to the acute effects of ANTU in rats can be induced by administering progressively increasing doses, and pleural effusions are not present in tolerant animals that die from large doses. ANTU produces a cross-tolerance to several other edemagenic agents, including inhaled irritant gases such as ozone and NO_2. Reaction of ANTU with sulfhydryl groups may be a necessary part of the mechanism of toxic action, since it has been reported that sulfhydryl group blocking agents are effective in rats in some experimental conditions.

Strychnine Sulfate

This alkaloid of the nux vomica plant is a potent convulsant poison with a lethal dose of a few milligrams per kilogram of body weight for most animals. It lowers the threshold for stimulation of spinal reflexes by blocking inhibitory pathways exerted by Renshaw cells over the motor cells in the spinal cord. As a result, poisoned animals go into tetanic convulsions in response to rather minimal sensory stimuli. Nux vomica was introduced into Germany in the sixteenth century for use as a rodenticide. Although its use has declined, it is still used in poisoned baits in control of vermin, and accidental poisonings in humans continue to occur. Strychnine nitrate has been used as a "bearicide" in Hokkaido, Japan. The minimal fatal dose for bears appears to be about 0.5 mg/kg.

Inorganic Rodenticides

A number of inorganic compounds are used in rodent control. Most of these are nonselective in their toxicity and are generally hazardous to man and domestic animals so that their use has declined in favour of more selective or less hazardous organic compounds.

Zinc phosphide reacts with water and HCl in the gastrointestinal tract to produce the gas phosphine (PH_3), which causes severe gastrointestinal irritation. Apparent insensitivity of dogs and cats has been attributed to the emetic qualities of zinc phosphide, in the presence of moisture, may evolve phosphate, which inhaled in sufficient concentration can cause fatal pulmonary edema.

Thallium sulphate is lethal to most animals in doses of 10 to 20 mg/kg. It apparently acts by reacting with free sulfhydryl groups, but the precise mechanism of poisoning is uncertain. Acute poisoning is accompanied by gastrointestinal irritation, motor paralysis, and death from respiratory failure. Lower, sublethal doses taken over a period time result in reddening of the skin and loss of hair. Pathologic changes include perivascular cuffing around blood vessels and degenerative changes in brain, liver, and kidney. Neurologic symptoms are prominent in repeated subacute poisoning and include tremors, leg pains, paresthesias of the hands and feet, and polyneuritis especially in the legs. Psychoses, delirium, convulsions, and other kinds of encephalopathy may also be noted. Dimercaprol (BAL) is of little benefit as a chelating agent in removal of absorbed thallium. Diethyldithiocarbamate has been demonstrated to accelerate the rate of excretion of thallium in experimental animals and to aid in the treatment of thallium-poisoned children. Use of 1 per cent thallium sulfate to control ground squirrels has resulted in outbreaks of thallotoxicosis in humans. In a 20-year period between 1935 to 1955, 778 persons were reported to have been poisoned by thallium-containing insecticides, rodenticides, and therapeutic chemicals, resulting in 46 fatalities. Because of its high, cumulative toxicity the use of thallium has been restricted to applications by qualified personnel, with a resultant marked decline in its use as a rodenticide.

White or yellow elemental phosphorus has caused poisoning because of the practice of spreading pastes containing this element on bread as a rodenticide bait. A dose of 15 mg of phosphorus can cause severe poisoning in humans and as little as 50 mg may be fatal. Shortly after ingestion phosphorus produces severe gastrointestinal irritation, and if a sufficient dose is ingested, hemorrhage and cardiovascular failure may prove fatal within 24 hours. The vomitus after phosphorus ingestion is luminescent and has a characteristic garlic odor. If the patient survives the initial gastrointestinal irritation phase, secondary systemic poisoning due to liver necrosis may ensure. Severe acute yellow atrophy of the liver is one delayed sequela that may ultimately prove fatal.

Barium carbonate and arsenic trioxide have also been used as rodenticides, but currently have little application for this purpose. Barium produces severe colic, diarrhea, and hemorrhage. It has a direct action on smooth muscles of the arterioles and cardiac muscle, which can result in increased blood pressure, cardiac irregularities, and death.

A variety of other compounds have some occasional application in rodent control. Carbon monoxide, methyl bromide, and hydrogen cyanide have been used as fumigants to kill rodents in enclosed spaces. These chemicals are generally toxic to all species. DDT, commonly thought of as an insecticide, is used as a poison for the house mouse and for bats. The principle of this treatment is to treat inaccessible areas where mice travel so that they will pick up a sufficient amount of DDT on their feet and fur, and ultimately, in preening, ingest the DDT and become poisoned. At best this seems an inefficient means of rodent control. Further discussion of action and therapy for poisoning by various rodenticides may be found in Hayes (1963).

Fumigants

Fumigants are used in the control of insects, rodents, and soil nematodes. They have in common the property of being in the gaseous form at the time they exert their pesticidal action and are used because they will penetrate to areas otherwise inaccessible for pesticide application (e.g., grain storage areas, rodent runways). Fumigants may be liquids that readily vaporize, solids that release a gas by chemical reaction (e.g., HCN from Ca $[CN]_2$ + H_2O), or gases contained in cylinders or ampules (e.g., methyl bromide). Thus they provide a potential hazard from the standpoint of inhalation exposure as well as in the case of solids and liquids, accidental ingestion or dermal exposure. Fumigants used in the protection of stored foodstuffs include acrylonitrile, carbon disulfide, carbon tetrachloride, chloropicrin, ethylene oxide, hydrogen cyanide, methyl bromide, and phosphine.

These chemicals have many other applications in industry and their toxicology has been discussed in other sections. In connection with pesticides it is worthy of comment that methyl bromide is said to have been responsible for more deaths in recent years among occupationally exposed persons in California than all of the more publicized organophosphate group of insecticides. During the period of 1957 to 1964, 62 systemic poisonings with five deaths were reported. In the usual case the early symptoms are malaise, headache, visual disturbances, and nausea and vomiting. Pulmonary effects included acute pulmonary edema, and neurologic effects in fatal poisonings included clonic and toxic convulsions. Several nonfatal cases resulted in persistent neurologic and psychiatric complaints ranging from muscular soreness and headache through decreased libido, mental depression, phobias, and paranoia. Although the neurologic and psychiatric symptoms resemble chronic poisoning by inorganic bromides, the serum bromide levels achieved in serious cases of methyl bromide poisoning are considerably lower than those required for poisoning by inorganic bromides. It has been suggested that this may be due to greater lipoid solubility of methyl bromide and hence greater penetration into the brain. However, since methyl chloride produces many of the same neurologic symptoms, it seems unlikely that the neurotoxicity of methyl bromide is due only to bromide ion. Methyl bromide methylates SH groups of cysteine, glutathione, and several SH-containing enzymes. Methylation of SH groups essential to cellular oxidation can be suggested as a possible mechanism for neurologic effects of methyl bromide and methyl chloride, and therefore BAL has been considered to possible usefulness in therapy. BAL given before exposure protected against lethal exposures in animals but had much less effect when given after exposure.

Phosphine, released from aluminum phosphate, although more acutely toxic than methyl bromide, is said to be safer for use as a grain fumigant under practical conditions. Use of acrylonitrile as a fumigant is limited by its flammability and high cost. Its toxicity has been attributed to release of CN ion *in vivo*, however, differences in symptoms and CN blood levels associated with poisoning by inorganic cyanides and acrylonitrile have led to some question about that mechanism. Chloropicrin (CCl_3NO_2) is a strong irritant, and sensory irritation gives early warning of its presence. It is, therefore, sometimes added in small amounts of other comparatively odorless fumigants to act as a warning agent. Ethylene oxide toxicity is also primarily due to its irritant actions in the lungs.

Ethylene dibromide in high concentrations (>200 ppm) produces primarily lung inflammation and edema is laboratory animals while repeated exposures to low concentrations resulted in histopathologic changes in their livers and kidneys as well. No abnormal signs were observed in rats and guinea pigs given 40 to 50 mg/kg/day for four months. A dose of 2 mg/kg/day given to bulls was reported to have resulted in impaired spermatogenesis within two weeks. Ethylene dibromide residues in fumigated cereal grains have been observed for up to two months after fumigation, and laying hens fed diets containing 10 ppm (daily dose of 1 to 2 mg/kg) had a decrease in egg weights. Investigation of the possible mechanism of this effect led to observation of impaired follicle growth apparently arising from impaired permeability of the follicular membrane to protein transfer. In a case of fatal human poisoning resulting from ingestion of 4.5 ml of ethylene dibromide, massive centrolobular necrosis of the liver and proximal tubular damage in the kidney were observed. Ethylene dibromide and 1,2-dibromo-3-chloropropane (DBCP), another nematocidal fumigant, were both found to rapidly produce highly malignant gastric squamous cell carcinoma in rats and mice.

DBCP also received considerable notoriety as a result of its being the probable cause of sterility and/or abnormally low sperm counts in workmen engaged in its manufacture. This resulted in a drastic reduction in its production and use. Studies in laboratory animals 16 years earlier had suggested the potential for this toxic effect when it was observed that repeated inhalation exposure to as little as 5 ppm of DBCP has an adverse effect on the testes and on reproductive function of male rats. Although the investigators, in that report, warned of the potential hazard, this warning was apparently not strong enough to prompt appropriate warning to workers and/or improve industrial hygiene practice sufficiently to protect workers. The future use of both ethylene dibromide and DBCP as fumigants will likely be served curtailed because of their strong carcinogenicity and their adverse action on reproductive function.

Special Problems

Interactions

Organophosphate potentiation

For several years following the observation by Frawley and coworkers (1957) of marked synergism of acute toxicity of EPN and malathion, the Food and Drug Administration Act required that all safety evaluations on anticholinesterase insecticides for which food residues were established should include tests of the toxicity of combinations. This led to routine tests for toxic interactions among this class of compounds. Most of these were acute toxicity tests using simultaneous administration. In 1961 DuBois reported studies in which the acute toxicity of various combinations of 13 different organophosphorus (OP) insecticides were tested in rats. Twenty-one pairs were additive in toxicity, 18 pairs less than additive, and four pairs synergistic. Since that time a few more pairs, involving new compounds, have been shown to be synergistic in acute toxicity tests. Combinations of several OP insecticides fed at recommended tolerance levels failed to produce significant synergistic toxicity in chronic feeding studies.

Malathion is one of the insecticides that has been observed most frequently as one constituent of a potentiating pairs of organophosphorus insecticides. This, normally, relatively safe insecticide is detoxified by carboxylesterases that are inhibited by other OP insecticides. The mechanisms of synergism among OP insecticides have been reviewed by DuBios (1969) and Murphy (1969). Two major mechanisms appear to be involved: (1) inhibition of detoxication by tissue carboxylesterase (aliesterases) and amidases, and (2) competition for nonvital binding sites that normally act as a buffer system to spare the vital acetylcholinesterase enzyme. Methods for screening for potentiating OP compounds by testing their potency as carboxylesterase inhibitors have been suggested as useful tests in acute studies and subacute feeding experiments. Compounds for potentiating OP compounds by testing their potency as carboxylesterase inhibitors have been suggested as useful tests in acute studies and subacute feeding experiments. Compounds that have a high potency as inhibitors of carboxylesterase relative to their anti-cholinesterase potency are likely to potentiate other OP insecticides or to alter the toxicity of other drugs and chemicals containing carboxylester or amide linkages. Pellegrini and Santi (1972) have demonstrated that impurities present in technical grade samples of malathion and phenthoate potentiate that toxicity of these compounds, thus accounting for the greater toxicity of technical samples as compared to highly purified samples. Synergism of malathion toxicity by impurities was offered as a possible explanation for the poisonings of malathion spraymen in Pakistan. This may account for the apparent "self-potentiation" of malathion reported by Murphy (1967). Noninsecticidal organophosphorus esters such as triorthotolyl phosphate are also potentiators.

These mechanism studies have demonstrated that simultaneous administration of compounds may not be the most suitable method for testing for interactions among OP insecticides, that carboxylesterases are much more sensitive than cholinesterases to inhibition by some compounds and that tissue carboxylesterase essays are suitable for detecting this subtle action in relatively short-duration feeding studies. The mechanism of competition of OP insecticides for nonvital binding sites has received less attention and should be subjected to further investigation. Measurements of relative carboxylesterase/cholinesterase inhibitory potencies may be a useful method of predicting potentiators, but they should also be corroborated with some *in vivo* toxicity tests.

Organochlorine insecticides

Tests of interaction among two or more pairs of organochlorine (OC) insecticides have usually involved measurements of the effects of one OC compound on the storage, excretion, and metabolism of another. Street's work on rats suggest that the storage of DDT and dieldrin in adipose tissue is reduced when they are fed in combination. This was attributed to accelerated rates of metabolism and excretion. Other indices of the toxicity of these compounds were not tested. A study of Diechmann and associates (1971) yielded the opposite effect with dogs; i.e. DDT fed with aldrin or dieldrin resulted in greater-than-expected residues of these compounds in fat and blood. Obviously additional work is required to determine if these represent true species differences, or if the discrepancies can be explained on the basis of differing experimental procedures.

Keplinger and Deichmann (1967) determined LD50s for over 100 mixtures containing two or three different insecticides. Most of the mixtures contained at least one OC insecticide. More than additive toxicities in mice were reported for endrin plus chlordane or aldrin, methoxychlor plus chlordane and dieldrin, and aldrin plus chlordane. Aldrin and chlordane were additive only in rats. Other potentiated mixtures included OC compounds with certain OP insecticides. The potentiations observed in this study were not striking (usually about twofold). It is possible that simultaneous administration of the compounds precluded the detection of some types of interactions.

Organochlorine insecticides protect against the acute toxicity of several OP insecticides. The mechanism of this protection appears to be due to the capacity of the OC insecticides to stimulate the enzymatic detoxification of OP compounds by liver microsomes or to increase noncatalytic binding sites for the OPs.

Other pesticides, drugs, and hydrocarbons that induce microsomal enzymes will, after an appropriate period of treatment, reduce the storage level of OC insecticides in rats and protect rats against acute poisoning by OP insecticides. Microsomal enzymes catalyze both the activation and detoxication of OP insecticides. In most cases it appears that the dynamics of the enzyme reactions and inductions favour detoxification. However, at least a few OP insecticides are potentiated by pretreatment with certain microsomal enzyme inducers. Caution should be exercised, therefore, in making broad generalizations concerning the effects of microsoma enzyme inducers on the toxicity of various classes of pesticides. Additional research is necessary to determine the specificities of various inducers (or inhibitors) on the several alternate pathways of metabolism of complex organic pesticides.

Although the above remarks have been primarily restricted to pesticide—pesticide interactions, they apply as well to other pollutant or drug effects on pesticide toxicities. In most cases where such interactions have been detected they appear to have been mediated through altered microsomal enzyme activities. Since at least 200 drugs and chemicals are known inducers of these enzymes, the number of possible interactions is tremendous. Relatively few have been subjected to toxicity tests in intact animals. Durham (1967) has reviewed many additional factors that may affect the toxicity of pesticides.

Pesticide-drug interaction

The capacity of organochlorine insecticides and certain herbicides to induce increased activity of liver microsomal enzymes that metabolize a variety of drugs is well established. However, attempts to correlate the increased capacity of tissues from pesticide-induced animals to metabolize drugs with effects of the pesticides on the intensity and duration of pharmacologic (or toxic) actions of the drugs are relatively few. Hexobarbital sleeping times or zoxazolamine paralysis times are often used as pharmacologic indices of altered drug metabolism *in vivo*, and in a few cases altered blood levels of drugs given to pesticide-treated animals have served as an *in vivo* index of pesticide-drug interactions. Conney and coworkers (1971) found that workers in a DDT factory had significantly higher excretion of 6-β-hydroxy-cortisol and a significantly reduced phenylbutazone half-life. This study suggests that at least occupational exposures can alter drug and steroid metabolism in man as well as experimental animals.

Unlike the organochlorine insecticides, OP insecticides have been shown to inhibit steroid metabolism by rat liver microsomes. Pesticide synergists of the methylenedioxyphenyl type such as piperonyl butoxide have been shown to inhibit or induce microsomal drug-metabolizing enzymes and to prolong or reduce hexobarbital sleep time and to potentiate or antagonize phosphorothioate insecticides depending on the dose and time of pretreatment with the synergist. When mice were pretreated with piperonyl butoxide, under conditions favourable to inhibition of microsomal oxidases, they were slightly more susceptible to the diethyl-substituted phosphorothionates, parathion and aziphosethyl, but were markedly resistant to the corresponding dimethyl-substituted compounds. The mechanism for this appeared to be, in part, due to the fact that glutathione alkyl transferase could serve as an alternate (to oxidation) pathway of detoxification of the dimethyl but not the diethyl-substituted compounds. Additionally, a rapid rate of reversal of dimethylphosphorylated cholinesterase (as compared to the diethyl compounds) allowed for reversal of injury to keep pace with the piperonyl butoxide-induced oxidative production of the active anticholinesterase metabolites.

The effect that microsomal enzyme induction or inhibition will have on the toxicity and action of a particular drug or chemical will depend not only upon the degree to which the enzyme activity is changed, but also upon the extent to which the enzymatic metabolism of the drug is the limiting factor in determining its intensity and duration of action and the relative influence on possible alternate pathways of metabolism.

Carcinogenic, Teratogenic, and Mutagenic Properties of Pesticides

Since other chapter have been specifically devoted to these pathologic processes, they have not, with a few exceptions, been considered in detail in this chapter. The report of the Secretary's Commission on Pesticides (1969) contains discussion and summaries of data on carcinogenicity, mutagenicity, and teratogenicity of pesticides.

Pesticides that the Panel on Carcinogenesis of the Secretary's Commission on Pesticides (1969) considered "positive" for tumor induction on the basis of tests conducted adequately in one or more species, the results being significant at the 0.01 level, included aldrin, aramite chlorbenzilate, p,p-DDT, dieldrin, mirex, strobane, and heptachlor (all registered for use on food crops), and amitrole, avadex, bis (2-chloroethyl) ether N-(2hydroxyethyl)-hydrazine, and PCNB. The recommendation of the panel was that human exposures to these compounds be minimized and that their use be restricted to purposes for which there was a clear health benefit. Many other pesticides were given priorities for further testing because the panel felt that they had not been adequately evaluated in experimental animals. Only three pesticides were considered to have been proven negative to tumor induction on the basis of "adequate" tests in experimental animals. Obviously this report has provoked much controversy, and the purpose of including these summary comments here is to make the reader aware of the problems. The situation for DDT is a case in point. The extensive use of this compound in industrial countries has not been associated with an increase in hepatic cancer in human populations, but many years ago Fitzhugh and Nelson (1947) reported that DDT fed in high doses to rats caused slight increase in hepatic cell tumors. Innes and associates (1969) reported a statistically significant increase in hepatomas in two strains of mice. Hepatic cell tumors in trout and tumors of several sites in F_2 and following generations of mice have followed DDT exposure. Additional studies sponsored by the International Agency of Research in Cancer confirmed the hepato-carcinogenicity of DDT in mice hepatomas were also increased in mice fed 250 ppm of DDE or DDD. While some oncologists feel that hepatoma induction is indicative of carcinogenesis, others feel that hepatomas are reversible lesions. The daily dosages ingested by animals in the experimental demonstrations of hepatomas are considerably greater than the dosage rate that man would receive, based on analyses of residues in typical meals. This, plus the failure of epidemiologic studies to demonstrate associations between DDT exposure and cancer in man, the controversy as to whether hepatoma production represents true carcinogenesis, and the fact that DDT has indeed been of great benefit in the control of malaria and other insect-borne diseases and in enhancing agricultural production, makes the administrative decision of whether or not to ban or greatly restrict its use especially difficult. It is not only a challenge to our scientific capabilities to adequately assess safety, but a challenge to social responsibility as well. Tomatis (1976) reviewed the program on the evaluation of the carcinogenic risk of chemicals to man of the International Agency for Research on Cancer. There were no pesticides among the 17 chemicals that he listed as having been found to have carcinogenicity in man or for which there was a strong suspicion of such action. Ten of the ninety-four chemicals, which the agency had determined to be carcinogenic in experimental animals only, were pesticides. These were amitrole, aramite, BHC, chlorobenzilate, DDD, DDE, DDT, dieldrin, lindane, and Mirex. The NCI bioassay program will not doubt continue to identify additional pesticides with carcinogenic potential and may exonerate some that IARC or others have branded as carcinogens. This is an area of great concern and one in which the compounds of greatest interest will likely continue to change.

Durham and Williams (1972) reviewed studies in experimental animals in which at least some mammalian species at some testable dosage of the following pesticides were reported to have produced teratogenic effects: carbaryl, captan, folpet, difolatan, organo-mercury compounds, 2,4;5-T, pentachloronitrobenzene (PCNB), and paraquat. Human consumption of organomercury compounds by pregnant women is known to have caused serious neurologic disorders in their offspring, which might be considered functional teratogenicity (or perhaps fetal toxicity). Other than this there is no confirmed relationship between exposure of pesticides and human terata. In the positive experimental studies the production of terata was usually demonstrated to be dose dependent, and the doses required were far in excess of what humans might be expected to receive under usual conditions. As with other toxic effects, pesticide teratogenicity and its relationship to human health must be considered from a dose-response standpoint and is subject to the same problems of interpretation and extrapolation as other dose-related effects, albeit a serious and tragic effect.

Recently proposed guidelines by the EPA for evaluating safety of pesticides include a battery of tests for mutagenicity. Durham and William (1972) reviewed the submammalian and mammalian tests available and commented on the problems of interpretation of these tests. Epstein and coworkers (1972) reported results of an extensive series of tests for mutagenic action of chemicals as determined by the dominant lethal assay in mice. Twenty-eight common pesticides were included in those tests. None of them was among the 16 chemical agents (out of a total of 174) that produced "unequivocal effects" on early fetal deaths and/or total implants, although TEPA (phosphine oxide, tris [1-aziridinyl]) and METEPA (phosphine oxide, tris [2-methyl-1-aziridyl]), which have been *proposed* as insect chemosterilants were positive. Durham and Williams (1972) reviewed reports of several pesticides that were mutagenic in nonmammalian systems (plants, bacteria, time culture, etc.), and they concluded that "from the present state of knowledge, it must be agreed that no firm conclusions can be drawn as to whether pesticides represent a mutagenic hazards."

Comparative Toxicity

A high degree of selective toxicity to target organism is a desirable goal in the development of useful pesticides. Metcalf (1972) has reviewed toxicity data for a large number of insecticides and calculated mammalian selectivity ratios, MSRs (mouse oral LD50/female housefly topical LD50). Considering only these two species and only acute toxicity it is apparent that there is an extremely wide range of relative toxicities. The situation becomes infinitely more complex when one considers a broader spectrum of non-target species.

Table 8.1. Relative toxicity of various insecticides to rats and houseflies.

Class	*Compound*	*MRS*
Organochlorines	DDT	59
	DDT	174
	Methoxychlor	668
	Chlordane	72
	Aldrin	27
	Dieldrin	24
	Endrin	2.4
	Heptachlor	72
	Lindane	107
Organophosphates	Parathion	4
	Methyl parathion	20
	Malathion	37.7
	Azinphosmethyl	4.1
	Chlorothion	85
	Dimethoate	390
	Ronnel	1,315
Carbamates	Aldicarb	0.175
	Carbaryl	0.60
	Zectran	0.60
	Propoxur	4.5
	Mobam	10.0

There are indeed occasional marked differences in susceptibilities of common laboratory test animals, but even more striking are species differences noted among wild animals of the same vertebrate class. For example, Hayes (1967a) compared reported single-dose LD50 values for 20 pesticides in five mammalian species commonly used in safety evaluation studies. The range of susceptibilities generally varied within a factor of less tenfold. All species were not compared for all 20 compounds, but in the majority of cases rats were more susceptible than mice, guinea pigs, rabbits, or dogs. Comparing the smallest single doses required to produce a serious effect in rats and man, man was more sensitive than rats (usually by factors of tenfold or less). In a similar comparison or reported acute insecticide toxicity values for five species of fish, Murphy (1972), calculated LD50 ratios of least to most sensitive of 2.7 for DDT, 4.7 for dieldrin, 246 for Guthion (azinphosmethyl), 49 for parathion, and 430 for malathion. A similar calculation for ten avian species gave least to most sensitive species ratios of 45 for dieldrin and 192 for parathion. The mechanisms of these species differences have received relatively little research, but there is evidence that they include both differences in sensitivity of target enzymes as well as differences in rats of biotransformation to either more or less toxic metabolites. Certainly, for a class of toxic chemicals that become as widespread in the environment as pesticides, for effects on a broad spectrum of nontarget species is reasonable. Since it is clearly unrealistic to except all pesticides to be tested for safety to all nontarget species that might be exposed, the only reasonable approach appear to be to attempt to understand basic mechanisms of species differences in susceptibility and, with this information base, to select or design compounds that will not only be safe for man but also be least likely to affect other nontarget organisms present in the specific areas in which they are applied. An impossible task? Perhaps. A worthwhile objective? Certainly.

9

TOOLS IN FORENSIC TOXICOLOGY

Guidelines for testing have long been issued by regulatory and interest groups. One of the most well-known efforts along these lines was published by the FDA in 1959. The "Appraisal of the Safety of Chemicals in Foods, Drugs, and Cosmetics" contains chapters on Chronic Toxicity as well as the well-known "Draize Tests." Since that time, guidelines for testing have been available in a less formal format. Since the 1960s, consumer and government interest in safety of foods, chemical work places, and the environment has nurtured the growth of many testing guidelines for diverse Federal regulatory agencies. In 1977, four regulatory agencies, the Consumer Product Safety Commission (CPSC), the Environmental Protection Agency (EPA), the Food and Drug Administration (FDA), and the Occupational Safety and Health Administration (OSHA) agreed to work together to reform the regulatory process. They formed the Interagency Regulatory Liaason Group (IRLG) to implement their agreement. The Food Safety and Quality Service (FSQS) of the Department of Agriculture (USDA) joined the IRLG in 1978. One of the working groups formed by the IRLG was the Testing Standard and Guidelines Work Group. This group was to develop comprehensive testing guidelines which would resolve differences in the many toxicological evaluation protocols.

In 1978, as this effort got underway, the EPA's Office of Pesticide Programs (OPP) proposed toxicology testing guidelines which were quite comprehensive. They were compiled for use under the Federal Insecticide, Fungicide and Rodenticide Act (FIFRA).

In 1979, draft toxicology testing guidelines were issued by the European Economic Community's Committee for Proprietary Medicinal

Products (EEC/CPMP). This set of standard, which is in concert with the guidelines of Canada's Health Protection Branch (HPB), supports the concept of an International New Drug Application. Also in 1979, the EPA issued proposed guidelines for toxicological evaluation of chemicals regulated by the Toxic Substances Control Act (TSCA).

In 1980, the IRLG, in concert with the Organization for Economic Cooperation and Development (OECD), revealed drafts of guidelines which addressed, toxicology testing issues. Presently, in 1981, the IRLG has issued the acute toxicology testing guidelines and the OECD has issued their complete set of guidelines.

There has been some consolidation of the diverse testing requirements since the United States regulatory agencies formed the IRLG, but differences still exist in the requirements for chronic testing of chemicals among the participating agencies. Even protocols (FIFRA and TSCA) produced by the same agency (EPA) differ in their provisions. Thus, some compounds which are covered by more than one regulatory blanket may find that a single standard testing procedure and protocol do not apply.

Facilities

There are obvious environmental qualities that a toxicology animal laboratory must have, including adequate temperature, humidity, lighting, and air movement. However, the facilities must also support offices for the technical staff, laboratory space for clinical and analytical operations, and storage space for animal feed, bedding and equipment. Without space devoted to these other areas, technicians will not have adequate ability or interest to keep records, animal caging will be stored in hallways, food and bedding will be kept in animal rooms, and support services will be conducted under inadequate conditions.

There are no rules of thumb for space allocation to the various phases of animal toxicology. This depends upon the types of testing being conducted by the laboratory. Acute testing requires the least laboratory support space because feed mixing, animal quarantine, clinical and chemical analyses, and data analysis are not performed extensively. In the other direction, subchronic and chronic testing require all of these supporting areas and the respective space allocated.

The astounding point to be noted is that fully one-third of the space devoted to the animal laboratory is allocated to nonanimal space—a fact that often goes unrecognized by laboratory administrative personnel. It is usual for an animal laboratory to be found wanting in these "nonproductive" areas.

The HVAC system (heating ventilation, and air conditioning) provides for the comfort of the laboratory animals. The creature comforts for humans and other animals should be regulated by separate systems according to the function of the various laboratory areas. These HVAC systems should have sufficient controls and sensing devices to maintain fairly constant conditions for maximum comfort of all life forms.

Because this "status" does not always remain "quo," it is highly desirable to have alarm and "back-up" systems available in the event of an emergency. Many laboratories have alarms to indicate temperature crises such as boiler or air conditioner failure, but conditions that create alarms may not be conducive to responding to the alarm, i.e., extreme weather conditions. In the winter, a boiler may not fire, so that outside air would be distributed to animal rooms without being warmed. In summer, lack of functioning air conditioning can result in hot air being distributed to the animal rooms. Thus any alarm system should also have an automatic ventilation cutoff along with the alarm so that animals will not freeze or overheat before someone can respond the alarm. Automatic switchover of standby boilers and generators will help to avoid anxiety that should normally arise under such alarm conditions. In an energy conscious society, it is also worth considering dual fuel capabilities for heating, at least. If one source of fuel becomes limiting, another can be substituted. This permits cost effective operation as well as the "fall back" position in case of fuel shortages.

Construction with materials that do not support combustion will negate a great concern for fire protection systems; however, extinguishers should always be immediately available in case of emergency. Fire extinguishers may contain any of a variety of materials, which may be, as bad for animals as they are for flames. Dry chemicals, foams, and CO_2 certainly would not be acceptable in extinguishing small fires in laboratory. Water sprinklers might do more harm (water damage smoke) than good. Consideration should be given to equipping the laboratory with HALON® extinguishers, which do not consume O_2 in the room as a method of limiting combustion.

The laboratory always exists within the placenta of the community—drawing in air and often water from this environment and discharging exhaust air and effluent into it. Intake air should be drawn in from the prevailing windward side in wind and exhausted downwind, even though systems may be devised to clean and filter the air before and after use. Some communities may have industries that contribute serious toxicants into the air, which may find then way into the laboratory. It is imperative to consider scrubbing or at least activated charcoal filtering of all incoming air if such a potential condition exists. In this regard, it is also essential that scientific personnel be altered to plans of major construction and renovation in the laboratory (or in the community). Solvents used in paints, cleaners, or adhesives can affect animals adversely. With embarrassment, these authors can vouch for the toxicity of pressurized paints applied in rooms containing bred female rats! Similarly, roofing solvents, insecticides from tree or lawn spraying, and other intentionally applied wide-use chemicals could inadvertently affect the conduct of many studies, and the scientific personnel must be sensitive to all situations that could place the laboratory animals at risk. The human nose is a sensitive and discriminating analytical tool—believe what it tells you—whether it be animal odors (change the filters) or chemicals/solvents introduced into the incoming air.

Safety Considerations

Chronic toxicity testing is not conducted without the possibility that the test material may affect humans as well as lab animals during the chronic exposure. For this reason, it is necessary to consider each test material as a dangerous entity, which could seriously affect technicians and other personnel with whom it comes in contact. Thorough training and dogmatic application of safety principles must be stressed for all individuals working in the laboratory. When in the laboratory, shoe coverings, bonnets, and lab coats should be worn regardless of the area. While this seems a bit rigorous, remember that the partial pressure of the animal rooms should be greater than that of the hallways. This means that hallways "collect" all materials which the rooms are able to void through louvers, cracks, or open doors. While this assures an even exposure to a single test article in each animal room, it equally assures a tossed salad of test materials in the hallways. Thus one cannot relax one's safety attitude once out of the animal rooms.

When mixing feed, handling test materials, or handling animals, it is important to wear protective polyethylene, polyvinyl, or latex disposable gloves. A full mask with appropriate filtration medium must also be worn at this time. Fiber "dust" masks are never acceptable in protecting the worker. Gloves should be removed and discarded and new gloves put on before entering another room, or reentering a room. These procedures represent common sense precautions to limit exposure to toxic best articles, but they are not fool proof! Latex or plastic gloves are not impervious to all test materials. When working with formulated pesticides and other liquid test articles be sure to test the gloves for porosity and strength following contact with test material. Remember, "safety clothing" is a two-edged sword. While it prevents materials from getting to the person, it also prevents materials from escaping from the skin once contact has been made. Thus a rip or hole in a glove should always be of concern. A new glove should be used immediately and the old grove discarded.

Since so many mechanisms and routes for accidental exposure to potentially hazardous materials exist in the laboratory, it is imperative that all employees (don't forget secretaries and receptionists) be trained minimally in how to respond to inhalation, dermal, ocular, or oral exposure. They should also have knowledge and training in first aid, while their supervisors should be fully trained in first aid. Procedures for emergency response and care should be reviewed and practiced.

Uniforms should be kept in the laboratory. Technicians should change into uniforms before starting the day and change back into street clothes at the end of the day. There is no good sense in transporting clothes-borne animal products and test materials to the home, nor is it reasonable to expose test animals to clothes-borne burdens of etiologic and toxic agents brought into the lab from home and street. Uniforms should include shoes, since all manners of contamination may be introduced into the laboratory by the feet.

Aside from outright toxic effects of test articles, technicians and laboratory personnel should guard the hazard of sensitization and development of allergies to animal hair, dander, and urine. Diligent use of masks and gloves will aid in the prevention of allergy development or allergic reaction.

Animal Requirements

Chronic and subchronic studies are commonly conducted using rats (24 months), mice (18 months), and dogs (12 months). The strains of these species are generally chosen to minimize or select for genetic variation and spontaneous appearances of lesions and/or tumors.

Feed

There are many types of animal feeds produced by major animal feed manufacturers. Semisynthetic feeds are formulated with chemically pure or refined ingredients. Vitamins, minerals, and carbohydrates of known purity are generally formulated with refined vegetable oils, starches, and casein to form a nutritious product capable of supporting all natural functions of the laboratory animal. Such diets may be designed and produced for any laboratory animal. The rationale for using semisynthetic diets includes constancy of ingredient mixture with low, controlled levels of contamination. Animal feeds formulated from vegetable products and fish and bone meals are not as likely to be of constant palatability or quality. These feeds are formulated to achieve a minimum guaranteed nutrient analysis by combining the same quality of stipulated ingredients in each batch (closed formula) or by combining any of several commercially available ingredients in appropriate levels to achieve the guaranteed nutrient analysis (open formula). Feeds of the latter type are often produced even by the large feed manufacturers to keep their costs down. The variable composition of open formula feeds leads to potential variation in protein, carbohydrate, and lipids, as well as palatability and compatibility with a test article. Even though the human diet is of the "open formula" type, this diet may give the investigator some problems in well-designed and controlled animal studies.

The type of diet used may affect not only palatability but also baseline plasma levels of liver enzymes. Glucose-6-phosphate dehydrogenase and alkaline phosphatase of the liver are reportedly lower in animals receiving semipurified diets than those receiving conventional commercial diets. What effect this might have on the outcome of a toxicity feeding study is not known. Regardless of the type of feed used, the diet is often used as a route of administration of the test materials, as stated.

Housing

Rodents are generally housed in metal (stainless steel or galvanized steel) or plastic (polyethylene, polypropylene, or polycarbonate) cages. Metal caging or floor pens are used for dogs. Minimum cages sizes for all species are stipulated in the *Guide for the Care and Use of Laboratory Animals* (DHEW publication, NIH 77-23) and compliance is monitored by federal and state health agencies. Since minimum sizes for cages are stipulated, only caging type remains to be decided. Two major types of caging are available.

Solid bottom (floor) cages, often called shoebox cages, and pens require bedding to be added to the cage to absorb urine. Such cages are usually used in reproduction studies but are not favoured for chronic studies because of the additional effort needed to clean the cages and changes the bedding. In addition, the use of bedding may introduce dust, pesticides or other contaminants. It must be recognized that clearance of the cage atmosphere is slower in this type of cage than in cages with wire mesh sides or bottoms, which may alter the outcome of the study. It has long been known that sawdusts and chips of some conifers induce liver mixed-function oxidase enzyme activity, which may affect the outcome of the study. Solid cages (plastic) can be fitted with filter tops to remove dust from the air. Added "isolation" is possible by HEPA filtration of the air flow passing over each cage.

Cages with metal, mesh floors are commonly used for rodent and dog studies. These cages have the disadvantage of allowing extremities, especially of younger or smaller animals, to be caught in the mesh. They also envelope the animal in room air on all sides so that there is no place for the animal to "bed down." This means that the temperature control in the animal rooms must be rigorous so that animals are not exposed to the stress of extremes in temperature. It may be evident that solid cages would be recommended if room temperature control was not stable. Solid bottom cages with bedding avoid "suspending" the animal in its environment.

Waste materials from animals housed on wire mesh floors is handled by collecting the waste on waxed paper, absorbent materials, or by flushing the wastes down sewer drains. Absorbent materials range from sheets of paper products to particulate absorbent such as expanded clay, wood chips, or ground corn cobs. The absorbent paper products rang from paper or cardboardlike products to highly absorbent pads with multiple layers of absorbent materials. While all of these materials adequately retain feces and urine, it is worth mentioning that these absorbent sheets and pads must lie flat on the shelves below the cages. Rodents have very few avenues for directing their activity. However, they will diligently go to great lengths to stretch and reach through the wire mesh flooring and pull fists full bedding paper into the cage to form a nest. The rodents most frequently achieve this with lightweight paper and padlike products. And while the resulting nest may be very satisfying to the rodent, it is the bane of animal caretakers and cage cleaners.

Some absorbent materials are sold with claims of deodorizing properties to keep the animal waste odors under control. Frequent replacement of soiled materials with new material will generally help to keep the animal room clean smelling. However, just as "nature abhors a vacuum," mice abhor a "clean smell." Thus the males will vigorously "mark" clean waste-collection materials so that the rooms quickly smell "properly marked" to the mice yet "pungently soiled" to the animal care staff. Frequency of paper changing for mice should be dictated by concerns for animal health and contamination rather than odor level, because mice seem to "mark" faster than man can change absorbent.

Dog cages must be cleaned daily and are almost always cleaned by spraying the wire floor and pans with water. Where bedding is used in pens, daily cleaning is absolutely necessary. Attempts to skimp on removal of wet bedding or replacement with fresh bedding will be rewarded with patches of dermal irritation and alopecia, as well as skin sores, possibly with maggot infestations.

Animal Environment

Temperature

The temperature for housing laboratory animals is often dictated by the comfort of technicians working in the rooms or by the limitations of the heating and air conditioning system. Temperatures of 70 to 72°F are common in rodent and large animals laboratories, but what temperatures do the animals prefer? Temperature recommendations for laboratory animals, published in 1971 in a National Academy of Sciences publication, *Defining the Laboratory Animal,* were presented as:

Laboratory animal	*Recommended temperature*	
	(°C)	*(°F)*
Hairless mouse	31-34	88-93
White mouse	26-31	79-88
Guinea pig	24-29	75-84
Rat	24-29	75-84
Hamster	21-26	70-79
Rabbit	12-21	54-70

It is perhaps more important that the temperature remain fairly constant, wherever it may be set, rather than fluctuate around a given temperature. The fluctuations probably cause more stress than a constant temperature, even if it is slightly outside of the recommended range.

Ventilation

Airflow through the animal laboratory must be sufficient to prevent the air from becoming stale and must provide a low-odor environment.

When more air is forced into a room than can be completely cleared by exhaust dusts, air flows through the cracks around the door, and the partial pressure of air in the room becomes positive with respect to the hallway or area outside the room. Establishing a positive room air pressure is an important method to reduce possible exposure of animals to test articles being offered in other animal rooms. If animal rooms were negative with respect to outside areas, foreign materials would be "sucked" into the animal rooms, thereby providing unplanned exposure to the test animals.

Room ventilation must be homogeneous throughout the room; this is generally controlled by adjustable diffusers. The ventilation of all rooms in a facility must be "balanced." That is to say, all rooms should have the same relative air flow and positive pressure with regard to hallways. Balancing airflow in an entire facility should always be performed by airflow control specialists, who document their achievements with airflow meters. Balancing should be done only after changing all air filters in the system. Balancing is not a "one-time" task; it is affected by progressive filter clogging and is therefore an ongoing process.

Relative Humidity

Stringent control of humidity is probably not important; however, if moisture in the air is too low, drying of the mucous membranes and eyes of the test animal occurs. If humidity climbs too high, the growth of bacterial and fungal populations may permit respiratory distress and dermal involvement such as ring-worm. In addition, urine and excreta do not dry, thereby increasing the room odor level.

Lighting

Common lighting schedules of 12 hr continuous light and 12 hr darkness are common. This schedule permits the animals to entrain upon the light cycle which, in turn, stimulates constant diurnal secretion of thyroid hormones, ACTH, and growth hormone. Regulated lighting cycles are necessary in reproduction studies since rodents enter constant estrus under condition of constant light phases without darkness. The importance of stringently controlled light cycles has probably been underrated in toxicology.

Cleanliness

Freedom from filth and vermin should be an inalienable right of all laboratory animals. Insecticides should not be used in the rooms, if possible. However, if infestations are threatened, AAALAC permits use certain insecticides in animal rooms. Electric insect traps and electrocution devices may be used in laboratories to control flying insects. However, the best insect control is prevention of infestation by limiting the amount of materials brought into the lab from uncontrolled sources, i.e., food, bedding, and supplies. Dust and dirt will normally build up in a room and must be removed. Recirculated dust may be observed around incoming air vents, indicating a need for changing filters.

A vacuum cleaner may remove this accumulation of materials providing that the machine noise is extremely low; otherwise, washing is the best method of removal so that the animal will not be stressed by the unusual noise. In this same regard, young technicians generally like to carry portable radios into animal rooms as they work. This practice should be discouraged for reasons known to the parents of every teenager.

Mapping of floors should be performed with a weak detergent solution with low volatility or known toxicity. Quaternary ammonium based detergents are generally acceptable. Nonscented products would seem to be the best alternative, thereby avoiding volatile components in the test area. It should be noted that any gradients in lighting, temperature, or airborne products in an animal room will occur vertically. Thus animals within groups should be distributed in cage racks in such a way as to be present equally at all vertical caging levels. This avoids confounding treatment group with cage level in the room.

The preceding section has hopefully pointed out some methods that can be used to minimize exogenous factors which can be affect the outcome of a long term toxicity study. The next section will cover some common laboratory procedures used in chronic toxicity studies including:

- Animal identification
- Cage identification
- Test material administration
- Data collection
- Body weight
- Food consumption
- Daily observations
- Organ weights

Animal Identification

Unique marking systems are necessary for conducting chronic toxicity studies, analyzing the results by animal and group, and retrieving data in the reconstruction of a study. Marking systems vary with species and type of study. Large animals can be tattooed, while smaller animals can be ear tagged or leg banded. Ear tags, which should be Monel metal rather than aluminum or steel to avoid irritation, have been and are being used in rodents, but tags may be lost during a study. The classical method for unique identification of rodents is the standard ear and toe clip system which allows for 999 animals without repetition. However, if rodents, particularly mice, are gang housed, they will attempt to cannibalize each others ears. Therefore, frequent checks and alternative marking methods should be standard operating procedure.

For acute tests in albino rodents, a saturated alcoholic solution of picric acid is used as a noninvasive marking system. The drawback to picric acid is its lack of permanence. Therefore, to be appropriate for chronic studies, the investigative team has to be willing to remark the animals once a month. A word of caution is necessary. If the alcohol evaporates and the picric acid becomes dry, it is incredibly explosive upon jarring or impact. Trained waste disposal experts should handle any vessels containing dried picric acid.

Cage Identification

Recent developments with computer "mark-sense" identification has proven to be a potential boon to the toxicologist with a computerized data gathering system. As computers become more available (less expensive), the "mark-sense" identification systems should become more widespread. For those investigators who do not have a computerized system, colour coded cage cards are a good alternative. By using a systematic colour coding, e.g., white for control, red for low dose, yellow for mid-dose, blue for high dose, the chances of treatment level mixups are minimized. With the colour code system, the cage, the container for the compound, and the page(s) in the note-books should all be coded.

Routes of Administration

Diet

Whenever possible, dosing should be accomplished by incorporating the test material in the diet. This lets the animal administer the material to itself according to its size and metabolism. It is the easiest method for the laboratory personnel since the animals do not have to be handled to administer the compound. If feed is used as the route by which a test material is administered, it is important to be assured that:

1. The substance is mixed uniformly throughout the feed at the specified level. The presence "hot" and "cold" spots will contribute to the variation in response seen in the study.
2. The substance is stable in the feed throughout the period of application. If the test material degrades in the oxidizing milieu of the feed, this route is clearly inappropriate.
3. The level of test materials is confirmed by acceptable analytical methods at stipulated intervals throughout the study. The extraction and assay of test materials from laboratory diets is a challenge to the analytical chemist. The establishment of adequate and appropriate analytical procedures is one of the first requirements for determining the uniformity and stability of the mixed feed.
4. The fortified feed is sufficiently palatable to permit normal intake of food for normal growth. If a loss of body weight and depressed food consumption is observed in preliminary tests, a split-plate palatability test should be performed. In this test, treated and untreated feeds are offered simultaneously for 4 days with the positions of the feed cups reversed daily. Preferential consumption of control feed indicates that the treated feed is not palatable, and either a paired-feeding study or another treatment route should be considered. Similarly, feed is not the preferred route when the test material must be administered in feed, or when it cannot be mixed properly.

Feed Mixing

Feed mixing is, at best, a messy operation, but it is also the foundation for many chronic studies. The techniques, equipment, and precautions used in feed mixing depend upon the properties of the feed and test material. It is obvious that no single statement can be made about the best method to use in all cases. But there are some principles to be applied across the board. The test material, if solid, should be ground as finely as possible; the smaller the particle size the better. If the test material is liquid or can be dissolved in an innocuous liquid vehicle, the distribution in feed may be made more easily and more uniformly. If mixing a diet that must provide 25 mg/kg rats, one will want to calculate the total feed required and total test material required. For instance:

For feed	*For test material*
120 rats eating	120 rats weighing
23 g feed/day; need	0.25 kg/rat (avg);
2,760 g total/day	30 kg total

Each day, 30 kg of rats will eat 2,760 g of feed. At a dose of 25 mg test material per kg body weight, these rats must eat 750 mg of test material in their daily allotment of feed. If feed is mixed once weekly, 5.25 g of test material must be mixed into 19.32 kg of feed with no wastage accounted for. Since losses always occur, one would make 25 of feed containing 6.8 g of test material mixed uniformly throughout. The very simplicity of these calculations could bore the dullest of students and is embarrassing to present except that it gives us a foundation to go on to a real-life situation.

In the laboratory, the situation is not always so simple. Feed is generally mixed a week before it is used so that the chemical analyses can be performed to confirm the intended test levels. A growing rat, depending on its sex, may grow 20 to 35 g in a week's time. Thus the situation becomes more interesting to the person calculating feed levels. What mean body weight will the rat achieve two weeks from now when the feed will be administered, and how much feed will the average rat be eating during the week? The answers that are selected for these questions will depend upon historical laboratory performance. It seems elementary that if dosing is calculated on a mg test material/kg body weight basis, the feed will have to be mixed separately for each sex getting the same dose level. On the other hand, if the feed for both sexes contains the same quantify of test material per unit of feed, the females will receive higher doses per unit body weight than will the males during adulthood.

In a recent study, 26 week-old male and female Fischer rats weighed 313 and 193 g, respectively. They ate 102 and 82 g of feed per week, respectively. If the diet for all animals contained 10 mg test material per kg, the males and females would have received daily doses 47 and 61 mg/kg body weight, respectively.

Returning to our example above, we have the responsibility to add 6.8 g of test material to 25 kg of feed. It would be unreasonable to try to stir a teaspoon of test material into 25 kg of feed—we would be much more confident if we were mixing 2.5 kg of test material into 22.5 kg of basal feed. Therein lies the rationale for making a premix, which is then added to the commercial, untreated feed to achieve a final dosing level. Premixes often comprise approximately 10% of the final diet. In our example we would add the 6.8 g of test material to 2.5 kg of feed to make our premix, with the knowledge that any error created in making the premix will be magnified 10-fold in the final feed.

The premix is often mixed in an bowl, stirring type mixer similar to a kitchen mixer. A powdered test material could be agitated into the air by mixing action or by electrostatic forces created by the friction of mixing in this system. Electrostatic forces can be overcome by adding a grounding wire to the mixer and adding 1% food grade oil to the feed to make it sticky. Other techniques for achieving a proper mix include the following. Layers of the feed and test material should be alternately added to the bowl. A bowl cover is recommended to prevent possible contamination or losses over the top, and most importantly, the appropriate size mixer must be used. If one tries to use a 2 quart bowl to mix 2.5 kg of premix, his efforts will be rewarded with spilled feed and a great sense of frustration. The 2.5 kg of premix should need no more than 5 to 10 min of mixing in the "kitchen mixer." So many labs use mixing times of 20 to 30 min that it is surprising that the feed an be mixed in a timely fashion. The bag and labels for the final feed should accompany the premix from this point forward.

The final feed is mixed using the premix in a similar way that the premix was developed from the test material. The 2.5 kg of premix is alternately layered into the mixing bowl with 22.0 kg of basal diet. One half kg of basal diet is held back to "rinse" the premix container. The principles concerning adequate size of equipment, use of absolutely clean equipment, and appropriate mixing time apply to the development of the final feed as well as to that of the premix. "Grab" several gloved handfuls of feed as it is poured into the final container. Save this sample of feed for analysis of the test material.

The open bowl, planetary mixer described above is only one of the types of mixers found in the laboratory. The other common type is the P-R or V blender. The V blender is named for its shape. The V rotates on an axis so that the feed flows back and forth between the "tip" and the "legs" of the V. Obviously, the feed is locked into this system so that spillage will not occur during the mixing process unless the ports are not tightened properly. This is an attractive feature when suspected carcinogenic or highly toxic materials are incorporated into feeds. A premix is still important when mixing feed with a V blender, even though it is an efficient blender.

If the test material is a liquid with an aqueous base, too much test material can dampen the feed and encourage the growth of microflora, which make the feed unpalatable. If the test material is in a volatile vehicle, allow the vehicle to evaporate before adding the premix to the final feed. Since many volatile vehicles are also explosive, provide sufficient ventilation to permit their evaporation from the feed. Evaporation is most easily performed from shallow pans, not unlike cage waste pans. The air movement around these pans must be gentle so that the test material is not carried off to the air filters.

Drinking Water

Drinking water is also an acceptable vehicle for administrating test substances. For soluble and stable compounds, this route may be preferred. This route is indicated when it simulates the route of human exposure. All of the caveats mentioned for feed are applicable to water. Close observation is essential because spillage is generally a more disasterous event when administering material by water. It cannot be recovered as easily as spilled feed. Losses of data because of this occurrence must be handled statistically.

Gavage

The French force feed geese to fatten them sufficiently to obtain the enlarged, fatty livers to make pate de foie gras, which graces the tables of the gastronomically fortunate. While compensory liver growth is an interesting toxicological phenomenon by itself, the subject is raised because the French word for "force feeding via stomach tube" is "gavage". Thus the word gavage has been adopted for "administer by stomach tube."

When the oral route is indicated, but feed and water are appropriate vehicles, gavage may be recommended method of administration. In this case, a test material is added to an appropriate vehicle and introduced into the esophagus with a tube attached to a graduated syringe. An appropriate vehicle is one which is compatible to both test material and animal. The most common gavage vehicles are water, water with suspending agents, and food grade oil—depending on the characteristics of the test material. When the test materials not soluble, a suspension is often formulated. Suspensions are made by increasing the viscosity of the vehicle with thickeners such as agar, carboxymethyl cellulose, or gum tragacanth. A wetting agent such as Tween 80 may also be used to increase the suspendability of the material. Stability assays will indicate the frequency with which the dosing formulation must be prepared during the test.

Dosing is commonly accomplished at a constant volume of 10 ml/kg body weight. In this way, a 260 g rat would receive a dose of 2.6 ml, and a 35 g mouse would receive 0.35 ml of material. Such ease of calculating the appropriate dose is important when many animals are to be treated daily for a long period of time. Errors arise if too much effort must be made to determine the quantity of test material for each animal. Body weights should be collected frequently during the growth phase of the animal, with dosing volume adjusted accordingly. Weekly adjustments are sufficient after the rapid growth phase.

Since rodents are nocturnal animals, they eat during the dark period. There is an increase in activity and eating just before lights on, at which time they become quiescent. Thought should be given to dosing animals after midmorning so that the food accumulation in the stomach will not interfere with dosing. It is not necessary to introduce the tip of the cannula into the stomach to obtain a good administration of the test material. Depositing the dose into the esophagus is quite sufficient in the rodent, which cannot regurgitate.

Other Methods

Other methods of administration of test substances in chronic studies include:

1. *Skin painting*. The test material is applied by inunction of a specified dose onto an area from which the hair has been removed. A portion of the dosing material must be considered to be ingested since animals frequently lick the foreign material from their skin.
2. *Subcutaneous injection*. This method is a frequently used testing route for pharmaceutical preparations; the site of injection is altered daily so that a single site is not constantly punctured. The dosing vehicle should be aqueous since the oil vehicle will track back along the needle path and be deposited on the skin and hair. If an oil vehicle must be used, "tracking" of the oil may be prevented by depositing the material under the skin of the inner thigh, having inserted the needle from the outer aspect of the thigh.
3. *Implantation*. Subcutaneous or intramuscular implantation is common for evaluating biopolymers for medical devices or prostheses. A clean surgical technique is necessary to avoid the complication of infection.

Data Collection

A word about data collection would seem appropriate. Computer logging of data now permits an observation, i.e., death of an animal, to be accounted for in all future records. However, where handwritten records are kept, separate laboratory books are often made for weekly body weights, food consumption, daily observations, and clinical test results. If an animal dies, the event is dutifully and properly recorded in the daily observation book, but the entry lines are still available in the other laboratory books. At subsequent weighings or observations, an entry may mistakenly appear in the dead animal's space and somehow the animal has reappeared. The more harried the technicians, the longer the reincarnation period. This is a serious problem which calls for appropriate care and vigilance.

The other aspect of manual data collection that promotes insomnia in Study Directors is transcription of data. Transferring data from a laboratory printout to a laboratory notebook is fraught with hazard, and in the end, the laboratory notebook cannot be considered the "raw" data. The printout or machine output is, in fact, the raw data. Yet, how many times have "units of enzyme activity per mg organ protein" been reported as raw data? Spectrophotometers speak in terms of optical density for percent transmission; scintillation counters report "counts per minute," not microcuries per vial. The arithmetic gymnastics that must be performed to transform machine data to understandable toxicological terms must be described fully and documented.

Daily Observation

It is a fact of life-looking at animals huddled in the depths of cages is not exciting. Even good technicians can be lousy observers. Every cage should be opened every day to assess the most gross state of the animal's well being, i.e., alive versus dead. The temptation to merely look into the cage each day without opening it is often irresistible, but in this case, if you've seen one you haven't seen them all. Rodents can die in the most lifelike poses, or they can get their appendages caught in the wire floor, and the technician will not know it if each animal is given only a glance.

If the technician does a good job of observing rats or mice, he will notice the amount, colour, and consistency of feces, and any spilled feed beneath the cage, the water level in the bottle (if any), evidence to urine on the paper or pan, and then he will look at the rat for any evidence of difficulty. Once the animal's condition is noted, the finding shall be reported in English, not medicalese. If the technician confuses miosis with mydriasis, the toxicologist will be completely misled! However, if the notebook states "pin-point pupils," there will be no misunderstanding even years later when the technician is gone. Do not encourage blepharospasm, epistaxis, and chromodacryorrhea when winking, bloody nose, and bloody tears give so much more confidence that the technician has diligently observed and recorded a finding.

If, in the course of taking daily observations, an animal is found dead, it must undergo autospy as soon as possible so that autolysis is minimized. If the autopsy cannot be performed right away, refrigerate the animal to retard autolysis. Since one of the major end-points in a chronic study is histopathological evaluation, every effort must be made to present the pathologist with the best samples of tissue from the experimental subjects.

Clinical Evaluations

Growth Rates

The true measure of growth rate of an experimental animal is the animal's response to the continued availability of food and water. Therefore, to evaluate growth, the investigator must record food consumption and body weight on a fixed schedule. Water consumption should be at least qualitatively compared between groups. This is particularly true when evaluating a diuretic or a salt of an acid.

Many protocols suggest that body weights can be recorded monthly after the rodent' weight plateaus at about 6 months. It is much better to weigh the animals weekly throughout the study. The weekly weighing assures the toxicologist that the animals will be examined closely and palpated at least once a week. Weekly weighings also give the investigator early warnings of the onset of disease or debilitation in aged animals. The latter consideration as a key factor in gathering data of toxicologic significance as the study winds down.

Food Consumption

Food consumption is often evaluated in chronic studies to assess the effect of a treatment be eating and food utilization, i.e., food consumed per unit weight gain. It is a widely collected and infrequently scrutinized item of data. Food consumption is measured by subtreeting the average daily weight to feed remaining from the weight of feed introduced into an animal's cage and dividing by the number of days in the feeding period. It is not always covious that there are three components to this value called "food consumption." It is comprised of food actually eaten plus food that is spilled minus fecal and urinary contributions to the feeder. Thus whenever "food consumption" appears excessive, account could be taken of the spillage of feed attributable to different treatment groups.

Organ Weights

Weighing the organs of treated animals may reveal a specific target-organ response. This is one of the first lessons taught in toxicology, yet there is an element of complexity in this lesson this not always described. The major organs weighed in a chronic study include the liver, heart, kidneys, spleen, gonads, brain, adrenal, thyroid, pituitary, and thymus (at early interval sacrifices). The procedures for obtaining the weights of these organs include removal from the body, dissecting free of adhering tissue, and weighing. Removal from the body requires no major considerations except to place the organ on a moistened surface so that it will not dry out.

Dissecting the organ free of adhering tissues does require a few words of caution. The most easily dissected organs are the liver, spleen, kidney testes, and perhaps pituitary. Very few decisions have to be made by the technician in preparing these discrete organs for weighing. The remaining organs have built-in hazards which have to be addressed.

Heart

This auricles of the heart to be addressed are so thin that they are often removed with the major arteries; in addition, the heart may contain unexpelled blood in the ventricles, which will add weight to the organ. The ventricles should be incised to remove blood and inspect the values and the endocardium.

Brain

While many organs are discrete, the brain continues posteriorly into the spinal column. In order to reduce variation in weights, necropsy and dissection procedures should be standardized. The spinal cord should be severed at the atlas joint before proceeding to the removal of the cranial cap. In this day, the brain will be cut in the same place each time. In addition, the olfactory lobes, which extend forward into the snout, are often left in the animal, thereby increasing variability.

Adrenals

The adrenals of the rodent are similar to colour to adhering fat. Without adequate training and care, the technicians may dissect the adrenals too closely, giving rise to a bimodal distribution of weights of adrenals. If one technician works on the control animals and another dissects the organs of a treated group, significant organ weight differences could arise due to differences in procedures and not treatment. This is another reason to insist on randomization of animals at necropsy.

Thyroids

The thyroid is a small organ in rodents with a colour similar to surrounding muscle. Like the adrenals, thyroid dissection requires care, training and practice.

An indication of variability in organ weight, whether contributed by the animal or the technician, is the coefficient of variability (CV). The formula for CV is

$$\frac{100\,(\text{standard deviation})}{\text{mean weight}}$$

Review of control groups of two mouse and four rat studies has shown the CV ranges of some organs to be approximately:

	Liver	Heart	Kidney
Mouse	10-15	15-20	10-15
Rat	10-15	10-15	10-15

Spleen	Testes	Brain	Adrenals
45-70	10-15	5-8	20-30
15-30	7-9	4-8	15-30

The contributions to variability are (a) animal variation, (b) technician dissecting variability, and (c) technician balance reading variability. It is interesting to compare the CV of the organs. The brain and testes have the least variability, followed by the major organs, the liver, heart, and kidney. The greatest variability was seen with the spleen and adrenals (and thyroid weights, 20-30, in one mouse study).

When organ weights are compared statistically, they are often expressed as weight per unit of body weight since animal size affects organ size. If body weights are greatly different between treatment groups, this expression of the relative size of the organ may not be valid. Calculation of relative organ, weights may not be appropriate because depressed body weight due to treatment is frequently due to depressed deposition of fat, not depressed development of lean body mass. If it were possible, we would choose to express organ weights relative to lean body mass, but we have no way to determine this value for each animal. However, since the brain weight is measured with low variability and is not greatly influenced by nutritional factors, it is a good, measurable monitor of lean body mass. Therefore, when significant treatment-related differences in a study are detected in many organ weights relative to body weight, organ/brain weight ratios should be analyzed.

Clinical Determinations: General Considerations

In the course of a chronic study, it is customary to monitor the state of the body fluids at several intervals i.e., 3, 12, 18 and 24 months in rats. At these intervals, blood is collected from one of all several sites (retroorbital sinus, tail tip, heart, or aorta, depending of the fate of the animal). Venipuncture is usual for large species, while blood is collected from the retroorbital sinus or the tail tip in rodents destined to continue treatment in the chronic study. Rodents may be bled from the abdominal aorta at the time of sacrifice. This permits greater amounts of blood to be collected for special purposes. Bleeding methods which require the technician to "milk" the blood out of the animal (such as cutting off the tip of the tail) run the risk of obtaining anomalous results on concentrations of microscopic or high molecular weight components. For routine hematological and chemical determination, no more than 1 to 2 ml of blood are required if newer microanalytical methods are used. This is important in mouse studies, in which it was once necessary to pool blood from several animals to provide enough blood to perform the desired analyses.

Clinical characteristics of blood are generally investigated in plasma obtained from blood mixed with an anticoagulant (heparin, EDTA, sodium citrate, sodium oxalate, etc.). The choice of anticoagulant depends on the analyses to be performed. For RBC cholinesterase and serum alkaline phosphatase determinations, heparin is the anticoagulant of choice since chelating anticoagulants interfere with the assay. Plasma to be used for clinical evaluation must be clear and straw coloured in appearance. Hemolysis always results in erroneous findings. Depending on the extent of hemolysis, the investigators will find lower hematocrit and red blood cell concentration, elevated serum lactic dehydrogenase, alanine and aspartate amino-transferases, alkaline phosphatase, potassium, and creatinine. These are the RBC components released into the blood. The hemoglobin released by hemolysis interferes with photometric measurements of bilirubin and with chemical reactions needed to measure lipase activity.

It is a good policy to submit duplicate samples from 10 randomly selected animals to the clinical laboratory. The data from these samples may be analyzed to provide an estimate of the laboratory repeatability. The samples which are coded as "duplicate" would not be included in the statistical analysis of the results.

Statistical analyses for hematological tests often reveal "statistically significant" results in *pretest* treatment groups. It is obvious that these results could not be "toxicologically significant" since treatment will not have been initiated. The "significant" results must be attributed to chance. The dilemma that this introduces is how to know which of the *post* treatment significant results are due to chance and which are due to treatment.

Significant treatment differences can arise from systematic error. It is not unusual for technicians to bleed (in sequence) control, low-, and high-dose animals. This practice is dangerous since endogenous diurnal cycles of blood constituents may be rising or falling during the period of bleeding. This would introduce a "dose-related" rise or fall in concentration of the affected constituent. It is obvious that blood constituents from nutrient sources often decrease with time after eating, e.g., lipids, so that animals are fasted to prevent this complication. But this does not eliminate the cycles of blood concentration found for glucose, for example. When control, young adult, male rats were fasted and bled throughout the day, the glucose level was highest at 10 A.M. and 2 P.M. with troughs at 11:30 A.M. and 4 P.M. Thus if control, low-, mid-, and high-dose groups were bled sequentially between 10 A.M. and noon (how often has that been done?) a dose related depression of blood glucose would be obtained. To avoid the needless mess provided by this situation, one should randomly distribute animals to be bled from all treatment groups across the duration of the bleeding period of

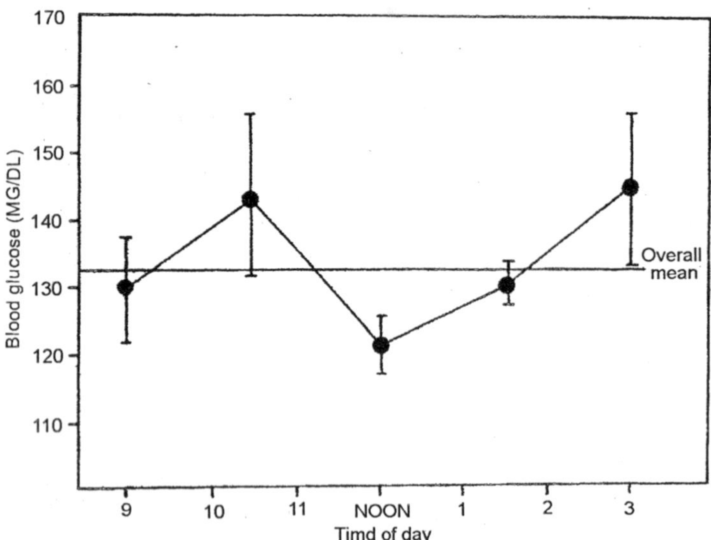

Fig. 9.1. Blood glucose levels of untreated male rats bled at different times of day.

the day. Some investigators claim that animals which were randomly distributed at the beginning of the study need not be rerandomized later because, after all, random is random. However, animals become "ordered" merely by being housed in a specific cage at a specific position in the room and must be randomized to eliminate the effect of being ordered; systematic error can arise if this is not recognized. Randomization may not eliminate all of the "chance" treatment effects to be seen. Some other precautions may be desirable.

Often five animals/sex/treatment group are sampled for interim clinical evaluation. Using so few animals encourages the occurrence of inexplicable results especially when the results are so often analyzed by a series of "T" tests, each pitting a treatment group versus its appropriate control. A better method of analysis would be an analysis of variance within each sex; better yet, one should employ a two factor analysis and determine the effect of *sex* as well as *treatment* on the parameters being studied. If statistically significant differences occur using analyses of variance, the response should be dose-related before attributing toxicological significance to the differences.

Care should be taken not to dismiss significant differences because the values fall in the "normal" range. For instance, the normal range

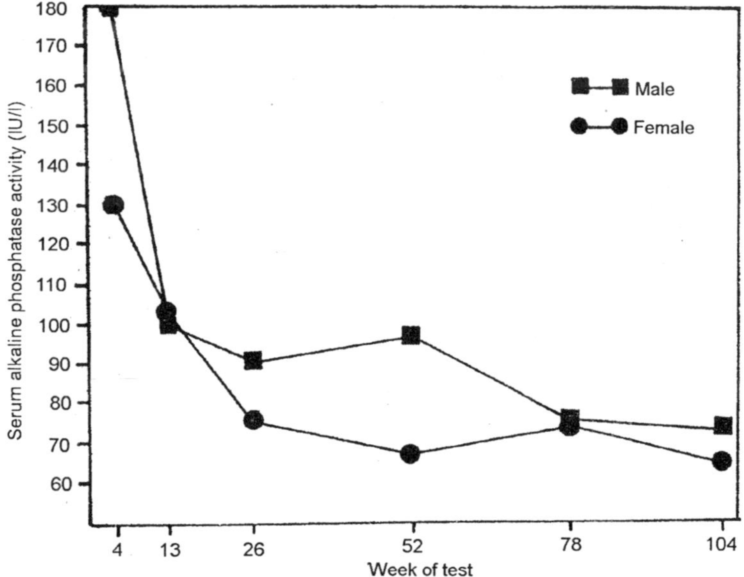

Fig. 9.2. Serum alkaline phosphatase activity of normal, untreated male and female rats over the course of two years.

for serum alkaline phosphatase (SAP) values of the rat are given as 56.8 to 128 IU/liter. This wide range is due to the ever decreasing SAP values with age after weaning. A high value in an aged animal may be clearly significant, even though the value may fall within the normal range that was generated by including young and old control animals in the historical file. SAP values for control rats evaluated at several intervals during a 2-year test are presented in Fig. 9.2.

Rules for decreasing "false significant" differences include:

1. Randomize animals.
2. Use sufficient numbers of animals.
3. Use appropriate statistical analysis.
4. Look for dose-response relationships.
5. Compare data to appropriate historical values from animals of similar age, sex, and physiological state.
6. Never use plasma samples which are hemolyzed.

Hematology

The classic hematologic parameters are the erythrocyte count, leukocyte count, differential leukocyte count, and hemoglobin, hematocrit, platelets, and reticulocyte counts. From these data, the mean corpuscular hemoglobin (MCH) and mean corpuscular volume (MCV) can be calculated. With the added concern for blood dyscrasias, it behaves the investigator to examine red cell fragility, sedimentation rate, coagulation factors, and to closely examine the bone marrow.

Generally, hematologic evaluations are carried out at several intervals throughout the study. These assays, along with the clinical chemistry assays, should be conducted on at least 10 to 15 animals per sex per group selected at random. It is critical that the blood be taken in the same manner for each sampling.

It is often desirable to perform pretreatment or time zero assay to establish baseline values. The value of zero time assays is underscored when one considers "early onset leukemia" in mice. This random phenomenon in some strains would be missed in initial hematologic evaluations were not conducted. Being unaware of the background leukocyte count could lead to a false positive finding of treatment-related leukemia.

Evaluation of bone marrow is a more tedious procedure. The most beneficial approach is to remove a section of a long bone at necropsy, allow the marrow to fix in the shaft, process the marrow, and examine its contents. The major variable in marrow examination is the site of sampling. In rodents, the epiphyseal plates of the femurs can be clipped and the complete shaft fixed. In larger animals, the femur is a good site for sampling but a standard distance from one of the epiphyseal plates should be selected.

A word of caution in handling long bones of dogs, monkeys, pigs, etc., must be offered. In general, the femur of the adult animal is well developed and must be sampled using a Stryker saw or hand saw. Do not place the bone on the table when sawing. The vibration causes scrambling and movement of the marrow and in some cases, complete loss of marrow from the shaft.

Differential White Cell Count

White cells are classed as neutrophils, basophils, lymphocytes, eosinophils, and monocytes. Occasionally, the relative quantity of one or more of these changes dramatically. Some specific changes are listed here with common interpretations:

1. *Neutrophils*. Elevated with acute infections (especially cocci), tissue necrosis (and hemolysis), strenuous exercise, convulsions, tachycardia, and acute hemorrhage.
2. *Lymphocytes*. Elevated with acute infection and chronic infection, e.g., hepatitis or malnutrition.
3. *Basophils*. Depressed in hyperthyroidism.
4. *Eosinophils*. Elevated with allergy, irradiation, pernicious anemia, parasitism, and some poisons, e.g., phosphorous or black widow spider venom.
5. *Monocytes*. Elevated with protozoal infection and some poisons, e.g., tetrachloroethane.

Nonspecific elevation of white blood cells, termed a leukemialike disorder, may be due to acute hemolysis or hemorrhage, severe burns, mercury poisoning, or stress. Leukopenia, or nonspecific depression of white blood cells, may be associated with some infections, inanition and debilitation, splenic disorders, and intoxication with chemical agents, e.g., sulphonamides or arsenicals. False leukopenia may also appear when automated cell counting is performed on white cells that have a tendency to clump or lyse. Unexpected occurrence of leukopenia is the obvious indication for manual counting to avoid errors in interpretation. It may be worth mentioning that mere shipment of animals is associated with leukocyte elevation in the blood. The elevated levels may persist for 3 to 8 weeks—the longer the transportation time, the longer the effect. Thus one should not use animals in one test which have been received on different dates.

Clinical Chemistry

Clinical chemistry evaluations have been a major area of concern to the toxicologist for several reasons. The first concern is the variability of results. Standardized techniques have to be applied within any one laboratory, and an intralaboratory variance has to be established before the values have meaning. The second concern is the value of the change observed. It is assumed that intracellular damage in the laboratory rodent manifests itself in the same fashion as damage or physiologic alternation manifests itself in humans. That is a basic assumption in animal testing—that the results reflect what will occur in the exposed human. The introduction of automated equipment in human clinical laboratories has channeled the toxicologist's approach to clinical chemistry by permitting almost effortless analysis of such classical serum enzymes as alkaline phosphatase (SAP), alanine aminotransferase, and aspartate aminotransferase (formerly known as SGPT and SGOT, respectively, which serve as indicators of liver toxicity. The electrolytes and blood urea nitrogen (BUN) along with creatinine are the major measures of renal function and remain major assays for the toxicologist. Several other enzyme systems have been suggested for aiding in diagnosis of organ damage, but the criteria of repeatability and interpretability in the laboratory animal must be followed.

Before selecting a "battery" of tests, it is better to evaluate organ specific activity during the early studies (acute and subchronic) and to focus on the area of concern in the chronic study. A thumbnail sketch of common clinical chemistry evaluations may be seen as follows.

Bilirubin

Arising from the breakdown of red blood cells, the major amount of bilirubin is bound to albumin in blood but is termed free bilirubin. Bilirubin is converted to the glucuronide form in the liver. In liver blockage, the yellowish cast to tissues is due to hyperbilirubinemia. Plasma bilirubin is also elevated with prolonged fasting and hemolysis.

α-Amylase

This enzyme hydrolyzes 1,4-glucosidic linkages of starch to form dextrins, maltotetrose, maltotriose, maltose, and glucose. This enzyme is elevated in pancreatitis and renal insufficiency and depressed in hepatobiliary toxicity.

Creatine and Creatinine

Known as methyl-guanacetic acid and its anhydride, respectively, these compounds are important in the physiology of muscle contraction.

Normally, creatine is found in muscle, while creatinine is the waste product found in the circulation. Creatine is found in urine in some muscular disorders. Values for creatinine are elevated in younger and more active animals. There is an elevation of serum creatinine after eating meat; this could be an important consideration in dog studies. Pathological elevation of serum creatinine occurs with renal failure.

Creatine phosphokinase

This substance is found in heart, skeletal muscle, brain, and testes, but not in liver. Elevated levels are found in muscular disorders, myocardial infarction, and pulmonary disorders.

Cholinesterase

True cholinesterase, found in red blood cells, can cleave only acetylcholine, while other esterases found in plasma and termed pseudocholinesterases, can cleave acetylcholine as well as other esters. Depressions of true and pseudocholinesterases accompany intoxication with some organophosphates and carbamates.

Nonesterified Fatty Acids

These are also termed free fatty acids and are elevated during fasting and depressed following ingestion of food or glucose and following insulin injection.

Glucose

Glucose is a nutrient in blood that is utilized by all cells of the body, including erythrocytes. For this reason, analyses should be performed soon after blood withdrawal. Samples may be stored for 48 hr if refrigerated and preserved with potassium oxalate. If a glucose oxidase method of assay is used, contamination of samples or glassware with ascorbic acid (vitamin C) will cause false negatives, while peroxide and hypochlorite detergents will result in false positives.

Serum Alkaline Phosphatase

This substance is found in most tissues, including bone, liver, and kidney; isoenzymes characteristic of different tissues may also be found. These enzymes catalyze the transfer of phosphate to suitable acceptor alcohols. The plasma levels decrease with age but are increased following eating. Elevations are also seen with osteoblastic activity, impairment of liver function, and obstruction of bile flow.

Total Protein

Depressions are almost always due to a fall in albumin concentration. This is complicated by compensatory increases in globulins. Thus determination of total protein is generally not very useful. Measurement of specific proteins could be more instructive, for instance:

Albumin; has colloidal osmotic function.

Metal binding proteins; ceruloplasmin, lactoferrin, metalothionine

Hemoglobin binding proteins; haptoglobin

Globulins; antibodies

Clotting factors

Trace proteins, hormones, enzymes

Electrolytes

These are sodium, potassium, and chloride. Normally, they are very stable components of blood. However, depressions accompany vomiting and diarrhea, while elevations in concentration are found in renal disorders, dehydration, and cardiac failure.

Aminotransferases

Aspartate and alanine aminotransferases, formerly known as glutamic oxalacetic (GOT) and glutamic pyruvic (GPT) transaminases, respectively, are elevated following tissue damage in which the cellular enzymes are dumped into the blood-stream. Aspartate aminotransferase is found in high levels in heart and liver, while alanine aminotransferase is most active in liver.

Uric acid

This endproduct of purine metabolism is classically elevated in humans with gout. It may also be elevated in renal toxicity and depressed with ACTH treatment.

Urobilinogen

This bacterial product of bilirubin metabolism in the intestine is partially reabsorbed and found in high levels in urine in liver toxicity or disease (cirrhosis and hepatitis).

Urea Nitrogen

Generally termed BUN, it is elevated in renal toxicity or disease and with increased protein catabolism but is depressed with overhydration and severe liver damage.

URINALYSIS

Urinalysis has been fraught with difficulty and cloned with controversy since the advent of routine analysis in toxicology studies. Generally, the crudest possible procedures are used in collection and analysis of urine. The results and their toxicological meaning generally correspond to the primitive methods employed.

Analysis of body fluids, be it blood, urine, lymph, or other, is conducted to determine if the source organ(s) is functioning properly or is being taxed beyond its capacity. If the techniques for gathering the fluid are not consistent, the interpretation will not be consistent. Urine is generally collected from troughs or trays placed below the cages in which the animals are housed. The urine so collected is then evaluated for colour and cloudiness, pH, specific gravity, and dipstick tests, as well as microscopic inspection for particulate matter.

pH values may differ by treatment but will not reflect the normal physiological situation since the dissolved CO_2 will have dissipated, resulting in an elevation of the pH. Hair, dander, and room dust often settle in the urine, to provide interesting viewing for the examiner and to contribute to the specific gravity of the urine. In addition, bacterial populations often develop in the urine collected in this manner. The addition of classical preservatives such as thymol or toluene is scarcely more than a symbolic gesture due to their lack of solubility. Other antibacteria or fungistatic agents would have to be evaluated for their interfering effects on clinical measurements before being used.

The results of urinalyses are generally so variable, especially with the current tendency to evaluate five animals/sex/group, as to be meaningless. If there is a real concern and reason to consider urinalysis important enough to characterize well, then it should be important enough to devote sufficient animals to the analyses so that the animals may be sacrificed with urine collected directly from the bladder and analyzed by sensitive means. Again, be sure to randomly select animals from different treatment groups throughout the day of collection, since first urine of the day may be decidedly different from that collected at other times of the day. As an example, the clarity of urine of saccharin-treated male rats is reported to be visibly diminished in the first urine sample of the "lights on" period, but clear at all other collection intervals during the day.

Finally, the clinical chemistry of urine may provide toxicological information as follows:

1. *Ketonuria*—elevated in starvation, low carbohydrate diets.
2. *Prophyrinuria*—elevated in lead poisoning and hepatic disorders, e.g., cirrhosis.
3. *Hemoglobinuria/hematuria*—elevated in toxicity, e.g., naphthalene, sulfonamides.

4. *Glucosuria*—occurs in diabetes.
5. *Osmolality*—usually crudely estimated by measuring specific gravity. Indicates degree to which kidney concentrates the urine. Osmolality decreases with some types of nephrotoxicity, e.g., "high output" renal failure.
6. *pH*—generally meaningless unless outside the range of 6.0 to 7.0. Urine in the bladder has lower pH than urine in the collection trough because dissolved CO_2 is liberated following urination.
7. *Crystalluria*—this occurs when urine becomes supersaturated in crystal forming molecule(s). May precede kidney stones or bladder stones.

Blood Levels of Test Material

The complex field of pharmacokinetics cannot be covered in this review, but one aspect should be mentioned. It is reasonable to check blood levels of the test material throughout the duration of the chronic test at a specified time after dosing or after "lights on." It is normal, in such tests, to administer the test material on a dose per unit body weight basis. One must understand that body weight is the sum of weights of all tissues and that these tissues do not vary allometrically (in the same ratio to body weight) over the life of an animal. Rats put on weight primarily in the form of fat after they are 2 to 4 months old. Thus increments in doses are largely in response to added fat. The dose of material thereby increases at a rate faster than the increase in lean body mass. If fat is not an active metabolizing or storage compartment for the test material, increases in blood concentration of the compound may be seen with age and increase in body weight. Such findings could easily be misinterpreted, for instance, as an inhibition of metabolizing enzyme activity. Thus once again, body weight is seen as a poor indicator of the quantity that the investigator is really in search of—lean body mass.

10

BIOETHICS AND TOXICOLOGY

Toxicology has aided us in establishing laws and in implementing regulations for our protection against all manner of poisonous substances. Our developing technology and growing population density aggravate existing environmental problems and create new ones. The growing unease regarding thee problems was expressed in 1960 in a symposium on "Problems in Toxicology". The dangers discussed included the usual environmental problems and the possible interaction of the various pollutants. Lay attention was drawn to the growing seriousness of these matters by publications such as *Silent Spring*. In the years since, the public has become more aware and better informed so that a number of legislative steps have resulted in necessary control measures. This discussion will be concerned with laws and agencies designed to regulate and control chemicals and other substances having poisonous or dangerous qualities.

Many useful and common substances, frequently contacted in our daily lives, may not be recognized as hazards, yet they are the cause of many poisonings. A causal look at our surroundings, at home or at work, will illustrate the need for consciousness of these hazards. Examples include solvents, cleaners, detergents, paints, paint removers, and household and garden pesticides. They would also include insect repellents applied to the skin, rat poisons, moth killer, mildew preventive, fireproofing chemicals, waterproofing chemicals, and polishes. Many of these useful chemicals are sold in pressure containers for aerosol dispersal. Some propellant gases have proved harmful when misused and some are also considered a threat to the environment.

Many drugs kept in the home are distinct hazards and need more regulatory attention For example, aspirin, sleeping, pills, iron tablets, and reducing pills have produced many serious or fatal poisonings, particularly in children. Other potential sources of injury include flammable fabrics and explosives. Such dangers are cause for concern for improvement of consumer protection.

The widely, distributed environmental poisons polluting our air and water are a serious problem requiring increased regulation. Air pollutants, including lead, CO, ozone, carbon solids, nitrogen oxides, and SO_2, increase with population and industrialization. However, earlier use of known techniques would have reduced our problems. The Environmental Protection Agency, in responding to these worsening problems, is emphasizing control. Beside industrial wastes, we have the growing problem of sewage disposal. These matters have received little previous attention because of apathy. Despite useful laws and a capable technology, progress has been made only as the result of strong public demand.

It is clear that we are constantly in contact with chemicals that are designed to serve a myriad of beneficial purposes. For example, products such as pesticides have made our lives easier and more comfortable, but we cannot have the benefits without accepting a degree of risk as well. Many of these products are highly toxic, even in low concentrations, and they often prevent difficulties in their application and disposal because of their persistent qualities and toxic breakdown substances. We have solution for some questions of safety concerning these; other questions remain unanswered. Additional information must be sought through research and experiment before we attain adequate regulations.

Regulatory Development

The intense interest in the health hazards of our environment, emphasized by the news media in recent years, has resulted in more effective legislation of their control. But public concern has not always been such a powerful factor in the passage of regulatory legislation. Before, 1900, neither the lawmakers, nor the manufacturers, nor others responsible for these problems left much pressure to correct them. There was at that time practically to legislation for protecting either the worker or the public form exposure to toxic materials, and injured parties had only limited recourse even in the courts. Two factors were mainly responsible for the changes that took place around the turn of the century. The first was the development of chemical methods sensitive enough to detect the presence of traces of poisons in food or in other materials. These aided in establishing cause-effect relationships.

The second factor was the recognition that workers are entitled to some protection against industrial hazards and that the responsibility for this protection rests with the employer.

Regulatory law has been developed over the years both by legislation and by administrative promulgation. Much of this, however, lacks coordination and often fails to keep pace with current needs, but reforming the law is difficult. In attempting reform, new laws are passed often without relation to the existing law, thus creating further confusion.

Regulatory Agencies

Of the many regulatory acts and agencies of the United States government a number are of minor importance from the standpoint of toxicology. These will be briefly described at the end of the chapter with adequate reference for further reading is desired.

The agency of greatest concern to most of us in recent yeas is the Environmental Protection Agency (EPA). It was established, by Executive Order, to govern matters concerning air and water pollution, the use of pesticides, and other matters affecting the environment. One primary purpose of its formation was to consolidate the functions of the several agencies relating to the environment in order to improve regulatory performance. The creation of this agency is an example of law reform and simplification that should result in better control of environmental hazards. The powers of the former regulatory agencies to control pollution were weakened by fragmentation. The Mark Commission cites an example in which the Food and Drug Administration was setting tolerance limits for pesticides, but had no power to prevent pesticide registration by the Department of Agriculture. The Reorganization Plan of 1970 now assigns both of these tasks to EPA.

All activities of the Department of Interior relating to water quality, water pollution control, studies of the effects of pesticides on fish and wildlife resources, and the Gulf Breeze Biological Laboratory were moved to EPA. EPA now controls the former functions of the Department of Health, Education, and Welfare relating to the Air pollution Control Administration and the DHEW's provision of technical assistance to the states. The Bureau of Water Hygiene, and with some exceptions, the Bureau of Radiological Health are also included. In addition, EPA assumed the activities of the Council of Environmental Quality (CEQ) that pertain to ecologic systems; those tasks of the Department of Energy, administered through its Division of Radiation

Protection Standards, establishing environmental standards for protection from radioactive material.

Toxic Substances Control Act

After the formation of EPA, the Toxic Substances Control Act (TOSCA) was added in an attempt to consolidate regulation of the chemical industry. Chemicals are all around us—in our air, our water, and our food, and in the things we touch. Many of these chemicals have become essential to our lives, and their production contributes significantly to our national economy. However, for many of these substances, we have little knowledge of the ill effects they might cause after many years of exposure. The Toxic Substances Control Act, which became effective January 1, 1977, regulates commerce and protects human health and the environment by requiring testing and the necessary use restrictions on certain chemical substances.

While we have enjoyed the extensive economic and social benefits of chemicals, we have not always realized the risks that may be associated with them. Many chemicals that have been commonly used and widely dispersed have been found to present significant health and environmental dangers. Vinyl chloride, which is commonly used in plastics, has caused the death of workers who were exposed to this chemical. Asbestos has long been known to cause cancer when inhaled. Mercury has caused debilitating effects in Japan. Perhaps the most vivid example was the careless dispersal into our environment of millions of pounds of polychlorinated biphenyls (PCB's), a highly persistent and toxic group of chemicals.

The new law promotes acquisition of adequate chemical data. It provides authority to regulate but says such authority shall not be used to create unnecessary economic barriers to innovation. It was passed following a five-year congressional effort. The Act requires the formation of the TOSCA Interagency Testing Committee. This is made up of representatives from eight agencies, which include the National science Foundation, the Occupational Safety and Health Administration, and the National Cancer Institute. There are also four nonvoting liaison agencies, including the Food and Drug Administration and the Department of Defense.

The primary purpose of TOSCA is to assure that chemical substances and mixtures do not present and unreasonable risk of injury to health or the environment. Yet when one considers that there are about 100,000 chemicals in commerce and that at least 1,000 new ones are added each year, it is obvious that the Agency faces a tremendous job. Think of the toxicologists needed! The early efforts of the Agency have resulted in a Toxic Substances List and four to eight chemical substances marked for study.

Food and Drug Administration

Another agency of great importance and interest to toxicologists is the Food and Drug Administration (FDA). In this consideration it is of interest to review briefly the background of the present law for protection of our food and drug supply. The first general food law was passed in Massachusetts in 1784, and in 1824 a Flour Inspection Act was passed in District of Columbia. In 1848, when it was discovered that the quinine for our soldiers in the Mexican War was adulterated, the Import Drugs Act was passed. From that time until 1905, more than 100 food and drugs acts were introduced but failed to pass the Congress. The many attempts do, however, show an increasing awareness of the need for such regulation. Early in this century a number of investigation of food and drug problems were carried out, including the effective efforts of Dr. Harvey Wiley and his so-called "poison squad," which operated mainly in Chicago. By exposing indescribably filthy conditions existing in some of the food-processing industries of that time. Dr. Wiley and his group, together with such writings as *The Jungle* by Upton Sinclair aroused great enough public demand that passage of effective laws resulted.

From 1906 until 1933 a number of improved food and drug laws were passed, but by 1933 it became clear that a stronger law was needed. A revised law, the Food, Drug and Cosmetic Act, was finally passed in 1938 following a drug-poisoning incident killing more than 100 persons. Besides establishment of the Food and Drug Administration, the new Act provided for (1) extension of coverage to cosmetics and medical devices; (2) requirement of predistribution clearance on safety of new drugs; (3) elimination of the Shirley Amendment requirement to prove intent to defraud in drug-misbranding cases; (4) provision for establishing tolerances for unavoidable or required poisonous substances; (5) authorization of standards of identify, quality, and fill of container for foods; (6) authorization of factory inspections; and (7) addition of the remedy of court injunction to previous remedies of seizure and prosecution.

Consumer protection against harmful food colorings began in 1907, when concern was expressed about the safety of the new coal tar colours just coming into use. Responsible food processors asked the government to set up a system for testing these colours and certifying them as pure and harmless. This voluntary system lasted until 1938, when certification was made compulsory by available when they were first listed as "harmless", were developed, colours were reevaluated. This retesting showed that, in fact, some of the colours in use were not completely harmless if used in unlimited amounts. So in 1960, the Colour Additive Amendments were passed, strengthening consumer protection in three ways.

First, the Amendments brought all colours (not just coal tar colours) under the jurisdiction of the law, Second, they required reevaluation-using new scientific tests—of all colours, even those previously listed and certified as harmless. (Any colour that produces cancer in a test animal is automatically ruled out). Finally, they allowed FDA to set limits on the amounts of colour used.

The Act also provides for the control of food additives as defined by the FDA: "A food additive is any substance that becomes part of food, or affects the characteristics of food, through direct or indirect use and with useful intention." They may be intentionally added to food to preserve, emulsify, flavour, add nutritive value, colour, or achieve other useful, desired purposes. Materials that might also get into foods while they are grown, processed, or packaged are called incidental additives. Before an additive can be used to improve a food product, it is subjected to toxicity studies by the food (or chemical) manufacturer, and it is evaluated and regulated by the FDA.

The Food, Drug and Cosmetic Act, under the Miller Amendment of 1954, also provided that the FDA establish tolerances for those registered economic poisons that appeared as residues in food products, and that the FDA maintain surveillance for conformity with the law. Thus, before a pesticide residue can be allowed to remain in or on food, the use of the pesticide on food crops must be approved by the Environmental Protection Agency. The pesticide is subjected to toxicity studies by the manufacturer and is evaluated and regulated by the EPA.

Food products are labeled with the required information to guide and protect the consumer. An amendment to the Food, Drug, and Cosmetic Act was passed in 1985 prohibiting the use of new food additives until the sponsor established safety and the FDA issued regulations specifying the conditions of use.

In 1962, much publicity resulted from the action of Dr. Frances O. Kelsey in keeping thalidomide off the American market. This drug produced thousands of deformities in babies born in western Europe.

The tragedy and attendant publicity created a great deal of public interest in drug problems. Subsequently, that year the Kefauver-Harris Drug Amendments strengthened new drug clearance procedures. As a result of this legislation, drug manufacturers had to prove effectiveness of drugs before marketing them. Further changes, including the amended versions of January 1971 and October 1976, have improved the law.

To summarize, the enactment of the modern Federal Food, Drug, and Cosmetic Act is aimed at assuring foods that are safe pure, and wholesome; drugs and therapeutic devices that are safe and effective; and cosmetics that are harmless. All these products must be honestly and informatively labeled and packaged. The FDA also requires that dangerous household products carry adequate warnings for safe use and are properly labeled, and that there be no counterfeiting of drugs.

Also of interest to toxicologists is the establishment by the Food and Drug administration of a National Drug Code Directory (NDC System). The system provides a unique ten-digit, three-part number for every drug. The system is computerized, and among other things it will provide a prompt identification of drugs in poisoning cases. This computerized information will be available for "those needing identification of the drug product, by-product, or generic name, dosage form, strength, route of administration, or legal status." It will also be of assistance for third-party reimbursement programs. This drug code system also has potential applications in hospitals for inventory control, billing, and medication records, and in government agencies for such diverse purposes as adverse reaction reporting systems, drug utilization reviews, poison control center operations, and drug product recalls.

The Drug Listing Act of 1972 dictated the expansion of the NDC System to include both human over-the-counter and veterinary drugs.

Occupational Safety and Health Act

A new law with wide-ranging effect and of great concern to industry is the Occupational Safety and Health Act (OSHA) of 1970, designed to assure that no employee will suffer diminished health, functional capacity, or life expectancy as a result of his work experience. The Act is administered by the Secretary of Labor. He is authorized to set mandatory occupational safety and heath standards for businesses in interstate commerce and to establish a review commission for carrying out adjudicatory functions under the Act. The Act calls for research in occupational safety and health to assist in the discovery of latent diseases, to establish the connection between diseases and the work environment where these exist, and to study other health problems. It also provides for training of personal engaged in the field of occupational safety and health. It stipulates enforcement and encourages states to adequately administer state and health laws. It is clear that toxicologists will be extensively involved in both administrative and compliance aspects of this Act.

National Institute for Occupational Safety and Health

The National Institute for Occupational Safety and Health (NIOSH) is the principal federal agency engaged in research in the national effort to eliminate on-the-job hazards to the health and safety of America's working men and women. The Institute was established within the Department of Health, Education, and Welfare under the provision of the Occupational Safety and Health Act. Administratively, NIOSH is located within HEW's Center for Disease Control of the Public Health Service. The portion of OSH administered by the Department of Labor is largely regulatory, but much of the Department's work will rest on the results of research conducted by NIOSH under HEW.

NIOSH is responsible for identifying occupational safety and health hazards and for recommending changes in the regulations limiting them. It also has obligations for training occupational health manpower and conducting research for new occupational safety and health standards. The recommended standards are transmitted to the Department of Labor, which then has the responsibility for their development, promulgation, and enforcement.

The institute's main research laboratories are in Cincinnati, where studies include not only the effects of exposure to hazardous substances used in the workplace, but also the psychologic, motivational, and behavioural factors involved in occupational safety and health. Much of the Institute's research deals with specific hazards, such as asbestos and other fibers, beryllium, coal tar pitch volatiles, silica, noise, and stress.

The establishment of both TOSCA and NIOSH has resulted in a strong demand for toxicologists. The increased activity in industry in attempts to comply with the law and the research and enforcement activities under OSHA have been powerful stimulants to all facets of toxicology. Perhaps the area of research and training will be most greatly affected. In this connection a program of grants for both training and research has been instituted.

Drug Abuse

Of great concern to all citizens, as well as to toxicologists and to legislators, has been the great increase in drug abuse in recent years. In an attempt to control the problem the Comprehensive Drug Abuse Prevention and Control Act of 1970 was enacted to provide for increased research into the prevention of dug abuse and drug dependence, for treatment and rehabilitation of addicts, and to improve law enforcement. The law makes available rehabilitation programs, research, medical treatment, education, control, and enforcement. This is another instance of a law that is administered by more than one agency. The National Institute of Mental Health has been designated to carry out the medical, educational, and research aspects of the law. Extramural research is supported by both a grant and a contract program administered by the Institute. This Institute also conducts an extensive public relations program. Toxicologists are involved within the Institute and as outside consultants for developing appropriate methods of treatment of addicts and solution of other problems.

Toxicologists may also be encouraged to know that an Office of Drug Abuse Policy has been established in the Executive Office of the President of coordinate the speed the work of the Federal agencies involved in drug control or drug abuse programs. The Director is to set priorities for federal drug abuse and related activities. The Office is to develop a comprehensive coordinated, long term federal strategy for all drug abuse programs conducted, directed, sponsored, or supported by any department or agency of the federal government.

Consumer Product Safety Act

Another law that will have considerable impact on consumer safety and poisoning cases is the Consumer Product Safety Act, passed late in 1972 and amended in 1976. The principal purposes of the act are to protect the public against unreasonable risk of injury and assist in evaluating the comparative safety and uniform safety standards for consumer products. The act is also intended to promote research of the causes and prevention of product-related deaths, illnesses, and injury. The term "consumer product" is defined as any article or part thereof for use, consumption, or enjoyment in or around a permanent or temporary household or resistance a school, in recreation or otherwise. The law specifically does not apply to tobacco, motor vehicles or their equipment, pesticides, aircraft or parts and appliances, boats, drugs, medical devices, cosmetics, food, or firearms, as all of these were controlled by law when the Act was passed.

The Act establishes an independent regulatory commission known as the Consumer Product Safety Commission (CPSC). The Commission is independent, not under a department of government. This relatively new law has proved something of a toothless cat in some danger of extinction. It is, however, the only agency of the government whose title contains the word "consumer". This, in the end, may save it. The exemptions from the Act noted above are considered by some to have been an emasculation. Nonetheless, the Act was given the responsibility for implementing several already existing laws, specifically.

The Flammable Fabrics Act (1972).

The Federal Hazardous Substance Act (1967).

The Poison Prevention Packaging Act of 1970.

The Refrigerator Safety Act of 1956.

Flammable Fabrics Act

The Flammable Fabrics Act had formerly been administered in part by HEW, the Department of Commerce, and the Federal Trade Commission. The functions of each department as they related to flammable fabrics were transferred to the Consumer Product Safety Commission (CPSC). The Act prohibits the marketing or interstate transport of articles of clothing or fabrics that are so flammable that they are dangerous when worn or when used for interior furnishings in homes and public buildings.

The law defines terms that apply and specifies what transaction are prohibited. It is of interest to toxicologists that the requirements of this Act led to the treatment of children's sleep wear with tris (2,3-dibromopropyl) phosphate. The subsequent discovery of the carcinogenic properties of this chemical required the removal of treated garments from the market at a high cost both economically and in terms of confidence in the federal bureaucracy.

Federal Hazardous Substances Act

The Federal Hazardous Substances Act of 1967 was also transferred to CPSC as noted above. The intent of the Act is to regulate "toxic" substances, defined as any substance (other than a radioactive substance) that has the capacity to produce personal injury or illness to mankind through ingestion, inhalation, or absorption through any body surface.

Other terms are given a legal definition for the benefit of he toxicologist and others who must administer the law. The term "highly toxic" means any substance that (1) produces death within 4 days in half or more than half of a group of ten or more laboratory white rats each weighing between 200 and 300 g; (a) at a single dose of 50 mg or less per kilogram of body weight, when orally administered; or (b) when inhaled continuously for a period of ne hour or less at an atmospheric concentration of 200 ppm by volume or less of gas or vapour, or 2 mg/1 by volume or less of mist or dust, provided such concentration is likely to be encountered when the substance is used in any reasonably foreseeable manner; or (2) produces death with 14 days in half, or more than half, of a group of ten or more rabbits tested in a dosage of 200 mg or less per kilogram of body weight, when administered by continuous contact with the bare skin for 24 hours or less. If it is found that available data on human experience with any substance indicate results different from those obtained on animals in the above-named dosages or concentrations, the human data shall take precedence.

"Corrosive" applies to any substance that in contact with living tissue will cause destruction of tissue by chemical action.

"Irritant" means any substance, not corrosive as defined above, that on immediate, prolonged, or repeated contact with normal living tissue will induce a local inflammatory reaction.

"Strong sensitize" means a substance that will produce in normal living tissue, by an allergic or photodynamic process, a hypersensitivity, evident on reapplication.

"Extremely flammable" shall apply to any substance that has a flash point at or below 20°F, as determined by the Tagliabue open cup tester.

"Radioactive substance" means a substance that emits ionizing radiation.

"Label" means a display of written, printed, or graphic matter on the immediate container of any substance. Labeling requirements are specified in detail with provision for declaring an item misbranded. In this revision of the law, additions are made regulating substances and toys used primarily by children. Branding of such items must include adequate direction for the protection of children from hazard.

A new term, "banned hazardous substance," is introduced that, besides several other meanings, includes any toy or other article intended for use by children that is hazardous substance or that bears or contains a hazardous substance that could be accessible to a child to whom such toy or article is entrusted. The Act lists various prohibitions, penalties, and other provisions, and repeals the Federal Caustic Poison Act with certain stated exceptions.

Poison Prevention Packaging Act

The Poison Prevention Packaging Act, as mentioned above, requires special packaging to protect children from serious personal injury or serious illness resulting from handing, using, or ingesting household substances, and for other purposes. One result of this law was the marketing or prescription and some over-the-counter drugs in containers having trick openings designed to prevent young children from opening them. Such common drugs as aspirin and iron compounds have been serious offenders in accidental poisonings.

Toy Safety

The Child Protection and Toy Safety Act of 1969 is not of much interest from a toxicologic standpoint except as it applies to the control of substances or objects that could leak or spray injurious material into an eye or be harmfully aspirated or ingested. Such toy or other article may be deemed to be banned hazardous substances.

Federal Hazardous Substances Labeling Act

In 1962 this law replaced the Federal Caustic Poison Act except for any "dangerous caustic or corrosive substance," as defined by the Federal Caustic Poison Act subject to the federal Food, Drug, and Cosmetic Act. The Act is essentially a labeling law, which specifies the label required on certain caustic substances. It is designed to regulate the distribution and sale of certain dangerous caustic or corrosive acids, alkalies, and other substances in interstate and foreign commerce. The law is largely of interest to toxicologists who might be acting as advisors or consultants to a business or industry interested in distributing such substances.

Lead-Based Paint Poisoning Prevention Act

This Act (January 1971) provides grants for detection and treatment of lead-based paint poisoning and for support of programs leading to the elimination of such poisoning. It prohibits the use of lead-based paints in any residential structures funded with federal assistance in any form. It is administered by HEW conjunction with the Secretory of Housing and Urban Development. The Act has provided support for a number of toxicologic projects.

Aircraft Spraying

The spraying of pesticides from aircraft is controlled by the Federal Aviation Administration under its regulations for agricultural aircraft operation. The operator must be certified; he must show by test that he is qualified in regard to safe handling of economic poisons. He must understand the proper disposal of used containers, the effects produced, and the symptoms of poisoning caused by the substances used and the appropriate measures to take in emergencies and the location of poison treatment centers in his locality. Other detailed specifications are given in the regulations for the safety of the operator and of the people on the ground.

Forensic Toxicology

The science of forensic toxicology is a hybrid of analytic chemistry and fundamental toxicologic principles. It is concerned with the medico-legal aspects of the harmful effects of chemicals upon humans and animals. Although the techniques for the isolation, detection, and estimation of toxic substances in biologic materials are primarily invoked for the purpose of aiding in establishing the cause or in elucidating the circumstances of death in a postmortem investigation, they are applicable as well to certain aspects of clinical toxicology, forensic determinations made on living subjects, and drug abuse monitoring programs.

Role of Chemicals in Fatalities

The harmful effects of exposure to chemicals have been established in the United States. Poisoning fatalities now approximate 10,000 annually; in 1968 about 3 per cent of all accidental deaths and 26 per cent of suicides involved poisons. In addition, it is estimated that for every successful suicide, there are 15 to 20 cases of attempted suicide, and that the total number of nonfatal poisoning exceeds 1 million per year. A particular class of chemicals, the barbituric acid derivatives, were implicated in 75 per cent of the suicides by drugs. Table 10.2 illustrates the frequency with which some selected toxicants were involved in fatal poisonings in California in a recent year. There, as nationwide, barbiturates are statistically prominent, accounting for 30 per cent of all suicides resulting from chemicals. Carbon monoxide, present in motor vehicle exhaust gas, represents an auxiliary means of suicide and additionally contributes to another sizable classification, death by conflagration, which is not generally categorized as a chemical means. Salicylates, although they are the principal; agents in accidental poisoning, do not represent a major cause of death. Toxicants such as arsenic, strychnine, and other classic poisons, of considerable historic significance in toxicology; are now rarely encountered in forensic analysis.

Table 10.1. The role of poisons in accidental and suicidal deaths in the United States in 1968.

	Accidents	*Suicides*
Poisoning by gases and vapours	1,526	2,408
Poisoning by solids and liquids	2,583	3,276
Total all poisonings	4,109	5,684
Total all causes	114,864	21,372

Ethyl alcohol, while not prominent as a primary lethal agent, is a truly ubiquitous chemical in the viewpoint of the analytic toxicologist. It has been held indirectly responsible for up to 50 per cent of the more than 50,000 annual nationwide motor vehicle traffic accident fatalities and is commonly detected in the bodies of many victims of homicide, suicide, and accidents.

Table 10.2. Selected data in fatal accidental and suicidal poisoning in California in 1976.

Causative agent	*Suicides*	*Accidents*
Barbiturates	374	109
Vehicle exhaust	185	21
Opiates and opioids	—	505
Salicylates	12	12
Arsenic	5	—
Strychnine	4	—
Total all poisonings	1233	1025

Most forensic laboratories today routinely analyze for alcohol in all the samples they receive. Of 25,000 coroner's cases investigated over a ten-year period, alcohol was found present in 16.7 per cent. If one includes tests performed on intoxicated drivers, the analytic determination of alcohol has been the forensic chemical examination most frequently executed over the past 50 years.

Forensic Analyst

It is the primary responsibility of the forensic toxicologist, as a member of the medicolegal team, to elucidate the nature and extent of chemical involvement in human fatalities. Inaugurated in this country by a handful of chemists performing crude chemical assays for arsenic and strychnine from the gastric contents of poisoning victims the profession currently includes several hundred toxicologists skilled in analytic chemistry, who utilize sophisticated instrumentation for the identification of potentially thousands of toxicants, which must be isolated from virtually every organ and body fluid.

Table 10.3. exemplifies the variety and frequency of substances encompassed in the domain of a coroner's toxicologist. While alcohol, carbon monoxide, the barbiturates, and morphine remain the substances most commonly encountered by the forensic toxicologist, it is the uncommon substances that constitute the greatest analytic challenge and probably require more of the toxicologist's time. These compounds are, for the most part, representative of the ever-increasing therapeutic arsenal of the physician, each new drug contributing to the complexity of the analyst's task. For instance, several years ago the antianxiety agents diazepam and chlordiazepoxide were the only benzodiazepine derivatives available therapeutically. The toxicologist, armed with the knowledge that these two drugs were among the most frequently prescribed to persons over the age of 65, would have equipped himself with a scheme for the isolation and detection of the compounds and their metabolites, and in certain areas of the country may have included this scheme in his initial or secondary search for poisons. Within the past few years, however, the number of benzodiazepine drugs on the world market has risen to 13, all close chemical relatives. To further complicate the situation, seven of the compounds—chlordiazepoxide, clorazepate, medazepam, diazepam, prazepam, temazepam, and oxazepam—have a common metabolic pathway. This, the chore of isolating and identifying a benzodiazepine derivative has been multiplied manyfold.

The example of the benzodiazepines has been and is being paralleled by other classes of drugs, such as the barbiturates, 25 of which are now prescribable in this country, and the phenothiazines, numbering approximately 16. The continued emergence of new drugs and chemicals that are made available to the public calls for perseverance on the part of the forensic toxicologist in the constant modernization of his analytic methodology.

While chemically very similar, the drugs within a class may vary widely in terms of pharmacologic activity, toxicity, and pharmacokinetic properties. Thus the goal of absolute qualitative identification of a compound isolated from a tissue sample becomes increasingly important with the continued availability of new and closely related chemical entities. Simply determining that a compound is a barbiturate, for example, does not justify interpretation of its blood concentration in

Table 10.3. Drugs and chemicals detected in Coroner's cases in orange county

Agent	*Frequency*	*Agent*	*Frequency*
Acetone	30	Meprobamate	126
Acetaminophen	20	Mesoridazine	2
Amitriptyline	44	Methadone	8
Amphetamine	28	Methamphetamine	9
Arsenic	4	Methane	4
Barbiturates	1,165	Methanol	5
Brompheniramine	2	Methapyrilene	27
Carbamazepine	3	Methaqualone	57
Carbon monoxide	354	Methocarbamol	8
Carbromal	9	Methyl bromide	2
Carisoprodal	4	Methylenedioxyamphetamine	1
Chlordiazepoxide	61	Methyphenidae	2
Chloroquine	2	Methyprylon	15
Chloropheniramine	2	Morphine	416
Chlorpromazine	35	Nitrous oxide	1
Chlorprothixene	2	Nortriptyline	11
Clorazepate	5	Oxazepam	4
Cocaine	11	Oxycodone	2
Codeine	92	Oxyphenbutazone	21
Cyanide	18	Papaverine	2
Desipramine	10	Paraquat	3
Diazepam	328	Pentazocine	13
Dichlorodifluoromethane	9	Perphenazine	13
Diethyl ether	1	Phenacetin	69
Diethylpropion	1	Phencyclidine	13
Digoxin	18	Phentermine	1
Diphenhydramine	5	Phenylbutazone	4
Diphenoxylate	1	Phenytoin	60
Doxepin	16	Procainamide	5
Ergonovine	2	Procaine	11
Ethanol	2,444	Prochlorperazine	10
Ethchlorvynol	63	Promazine	6
Ethinamate	2	Promethazine	6
Ethoheptazine	5	Proparacaine	1
Fluphenazine	1	Propoxyphene	112
Flurazepam	17	Propranolol	5

Furosemide	11	Pyrilamine	1
Glutethimide	31	Quinidine	11
Halothane	2	Quinine	2
Hydromorphone	1	Salicyclic acid	263
Hydroxyzine	7	Scopolamine	1
Hydrochlorthiazide	4	Strychnine	3
Imipramine	23	Theophylline	16
Isopropanol	3	Thioridazine	47
Levallorphan	1	Trifluoperazine	18
Levaorphanol	1	Trichloroethane	3
Lidocaine	7	Trichloroethylene	3
Malathion	3	Trichloromonofluoromethane	8
Meperidine	10		

terms of clinical symptoms. And often-requested estimates of the amount ingested, time of administration, and time of death are unattainable without explicit knowledge regarding the rate of absorption, pattern of body distribution and extent of metabolism and excretion of a compound.

Obviously, the forensic toxicologist must be a first rate chemical analyst, intimately acquainted with the modern equipment and techniques that can furnish him with the qualities of speed, sensitivity, and specificity he requires. Further, he must be equally skilled in the application of toxicologic principles and pharmacologic facts to the interpretation and assessment of his findings in order to form conclusions regarding the circumstances of death.

Objectives of Toxicologic Analysis

Besides playing a major role in postmortem medicolegal investigations, the forensic toxicologist serves another equally important, although not so apparent, purpose. The data on human toxicology accumulated by him and his colleagues are often lifesaving to others, in that they lead to recognition of particular hazards in regard to drugs or chemicals either accidentally contacted or intentionally abused.

A dramatic example involves the recent epidemic of halogenated hydrocarbon inhalation by youths. Some early reports by toxicologists of fatalities resulting from this abuse gave rise to a nationwide epidermiologic study that turned up 110 similar deaths over a seven-year period. The predominantly sudden deaths, which generally lack conclusive autopsy findings, have recently been attributed to ventricular fibrillation due to cardiac sensitization to epinephrine. It is hoped that education of the public through continued publication of the potential dangers of these chemicals will lead to a decrease in the incidence of abuse.

Recognition of the heroin epidermic that has plagued the metropolitan areas of the United States may be partly ascribable to the work of forensic toxicologists. The geometric progression in the incidence of death due to heroin overdose in large cities over the ten years from 1960 to 1970 was a major indicator of the impending heroin crisis. Heroin fatalities in Philadelphia rose from five in 1962 to over 170 in 1970, while narcotic overdosage was the leading of death for those between 15 to 35 years of age, which reported over 1,200 such deaths in 1970. The Baden formula, which is now used by many cities in calculating their total addict population, is based on a city's annual heroin fatality rate. Through the application of this formula and increased surveillance on the part of the district coroner's toxicologist, the District of Columbia adjusted its estimated addict population upward to 16,800 from a previous figure of 4,200.

Rise of Forensic Toxicology

Although attempt at tracing the early foundations of forensic toxicology must necessarily focus on the Spanish chemist and physician Mathiew J.B. Orfila (1787-1853), whose extensive influence on the development of this discipline is undeniable. An interest in forensic medicine and knowledge of analytic chemistry led Orfila to devote several years to experimentation with the poisons of that period, culminating in his textbook of general toxicology. *Traite des Poisons*, in 1814. As professor of legal medicine at University of Paris, he devised analytic methods for the detection of poisons in human viscera, investigated the reliability of antidotes to poisons, and authored numerous other monographs on various phases of forensic medicine and toxicology. Orfila served as expert witness in the courts of Europe for many years, espousing his firm belief that only through the use of chemical analysis could a case of criminal poisoning be properly adjudicated.

Undoubtedly his most noteworthy contribution to modern forensic toxicology was his discovery that poisons, after administration via the oral route, were absorbed from the gastrointestinal tract and distributed to the various organs, in which they could be detected by chemical analysis. Fundamental as this concept seems today, the chemists of Orfila's time, having failed to find a poison in the contents of victim's stomach or intestines, would have concluded that poisoning was not responsible for the death.

Orfila also served to arouse popular interest in the infant science of toxicology, notably through his role as expert witness in the murder trial of the infamous Marie Lafarge in 1840. Utilizing a technique developed by the English chemist James Marsh several years earlier, Orfila demonstrated the presence of arsenic in the tissues of a victim of poisoning and for the first time toxicologic data was used as evidence in a medicolegal trial. His testimony resulted in the conviction and life imprisonment of Madame Lafarge and stimulated a furor of worldwide disputes over the validity of toxicologic premises. The aftermath of this trial saw the arrival in Paris of numerous young chemists eager to study under orfila and other French toxicologists.

Orfila's influence was extended to England by Robert Cristison (1797-1882), a physician who had studied toxicology under the master in Paris. Returning to the University of Edinburgh, Cristison was appointed professor of forensic medicine and thus became the first British toxicologist. His excellent *Treatise on Poisons*, incorporating many of the toxicologic concept of Orfila, was published in 1829 and survived a number of revisions, the fourth of which became the first American edition in 1845.

The next 60 years witnessed the further development of qualitative and quantitative assays for the detection and estimation of small amounts of poisonous chemicals. One of the most noteworthy advances is attributed to Jean Servais Stas, professor of chemistry at Brussels and former student of Orfila, who in 1850 was requested by a Belgian magistrate to perform an analysis for poison in a case of suspected murder. Stas succeeded in isolating the alkaloid nicotine from the dead man's tissues. In so doing he developed a means of extraction and purification, which after numerous refinements and modifications, forms the basic for the method of solvent extraction used universally by toxicologists today in isolating a wide variety of toxicants from biologic samples.

While the methodology was fast becoming available, toxicologic analysis for medicolegal purposes was not to become an accepted and routine procedure in the United States until well into the twentieth century. In 1918 the coroner system in New York City was replaced by a medical examiner system. Simultaneously, a laboratory of forensic toxicology was established, the first in the United States, under the supervision of A.O. Gettler. Over the years the numerous associates of Dr. Gettler have radiated out to establish many of the laboratories presently operating within coroners' and medical examiners' offices in the urban centres of this country.

The American Academy of Forensic Sciences was established in 1949 to uphold and further the practice of all phase of legal medicine in the United States, the present 300 members of the toxicology section represent the majority of the analytic toxicologists in the century, including a number of hospital and private clinical laboratory analysis. The annual meetings of the Academy and its quarterly publication, the *Journal of Forensic Sciences*, serve an important role as forum for all matters of professional interest to forensic toxicologists. This Academy, together with the Society of Forensic Toxicologists and the California Association of Toxicologists, sponsors the American Board of Forensic Toxicologists, which certifies properly trained and qualified forensic toxicologists in their chosen speciality.

Forensic science organizations such as that have evolved concurrently in other countries such as Great Britain and Australia, and in order to bridge these gaps the International Association of Forensic Toxicologists was formed in 1963. With more than 500 members from 45 countries, the Association publishes an informal bulletin that presents analytic techniques and scientific data on cases involving new or infrequently encountered drugs and other chemicals.

The number and variety of poisons met with in the practice of forensic toxicology today provide a formidable obstacle to any one person attempting to master the art. With a view toward alleviating this problem by providing an opportunity for promulgation of pertinent professional information on an interpersonal basis, several informal organizations have been formed throughout the country. The California Association of Toxicologists, for example, whose meetings are open to any person demonstrating an interest, holds quarterly workshops involving lively discussions on timely topics.

From the Death Scene to the Laboratory

Approximately 20 percent of the population die under circumstances entailing an official inquiry into the cause of death Deaths that warrant investigation under the laws of most states are those unattended by a physician, or occurring under violet, unusual, or sudden circumstances. Determining the cause of death in these cases becomes the responsibility of the medical examiner or coroner and much depends on the accuracy of his determination. The innocence or guilt of the accused in many cases may depend solely on the proper postmortem diagnosis of the cause of death of the victim. Other legal problems hinging on the final classification of a death include insurance benefits, workmen's compensation benefits, and civil accident liability. Aside from the legal aspects, there is to be considered the emotions of the living. Interpretation of a case due to drug poisoning as accidental or suicidal, for example, should not be taken lightly. The forensic toxicologist plays a paramount role on the evaluation of a significant proportion of unclassified deaths. Prerequisite to the comprehension of this role is a basic understanding of the mechanics of a medicolegal investigation.

Medicolegal Investigative Team

In order to properly evaluate case, the coroner, who may or may not be a physician, or the medical examiner, who is trained in anatomic and clinical pathology as well as forensic pathology, must depend not only on his expertise but on the help of the best-qualified team available. This team consists of a homicide investigator, a medical examiner's investigator, a forensic pathologist, a forensic toxicologist, and, in certain cases, specialists trained in hematology, microbiology, sociology, odontology, anthropology, or criminalistics.

Homicide Investigator

In cases of sudden and unexplained death, the first investigator called and consequently the first to arrive on the scene is the police homicide investigator. The rule of preservation of the death scene must be enforced until all details can be photographed and any witnesses interrogated. The homicide investigator will fingerprint the victim and collect such evidence as firearms, knives, and other articles relevant to the case that will later be examined by appropriate specialists. Other experts will be called to assists as needed, including identification technicians, police photographers, and criminalists.

Medical Examiner-Coroner's Investigator

Two types of investigators are found in medical examiner and coroner systems in the United States. The first is the medical investigator or deputy medical examiner, a physician who has been trained in forensic medicine. The second is the lay investigator who has a suitable academic background and has gained experience through on-the-job training while serving an apprentice-ship under a senior investigator. The increasing complexity of present-day cases makes it imperative that the investigators possess highly specialized skills and expertise not found in other areas of medicolegal investigation. In cases of sudden and unexplained death, he is frequently the only member of the medicolegal team to actually view the scene and collect the evidence that other members of the team will need to assist them in their investigation.

The medical examiner-coroner's investigator is responsible for the identification of the decedent, the documentation of circumstances surrounding the death, the collection and preservation of evidence including medications and other toxic substances; in the area, photographs of the body and the total scene, interviews with witness, family, and friends as indicated by the nature of the case, and a complete medical history. All information is incorporated into a formal report, which becomes a part of the case record.

The information given the pathologist must also be given orally or in formal report to the toxicologist at the time the tissues and the preliminary pathology report are submitted to the laboratory. The investigator will also make the photographs available to the toxicologist and will submit all medications and other toxic substances directly to him.

Forensic Pathologist

The forensic pathologist differs from the clinical pathologist in that the latter specializes in death due to natural causes while the former specializes in sudden and unexplained deaths. The forensic pathologist can make dead men tell tales by being cognizant of the pathology associated with various injuries or poisons. For example, a murder might smother his victim and then burn the building to disguise the death. A forensic pathologist, with proper laboratory support would be alerted to this ruse by the lack of carbon particles in the lungs and the absence of carbon monoxide in the blood.

The possibility of death due to a poisonous substance arises whenever the cause of death is not readily apparent from the gross examination of the body at autopsy. Any unmarked body without stab wounds, gunshot wounds, or crushing injuries is potentially a case of poisoning. Although the majority of cases referred to the medical examiner-coroner are finally resolved as natural deaths, many of these do not exhibit characteristic and recognizable morbid anatomic changes and may be difficult or sometimes impossible for the pathologist to ascertain unaided. Among these are metabolic disease such as "thyroid storm," porphyria, addisonian crisis, and diabetes mellitus and functional disorders such as epilepsy and cardiac irregularities, including sudden ventricular fibrillation in the presence of only moderate arteriosclerotic heart disease.

The autopsy report prepared by the pathologist consists of the gross findings, negative as well as positive, describing the body both externally and internally in great detail followed by the results of the histochemical or microscopic studies. On the basis of the gross and microscopic examinations the pathologist will give his opinion as to the cause of death. In those cases in which the cause of death is not evident and in those cases in which there is pathologic and/or historic determinations are both expensive and time-consuming, and the toxicologist should not be expected to begin his task until all preliminary investigation has been completed. If an adequate history has been obtained and a thoroughly complete necropsy has been performed, the toxicologist need not be faced with a "general unknown."

The complete autopsy report often provides information pinpointing a toxic substance or class of substances. If multiple needle marks are found, for instance, the toxicologist will suspect the use of opiates and direct his initial efforts toward the disclosure of this group of compounds. The report will also allow the toxicologist to omit the search for poisons obviously not suspect. If the gastrointestinal tract is normal, one does not analyze for corrosives. If the liver and kidneys show no gross or microscopic damage, one omits the search for heavy metals.

Collection and Preservation of Postmortem Specimens

The forensic pathologist additionally is experienced in the practice of the rule of evidence, thereby ensuring that specimens for toxicologic analysis arc properly obtained, placed in appropriate containers, sealed, signed, and dated. These specimens are taken immediately to the laboratory, where the toxicologist will sign or initial the seal on each container and record the hour and dater received. The chain of possession, in all cases, must be intact, guaranteeing complete chronologic accountability of the samples in the expectation of judicial proceedings.

Tissues Required for Analysis

Inasmuch as it is usually impossible to determine at autopsy what tissues the toxicologist will need in his analysis, adequate samples of all tissues should be taken. These can be disposed of later if not required, whereas the possibility for disinterment of a body is remote. The pathologist should confer with his toxicologist to establish the quantity of tissue needed, since this will largely depend on the methods and instrumentation used for analysis.

Blood

Great care should be exercised in the collection of the blood sample to ensure freedom from contamination. Heart blood is preferred and peripheral blood is acceptable. Under no circumstances should the sample be "scooped up" from the body cavity since this blood may be contaminated with fluids from the viscera and/or the stomach contents. A 100 ml sample will usually suffice for routine studies. Alcohol, cyanide, carbon monoxide, barbiturates and other depressants, and tranquilizers are among the poisons easily and readily detected from the blood.

Brain

At least 50 g should be collected. This tissue is especially useful in the demonstration of a alcohol and other volatile poisons.

Liver

A sample of 100 g is a minimal requirement. The liver is the site of biotransformation for the majority of toxicants, and the levels found in this tissue may be up to several hundred times higher than found in the blood. In many instances, the liver may be the only tissue in which the toxic substance will be found in sufficiently high concentration for absolute identification and quantitation.

Lung

At least 100 g of lung should be obtained. This tissue will be especially useful in fatalities due to substance inhalation. It may likewise be a strategic tissue in certain instances of injection or ingestion of a poison. It has been experience of the authors that in acute deaths resulting from the intravenous injection of heroin, morphine, the principal biotransformation product, is found in significant concentrations in the blood and lungs and may not be present at detectable levels in other tissues.

Bone

Bone should be collected if there is any indication that a pesticide or metal is suspected. A total of 100 g should be prove adequate.

Hair and fingernails

These specimens should be taken if chronic metal poisoning is suspected.

Adipose

A minimum sample of 50 g should be taken routinely. In cases in which the victim has survived some days following ingestion of an unknown poison, or if pesticides or insecticides are suspected, adipose tissue should be analyzed. Among the drugs that will accumulate in the fat are thiopental, glutethimide, and ethchlorvynol.

Urine

All available urine should be collected, and if the bladder should be submitted intact. A small amount of urine will be present in the empty bladder and this can be utilized for a micro sugar and acetone determination. Postmortem blood sugar levels are of little or no value, but the urine analysis may give evidence of diabetes. Urine often provides a concentrated, relative unadulterated form of a poison and its metabolites and is applicable to a variety of preliminary screening tests.

Bile

The gallbladder should not be opened at the time of autopsy but, rather, should be removed intact and placed into a separate container. Biliary excretion is an important route of elimination for a number of foreign compounds, including drugs such as morphine, methadone, and glutethimide.

Stomach and contents

The stomach should be ligated at both ends and disturbed as little as possible en route to the laboratory. The pathologist may wish to be present when it is opened and emptied so that he may take it back to his laboratory for closer inspection. Tablets and capsules are frequently found intact in cases of overdosage and may be easily and quickly identified. The volume of the stomach contents should be recorded so that the total quantity of drug(s) present may be calculated. This value, together with the tissue concentrations, is necessary for an estimate of the amount of a compound actually ingested.

From the Laboratory to the Courtroom and Beyond

Analysis

As previously stated, on the basis of a good investigation and autopsy the toxicologist may be able to proceed directly to the tissue of choice and expeditiously elucidate the nature of the poison in question. The cherry red colour of blood taken from the victim of a fire would suggest that a carbon monoxide determination should be performed first. Other obvious (but rare) examples are toxicants with characteristic odors, such as cyanide and organic solvents, or materials producing distinctive pathology, such as the corrosives.

In those cases in which the medical history is sparse and the autopsy shows little other than visceral edema and congestion, a number of toxic substances must be searched for as matter of routine. The techniques involved in this search often necessarily compromise sensitivity or specificity in favour of speed, reliability, and comprehensiveness. While it is not the purpose of this chapter to provide a detailed modus operandi for toxicologic screening, a brief presentation of a general approach to the problem is in order.

Analysis of the stomach contents

The intact stomach should be emptied into a large flat container for careful inspection of the gastric contents. If death has been rather rapid, the dosage forms of ingested drugs may be discrete and readily identified. The contents should be checked for odor, colour, and gross appearance and the pH measured. Sodium salts of weakly acidic drugs may give an alkaline pH. Description of the contents should include any recognizable food as well as foreign materials.

The contents are then weighed and a portion taken for analysis. The stomach contents may be examined for heavy-metal compounds using the Reinsch test, which consists of boiling a short spiral of copper wire in the acidified contents. Any metals depositing on the wire must be confirmed by further testing.

A weighed sample of stomach contents can be extracted for acid, basic, and neutral drugs by direct extraction with organic solvents. Ultraviolet spectroscopy and thin-layer or gas-liquid chromatography offer a means of rapid screen for the majority of drugs.

Analysis of the urine

A battery of screening tests can be rapidly accomplished directly from the urine.

1. Sugar and acetone determinations using Clinistix and Ketostix.
2. Tumeric paper test for borates.
3. Furfural spot test for meprobamate and other carbamates.
4. FPN spot test for phenothiazines and related compounds.
5. Five percent ferric chloride reagent for salicylates.
6. Fujiwara test for chloral and other halogenated hydrocarbons
7. Reinsch test for heavy metals.

A sample of urine is also extracted for acidic, neutral, basic, and amphoteric drugs and analyzed utilizing methods corresponding to those for the gastric contents.

The information gained from the analysis of the stomach contents and the urine will often provide all the information necessary to determine what procedures to follow with respect to the viscera. As a general rule the toxicologist should analyze the blood, brain, lung, liver, kidney, and bile for the purpose of establishing toxicant concentrations. It may be effectively argued that complete body distribution studies are not necessary in all cases. Certainly in the case of death due to acute alcoholism the blood, brain, and stomach contents offer all information of relevance and no other tissues are really satisfactory. Likewise, in the case of death due to the intravenous injection of heroin it may be impossible to demonstrate its metabolite, morphine, in many of the tissues. However, following overdosage of the majority of drugs, concentrations in the specimens mentioned are substantive to valid estimation of the amount administered.

Curry (1976) states that three questions will be asked of the toxicologist upon completion of his analysis. These are (1) Did you find any poison, and if so, what was it? (2) When and how was the poison taken into the system? (3) How much did you find? To these queries should be added: (4) Are the levels found consistent with death? To answer these questions the authors feel that the analysis of blood, liver, urine, and stomach contents will be minimally required.

Report of Findings

The format of toxicology reports will vary from laboratory to laboratory, but authorities appear to be in agreement as to the information the report should contain. The case number, name of decedent, tissues taken at autopsy, drugs, and other physical evidence found at the scene and the chain of possession of these samples must be clearly stated. The body of the report must list the concentrations of any toxicants found present in the tissues as well as toxicants analyzed for but not present in levels above the limits of detection for the methods used. Methods applied in the analyses should be briefly described or a reference given if the method has been published. This information will enable medical examiners, forensic pathologists, and other toxicologists to form an opinion concerning the validity and reliability of the analyses performed.

Since many persons who are not forensic medical specialists or forensic toxicologists may be concerned with the report, an interpretation of the findings is essential. This is a most difficult task for the toxicologist since he is reasoning from data collected from other fatal cases from his case files as well as data collected by other workers that have been published in the literature. Therefore, the interpretation given by the toxicologist is his "opinion" based on these data. This opinion must be an honest one. If all data lead to one conclusion, it should be so stated. The majority of cases, however, are not that simple, and in cases liable to more than one interpretation the toxicologist should state the arguments both for and against each and, if possible, weigh the relative probabilities. A statement on the toxicity of the chemical compound found may be included with an opinion as to whether this represents a therapeutic level, or a moderate or large overdose. If the case involves a new toxicant, the interpretation may have to be deferred until more data are available.

Interpretation of Findings

One of the most difficult problems facing the forensic toxicologist is that of interpreting his analytic findings. While the task of isolating, identifying, and estimating the level of a toxic substance from biologic specimens is not to be considered common place, with present-day instrumentation and the toxicologist's chemical expertise this aspect is not insurmountable.

An approach to the problem of interpretation usually begins with a review of data abstracted from the literature or culled from previous cases investigated by the toxicologist and his colleagues. The former often supplies information concerning blood levels resulting from therapeutic administration of a drug or from overdosage in which the patient survived. The latter concerns statistical data on body distribution studies from fatalities known to have arisen from a particular compound. An experienced analyst will usually have available a substantial body of information that greatly enhances his ability to evaluate toxicologic findings. Information from well-documented and well-investigated cases that the toxicologist personally obtains is of the foremost value in understanding toxic and fatal levels. In evaluating data received from outside sources, one must bear in mind that there is no uniformity or standardization of toxicologic procedures among clinical and forensic laboratories. Methods for isolating, identifying, and quantitating toxic substances from tissues often differ greatly in their degree of specificity, sensitivity, and accuracy.

Recovery alone poses a problem since drug-protein complexes formed in plasma and other tissues may be difficult to break down without substantial loss of the drug. Thus, the values reported are indicative only of the amount of a compound recovered and do not necessarily reflect the amount actually present in the tissue.

Since for the majority of drugs and chemicals the blood or plasma level most clearly reflects the clinical state of the patient, it is this level that is most often cited in the toxicologist's report as the deciding factor in case of possible overdosage. It is certainly true that in clinical studies involving naive subject, individuals do not vary significantly with respect to the pharmacologic effects produced in certain well-defined blood concentrations of most drugs. However, in interpreting levels exceeding these therapeutic concentrations the toxicologist should be aware of modifying factors likely to be encountered.

Factors affecting the clinical state at a given blood concentration of a drug

Tolerance, a state of decreased responsiveness to a drug, is a result of prior exposure, usually long term, to a given drug or its congener. Cellular adaptation is one type of tolerance in which ever-increasing blood concentrations of a drug are required in order to maintain a certain pharmacologic response. This situation is exemplified by the methadone maintenance patient who may be receiving a daily oral dose of 100 mg of methadone hydrochloride. This same dose, although it produces no noticeable narcotic effects in the tolerant patient, could easily prove fatal if ingested by a nontolerant individual. While it is tempting, the toxicologist should refrain from classifying a blood level as consistent with death accord'ng to literature values until the decedent's history of drug usage has been determined.

The problem of drugs in combination is a frequent obstacle to interpretation of toxicologic findings. The possibility of antagonism of

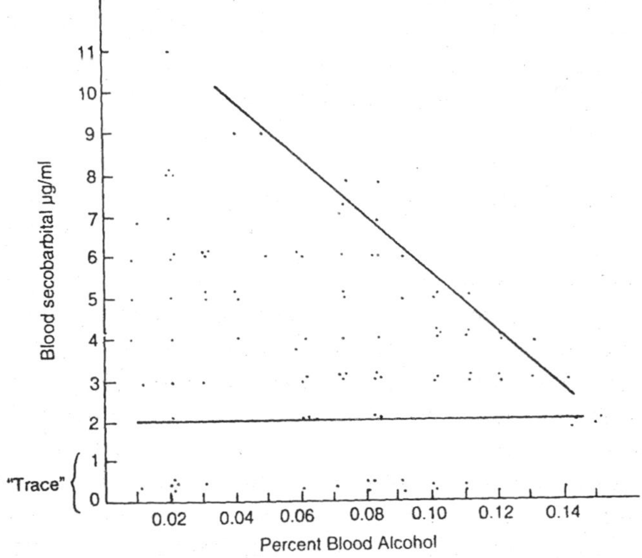

Fig. 10.1. Blood concentrations of secobarbital and alcohol in 102 drug abusers ranging in age from 12 to 25 years.

one drug by another, although rare, should not be overlooked. More often the additive or synergistic effects produced by the interaction of two or more depressant drugs may result in coma or death, although none of the drugs is present in toxic levels. The combination of alcohol and secobarbital is commonly employed for purposes of intoxication or as a means of suicide and has been well investigated.

Unfortunately, the effects of many other drug combinations are not known. A significant number of coroner's cases are those revealing no pathologic changes, in which the toxicologist has isolated several drugs, each in relatively low levels. In these cases only previous reports can help elaborate on whether the effect created is that of addition, synergism, untoward reaction to one or more of the drugs, or some other mechanism. However, if the chemical findings constitute the only positive findings in a case in which a complete autopsy and investigation have been performed, it may be reasonable to conclude that the terminal episode was produced by the chemicals found. However, this conclusion may occasionally assume a degree of competency on the part of the toxicologist and pathologist that is not justified.

A further, possibly obvious, factor in the interpretation of blood levels is the likelihood of the analyst mistaking a pharmacologically inactive metabolite for a parent drug and thus recording an inordinately high test result. While this problem is usually avoided with the newer chromatographic techniques used in toxicologic analysis, many of the traditional visible and ultraviolet spectrophotometric methods are less specific and will yield positive results with certain products of drug metabolism, such as the hydroxylated barbiturates.

Factors affecting blood concentrations of drugs

Quite often the forensic toxicologist is requested by the coroner or the court to estimate the amount of drug ingested by a decedent strictly on the basis of a given blood concentration. This information could be invaluable in classifying a death as either suicide or accidental. Or assuming that the dosage and blood level are known, the toxicologist may be asked to predict the elapsed time between drug administration and death.

There are many variations of this theme, but in essence it requires an assumption on the part of the toxicologist that there exist for this drug both a well-defined dose-blood concentration relationship and pharmacokinetic constants for its rates of metabolism and excretion. Any estimate of dosage or of time until death on this basis is at best

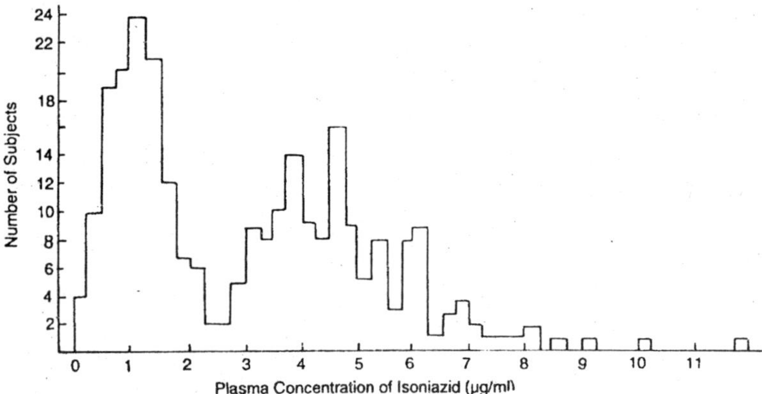

Fig. 10.2. Plasma concentrations of isoniazid in 267 human subjects six hours after oral administration of the drug at a dose of 9.8 mg/kg.

a gross approximation, and the toxicologist should approach this field of speculation with great caution.

The primary factor determining blood concentration produced by a given amount of most drugs (assuming standardization as to weight of the subject and route of administration) is the rate of drug metabolism. This is largely controlled genetically and is subject to significant individual variation. For instance, administration of a standard dose of isoniazid to 267 subjects resulted in a very broad distribution pattern of plasma levels of the drug. This type of individual variation may be an important cause of idiosyncratic drug reactions, although disease conditions can certainly predispose individuals in these unpredictable responses.

Aside from genetic differences, there are the factors of induction and inhibition of the drug-metabolizing enzymes found in the liver. Many drugs can inhibit the metabolic inactivation of other drugs and thus cause an increased pharmacologic response. Of more practical importance is the phenomenon of enzyme induction, or metabolic tolerance, a condition of accelerated drug biotransformation attributable to chronic administration of the same drug, its analogs, or a nonspecific inducing agent. Among these nonspecific agents are such ubiquitous compounds as phenobarbital and ethanol, which can enhance the metabolism of many other drugs and endogenous compounds. Of special relevance to the forensic toxicologist is ethanol, which is known to induce its own metabolism. This action may serve in part to explain the tolerance of chronic users to large amounts of alcohol, although there is certainly a cellular adaptation vector present as well.

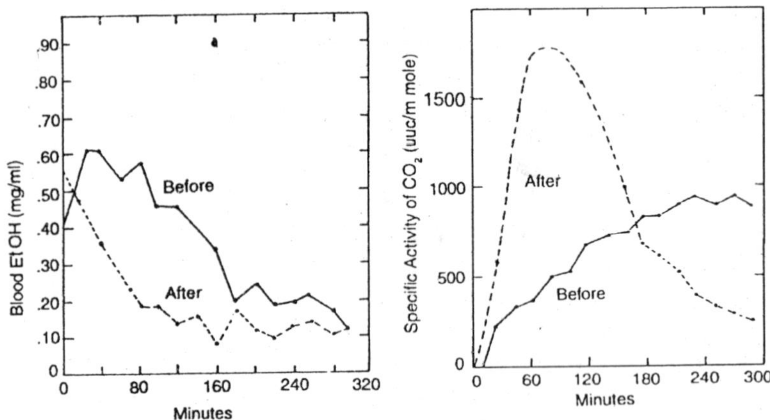

Fig. 10.3. Blood alcohol concentrations and expiration of $^{14}CO_2$ in a human subject after a test dose of ^{14}C-ethanol, before and after a seven-day period of ethanol administration (3.2 g/kg/day).

The rate of urinary excretion of unchanged drugs may also have an important influence on the establishment of their blood concentrations. Although this may be kept constant under controlled conditions, it is theoretically possible to effect tenfold change in the rate of clearance of weakly acidic and basic drugs for every unit change of urinary pH. This pH-dependent excretion has been demonstrated for a number of psychotropic drugs, including amphetamine and methadone.

In certain instances other parameters than blood concentrations may be used to affix the time of survival following a drug overdose. Wright (1955) originally suggested that when death supervenes after the ingestion of a barbiturate, the concentration of the drug is significantly higher in the liver than in the blood. This observation was extended by Curry and Sunshine (1960), who showed that for the majority of cases the liver/blood barbiturate ratio is greater than four when death occurs within five hours of ingestion and less than four when the time interval exceeds five hours.

Other factors bearing on interpretation of findings

The route of administration of drug must also be considered in interpreting fatal cases. Most cases of overdosage in the past have involved administration by the oral, buccal, or inhalation routes, whereas in recent years the parenteral, and especially the intravenous mode has increased in popularity among abuses of narcotics, barbiturates, and amphetamines. Due to the rapidity with which the drug enters the circulation after intravenous administration and the high initial concentrations that are produced, toxic effects may occur that would not be expected after administration of the same dose orally. Additionally, acute allergic responses are more likely to be observed following intravenous administration than by other routes. Therefore, levels in fatal cases due to intravenous injection may be quite low compared with levels found after oral ingestion. A review of further miscellaneous factors that may affect interpretation of toxicologic results is to be found in Gonzales and coworkers (1954).

Delivery of Expert Testimony

The forensic toxicologist is frequently called upon testify in court and should be well prepared for such testimony as applies to one of his cases. His role in the legal process begins with the acceptance of biologic specimens and other evidence. The toxicologist must make certain that the individual delivering the specimens has signed and dated the coroner's seal or evidence tag, thus ensuring an intact chain of custody. He must, in turn, sign and date all evidence and record the hour received. The specimens must be maintained under lock and key and be available only to authorized laboratory personnel.

The toxicologist will be asked to testify as to the procedures undertaken by him and the results obtained and to form an opinion as to the relevance of his findings to the case in terms of reasonable scientific certainly. He will be required to explain what toxic substances were isolated from the tissues and how they were identified. One man's proof is another man's probability, and knowledgeable attorneys will seek disagreement among experts. Positive identity of a compounds is not always a simple matter, and the forensic chemist must be prepared to give scientific evidence explaining why he is reasonably certain that he has identified a specific substance and not a closely related compound. For example, one toxicologist may be satisfied to testify as to identity based on an ultraviolet spectrophotometric scan and a single thin-layer chromatographic analysis, while another would require additional gas-liquid chromatographic, infrared, or mass spectrometric data.

Iron-clad rules cannot be laid down for what constitutes proof of identity and so the toxicologist must rely on his chemical background, experience, and opinions. He should be absolutely certain of his findings before presenting them in a court where the very life of he defendant may be dependent on the accuracy of his testimony. The forensic toxicologist must be prepared to present all his findings upon proper queries from the court. He is not an advocate. He is a searcher and relater to facts and his conclusions are based on fact, not on conjecture or speculation.

Pretrial conference

The quality of expert testimony depends not only on the ability of the toxicologist to maintain a chain of custody, positively identify chemical compounds, and interpret these findings for the court, but also on resolving misunderstandings and misconceptions that may exist between the lawyer and the toxicologist. A pretrial conference is, then, an absolute necessity. The toxicologist should explain his findings and his interpretation of his findings to he lawyer. If his interpretation is based on textbooks of recently published work in addition to his own past cases, the lawyer should be told this and given a list of the books and papers. The toxicologist and the attorney must consider all the evidence and complexities. If the toxicologist is testifying for the prosecution, he should also permit the defense to interview him prior to the trial. The governing concern of the forensic toxicologist should be impartiality to both sides. He should be interested only in justice and truth.

Voir dire

Prior to actual testimony the toxicologist must be qualified to the court as an expert witness. The legal profession has a procedure known as voir dire (to see, to hear, to speak the truth) that permits the attorney who calls an expert witness to introduce this witness to the jury or judge, thus enabling the court to decide if he is indeed an expert in the field and if he should be heard as a witness. It is obvious then that the responsibility for properly qualifying the witness lies with the attorney's direct questioning. This should consists of specific questions concerning pre-professional as well as professional training. Degree, licences, internships, residencies, postgraduate courses, certifications by boards of specialists, awards and affiliations with professional scientists should be cited. The attorney should elicit information concerning the number of years the toxicologist has practiced his art as well as the frequency of the particular type of case in question in the experience of the witness. The emphasis should be on the training, experience, and specialized knowledge of the subject to be offered in evidence, but other pertinent information may be offered, such as teaching affiliations or professional publications.

Examination and cross-examination

From the strictly legal standpoint, when the expert testifies to a reasonable scientific probability, he has satisfied his obligation to the court. He is not required to satisfy a party's burden of proof, although the toxicologist's testimony may be quite persuasive when that question arises. If a pretrial conference has been held question asked by the attorney who has called the expert will be based on such a conference and will hold no surprises.

However, cross-examination may be a different matter since it is the aim in this procedure to impeach the witness if at all possible. This may be done in a number of ways. For example, the attorney may be able to prove lack of training or experience or a lack of knowledge on the part of the toxicologist concerning the specific type of poison involved in this case. It is of utmost importance to convey an attitude of independence and objectivity in these proceeding and to avoid personal involvement. Starrs (1971) has cited seven ethical guides for forensic scientists in a recent symposium to which the interested reader is referred. These cover responsibilities in the handling of evidence and in tendering testimony to both the prosecution and defense. Additionally, Gerber (1961) described some concise rules of conduct for physicians in court that apply equally well to the toxicologist. Among these are:

1. Notify the court attendant that you have arrived and ask him to pass the information along to the counsel table.
2. Be conscious of your dress, appearance, and bearing.
3. Display dignity, confidence, and humility.
4. If you do not understand a question, or do not know the answer, say so.
5. Combat the temptation to use technical terms. Many scientists cling to the idea that technical terms impress the jury, but actually most juries resent them.
6. Do not partisan in attitude.
7. Do not try the case; allow the attorney to do that.
8. Be convincing but do not be prejudiced or belligerent.

Future of Forensic Toxicology

The forensic toxicologist depends heavily on information obtained from previous experience with poisonings, both fatal and nonfatal. He must also have ready access to information pertaining to methods used for the definitive identification of toxicants and for the isolation and identification of toxic substances from biologic specimens. Recent advances are making this crucial information and the means to obtain it more readily available.

Data from Fatal and Nonfatal Cases

In January, 1967, the Toxicology Information Program was established at the National Library of Medicine in Bethesda, Maryland. The library contains a computer-based file of toxicologic information and is responsible for disseminating this information. As a result of this endeavor, the Library's computer-based MEDLARS compiled and produced *Index Medicus* and other discipline-oriented biomedical bibliographies. Among these was *Toxicology Bibliography*, published on a quarterly basis to provide professionals working in toxicology access to the world's relevant and significant journal literature in this field.

A similar program has been instituted at the Home Office Central Research Establishment in Berkshire, England, with respect to computerizing information from the world's scientific literature, and has been extended to the computerization of certain analytic data.

Fatal case data compiled and submitted by members of the toxicology section of the American Academy of Forensic Sciences are disseminated annually in the Registry of Human Toxicology. At present, the Academy is approaching computerization of these data.

Storage and Retrieval of Analytic Data

With the massive number of new pharmaceuticals, pesticides, and other potentially dangerous compounds introduced annually to the market, the problem of identification has reached such proportions that it is unmanageable by conventional means. In 1968, the California Association of Toxicologists began accumulating their combined toxicologic analytic data for future use by any toxicologist in the state. The data, translated into simple digital codes for ultraviolet, infrared, gas chromatography, thin-layer and paper chromatography, and crystal test parameters, will ultimately be computerized. A more desirable approach would be a national consolidated case and analytic data bank reinforced with pathology and investigative data.

Instrumentation in Identification

Until the late 1950s, most toxicologists were limited to ultraviolet, visible, and infrared spectrophotometry in terms of instrumentation. Many laboratories relied almost totally on time-tested thin-layer and paper chromatographic procedures, certain chemical reaction products, and crystal tests. With the advent of gas chromatography, the analyst was provided with a useful tool for the separation of complex mixtures and rapid identification of toxic compounds and their metabolites from biologic material. Recently computers have been added to the gas chromatographic systems to provide analytically meaningful interpretation of the chromatogram.

Early in this decade the combination gas chromatograph/mass spectrometer/data system gained wide acceptance among toxicologists since it provided a quickly and positive identification of unknown substances. The versatility of modern GC/MS/DS provides for changing the dual ion source configuration to operate in either the electron ionization (EI) or chemical ionization (CI) modes. Comparing both the EI and the CI spectra of an unknown can provide very rapid confirmation of the identity of a toxin.

Among other instrumental techniques currently used and accepted in the forensic laboratory are atomic absorption, radioimmunoassay, and spectrophotofluorometry. Nuclear magnetic resonance, Raman spectrophotometry, and high-pressure liquid chromatography are techniques more recently under investigation by the forensic toxicologist. Of these latter techniques, liquid chromatography may be the analytic technique come of age. It would appear to be a perfect complement to gas chromatography and thin-layer chromatography for the separation of complex mixtures. It has the advantage of having the capability of separating polar materials such as many of the drug metabolites that are not readily amenable to gas chromatography.

Automated Analysis

If the clinical and forensic laboratories are to keep pace with the present demands, some degree of automation will be a necessity. The Home described an automated method for extracting, identifying, and quantitating drugs for up to 20 samples an hour as early as 1971. Their instrumentation included ultraviolet spectrophotometry, visible spectrophotometry, and spectrofluorometry.

Totally automated instruments for radioimmunoassay are now marked. No operator intervention is required once the instrument is loaded with biologic samples and reagents and started, until the results are printed in digital form on a paper tape.

INDEX